stage
costume
techniques

Joy Spanabel Emery

University of Rhode Island

Drawings by
Jerry R. Emery

stage costume techniques

Prentice-Hall, Inc.
Englewood Cliffs, New Jersey 07632

Library of Congress Cataloging in Publication Data

EMERY, JOY SPANABEL.
  Stage costume techniques.

  Includes bibliographies and index.
  1. Costume. I. Title.
PN2067.E48   792'.026   80-21385
ISBN 0-13-840330-9

PN
2067
E48

*Editorial/production supervision and interior
   design by Linda Schuman
Jacket design by 20/20 Services Inc.
Manufacturing buyer: Edmund W. Leone*

© 1981 by Prentice-Hall, Inc., Englewood Cliffs, N.J. 07632

Printed in the United States of America

10 9 8 7 6 5 4 3 2 1

PRENTICE-HALL INTERNATIONAL, INC., *London*
PRENTICE-HALL OF AUSTRALIA PTY. LIMITED, *Sydney*
PRENTICE-HALL OF CANADA, LTD., *Toronto*
PRENTICE-HALL OF INDIA PRIVATE LIMITED, *New Delhi*
PRENTICE-HALL OF JAPAN, INC., *Tokyo*
PRENTICE-HALL OF SOUTHEAST ASIA PTE. LTD., *Singapore*
WHITEHALL BOOKS LIMITED, *Wellington, New Zealand*

contents

part   3
the costumer's crafts and techniques

illustrations

three

four

five

six

sixteen

seventeen

eighteen

nineteen

twenty

foreword

At last, here is a source book to save the harried costumer hours of explanations and years of grey hairs. The extensive information that Joy Emery offers was not born in an ivory tower of theories, but in the basement of practicality. Her logical approaches to the challenges confronting a costumer have been created out of the needs of real working situations and reflect the ambiance of teacher and student working together toward solutions.

The book provides a quick reference for the experienced costumer and a detailed guide for the neophyte. It not only guides the reader beyond the designer's sketch through the needles-and-pins realities of theatrical costuming involving the selection of fabrics, creation of patterns, decorations, and maintenance, but it also includes frequently overlooked discussions concerning the effect of the costume on the body, shop equipment, the requirements of a fitting space, and fabric modifications. Nor does Joy leave you dreading the fact that actors have, in addition to a body, not only a head to be covered, but two feet as well. She offers sound directives for creating millinery and footwear in addition to the garments to cover the body.

Since I have had to learn most of the organizational aspects of costuming by experience, I can only feel glad for those who will benefit from this comprehensive manual.

Irene Corey

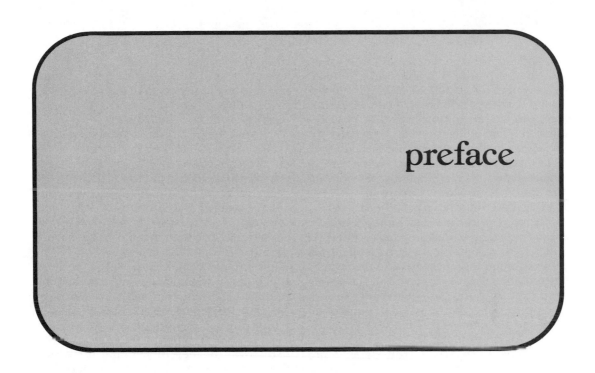

preface

The subject of this book is theatrical costuming—creating garments, accessories, and related items to establish the illusion the costume designer envisioned for the characters and the production. This is not a book on costume design. Several books relating to design can be found in the bibliographies throughout the book. This is a book that is concerned with the fundamental skills and crafts required for preparing costumes and getting them on stage, complete and on time.

The field of costuming is quite broad, and the challenges it presents are always new and exciting so that a single volume cannot cover all of the variables that are part of the field. However, it is possible to deal with these variables if a strong basic foundation in costume crafts has been built. The intention here is to set forth information and techniques that will provide the materials for building that strong foundation to meet the challenges and to solve the problems inherent in all of the variables.

In addition to designing and costuming shows, I have been teaching the subject for a number of years. The information that is compiled here is the result of the approach to teaching costuming that has evolved.

The craft of costuming requires many skills; the ability to sew is just one of those skills. Teaching someone how to create costumes is a multifaceted project. Much of what a costumer does is the result of experience with fabrics, a strong tactile sense, and an eye for proportions and relationships of parts and décor within the given costume. A great deal of the work is done by "eyeing" something into place, by sensing what looks right, and by using a knowledge of what the materials being worked with will do. All of this, of course, relates directly to the play script; therefore, everyone working on the construction of costumes for a show needs to read the script before the work is begun.

Beginning students need to gain experience and to develop the tactile sense and the ability to see the scale required in costumes for the stage and the character. To develop these abilities, students need to begin with the rudiments of costume crafts and often need to unlearn other practices that may have been developed when considering streetwear or commercial patterns. They also need to develop confidence in their ability to create any shapes and appearances from various materials.

For these reasons, I have been working with the method for developing students' awareness that is set forth here. The first phase is to acquaint them with the materials and techniques that are basic to the field by introducing the various facets of costuming and then defining and describing the various materials, methods, and equipment that are fundamental. The next phase, in order to develop the sense of what looks "right" and to free them from dependence on modern commercial patterns, is to explore basic flat pattern drafting techniques. The students then fit and adjust the patterns for future uses.

I have found that students can draft, cut, and baste together the basic bodice pattern in two to three hours. Fitting the basic pattern and making the necessary adjustments usually takes less than an hour. This exercise accomplishes several objectives. Primarily, it inspires confidence in working with fabric and patterns on the body. In addition, the students gain insight into how a pattern functions, including important features of how a flat pattern adapts to the round contours of the body and how to use the various drafting, cutting, and construction tools. Students with some background in pattern and sewing skills usually complete this exercise very quickly and can move on to any of the pattern drafts, thus allowing them to proceed according to their own aptitudes and interest levels.

Next, we explore several of the variations that are possible with these basic patterns. The purpose of these exercises is to awaken their thinking and to free them

from dependence on basic modern patterns. The confidence gained through these projects prepares them for working with more complex period patterns and developing patterns of their own.

Fitting the patterns is fundamental to each drafting exercise. It strengthens the sense of how things work on the body and what shifting of the cut (and, thereby, the grain of the fabric) will do to garments and begins to develop a "feel" (the tactile sense) for shaping garments to achieve the proper appearance for the costume, whatever the period.

The approach described here is meant to function as a teaching tool, a device for preparing students for the more advanced work of creating proper silhouettes through patterning for any period or type of clothing required. It is intended to allow students to discover the incredible range of possibilities that can be achieved by properly manipulating fabrics and other materials. The intention is to help prepare this sense of awareness and to build confidence to explore the various phases of patterning, specifically, and the related crafts of costuming, generally.

The third segment of the book relates to these crafts. The information included here is meant to serve as a springboard for students. The material is intended to provide enough information for them to begin to explore the techniques for individual projects or through practical application for a given production, but, needless to say, nothing like the full range of possibilities can be covered in a few chapters in a single book.

While a primary focus of this book is on drafting contemporary patterns from actor's measurements, it should be understood that drafting and working with modern patterns is a tool, not a goal, in developing skills for more advanced costuming work. The flexibility of modern patterns, as demonstrated in Chapter 13, provides a series of exercises which have a direct carryover to period and created patterns. Developing basic techniques, through analysis and exercises, for working with period patterns then becomes a logical progression in patterning since the rudiments of pattern drafting have been developed through the basic pattern drafts. Once the basic theories of pattern drafting have been mastered, it is an easy step to carry these theories over into working with specific period patterns (several sources are cited throughout the book) or to create patterns to capture the intended appearance of a specific costume design.

Experimentation, a fundamental element of costuming, is often necessary in order to find solutions that will provide the desired appearance of the costumes. I have attempted to provide the foundation for experimentation by setting up rules-of-thumb, guidelines, and examples throughout the text. Glossaries have also been included which define and identify terms, techniques, and functions, so that these can be applied when the need arises. This book is intended to serve as a teaching and learning manual, one that provides the information that will allow those being introduced to the costuming field to acquire knowledge and skills for a solid foundation for the exciting and rewarding work involved in it. Hopefully, it will also provide a handy and useful reference source for those already working in the field.

While I have worked as a costumer for other designers, most of my experience has been working as a designer myself. In many situations, I have functioned as both designer and costumer, and this experience is reflected in the approach taken here. The underlying philosophy is that costuming is an art, as well as a skill, insomuch as those in the costuming field interpret the design, gather information, and translate the information and impressions into the theatrical medium of the costume. Many people become involved in the process of creating the total costume, and numerous skills are brought into play in order to complete the visual effectiveness of the costume. Creative thinking, creative problem solving, and creative application of the acquired skills all go into the making of a costume.

There is an obvious transition here, since many people were also involved in preparing this book. My students, for several years, have been working with and testing the pattern drafts and other materials in the book. Their efforts and guidance have been most helpful and extremely important. Constance Meiklejohn, the former Costume Shop Manager at the University of Rhode Island, has also been of great assistance; she not only prepared the weaves for the illustrations in the chapter on fabrics but has also given much valuable advice on several other subjects included in the book. I also wish to thank Irene Corey for her invaluable assistance and inspiration; Dr. Patricia Helms, Associate Professor of Textiles and Clothing at U.R.I., for her assistance in preparing the technical information on fabrics; and Robert J. Izzo for practically all of the photographs taken especially for the book. Finally, and most particularly, a special acknowledgment to Jerry R. Emery whose contributions to the text cannot even be calculated; he was both a major consultant and editor in the preparation of the manuscript and his beautiful line drawings speak for themselves.

stage costume techniques

the costumer
and the
costuming process

part 1

one

the theatrical costume and the costuming process

The word *theatre* is derived from the Greek word which means "seeing place." In the visual aspects of a production, the theatrical costume is a vital element which is created to enhance the particular characteristic qualities of the play and of the character who is dressed in it. On one hand, it supports the interpretation of the script while it helps to establish locale, mood, and time frame; on the other hand, it helps to define character, indicating social status, age, personality traits, and, sometimes, relationships to other characters.

The theatrical costume is unique. It must fulfill a combination of requirements with which no other form of clothing and adornment needs to be concerned. It must express a quality that is "larger-than-life" and be organically in tune with the script and the production; that is, it must fulfill the playwright's intentions and dramatic statement, and it must be in accord with the director's concept and interpretation. In order to project those elements, the scale of the theatrical costume and the detail in it must be exaggerated, simplified, and clearly defined. In addition to meeting these requirements of projecting script and production concepts and of expressing visual qualities of the individual character, the costume on stage is viewed from varying distances and under strong, often intense, and usually colored light. It must also be durable enough to withstand the heavy strain of performance and is often called upon to serve again in other productions.

By contrast, clothing intended for street-wear is designed and constructed to be viewed much more closely, under natural light or softer lighting conditions than those found on stage. Street-wear is subject to strains and activities that are different from those imposed by an actor in a dramatic performance; therefore, it must meet a different set of requirements in design, materials, construction, and use.

Theatrical costuming not only encompasses the entire range of clothing history from the advent of clothing to the present, it also includes, for such things as fantasy and other nonrealistic plays, the development of styles of clothing the body which have no precedent in clothing history.

A theatrical costume becomes a visual extension of the actor and the character as portrayed. It enhances the illusion of the environment of the play while aiding the actor in projecting the period and style of the production. The costume is a visual statement of a dramatic, theatrical *idea;* therefore, costumes exist beyond the realm of "clothing."

The *design* of the costume develops all these elements for a production; the *execution* of the costume renders each design in its three-dimensional form.

A coverage of methods and techniques for the execution of theatrical costumes is the theme of this book. However, in order to grasp all that is involved in that process, we need to review briefly the areas of responsibility which customarily fall to the costume designer before exploring, in more detail, the responsibilities and functions of the costumer. There are, of course, overlaps in the areas of basic responsibilities. Both, for example, must read the play and be familiar with the requirements set forth by the script; both also need to know the style and the approach to the production that have been determined beforehand. But in the practical consideration of the sequence of processes involved in realizing a costume from an idea to the stage, certain working responsibilities can typically be ascribed to each person.

THE COSTUME DESIGNER'S RESPONSIBILITIES

The design of the costumes is the costume designer's primary responsibility. The designer begins by working with the script, exploring the dominant ideas the playwright has incorporated in it. In conjunction with the director, the production concept or predominant idea for the specific production is developed. This concept provides the framework in which the designer works. It defines the area of research and provides the key for the style, mood, and detail of the costumes. The designer also works with the scenic designer and lighting designer to coordinate the more specific elements of style and of colors, textures, and other compositional concerns. Once the basic ideas are agreed upon with the director and other designers, the costume designs are ready to be finalized in consultation with the costumer who is responsible

for making the costumes look like the designer's sketches.

The costume as designed should incorporate everything the actor wears: from head to toe and from skin to final layer, as well as many of the things the actor carries, such as parasols, purses, canes, or other accessories. This information is necessary in order to develop a complete inventory, or *costume plot,* of everything that is required by the script and the designer for each character. This inventory provides the specific means for determining both the cost of each total costume and the cost for all the costumes. The inventory forms the basis for calculating the costume budget for a production or, if the budget has already been established, defines what adjustments will need to be made to complete the costumes within the budget.

The design is usually developed from a series of "idea" sketches (Fig. 1–1A) and then developed and rendered as a full-color drawing after the ideas have been consolidated and approved by the director. This costume plate (Fig. 1–1B), or "sketch" as it is commonly called, also includes any pertinent information on materials (fabric swatches are included on the plate), structure, or specifications for any peculiarities which must be provided to the costumer by the designer.

The designer must also be available to answer the thousands of questions that arise during the construction and fitting processes. The questions range from the fabric to be used to the size, shape, and color of the boutonniere in the lapel of an extra in the final scene. Quite often the designer is also called upon to work with the actor in the costume to develop proper movement and posture for the era and the character.

The designer's responsibilities also include solving the problems of any quick changes in a production, creating special effects such as "breaking down" (artificially aging) costumes, and working with the costumer in making any adjustments and corrections during the dress rehearsal period.

Figure 1–1A Examples of designer's idea sketches for *Rosencrantz and Guildenstern Are Dead*. Segment from the author's notebook.

Rosencrantz and Guildenstern
· Gertrude

THE COSTUMER'S RESPONSIBILITIES

The execution of the designs is the costumer's major responsibility. (Oftentimes the designer and costumer are one and the same individual, especially in the educational theatre and many repertory operations.) To execute the designs successfully, a costumer needs to develop an extensive background in costume history, patterning methods, and construction materials and techniques. The costumer must also be able to analyze the design specifications on a costume sketch and determine the best methods for realizing the costume in its final form. Figure 1–2 shows the completed "Gertrude" costume as realized from the designer's sketch.

The major elements involved in the process of realizing the designs are more far-reaching than may appear at first glance. Basically, the costumer must know how to pattern garments and accessories, how to put them together, how and when to decorate them, how to complete them in the given time period and within the budget, and how to maintain them for all the performances. This entails more than knowing how to sew; it involves organizing all the elements and activities that go into

Figure 1-2 The completed "Gertrude" costume on stage as produced at the University of Rhode Island. An example of the development of a costume from the designer's sketch. From the author's collection.

producing the costumes, with all the appropriate accessories, to create the total appearance of the costume design. Therefore, in order to function as a costumer for a production, an individual must be able to coordinate and direct the development of the total costume within the given time period and be able to coordinate the execution of the skills necessary to prepare and maintain costumes.

Of course, knowing how to sew and having experience in making clothing is fundamental to costuming, but, since the theatrical costume is unique, many other skills must also be developed. The processes involved in acquiring these skills are discussed in subsequent chapters; this chapter will concentrate on an overview of the various elements that are basic to developing a costume from a designer's rendering.

Coordination with the Designer

Designers' rendering techniques and styles are quite individualistic; therefore, costume designers depict the costume in numerous ways. Some designers are meticulous about showing detail in a costume plate, even including seam locations, the number of buttons on a garment, and other details. Other designers are more concerned with capturing a mood or a moment in the play and do not include as much detail in the plate. The costumer, ultimately, must have information on the details in order to execute the costume. This information is acquired through constant consultation with the designer, plus a solid understanding of the costume crafts on the part of the costumer. One of the basic elements of costuming is knowing what questions to ask and when to ask them in order to acquire the necessary information to complete the costumes.

As a part of the design process, the designer will determine the number of costumes, the accessories required, and any special items that will be needed. The designer and costumer must then coordinate this information so as to determine exactly what has to be done in order to produce everything that is needed. This includes determining what is to be made in the workshop, what can be found and/or purchased, and how to accomplish these objectives. This means that timetables and a costuming production schedule will need to be developed in order to complete the work on time. The various aspects of drawing up and working within the production schedule are discussed in Chap. 20.

Coordination and consultation between the designer and costumer are ongoing procedures, since the designer must be in regular contact with the costuming process to answer questions and to attend the costume fittings. A designer will often want to supervise or actually do some of the finishing details such as painting or otherwise dirtying up the costumes, ornamenting or working out decorative details on or for the costumes, or any other special details that are part of the costuming process.

The costuming process can be divided into three major phases: patterning and cutting; constructing, fitting, and finishing; and maintaining the costumes. Each phase has several facets that are part of fulfilling the requirements of that phase.

Patterning and Cutting Costumes

Patterning can be defined as the manipulation of the garment fabric on the body to coax the grain of the fabric to fall straight and smoothly, or in folds, as specified by the design. It also involves developing appropriate patterns for accessories, including hats, shoes, jewelry, and any other items an actor wears (or sometimes carries) that need to be made or altered in the costume shop. While most patterning is done with fabrics, other materials will also be involved in order to meet the requirements of the design.

Cutting is part of the patterning process, since it is the act of taking the pattern ideas and cutting the costume to fit a specific actor or size. An individual who is proficient in this area is in demand, and there are many who specialize as "cutters." A cutter develops patterns to create the desired appearance, drafts them, and cuts the costume; consequently, this individual must have a very solid knowledge of pattern techniques, fabrics, and other materials and be able to visualize how the garment will look and move when it is worn on stage.

Costumes can be patterned with flat patterns or draped patterns, or a combination of these. As the term implies, flat patterns are shapes that are developed on a flat surface. The pattern can be drawn on paper or on fabric, with allowance for the round contours and bulges of the body included in the flat shape through fitting darts and the curves and angles of the seam lines. Draped patterns are developed on three-dimensional forms, using either dress forms or the human body. The allowances for body contours are developed directly on the form. The draped pattern can also be marked for fitting darts and seam lines and then be spread out to be used as a flat pattern. Both approaches require an accurate set of measurements, an awareness of the grain of the fabric, and an understanding of how to manipulate fabric. Each method also requires constant observation of the material, since only a certain amount of manipulation is possible before undesirable distortion takes place.

Flat patterns are available for contemporary clothing. These commercial patterns are often valuable for modern-dress shows, and paper patterns from previous decades are invaluable as part of a pattern library collection. Flat patterns can also be drafted from an actor's measurements by using contemporary pattern shapes as a point of departure, or they can be drafted from period patterns that are available from various sources. Several of these sources feature patterns, taken from authentic garments and tailoring books of the period, that are drawn to scale. Using the actor's measurements as a guide, these scaled-down patterns can be enlarged to fit the full-size body. The use of period patterns (techniques and sources are cited in Chap. 14) is an important element for capturing a sense of the period. For costumes that present problems for specific flat pattern techniques, draping the fabric on a form that matches the actor's measurements and clearly marking darts, pleats, seams, and the like will provide the necessary pattern for cutting and constructing the costumes.

Essentially, all patterning is based upon the actor's measurements. A complete, accurate, and up-to-date set of measurements for each actor is necessary when cutting patterns in order to assure proper fit. Chapter 5 details the measurements needed, with a description of how to take them.

Basic patterns that have been fitted and adjusted should be clearly identified, catalogued, and kept in a pattern library for future use. A well-developed pattern library is invaluable when preparing a production because it saves hours of patterning time. A good practice to adopt if the acting pool remains relatively constant, as is often the case in educational and regional theatre companies, is to make and maintain basic patterns that have been fitted to a specific actor.

Constructing, Fitting, and Finishing Costumes

A great many of the costumer's responsibilities are involved with constructing, fitting, and finishing the costumes. These three aspects intermingle; construction involves seeing the garments and accessories through to completion, and this requires several fittings during the development of the costumes to make sure the items fit the actor and are properly coordinated with each other. As the costume items are put together, various elements will need to be finished prior to the final assembly of the costume, with final finishing details added as the costume unit is completed. For example, a heavy, decorated sleeve may need to be finished before it is set into a long, heavy robe since the units will be easier (and lighter) to work with separately.

Since many costume patterns are drafted, and the fabrics and materials that are used differ from those traditionally used for street-wear, costume construction means more than just sewing garments together. The costumer must figure out the step-by-step process for assembling each item and then communicate that information to those working on the costumes. This means synchronizing the preparation of each and every costume and accessory so they will all come together, in completed form, at the right time. For example, this can range from determining whether fabric needs to be treated (dyed, silk-screened, or whatever) before it can be cut to specifying what seams need to be joined and when in the process this needs to be done. The costumer, then, must have a complete picture of exactly what is needed for the costumes of the production and must devise the means for accomplishing it.

The costume fittings fall under the jurisdiction of both the costumer and the designer. Generally, there are at least three

9

fittings for a costume, although more may be required for specific costumes. The first two fittings are to check the fit of the garment and to define details required by the design. The final fitting is to pull all the elements of the total costume together for the designer to approve. A major objective of the fittings is to make sure the costume fits comfortably, that it is well supported on the body, and that the actor can move while in the costume and execute all the activities required by the role being played. A detailed discussion of the fitting process is in Chap. 12.

Finishing includes completing all the items with decorative detail, appropriate fastenings, and the like. The garments should be completed so they are secure enough to withstand the strains of performance; all stitching should be permanent and all attachments secured. The inside of the garment, although not usually finished with the same type of detail as street-wear, needs to be neat and free of hanging threads, rough edges, and, of course, pins. The garments and other items should be labeled to identify who wears or uses them; however, the labels should be attached inside the garments or placed on the accessories so they will not be visible to the audience.

Maintaining Costumes

The third phase of the costuming process is to maintain the costumes during the run of the production. This is as important as the other phases but is often overlooked. Actors all too often appear in wrinkled,

torn, or pinned-together garments, negating the careful preparation of the costumes. Before the show has opened, a schedule needs to be prepared for washing or cleaning the costumes and for keeping them pressed and in good repair during the run of the show. The information on the schedule should include the names of the people who will do the work as well as detailing the times when the work will be done.

The specific activity required by the production as well as the manner in which the costumes are treated by the actors and the wardrobe crew (who work with the costumes through the run of the show) will determine how extensive the schedule needs to be. For example, a production that requires dirty-looking "rags" for clothing, such as *The Threepenny Opera* or *Mother Courage,* will not need as much ironing of the costumes as will one that requires elegant, well-kept costumes for a production like *The Would-Be Gentleman.* In both instances, however, the costumes need to be kept clean for the actors to wear.

In addition, costumes that are carefully hung up and not crushed together on a rack require less upkeep than those which are shoved together or tossed on a hanger or on the floor. Providing containers for jewelry, shoes, and other accessories, as well as an adequate number of hangers that are suitable for the weights of the costumes and adequate space for keeping the costumes, is as important in properly maintaining the costumes as an iron and ironing board or sewing kit.

THE COSTUMER'S ANALYSIS FOR DEVELOPING COSTUME PATTERNS

To determine how best to pattern the costume, the costumer studies the sketch with several questions in mind: What is the general shape of the costume? Where does it

conform to the body? Where does it fall away from the body? Where and how does it close? How do the unseen portions of the costume (usually the back and undergarments) look? There are several aspects that need to be considered during the analysis. How the garment is fitted to the body is very important in achieving the appropriate appearance. The number and location of fitting darts, for example, have considerable influence on how the fabric looks on the body, as do the number and placement of seams. The costumer must also consider the types and amounts of fabric required to make up the total costume.

When analyzing and determining the type of pattern required to create an effective theatrical costume, common sense becomes a key factor. Garments which were worn and lived in by people of previous eras were made for bodies not too unlike the modern body. Proportions and sizes have altered somewhat over the centuries, but the basic characteristics remain unaltered. Therefore, a great deal is learned by studying all types of garments and patterns.

A good exercise to help develop an awareness of how garments need to be patterned is to select some clear illustrations of both modern and period garments and study them with all these considerations in mind. A study of pattern books for modern and period garments to see how the pattern shapes vary and how these variations affect the appearance of a given garment helps sharpen one's awareness of how to pattern particular items. Utilize every possible source to become familiar with patterns and the cut and construction techniques which are involved. A great deal can be learned through observation of modern garments, and many museums or universities have authentic clothing collections which are helpful in learning more about the patterns, cut, and construction of garments of other eras. Other sources are cited in the bibliographies at the ends of several chapters which will help to expand your understanding of the techniques involved in patterning.

Research for Historical Appropriateness

Research is a major factor in determining how to pattern a costume to meet the designer's specifications. Knowledge of costume history for general information on styles of garments and accessories, appropriate fabrics and colors, and characteristic detail is a necessary aspect of costuming. When looking at the fashions from any era, it is easy to determine skirt lengths, waist positions, fullness in the garment, predominant materials, colors, and textile decorations. It is less easy to determine what the pattern for the garment needs to be in order to capture the total appearance of the garment for a given character. To acquire this knowledge, it is necessary to study patterns from the specific era and whenever possible, to examine actual garments from the era.

In addition, it is important for the costumer to research the customs and manners of the society the garments reflect. For example, it is important to have a grasp of the restrictive society inherent in late seventeenth-century Salem in order to make effective costumes for the characters in *The Crucible*. It is equally important to know the sources for the fabrics used and the types of dyes available to those people. On the other hand, consider the society reflected in Congreve's *Love for Love*. Although the time period is essentially the same as in *The Crucible* (it was written in 1695), the mores and manners of the characters in this play are entirely different, with emphasis being laid on the foibles of man. Therefore, the garments, decoration, fabrics, and cut of the costumes will need to be entirely different from those for the Salem of 1692. While this type of research is ascribed to the designer, research is equally important for the costumer in order to interpret the designs and to determine the type of patterning required.

Utilizing sources such as books on the history of costumes, paintings, fashion magazines, period pattern books, and social and cultural histories provides a strong general background. But, since each show will present a different challenge, some specific research is always necessary for each new set of costumes.

During the research process for a specific show, the costumer will need to concentrate on the silhouette created by the garment and undergarments, on the characteristic detail and decoration, and on posture and movement in the garments to determine how best to pattern the costume.

SILHOUETTE. The silhouette incorporates the total figure in relief against the surrounding space. It refers not only to the general outline and shape of the garment but also to the combination of body shape, posture, and garment units that creates the characteristic outline. The silhouette is made up of the contours created by the garments and supporting devices which give the clothed body its characteristic shape. In order to suggest the proper silhouette, it is necessary to learn what garments are involved and how they were worn.

It is usually necessary to work from the inside to the outside, from the invisible undergarments and body supports to the visible garments. The necessity of proper undergarments cannot be overstressed. For a modern example, notice that it is impossible to capture the "Lana Turner" bust-line silhouette of the late 1940s by using the "no-bra, natural look" brassiere of the 1970s; therefore, it is necessary to start with the correct brassiere style to achieve the 1940s "sweater-girl" look.

Capturing the proper silhouette of another era often necessitates the use of corsets to support the body and the costume, full or partial hoops to support the skirts, or padding to round or distort the natural body line. Consider the silhouette created by the dress of Queen Elizabeth I (Fig. 1–3). In her garments, the bust was flattened, the torso was heavily corseted (we even have examples of hinged cast-iron corsets worn at that time), and the hips were often extended with hoops (called *farthingales*). Collars were high and stiff, sleeves were large, resembling an enlarged drumstick, and the garments contained volumes of rich, heavy materials. To achieve the proper silhouette, these elements must be simulated in the cut and construction of the costume if the actor is to achieve the illusion of the Elizabethan era.

A review of the history of fashions quickly reveals that throughout the centuries there has been an inherent urge to improve or "correct" the natural body line, and, in so doing, numerous means of distorting that natural line have been devised.

CHARACTERISTIC DETAIL AND DÉCOR. Textile designs, decorative trims, elaborate detail, and the use of elegant furs, jewels, buttons, and bows are equally important in defining elements of costume that are characteristic of a given period. This includes elements on the garment, accessories that augment the effect, and hairstyles that cap the silhouette. All these details are important in capturing the characteristics of a given era and appearance.

In addition to layers of undergarments, outer garments that are revealed only at the neck, sleeve and hem must be considered and incorporated into the total costume for completion. These may be separate garments, as they often were originally, or they may be built into the costume to give only the appearance of the layers. The theatrical costume is intended to create the illusion of the given period or style and is not intended to duplicate the historical garments. If, for example, a shirt is revealed by a neck or cuff ruffle only, there may be no need to have a full shirt

Figure 1-3 An example of the corseted torso of an Elizabethan lady. Notice the flattened bust, the high collar (called a *ruff*), the drumsticklike sleeves, the V-shaped waistline, and the width of the skirt.

under the visible garment. A ruffle (called *ruching*) attached at the collar and wrist of the garment may well be sufficient.

Any decorations and costume accessories to be added will need to be considered, as will the stage business with and in the costume. For the costumer, these elements are worked out in consultation with the designer and will vary in degree of importance with each production. Examples of this aspect are cited in the discussion of the Costume Plates later in this chapter.

POSTURE AND MOVEMENT. The type of posture and movement that is required for the garments of different periods is an important aspect in determining how to pattern a garment. For any given period, the appropriate attitude of the body, how it stands, and how the garments influence the movement are important factors to observe during the research process. While the actor is mostly responsible for posture and carriage on stage, the proper cut and construction of the costume will assist the actor a great deal in achieving the proper movement in the costume. Therefore, it is necessary to be aware of the posture and movement characteristics for the period the costume is to reflect in order to determine how the cut of the garment and how its fabric and weight will influence these characteristics. For example, posture and movement in a soft, clinging formal gown typical of the 1970s is quite different from the posture and movement when wearing a strapless, stiff-net formal gown of the 1950s.

To analyze some of the factors involved in determining posture and movement that are characteristic of a given era, picture a woman of high fashion in the early fifteenth century. Her head is crowned with a large "hennin" with gossamer drapery trailing from it. The neckline is wide to the shoulders, the waistline is high, just under the bust, and the skirt is floor length with a long train dragging behind (Fig. 1–4). The skirt has volumes of material and is probably either lined with fur or at least edged with it. The sleeves are long, usually over the hand, fitted to the arm, and there is often an additional fur-lined wide sleeve that reaches the floor. In order to support the weight, a woman of the fifteenth century had to stand with her back slightly curved and pelvis pushed forward, referred to as the "pelvic thrust." This posture was dictated by the garments and was the standard of the day as depicted by Van Eyck in the nude Eve in the *Ghent*

Figure 1-4 The character of "Agnes" in Anouilh's *The Lark* as produced at The Ohio State University. The actress's posture and "pelvic thrust" is influenced by the cut, weight, and distribution of the fabric in the gown and by the headdress. From the author's collection.

waist is high, the hands are held high; if low, the hands move down. Consider what happens to hands and gestures in a pair of hip-huggers as opposed to natural waist-line pants.

Another example of what to observe is how the legs are defined. When the line of the legs is defined in tight-fitting hose or pants, the leg becomes a strong focal point and is displayed (referred to as "making a leg"). If the legs are hidden under fabric, the posture often is such as to allow the outline of the leg to be seen. Examine Hellenistic Greek sculpture and observe the

Figure 1-5 An example of the "pelvic thrust" that was typical of the "ideal" figure and the posture of the fifteenth century. Drawings are taken from Van Eyck's "Eve" in the *Ghent Altarpiece* and the bride in *Giovanni Arnolfini and His Bride.*

Altarpiece and in the clothed bride in *Giovanni Arnolfini and His Bride,* as shown in Fig. 1-5.

Many things concerning posture and movement can be learned by examining paintings from other eras and applying certain criteria. The high waistline of the fifteenth-century lady dictates where the hands go, since we all unconsciously accent waistlines with the hands. Her hands rest high, under the bust to accent the waist (Fig. 1-4); an Elizabethan lady, with the deep V over the abdomen, rests the hands, gently clasped, just below this V (Fig. 1-3). Waistlines or decorative detail are focal points in a costume and strongly influence what one does with one's hands; if the

14

typical stance and how one of the legs is in evidence through the drapery. When volumes of fabric cover the legs, the wearer sits with the knees apart to support the fabric, something that was highly frowned upon for a "respectable young lady" after the 1920s when skirts became short.

There are certain key factors to observe when analyzing posture and movement for the various eras. Review the type of garment and undergarments, the amount of fabric and fullness in the clothing, how the weight and fullness are supported by the body, and where the focal points are located. The position of the waist, the outline of the body, where the flesh is revealed, and where there is strong decorative detail all influence the posture and movement.

Also consider the various points of contact of the garment on the body. Determining how and where the body supports the garment is basic to posture and movement in the costume and, consequently, to selecting the appropriate patterns for the costume.

CONTROL IN THE GARMENT. How and where the body supports the costume is basic to the silhouette and to a large extent is fundamental to how the costume is worn and the manner in which it moves. All this can be referred to as *control of the garment*. Control includes manipulating the fabric and garment pieces to achieve the appearance that is appropriate to a given period or even to the nature of the specific character. Control is basically achieved by the placement and direction of the seams and the distribution of the weight and fullness of the garment.

Consider the gentleman's coat of the mid-eighteenth century, one like George Washington might have worn (Fig. 1–6). The silhouette emphasizes a slightly rounded chest and sloping, but not slouching, shoulders; the rounded chest is accented by the neck ruffle (*jabot*) which falls over the chest. In order to capture this

Figure 1-6 An example of the posture created by the garments of a gentleman in the mid-eighteenth century.

rounded chest line with the sloping shoulders, the shoulder seam must be moved from the top of the shoulder, where it is located in the modern suit coat, to the back of the shoulder, near the shoulder blade. This shift alters the grain line of the fabric on the body, and the fabric rounds the top of the shoulder smoothly, creating the sloped shoulder, and falls in such a way that it creates a rounding effect for the chest. To accentuate the effect, the armhole of the coat is altered by shifting the shoulder seam to the back. The front shoulder seam is lengthened, and the back seam is shortened (see Fig. 13–8). The

Figure 1-7 Examples of eighteenth-century costumes for *Rule, Rhode Island!*, an original play as produced at the University of Rhode Island and the Edinburgh Fringe Festival. Photo by Robert Izzo.

two-piece sleeve for the coat is also cut to accentuate the silhouette; the pattern features a forward curve at the elbow (a modern pattern is cut without a curve), and the sleeve cap at the top of the sleeve is adjusted slightly.

These alterations combine to hold the shoulders back, and the arms are nudged into a slightly forward position rather than held straight at the sides as in the modern coat. With this type of pattern, the weight of the coat is distributed evenly over the shoulders (Fig. 1-7). This approach creates a coat that is controlled by the patterning process and can, therefore, be worn effectively by the actor. If this process is not utilized, the control of the coat is lost, and the garment will tend to hang from the shoulders so that the desired silhouette will not be achieved.

Learning how and when these pattern variations for control are necessary in order to capture the proper silhouette is an important aspect of the patterning process and requires a solid understanding of the basic pattern shapes and their functions. This understanding is necessary to the process of gaining proper control of the costume, and proper control is important in achieving the appropriate silhouette while assisting the actor in gaining the correct posture and movement.

Application of Modern Materials and Costume Crafts

Research for theatrical costumes is carried out in two directions. One is the study of a given historical period to learn the characteristics of garments and accessories, and the second is the study of modern techniques and materials to apply to those characteristics. Since the total costume incorporates more than just the clothing that is seen by the audience, research into modern materials and techniques is as important as the historical research. Duplicating a cast-iron corset for an Elizabethan silhouette, for example, is unnecessary and impractical (besides, no actor would wear it); however, creating a stiffened torso and flattened bust line is necessary and practical since a corset can be made which is not uncomfortable to wear.

Making corsets, along with several other costume crafts for creating illusions with modern materials and techniques, is discussed in Part 3. Here we are concerned with the garments as depicted in the designer's sketch and the basic elements of patterning and cutting these garments.

FABRICS FOR COSTUMES. The selection of appropriate fabrics for theatrical costumes requires an awareness of the fabrics used in a given period and an understanding of which modern fabrics can accomplish the desired visual effect. In order to select the most appropriate fabric for the costume, several questions need to be posed and answered. Should the fabric be soft or stiff? Should it be lightweight or heavy? In other words, determine what type of body, or "hand," is required for the costume. Consider the texture of the fabric: Is the fabric to be smooth or rough? Is the appearance to be shiny or a matte finish? How is the fabric to react to light? What colors and textile designs are appropriate for the given era? Does the costume require several textures and textile designs to achieve the desired visual effect? Colors and textile design are influential in depicting the style of an era.

Additional practical questions also must be considered with regard to what needs to be done to the fabric and to the costume when it is finished. Does the fabric need to be dyed or require any other special treatment for a specific textile design? This is important since some fabrics react better to dyes or other treatments than do other

fabrics. Will the upkeep of the costume require frequent cleaning, and, if so, does it matter whether it is laundered or dry-cleaned? This becomes particularly important when maintaining the costumes for a show. A final consideration is the cost of the fabric. Less expensive fabrics can often be used to simulate expensive cloth; corduroy, for example, is often used instead of velvet, and less expensive upholstery fabrics can be substituted for more expensive brocades or jacquards. At other times, the more expensive fabrics are necessary in order to achieve the appropriate appearance for the costume. The final choice with regard to cost is determined by what needs to be done to the fabric; whether it will give the right appearance for the design; if it is durable enough to withstand the strains of performance; and its relationship to the total show and budget.

Usually the costume designer selects the fabric for each costume, but it is also necessary for the costumer to be familiar with fabrics and to know which will best fulfill the costume requirements. The Fabric Glossary in Chap. 4 is a guideline for becoming familiar with the properties and functions of fabrics used for costumes.

LININGS FOR COSTUMES. The type and function of linings for the costume should also be considered for both durability and appearance. The factors which influence the selection of lining fabrics include whether or not the good fabric needs more body or weight in order to fall properly, often the case when trying to suggest something like the fur-lined robes of the fifteenth century. In this instance, a heavyweight canvas, or even felt, is appropriate as a lining. If the function of the lining is just to add durability to the costume and to protect it from abrasion and perspiration when worn, an unbleached muslin works very well. If the lining is going to be revealed in movement or purposefully revealed, as in the case of an open, flowing sleeve, the appearance of the lining needs to be carefully coordinated with the garment.

The method of attaching the lining to the garment is determined by how much of the inside of the garment will be seen by the audience. If the wrong side of the garment is to be visible, the lining should be coordinated and put in so that the seams are concealed. If the inside of the garment is not going to be seen, there is no need to conceal the seams or to use coordinated linings; the lining can be selected for its durability qualities since that is all that is required.

Again, how often the costume is to be cleaned and the method to be used must be included in the consideration and the selection of linings. If the garment is to be laundered, the lining must be a washable fabric and may have to be preshrunk before it is used in the costume.

CLOSINGS IN COSTUMES. Yet another consideration in determining the require- ments for the execution of the costume is the placement and type of closing for the garment. Where does it open so the actor can get into it, and how is it to be fastened? Does the garment need to be changed quickly? The position of the closing and the type of fastening have a considerable influence on the design and construction of the costume. Many periods accented and decorated the fastenings, thereby indicating the placement of the closing; other periods concealed the fastenings.

The most common method of closing modern garments is the zipper. However, the zipper was not invented until 1893 and was not popular until the 1940s. Therefore, it is generally inappropriate for most period garments; a flash of metal down the front of Hamlet's doublet can be quite disconcerting. Various types of closings and the appropriateness of the different ones are discussed more fully under Construction Supplies in Chap. 2.

INTERPRETING THE COSTUME PLATE

Ultimately, the most important responsibility in the costumer's work is to make up the costume to fulfill the requirements of the design and the production. To exemplify the processes involved, two costume plates have been selected for analysis for patterning and construction procedures. The selections illustrated were chosen because there is not a great deal of detail involved, and the patterning for the garments is not complex; both can easily be patterned and constructed using the basic principles of costuming and the selected costume crafts which are detailed throughout the book. In both instances, patterns can be developed using variations of the basic pattern drafts described in Part 2.

The analysis is based on observations of what is suggested in the sketch and the re- quirements of the production; it becomes a summation of what is necessary to assemble the costume.

Analysis of the "Isabella" Plate

The Isabella Plate (Fig. 1–8) is a design for a *Commedia dell' Arte* production and is a romanticized version of a pseudo-Elizabethan silhouette. The script for the production was actually a compilation of three Commedia scenerios; specific dialogue and stage business were developed in rehearsals by the director and the actors. Isabella is the stock ingénue lead whose love for Oratio is thwarted at every turn. Ultimately, through perseverance and a bit of trickery, she wins the day and is united with her lover.

Figure 1-8 A simplified costume sketch for "Isabella" to show details for analysis of the sketch for construction purposes. From the author's notebook.

The premise for the production was that of a touring company of players who would arrive (somewhat mud-spattered) on the scene, set up their equipment, and prepare for the performance as an overture to the show. To support this, the actors would arrive in a simple form of dress, and pieces of costumes would be added as part of this preparation so the audience would see the transformation from weary travelers to sparkling performers. For the character of Isabella, this meant arriving in a cape over a simple blouse and skirt; the over-gown, mask, and hair decoration would be added (with the assistance of the

actor who played her maid) on stage. Some of the stage business would include dressing the hair and a Scarlett O'Hara type of routine of lacing Isabella into the over-gown (Fig. 1-9).

SILHOUETTE. The body line is accented by a smooth torso, small waist, and extended hips, with a full skirt line over the legs. The line of the torso requires a corset to support the body and create the smooth line of the bodice. The corset should not be true to the Elizabethan line since the bust is not flattened; it is lifted and rounded, but the corseting should accent a small waist and smooth torso.

Hip-padding (in this instance a *bum-roll,* as described in Chap. 16) will be needed to

Figure 1-9 Completed "Isabella" costume for a *Commedia dell'Arte* production as produced at Rhode Island Junior College. From the author's collection.

19

help create and support the fullness of the skirt. In addition, one petticoat is visible, and at least one other petticoat will be needed to support the fullness of the skirt. It should also be noted that the use of the hip-padding will necessitate additional length for the skirt and petticoats to compensate for the amount of take-up over the padding. The type of shoe to be worn and its heel height will need to be determined before the skirt lengths can be cut.

CHARACTERISTIC DETAIL AND DÉCOR. The projection at the top of the armhole suggests a variation on the crescent-shaped "wing" that is characteristic of the Elizabethan silhouette; this will need to be cut separately and attached to the armhole to capture the correct shape. The sketch also suggests that welting (or piping, often used in upholstery) be added to accent the over-grown neckline and waistline.

The ruffling at the neckline could be just that rather than the full blouse it represents; however, since the over-gown is added on stage, the full blouse will be seen and is, therefore, necessary.

The décor is quite simple, consisting of a neckband for the neck and bows for the front of the garment and for the hair. The bows will need to be graded in size for the appropriate proportions in the costume.

POSTURE AND MOVEMENT. The garment requires erect posture, the arms need to be held slightly away from the body to help accentuate the small waist, and the head must be held high. The corset will assist in the erect posture, the hip-padding will influence the arm positions, and the neckband will aid the actor in holding the head high.

CONTROL IN THE GARMENT. The over-gown fits the upper torso very snugly, dropping in a V-shape over the abdomen in front, a characteristic detail of the Elizabethan silhouette. The design of the bodice, as well as bodice patterns of

the period, indicates that this is controlled by seams rather than by fitting darts (see Chap. 13) and that the torso needs to be corseted to achieve the smooth line in the bodice.

The blouse is gathered into a low neckline and features full sleeves with a puff at the upper arm. While we cannot see the length of the blouse, it needs to be long enough to tuck into a skirt since the actor will be seen in only the skirt and blouse at the beginning of the performance.

The skirt of the over-gown falls out and away from the waist; it is very full, cut on the straight grain, and is controlled by pleating. In this instance, the pleating is cartridge pleating (described in Chap. 9), which is another characteristic of the period. The plaid petticoat is full and is controlled by pleats, but the center front of the garment is left flat and unpleated. These pleats will need to be regular overlap pleats, and they will be controlled with a waistband so the petticoat can function as a simple skirt at the opening of the show. The additional petticoats can be made in the same manner, or simply gathered onto a waistband since they will not be visible to the audience.

FABRICS AND LININGS. The fabric of the over-gown needs to have a degree of body and weight as well as a textured, matte finish. A pin-wale corduroy was selected for the over-gown. The plaid petticoat also needs a certain amount of body but needs to be of a rougher texture than the over-gown to help support the traveling player image. Something like a butcher cloth or imitation linen will provide the body and the texture needed.

The blouse needs a soft fabric that is lightweight and washable. A simple cotton blend will work nicely.

The blouse and petticoats will not need to be lined, as the blouse must be kept soft and lightweight, and the petticoats serve as a lining to the total garment. The over-gown bodice will need to be lined; a canvas lining will add to the stiffened quality of the bodice. Since the over-gown skirt is opened in an inverted V at the front, it will kick open to reveal the lining. A colored lining taffeta, attached so as not to reveal the seams, is appropriate.

CLOSINGS. The stage business requires that the over-gown be laced closed in the back. This will require grommets (for the ties to go through) set into the bodice back, and snaps will be needed on the skirt portion of the gown.

The neckline of the blouse is large enough to go over the head without the aid of an opening, and the sleeves will be gathered with elastic to expand over the hand, so that no opening will be necessary at the wrists.

The petticoats can be closed with hooks and eyes at the side or back, whichever is most convenient, since the closing will be hidden in the pleats.

Analysis of the "Mr. Twinkle" Plate

Mr. Twinkle (Fig. 1–10) is a budding young poet in Anna Cora Mowatt's *Fashion*. He, like most of the characters in this satire on the foibles of fashionable society, is superficial and more concerned with the image he projects than with his poetry. The production was set in the 1830s and uses the era's extremes in silhouette and detail to underscore the frivolous preoccupations of the character.

SILHOUETTE. A small waist that is accentuated by fullness at the chest and hips is the basic silhouette of the 1830s. This does not require any particular body support items since the rounded chest and sloping shoulders can be accented with the cut and detail of the upper costume and a sufficient amount of fullness over the hips can be created by pleating the pants at the

Figure 1–10 A simplified costume sketch for "Mr. Twinkle" for *Fashion* by Anna Cora Mowatt. From the author's notebook.

waistline and tapering each leg of the pants to accentuate the leg.

CHARACTERISTIC DETAIL AND DÉCOR. The collar is wide to help accent the sloping shoulders and is finished with a decorative edge. There is also a large bow tied around the neck. The pant legs are long and are caught under the foot by means of a strap or stirrup.

POSTURE AND MOVEMENT. There are no specific movement requirements which are directly influenced by the costume other than the accent on the legs. This is enhanced by the stripe in the pant fabric and the length and shape of the bottom edge of the pants as well as the tapered toe of the shoe.

CONTROL IN THE GARMENT. There is some fullness indicated in the body of the shirt; the use of a yoke at the back of the shirt will enhance the smooth shoulder line and the appearance of the shirt. The sleeves of the shirt are full and will be gathered into the armhole and the narrow cuff.

The fullness at the hips of the pants is controlled by pleating the pant waist into a waistband. The accented pocket line on the pants can be false if no real pockets are required. Since this would be a stage-business concern, it should be checked with the designer and director.

FABRICS AND LININGS. The fabric of the shirt is specified by the designer as velveteen; the collar is white piqué, edged with eyelet, and should be removable for easy cleaning. A heavyweight green-and-white–striped duck cloth is indicated for the pants; the bottom of the legs will require extra length for the stirrup.

The weight of the duck in the pants is sufficient to create the line of the garment, so no lining is required. The shirt can also be unlined, with the exception of the yoke, which needs to be lined for extra durability. Unlined velveteen will fall softly in the manner shown in the sketch.

The actor will need a T-shirt under the shirt for his comfort, and dress shields should be set into the underarms of the shirt to protect it from perspiration.

CLOSINGS. The closing for the shirt is in the front and features buttons that are covered with the shirt fabric, called *self-covered buttons*. The pants have a traditional fly-closing, but the zipper will have to be carefully concealed since zippers were unknown during the period in which the play is set.

ACTION IN COSTUME

There is one final note with regard to specific costumes as illustrated by the designer in the costume plate. The drawing shows how the costume is to look in a posed position, but the costume will only be seen on stage in that position very briefly, if at all. The rest of the time it will be moving as the actor performs. Therefore, the costumer needs to know how the costume is to be utilized in movement, if it is to be changed quickly, if pockets or additional items are necessary, or if any unusual features are required. Much of this information is to be found in the script, so the costumer must be familiar with the requirements of the script.

Since the onstage action will considerably influence how the costume is assembled, both the designer and the costumer must know what the director and actors are preparing in the rehearsals and what the stage business of each actor is to be. Observing rehearsals, then, becomes an important aspect of the costuming process.

The information derived from the script and the stage business becomes part of the analysis and construction process. The specifics of all the stage business cannot be known from the outset because the performance is developed during the rehearsal process. However, key factors can be determined early. For example, if the script indicates that two properly dressed young men engage in fisticuffs, it is usually safe to assume that their suit coats will be removed for that exchange. Another script may have one character giving money to another; this means that there must be some means provided for carrying that money for both characters, whether it be a pocket or a purse.

The developmental nature of preparing a production for performance requires coordination between all concerned. In assembling costumes, this coordination is primarily concerned with what the costumes are to look like, how they are to move, and what the actors need to be able to do in them.

ADDITIONAL SOURCES

There are numerous books on the history of costume and of fashions that are valuable for research into various periods. These books can be found in the costume bibliographies cited in Appendix B. The following selected sources are useful for exploring the facets of costume design and movement in period garments.

ARNOLD, JANET, *A Handbook of Costume.* London: Macmillan London Ltd., 1973.

COREY, IRENE, *The Mask of Reality: An Approach to Design for the Theatre.* Anchorage, Ky.: The Anchorage Press, 1968.

GREEN, RUTH M., *The Wearing of Costume.* London: Sir Isaac Pitman & Sons, Ltd., 1966.

MOTLEY, *Designing and Making Stage Costumes.* New York: Watson-Guptill Publications, reprint 1974.

OXENFORD, LYN, *Playing Period Plays.* Chicago: The Coach House Press, Inc., 1959.

RUSSELL, DOUGLAS A., *Period Style for the Theatre.* Rockleigh, N.J.: Longwood Division, Allyn & Bacon, Inc., 1980.

——, *Stage Costume Design: Theory, Technique, and Style.* Englewood Cliffs, N.J.: Prentice-Hall, 1973.

SMITH, C. RAY, ed., *The Theatre Crafts Book of Costume.* Emmaus, Pa.: Rodale Press, Inc., 1973.

two

the costume workshop

The costume shop is the hub of all costuming activities. Since a number of people spend many hours in the costume shop, and there is always a degree of pressure to get things done well and on time, the space should be made as pleasant as possible. Part of this can be achieved by the color and décor on the walls. Light pastel colors which create a greater sense of space are preferable to dark enclosing colors or "hot" colors such as reds or yellows, which seem to create tensions. As illustrated in Fig. 2–1, hanging plants, masks, or other interesting items from previous productions, or even a collection of long, colorful beads, can be used to decorate the walls and create an interesting space in which to work. Floors that are easy to clean, and easy to retrieve the inevitable box of spilled pins from, are a great advantage. Tiled floors provide a hard surface that is easy to clean and are comfortable for those who stand for long hours at the cutting table. They are preferable to ce-ment floors or even carpeting. In addition, a radio to provide pleasant background music also increases the congeniality of the workshop. Of course there should be a space set aside for the essential coffee pot, and we have found that a small refrigerator is very useful.

There is an old catch phrase that specifies "a place for everything, and everything in its place"; this is a worthy motto for any costume shop. Ideally the workshop should provide adequate work space for cutting and sewing, space with good ventilation for dyeing and painting, and space for accessory fabrication that is also well ventilated. There should be a laundry area with washer, dryer, sinks, and running water, and there should be space within the shop for storage of fabrics, notions, and other supplies. A fitting area that is apart enough to be private is very important, and a separate, large, dry storage area for costume stock and other items is invaluable.

Figure 2-1 This view of the costume workshop at the University of Rhode Island shows the arrangement of the equipment in the shop. Notice the wall decorations, hanging plants, and the thread and bead storage facilities on the walls that also provide additional color. Photo by Robert Izzo.

All should be readily accessible to the dressing rooms and performance areas for easy transportation of costumes. If the workshop, storage space, and performance-related areas are not on the same level, there should be a large elevator to transport rolling racks of the costumes. The workshop should be supplied with sufficient electricity to operate all equipment simultaneously, and the working areas should be well lighted, preferably with incandescent lighting for truer color.

Of course, the ideal workshop is a rare thing indeed. The costumer rarely has the opportunity to design the workshop space and its relationship to other necessary areas. In real life, the actual workshop is usually less than ideal, and the space available dictates the arrangement which will provide the most efficient method of operation.

The actual space, combined with personal preferences, methods of working, and the type and amount of equipment, will influence how each shop is organized. However, the specifications of an ideal workshop can provide the fundamentals for setting up and organizing a very usable workshop. Necessary and optional equipment and tools for the workshop are cited and defined in the Workshop Glossary later in this chapter.

WORKING AREAS. The costuming activities which occur in the workshop are numerous and varied, with each activity requiring slightly different features. The cutting space needs to be fairly large and free of clutter, with easy access to the drafting and cutting tools. New fabrics for a show should be close by and there should be bins or boxes in which to collect usable

25

scraps of the fabric being cut. The sewing space should provide room for machine-sewing, a hand-sewing area, and ironing space. The machines need to be set up so there is clearance for large amounts of fabric in the front, back, and side of each machine as well as floor space for a sturdy straight-back chair for the operator. A separate hand-sewing area provides seating for people working on this phase of the costumes and keeps the machine space free. The ironing areas should be easily accessible to encourage pressing during the construction process. There should also be rack space for hanging the costumes in progress.

The accessory fabrication area also needs to have a clear working space with easy access to the jewelry, millinery, and other special tools. This area requires good ventilation since the fabrication techniques often call for the use of caustic or volatile materials (see Chaps. 15 and 19). Ideally, this area would be in an adjoining room so that the fumes and activities there do not interfere with the other costuming work.

The dyeing space is often the same as the laundry area. This area should be well ventilated; it should have hot and cold running water and a double sink for washing and rinsing. A floor drain and easy-to-clean surfaces on counter and floor will make maintenance easier, and storage shelves or cabinets for supplies will keep it neat.

Laundry equipment is detailed in the Workshop Glossary, and dyeing equipment, tools, and supplies are discussed in Chap. 15.

STORAGE AREAS. The number and location of storage areas is determined by the space available and the uses of the items to be stocked. The lack of adequate storage space is a constant lament in most theatres and workshops. One's inventiveness is often taxed when trying to figure out where and how to store things, but the basic criterion of storage is simply being able to find things when you need them and knowing or remembering if you have a particular item.

Sewing supplies, notions, drafting tools, trims and decorative items, fabrics, and related accessory tools should be readily accessible in the workshop. The space under the worktables is very useful for storage. If drawers and shelves can be custom-built, that is ideal; if not, chests of drawers and ready-made shelving can be placed under the tables. Various types of dividers in drawers will keep things straight. We have found, for example, that a divider as simple as an egg carton is valuable for storing pairs of earrings and bits and pieces of jewelry. Shelving for fabrics and other tools provides ready access, and nails driven into the walls will hold strings of beads, ribbons, spools of thread, bobbins, and numerous other items.

Storage arrangements need not be fancy, but they must be usable. If stored items are easy to reach when needed, if containers are clearly labeled as to contents, and if items are put back where they belong between uses, very simple storage arrangements will do.

Of course, items necessary to the fitting process should be readily accessible to the fitting area, just as laundry items and the dyeing and painting materials should be accessible to those work areas.

There should also be a large area for storing costumes and accessories that are not in use for specific productions. Heavy-duty, permanent racks for hanging costumes should be 6 ft high to accommodate long garments; double racks, as shown in Fig. 2-2, are useful for storing men's suits and other short items. The racks should be capable of supporting a great deal of weight; we use 1 in. "black pipe" for our racks. The racks should be spaced to allow each rack the width of a coat hanger plus clearance for the fullness of the garments to be hung there. If the

Figure 2-2 Examples of permanent costume storage racks, one of which is a double rack. The wall space beyond the single rack is used for storing shoes. Photo by Robert Izzo.

urement. These boxes can be stacked on top of one another since the weight of each is not great, and each can be pulled out like a drawer when needed. All boxes used for storage should be sturdy and have covers to protect against dust. It is advisable to reinforce the box corners with strong packaging tape. Each box should be clearly labeled to identify the contents. If the storage space has a high ceiling, use high shelves but store only light items, such as hats, on the top shelves and be sure you have a ladder handy.

Walls are also useful for some types of storage. For example, we have made shoe hangers out of heavy cloth and hung them on the walls in the storage area as shown in Fig. 2-2. They take up very little space in the room and allow for quick, easy access to the shoes. Clear floor space and a worktable are also valuable in the storage area for sorting items, labeling boxes, and other work.

FITTING SPACE. Specific requirements for the fitting space are discussed in detail in Chap. 12. Briefly, though, in regard to planning the shop layout, keep in mind that this area should be separated from the other work areas in order to provide the needed privacy. It can be very uncomfortable for the actor to go through a fitting while being watched by those working in the shop. If a separate space is not available, use a folding screen to partition off an area. Allow for shelving and cabinets sufficient to hold the tools and materials needed in the fitting process. There should also be a full-length mirror in the fitting space.

racks are placed close together in pairs, with walkways only between the pairs instead of on either side of each rack, there will be full freedom of access to all the stored items, but less floor space will be taken up by the access paths.

Shelving is useful for storing small or flat items. Sturdy dress boxes are good for men's shirts sized according to neck meas-

GLOSSARY OF WORKSHOP EQUIPMENT AND TOOLS

In order to produce costumes efficiently, the workshop needs certain basic equipment and supplies. While each production may require additional special supplies,

these can be added to the stock as the occasion arises. Many of the more "specialized" supplies and tools are discussed in subsequent chapters that deal directly with the

methods involved in creating certain costuming effects.

The basic tools and supplies for a well-equipped costume shop are enumerated and described in the following glossary. The glossary is divided into categories based on the primary functions of the items cited. The categories are

> Workshop Tools and Supplies
> Drafting and Cutting Tools
> Machine-Sewing Equipment and Supplies
> Hand-Sewing Notions and Supplies
> Construction Supplies and Notions

Each entry gives a general definition of the item, suggests some of its functions, and includes information for selecting a specific type or make for the workshop. In some cases there are suggestions for locating the item if it is not available in a local store. Appendix B gives many sources for supplies and equipment, and an additional resource for discovering suppliers in your own area can be found in the Yellow Pages of your phone book.

Workshop Tools and Supplies

CUTTING TABLE (Fig. 2–3). This large table used for drafting patterns and cutting garments is a major item in the workshop. The specific height and size of the table depend on personal preference and available space. Such tables are usually about waist-high, but the exact height should be determined for comfort while cutting to minimize strain on the user's back. The width of the table should be sufficient to accommodate 45 in. (115 cm) wide fabric and the length should be convenient for cutting long fabric lengths and still allow some space for the drafting and cutting tools being used. A table 4 ft wide by 8 ft long is sufficient for most drafting and cutting needs.

A thin layer of cork, ⅛ in. to ¼ in. (0.3 cm to 0.6 cm) thick, adhered to the top of the table, makes a good working surface. The fabric will not slip on this surface and can be pinned directly into the soft top layer. A sheet of homosote will work in place of the cork. Its surface is not as nice to work on, but it is cheaper.

Drawers in the table for storage of cutting and drafting tools are recommended. The space under the table is good for additional storage drawers or shelves and scrap boxes.

An interesting variation for the cork-top table is to make the soft working surface a separate, removable panel. This can be accomplished by adhering a thin layer of cork on a sheet of ½ in. plywood which matches the dimensions of the table and mounting a strip of wood along the length of the table on one side. The edge of the wood should be slightly above the surface of the table with the cork top in place, similar to a pencil rail on a drawing table. This independent cork top can then be used flat, tilted with supports at the back (Fig. 15–7), or it can be removed if heavy work which would damage the cork is to be done on the table surface.

DRESS FORMS. Several types of forms are available, but the inexpensive adjustable forms which are popular for domestic use have proved to be too fragile for use in a costume shop. Commercial padded forms on heavy-duty adjustable stands are durable and most preferable. A minimum of three female forms, sizes 10, 12, and 14, should be on hand. These forms can be somewhat enlarged to match measurement variations or be converted into male torso configurations by wrapping the form with thin sheets of foam rubber. Commercial padded male forms on heavy-duty stands are also available; sizes 38 and 42 are recommended as a minimum. Moldable forms are available in many fabric shops. These can be molded into various body configurations and sizes; however, they are almost as expensive as the more durable

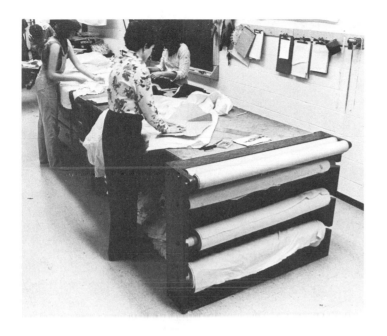

Figure 2-3 An example of a cutting table with bolts of fabric stored at the end. Storage shelves and drawers are under the table, and work notes and shopping lists are on the wall behind. Photo by Robert Izzo.

commercial forms and have a shorter life span. Plastic mannequins can be valuable as units or separate pieces. Mannequin legs, for example, make good forms for painting or aging tights.

HAMMERS. Used for anything from setting grommets to driving nails on which to hang bobbins, a claw hammer that pries crates open and pulls nails has general usefulness, and a ballpein hammer can be invaluable for bending and shaping materials for props and accessories. A tack hammer is also worthwhile for setting upholstery tacks and similar items.

HANGERS. A good supply of heavy-gauge wire hangers should be on hand. Wooden hangers are good for heavy costumes, and specialty hangers such as skirt and pant hangers help maintain individual costumes during the run of the show. Dry-cleaning suppliers are good sources for hangers.

IRONS (Fig. 2–4). Heavy-duty steam irons with portable tanks that hold up to three gallons of water are available com-

mercially and are valuable in a workshop. These irons are designed to be left on for the entire workday without burning out the iron or damaging it. Distilled water is held in the tank and is forced into the iron under pressure. The hot iron converts the water into steam which is released manually. This iron provides a greater concentration of steam and more efficient results than domestic irons. Domestic irons have a very short life span in a workshop and need to be replaced regularly. Our heavy-duty irons have been in use over six years and have required virtually no repair. These units are available from several sources cited in Appendix B.

A common problem with steam irons is dripping and spitting water, which generally comes out rusty and always on the center front of the costume. The major cause of this problem is that the iron is too cool to convert the water to steam. Always make sure the iron is hot before setting the iron to release the steam. A second cause of water spotting is mineral deposits in the iron. Always use distilled water to prevent

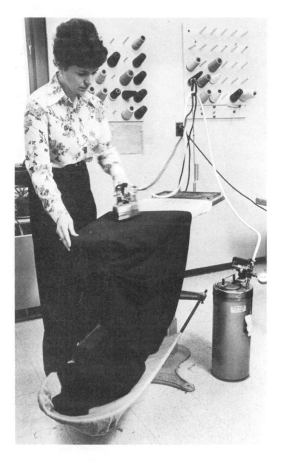

Figure 2-4 An example of a heavy-duty steam iron with portable tank on the floor. The ironing table is a heavy-duty and noncollapsible model with a fabric sling to keep the fabrics being pressed off the floor. Note the thread and bobbin storage on the wall. Photo by Robert Izzo.

rust buildups and never leave water standing in the iron when it is not hot.

IRONING TABLE (Fig. 2-4). Heavy-duty, noncollapsible ironing tables are available commercially and are very durable; consequently, they are preferable to portable domestic ironing boards which have a short life span in a workshop. Domestic boards are valuable, however, when mobility is necessary.

IRONING SUPPLIES (Fig. 2-5). Certain items are valuable for special ironing problems such as curved seams and sleeves.

A *sleeve board* is a small ironing board shaped to slip inside sleeves and other tubular shapes for easier pressing. It is available at most notion counters.

Tailor's hams are made in several sizes and are stuffed shapes which are used to slip inside curved seams and difficult-to-reach areas for easier ironing. They are available at most notion counters.

A *velvet board* has a surface that looks like a miniature bed of nails and is used for pressing velvet. The velvet is placed on the board, pile side down; the board surface supports the cloth without crushing the pile. These boards, also sold by the name "needle board," are available through major notions supply houses.

METAL FILE. A hand tool specifically for metal work, this tool is used to smooth rough metal edges on jewelry or corset stays and is available in hardware stores.

MIRROR. A full-length mirror in which the actors may see themselves in costume during fittings is valuable. It also helps the costumer keep track of wrinkles, straightness of seams, and the level of hems during the fitting process. It should be located in the fitting area.

PAPER. A roll of heavy brown wrapping paper for making patterns is indispensable.

PLIERS. Several types of this hand tool are needed.

Sheep-nosed pliers with slip-joint hinge and toothed jaws are useful for holding, gripping, or bending a variety of materials.

Cutting pliers which have a cutting edge as well as a flat surface are necessary for cutting wire, trimming corset stays, and many other uses.

Needle-nosed pliers with long, thin jaws are essential for bending wire into small shapes and for reaching areas too small for fingers or other pliers.

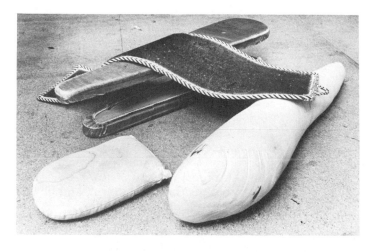

Figure 2–5 Examples of selected ironing supplies: *above,* velvet or needle board over a sleeve board; *below left,* a tailor's mitt; *right,* a tailor's ham. This particular ham is actually a muslin fitted sleeve that has been stuffed and finished at the ends; this can be pinned to a dress form to add arms to the form where necessary. Photo by Robert Izzo.

RACKS. Rolling costume racks 5 ft 6 in. (165 cm) to 6 ft (180 cm) high by 4 ft to 6 ft (120 cm to 180 cm) long with a shelf across the bottom are valuable for hanging and shifting costumes into workshops and dressing rooms. Permanent standing racks or racks suspended from the wall can be used in the workshop but have less flexibility.

SCREWDRIVERS. Several assorted sizes of this hand tool are essential: small sizes for machine adjustments and repair and larger ones for work on props and other projects. There should be at least one small screwdriver for each sewing machine for replacing needles and removing cover plates for cleaning.

SEWING MACHINES. The number and type of machines depend on space available, general workload of the shop, and personal preference. Several types of machines are available. See Machine-Sewing Equipment for a more complete discussion.

STEPLADDER. Small or medium-height, lightweight ladders are useful to reach high storage areas.

STORAGE SHELVES, BOXES, AND CHESTS OF DRAWERS. These units are necessary for storage of the general workshop items. Inexpensive heavy-steel shelving 6 ft (180 cm) high by 3 ft (91.5 cm) wide with 18 in. (46 cm) deep adjustable shelves is recommended. Strong boxes uniform in size with lids or covers give the most efficient storage; book cartons or liquor shipping boxes are good strong containers. Chests of drawers can be found in the prop shop or at yard sales.

TAPES. Various adhesive-backed tapes are multipurpose.

Adhesive tape. The regular half-inch tape is handy for quick labeling of accessories and garments, but it will generally fall off garments when they are washed.

Cellophane tape. The "magic" type that does not yellow or peel is the most desirable. It has many uses including piecing patterns together.

Masking tape. The ¾ in. or 1 in. tape has many functions, including labeling spaces on costume racks and blocking out areas when painting.

WASHER AND DRYER. Top-loading large-capacity washing machines and front-loading dryers are a great asset in a shop. The small apartment-size washer with a spin-dry chamber is valuable for dyeing and as a substitute for the larger laundry units if they are not available or if space is limited.

WASTE CANS. Large trash cans are essential, and small waste cans set by each sewing machine save a lot of cleanup time.

Drafting and Cutting Tools (Fig. 2–6)

FRENCH CURVE. Dressmaker's french curves are useful for drafting necklines and armholes. They are available at most notion counters.

SCISSORS. Several sizes are recommended: small for clipping threads and seams, medium for trimming fabrics, and large for cutting garments. All scissors must be kept sharp and in good condition. Oil the hinge occasionally for smooth operation, but excess oil must be wiped off before cutting fabric. A cardinal rule for the use of scissors is: Fabric scissors are for fabric only. Keep separate scissors for paper and other materials which dull scissors quickly.

Dressmaker's scissors have a raised handle on an angle from the blade to allow the blade to rest on the cutting surface while the hand is raised above the fabric for easier cutting. These are available in 8, 10, and 12 in. lengths for either the right or left hand; both should be part of the supplies.

Pinking shears are used for fabrics that ravel easily. The cutting edge cuts a sawtooth pattern which interferes with long threads pulling out of the fabric. However, they are difficult to keep sharp and are of minimal value in a costume shop since overcasting or hemming provides more durable securing of cut edges in a stage costume.

Paper scissors are any pair of old scissors which are reserved for cutting paper. No fabric scissors should ever be used for cutting paper.

TAILOR'S CHALK. The flat wax-compound type, available in white, black, red, yellow, and blue, is recommended over the regular pressed-powder type which tends to brush off prematurely. The wax-compound type is used to draw pattern and alteration markings and can be removed by melting the markings off the fabric with a hot iron. It is necessary to check the chalk on the fabric prior to use; it leaves an oil-type stain on some fabrics, and the pigments stay in the fabric. The white chalk is the most useful, and all are available from notions suppliers.

TAILOR'S SQUARE. A rectangular ruler 15 in. (38 cm) by 4 in. (10 cm) that is used to establish right angle lines on fabric. The square is made of clear plastic for easy alignment on the fabric. Available from notions suppliers, several should be kept on hand for all pattern drafting.

TAPE MEASURE. Several flexible plastic measuring tapes with large numbers are indispensable for taking measurements and drafting patterns.

TRACING PAPER. A heavy paper with a waxed, colored surface used to transfer pattern and alteration markings is available in packages of assorted colors.

TRACING WHEEL. A tool that resembles a miniature pizza cutter with a saw-tooth edge, it is used like a pounce wheel with the tracing paper to transfer pattern marking and alterations and can be found at notions counters.

TRIANGLE. A large, clear-plastic right-angle triangle for drafting patterns is very helpful and can be found at artist supply houses or notions counters.

YARDSTICK. Metal ones are more durable than the wooden yardsticks, but either will work. They are essential for laying out straight lines on patterns and can be found in hardware stores.

Figure 2-6 Examples of selected drafting tools and notions: *above,* dressmaker's french curve, large cone of thread, tape measure, and button thread; *middle,* tailor's square over tracing paper, mat knife, and tracing wheel; *below,* seam ripper, T-pins, and beeswax. Photo by Robert Izzo.

Machine-Sewing Equipment and Supplies

Bobbins. Several bobbins for each machine are necessary and will save a good deal of time. Only one color of thread should be on a bobbin at one time. Bobbins can be stored on nails in the wall near the machines. This type of storage allows for quick selection of color and eliminates tangled thread between bobbins as may happen when they are stored loose in a drawer. Several are usually provided with the machine; additional ones can be purchased from the retailer.

Brushes. Stiff-bristled brushes are used to remove lint and threads from the sewing machines. In order to function properly, the machines must be kept clean and lint-free. Brushes are usually provided with the machines, and additional ones are available from the retailer.

Buttonhole Attachment (Fig. 2-7). This attachment is used on straight-stitch sewing machines to make buttonholes of various sizes. Operating instructions come with the attachment which is valuable for making consistent, error-free buttonholes. Buttonholes can be made on a zigzag machine without this attachment.

Knitting Machine. Used to manufacture knitted cloth or garments, a knitting machine provides additional versatility in

33

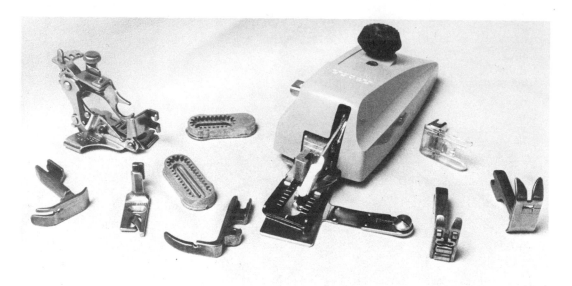

Figure 2-7 Examples of selected presser feet: *from left to right,* straight stitch foot, pleater foot (*above*) roll hemmer, cams for buttonhole attachment, cording foot which can also be used as a zipper foot, buttonhole attachment, clear plastic foot, roller-bar foot, and zigzag foot. Photo by Robert Izzo.

creating a variety of textures and colors. Sources are cited in Appendix B.

MANUAL.   The manual that is supplied with each machine provides essential information for the operation and care of the machine. It must be studied carefully and kept with the machine for reference. Most problems with machines can be avoided or at least corrected by following the instructions in the manual.

NEEDLES.   Two types are available—the standard, or sharp-pointed, needles and ball-point needles which have a rounded tip and are designed for use with polyesters and knits in order to prevent the needle from pulling the threads. The rounded tip slips between the fibers of the fabric rather than through the fiber, thereby preventing snags and pulls in the cloth. Ball-point needles can be used on all fabrics and are available in the same sizes as standard needles. Both American and European sizing of needles is shown in Fig. 2–8.

Machine needles are also sized according to the length of the needle. Since all needles do not fit every machine, the manual will designate the proper needle for the given machine. If the needle length is incorrect, the machine will not function properly. If the needle is too long, it will break; if it is too short, it will not pick up the bobbin thread to complete the stitch.

Most needles have a flat side at the top of the shank, and all needles have a long groove on one side which is the side the thread goes through first. A simple method of determining how to place a needle in the machine and how to thread it is to remember that the long groove generally follows the line of the last thread guide. If the last guide is in the front of the machine, the long groove faces the front, and the needle is threaded from front to back; if the guide is on the left side, the long groove is on the left side, and the needle is threaded from left to right. To be sure, check the manual for the particular machine, since a needle inserted the wrong

Fabric	American	European
Lightweight	9–11	70
Medium Weight	14–15	90
Heavyweight	16–18	100

Figure 2–8 Sewing machine needle size chart shows American and European equivalents and the appropriate needle sizes for various fabric weights.

way will keep the machine from completing stitches.

OIL. Lightweight sewing-machine oil is essential for lubricating the machines and is available from the retailer. The manual will indicate when, where, and how often to oil the machine. Do not use the heavier, general-purpose "household" oils.

PRESSER-FOOT ATTACHMENTS (Fig. 2–7). These pieces control the fabric under the needle when sewing. Several types usually come with the sewing machine, and additional types are available from the retailer. The manual will give complete operating instructions for each attachment. The following are the most useful in the workshop.

Even-feed foot has a sawtooth bottom surface to give a better and more even feed to fabrics, such as velvet, which tend to slip or slide with a conventional presser foot.

Pleater foot is a complex-looking attachment which is valuable for pleating narrow, lightweight lengths of fabric for decorative edgings called "ruching." They are fragile and do not always function properly, but when they do, they save hours of time.

Roll hemmer foot rolls the fabric over while stitching to make rolled hems.

Roller-bar foot is used for stitching stretch fabrics and glossy finished fabrics such as the "wet-look" fabrics. The prongs and base of the foot have small wheels which roll.

Straight stitch foot is a narrow double-prong foot used for straight stitching.

Zigzag foot is a wide double-prong foot with a wide needle slot used for zigzag stitching on zigzag machines only. It can also be used for straight stitching.

Zigzag clear-plastic foot is particularly valuable for buttonhole work on a zigzag machine because the clear plastic allows you to see the work directly under the needle.

Zipper foot is a single-prong foot that is made to allow the prong to adjust from side to side to permit stitching next to the zipper teeth. A *cording foot* is similar in shape but is not adjustable.

SEWING MACHINES. The number and type of machines in the workshop depend on the space available, general workload of the shop, and personal preference. Regardless of the type or brand of machine, it must be properly used and cleaned. Each machine comes with a manual that must be carefully studied and kept with the machine for reference. Each machine seems to develop its own personality, and a costumer needs to become familiar with the machines in the shop and be able to do simple repair work on them. The manual is the guide for repair work and general maintenance. It is important to remember that a clean, well-oiled machine is a "happy machine." Sources for machines are listed in Appendix B, and local sources can be found in the Yellow Pages of the phone book.

Domestic machines are made for home use and range from simple straight-stitch machines to complex multifunction machines. Domestic machines with the following features are valuable in the workshop: reverse stitch, zigzag stitch, stretch stitch, and blind-hem stitch.

Free-arm machines (Fig. 2–9), with the larger sewing surfaces removable, are valuable for stitching tubes such as sleeves and pant legs.

Additional features that are found on some domestic machines are virtually use-

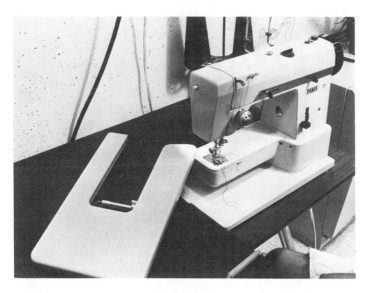

Figure 2-9 An example of a portable, domestic free-arm machine with the larger sewing surface removed; the free arm is valuable for stitching tubes such as sleeves or pant legs. Photo by Robert Izzo.

less in a costume shop and only complicate the mechanism of the machine. The more complex the mechanism, the more readily the machine will break down.

Industrial machines (Fig. 2-10) are durable heavy-duty machines which are available with straight stitch and zigzag stitch features. Industrial machines are built to operate at very fast speeds, but they can be geared down for slower operation by less-experienced people. These machines are made for heavy use and have a long life span. They can be used on all weights of fabric and have a durability and versatility which make them very useful in a workshop. The mechanism for the machines is simple and easy to maintain, and the cost is comparable to many domestic machines.

Industrial blind-stitch machines (Fig. 2-11, p. 38) make a chain stitch with one thread (there is no bobbin) that is barely visible on one side of the fabric. Primarily used to hem garments, this machine can save hours of hemming time.

Lock-stitch (*merrowing*) *machines* (Fig. 2-10) are available in industrial and domestic models. A lock-stitch machine trims seam allowance while overcasting the edge and lock-stitching the seam all in one operation. These machines are excellent for use on knits and jerseys and for making strong finished seams on items like corsets.

Hand-Sewing Notions and Supplies

BEESWAX.   Used on thread to strengthen it and to prevent knotting, it is available in chunks at most notions counters. The thread is coated with the wax by pulling it through the wax.

CARPET AND BUTTON THREAD.   A waxed heavyweight thread that is strong and durable, it is used to attach buttons, snaps, and hooks and eyes. It is also good for hand-gathering heavy fabric. The color range is generally limited to black, brown, tan, and grey; it is available at notions counters.

NEEDLES.   Regular hand needles come in a range of sizes; the higher numbers indicate the finer or thinner needles. Sizes 9 to 10 are good for sheers, sizes 3 to 5 for medium-weight fabrics, and sizes 2 to 4 for heavyweight fabrics. Since needles have a

Figure 2-10 An example of an industrial sewing machine in the foreground and a domestic lock-stitch (merrowing) machine in the background. Photo by Robert Izzo.

way of disappearing, a large supply is recommended. Once in use, needles should be kept in a pincushion; sticking needles into spools of thread damages the thread and causes it to knot and break. Certain specialty needles should also be kept in stock.

Bodkin is a large needle with a rounded tip used for heavy knits, work with yarn, and prepunched leather.

Curved (upholstery) needle has a heavy curved shank and is used for special work on padded pieces.

Leather needle has a triangular-shaped shank and is used for stitching leather and furs.

PINCUSHION. Several in large sizes are needed for needle and pin storage. The type with the emery bags attached is useful for removing burrs from needles.

RAZOR BLADES. The single-edge blade or one that can be inserted in a handle is preferable. Razor blades are useful when cutting leather or fur but should not be used for ripping seams. The blade will cut

37

Figure 2-11 An example of an industrial blind-stitch machine that is used primarily to hem garments. Photo by Robert Izzo.

through the fabric as readily as it will cut the stitching. Use a seam ripper.

SAFETY PINS. Assorted sizes are essential and can be purchased in bulk from notions supply houses.

SEAM RIPPER (Fig. 2-6). A single-prong tool set in a handle, it is used for ripping out seams and unwanted stitches. It is an essential tool, and several should be kept in stock. They are available at notions counters.

STRAIGHT (COMMON) PINS. Steel pins, rather than brass, are advisable because after the inevitable spill, they can be picked up with a magnet. Pins should be purchased by the pound, a more economical packaging, and are available at notions supply houses. Three sizes are recommended: lightweight (no. 10 to 15) for sheer fabrics, medium weight (no. 17 to 20) for general use, and heavyweight (no. 32) for heavy fabrics, leather, fur, or millinery. Straight pins are sized in $1/16$ in. increments so that a no. 10 pin is $10/16$ in. long, a no. 17 pin is $1 1/16$ in. long, and so forth.

T-PINS (Fig. 2-6). This is a heavyweight T-shaped pin that allows the pin to be pushed through wigs or heavy materials easily. The shape keeps the pinhead from getting lost in material such as hair or fur. They are available at notions counters.

THIMBLE. A metal or plastic guard for the finger tip is a must with hand-sewing to protect the finger used to push the needle through the fabric. They are available in a range of sizes; several should be kept in the shop since one size does not fit all.

THREAD. It is available in cotton or synthetic fibers; mercerized cotton thread

38

is preferable but is often difficult to find. Polyester thread has some degree of stretch and will work well on most fabrics, but it will not take a dye and often frays on the sewing machine. Nylon thread can be a problem since it can cut fibers and other threads. It is difficult to work with and is not recommended for general use.

Large cones (Fig. 2–6) of 1200 yards are the most economical and can be found at notions supply houses. Spools with less than 600 yards are not economical except in unusual colors for short-term use. The large cones of thread will not be supported by the normal thread spindle on machines; however, holders for the cones are a worthwhile investment and are available from industrial sewing-machine vendors.

Thread is available in several sizes or weights. The medium-weight 50 or 60 is the most commonly used. Thread sizing uses high numbers, 70 to 100, for light-weights, and low numbers, 8 to 20, for heavyweights. Lightweight threads are seldom used in a costume shop, unless the fabric is very sheer, because of the lack of strength.

A range of colors including black and white should be kept in stock. These basic colors include red, yellow, orange, light and dark greens, blues, greys, and browns. Special colors to match unusual fabrics should be purchased with the fabric.

Construction Supplies and Notions

ADHESIVES. There are many types and brands of adhesives on the market. For general purposes, two types should be kept in stock: an all-purpose glue for solid objects and a flexible glue that will not crack or peel on fabrics as they move. Additional special adhesives may be required for certain plastics and other materials.

All-purpose adhesives. A white clear-drying glue, such as Elmer's Glue, has many uses, particularly for costume prop-erties and accessories. These glues also make an excellent sizing for hats when mixed with equal parts of dry starch and water (see Chap. 18).

Flexible adhesives. There are several types of flexible adhesives, each of which has properties that are applicable to a variety of costume projects. A sample of the type selected should be tested on the actual fabric prior to use to determine the degrees of adhesion and flexibility.

Barge Cement (brand name) is a flexible contact glue that is used primarily for leather, but it is also usable on other fabrics and materials such as foam rubber. Barge thinner should also be kept on hand to extend the glue which thickens with evaporation. Both are available at hardware stores and leather supply houses.

Contact spray flexible adhesive, such as 3M Spray Trim Adhesive, is effective for adhering foam rubber, fabrics, and/or trim together. The glue comes in an aerosol can and is available from craft supply houses.

Hot-melt glue is indispensable because it has so many uses such as gluing sections of hats together, applying trims, or used by itself as three-dimensional decoration. The glue is applied with a glue gun, and there are several models on the market, any of which will serve the purpose. The glue melts to a semifluid state at 300 to 400 degrees F. and hardens and cools within 60 seconds. The glue comes in stick form and is available along with the gun at most hardware stores.

Ply-On Film (brand name) is used to laminate fabrics together. The film is a sheet of plastic backed with heavy paper; the plastic serves as the adhesive in the lamination process. The fabric is pressed with a dry iron at a low setting onto the shiny (plastic) side of the sheet. When cooled, the fabric and film is cut to the design shape, and the paper backing is peeled away. The plastic-backed fabric will not ravel and the shape is ready to be ironed in place as an "iron-on patch" or appliqué. Since the cut fabric will not ravel, it can also be used to make flowers and other fabric items. Ply-On Film is available from theatrical supply houses.

Stitch Witchery (brand name) is a material used to laminate fabrics together. It looks like a very sheer pellon and is cut to match the shape of the piece which is to be laminated to the fabric. It is then sandwiched between the fabrics and pressed with a hot iron. The heat from the iron melts the Stitch Witchery so that it impregnates both fabrics to hold them together. It is available under several brand names and can be purchased by the yard or in prepackaged amounts at notions counters. The package also includes instructions on how to use the material.

Transparent polyvinyl glue, such as Swift's Flexible Adhesive no. 3917, is often used to coat industrial-weight felt to mold a shape for something like armor (see Chap. 19). The glue can be stained with dye, metallic powders, graphite, or paint to look like leather or metal. This glue is also an excellent sealer for styrofoam before the foam is painted.

BUTTONS. Decorative buttons can be purchased as necessary. A supply of assorted sizes for making fabric-covered ("self") buttons is advisable along with the collection of assorted buttons which accumulate over a period of time.

CORSET STAYS (Fig. 2–12). Available in several lengths, corset stays are thin flexible bands of spring steel coated with paint and tipped with plastic so there are no sharp edges. One-half inch wide stays in 6 in., 8 in., and 12 in. (15 cm, 20.5 cm, and 30.5 cm) lengths are recommended. The stays can be cut, filed smooth, and dipped in liquid plastic (available from craft suppliers) to shorten the lengths. Stays made of wire in a flattened spiral pattern are also available, but the length of these stays cannot be trimmed down as easily.

The stays are used for the construction of corsets and period bodices (see Chap. 16). Large notions and surgical supply houses stock a range of sizes in corset stays.

ELASTIC. Available in various widths, both black and white elastic that is ½ in. wide is recommended for general use. It can be purchased by the bolt from large notions supply houses.

FABRIC TAPES. There are several types of cloth tape which are used for different purposes.

Bias tape is a bias-weave tape, with a single or double fold, used for finishing curved edges in garments. It can be purchased by the bolt in black, white, and colors from notions supply houses. Small amounts prepackaged in a range of colors are also available but are not as economical as the bolts.

Hem or *rayon tape* is a flat lightweight tape with finished edges and is available in a wide range of colors. Used to finish hems, this tape has somewhat limited use in a shop since it is not very durable. It is available in packages at notions counters.

Lacing is the tubular lacing manufactured for shoe laces. White cotton lacing is useful for lacing garments closed, and it can be dyed any color. It is available by the bolt from cording manufacturers.

Twill tape is a herringbone-weave tape with finished edges. It can be used for ties, drawstrings, corset-stay casings, and other casings on the straight grain. It is available in a range from ¼ in. to 1 in. (.6 cm to 2.5 cm) widths and can be purchased by the bolt from notions supply houses. Both black and white ¾ in. (2 cm) wide tape is recommended; the prepackaged twill tape is not as economical as that purchased by the bolt but is available in a range of colors.

FEATHERBONING (Fig. 2–12). A lightweight flexible boning covered with fabric, featherboning can be stitched directly onto the garment and does not require additional casings as do the corset stays. It

Figure 2-12 Examples of coiled feather boning, spring steel corset stays, and a grommet set with grommets. The fabric is cut with the cutter (*left*). The grommet stud is set on the stand, and the washer is placed over the stud with the fabric sandwiched in between. The grommet is set with the setting rod (*center right*). Photo by Robert Izzo.

does not give as firm support as the stays, but it does work satisfactorily for minimal corseting in a bodice and modestly sized hoop skirts. It is available in black and white and can be purchased by the yard from most notions supply houses.

GROMMETS AND GROMMET KIT (Fig. 2-12). The grommet is a two-piece (top and bottom) metal ring that reinforces the lacing holes in garments. The color range is limited to brass and silver, but they are available in a range of sizes; for use in costumes, sizes 0 and 1 are best. Grommets and grommet kits are available at most hardware stores. Grommets are more secure than the multicolored eyelets which are one-piece units that pull out of cloth easily.

HOOKS AND EYES. Black and silver hooks and eyes, sizes 3 and 5, purchased by the gross from notions supply houses are the most economical. Larger sizes such as the number 306 hook or the large cape hooks and eyes are valuable for use on heavy garments. Some small sizes may be needed for sheers. Hooks and eyes are used on a closing that has some stress or pulling against itself. If the closing is loose, without any stress, the hook and eye will not stay closed. Flat or straight eyes are used for overlapped closings and are the most commonly used; the number 8 eye matches the 306 hook. Round eyes or loops are used for edge-to-edge closings, with the loop of the eye extending just beyond the edge of the fabric; the number 6 loop matches the 306 hook.

HOOP SUPPORTS (Fig. 2-13). A variety of materials can be used to make skirt supports and hoop skirts. The selection of materials is determined by weight, size, and amount of flexibility required. For instance, a farthingale for Queen Elizabeth I is intended to be rigid; a hoop skirt for Scarlett O'Hara needs to be flexible.

Copper tubing is lightweight and pliable, but it will not bend out of shape as easily as wire. Three-sixteenths inch tubing is

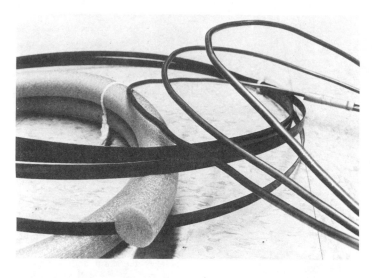

Figure 2-13 Selected hoop-support materials: foam rod, spring steel, and copper tubing (*left to right*). Photo by Robert Izzo.

effective for making farthingales and eighteenth-century panniers. The tubing is easily flattened and riveted at the joints. It can be obtained through plumbing suppliers.

Foam rod is a packing for large caulking jobs such as expansion joints in concrete buildings. It is lightweight, resilient, and durable; ½ in. to 1 in. (1.3 cm to 2.5 cm) diameters are appropriate sizes to use. Foam rod is easy to cut, and joints can be hot-melt glued together. It is available from building suppliers.

Spring steel is made of flattened, tempered steel that "springs" back into its original shape. It is lightweight and durable and is most effective for large hoop skirts that must have flexibility in order to get through doors. See Appendix B for sources.

HORSEHAIR BRAID. Now made from nylon, the braid is used for stiffening edges such as hems and for making hats. It is available in various widths from notions supply houses.

JEWELRY FIXINGS. Assorted junk and costume jewelry is a valuable and necessary asset for a workshop. A collection of complete and broken jewelry should be kept in stock. Special plastic or glass stones, settings for stones, heavy chains and links, and assorted other items can be purchased in bulk from costume supply houses or hobby shops. These items are used in constructing stage ornaments as discussed in Chap. 19.

MAGNET. Small magnets which are readily available should be kept in the shop for picking up pins and other metal items that always seem to be on the floor.

MILLINERY WIRE. Used primarily in hat construction, this wrapped wire is available in black and white from millinery supply houses.

RHINESTONES. Available in clear and in a range of colors, they are used to add glitter to a costume or an accessory. They are made in a range of sizes and are available from craft supply houses.

RHINESTONE SETTER. A tool used to set rhinestones in fabric, it is available from craft and theatrical supply houses.

SNAPS. Generally used for closings that are not taut and are not subject to stress, snaps are available in a range of sizes: 000 and 00 are useful for sheers and lightweight fabrics, while size 3 is valuable for heavy garments. Bulk purchases from notions suppliers are the most economical.

SOLVENTS. Liquids that are used for thinning and dissolving, solvents include water for thinning acrylic and other water-soluble paints and several other liquids which are applicable to costuming, many of which are detailed in Chap. 15. In all instances, check labels or instructions for the materials prior to use, and test the materials and fabrics first.

Acetone is a flammable liquid used as a general solvent and is needed for work with Celastic (see Chap. 19). Only small amounts should be poured into an open container at a time since it evaporates quickly. The container should be glass or metal because acetone will dissolve many plastics. Always wear rubber gloves when working with acetone and work in a well-ventilated area. Acetone is also known as dimethylketone and is available from drugstores and chemical supply houses.

Alcohol is used as a solvent for some dyes and for shellac. Denatured (not for human consumption) alcohol is available from hardware stores.

Turpentine is used to thin some paints and is a standard solvent to stock in a shop. It is available from hardware stores.

STEAMER. A tabletop unit which makes steam is valuable for millinery work. Felt, for example, can be steamed into a desired shape as described in Chap. 18. See Appendix B for sources.

VELCRO. Used to close garments, Velcro has two pieces of tape with a napped surface which adhere to one another when pressed together. Velcro is readily available by the yard in widths from ½ in. to 1 in. (1.3 cm to 2.5 cm) in assorted colors. It is expensive, bulky, and noisy for closings; however, it proves to be the simplest solution to many fast-change problems. It is reusable, which reduces some of the ex-

pense. A stock supply of ¾ in. (2 cm) Velcro in black and white is advisable.

Velcro Adhesive 40 (brand name) is a flexible glue for attaching Velcro in places where stitching is difficult or impractical. It is a very durable adhesive.

WEIGHTS. Used to control drapery or hems in garments, a variety of weights is available. These range from hardware items, such as nuts and washers, to cloth-covered lengths of drapery weights, to fishing-line weights. Weights can be concealed inside a garment or used decoratively.

WIG BLOCKS (Fig. 17-5). There are three types of blocks, each of which serves a slightly different function.

Styrene wig blocks are inexpensive and are valuable for hat construction, wig work and storage, and mask construction. These multipurpose blocks are readily available at notions counters.

Canvas wig blocks are available in a range of standard sizes from 21 in. to 24 in. (53.5 cm to 61 cm) head sizes. Canvas blocks are more expensive than styrene but offer many advantages, including durability and more accurate headshapes. They are available through theatrical supply houses.

Wood wig blocks, made of soft wood, are essential for making wigs and other hairpieces. These can also be used for hat construction and are available from theatrical supply houses.

WIG STANDS (Fig. 17-5). The stands clamp onto the edge of a table and support the wig block. The type with the vertical extension which can be locked into different angle positions offers the most versatility and is available from theatrical suppliers. Doweling set into a wood base provides an easy-to-make stand for storage and some construction work.

ZIPPERS. Metal zippers are available in a range of lengths and colors, and they are far more preferable than nylon for costumes. Nylon zippers twist out of shape, melt, and cannot be repaired. Metal zippers are more durable and can be repaired. For example, if the zipper pull has come off the track, use pliers to remove two or three teeth at the bottom of the zipper on the side without the pull. Guide the pull onto the tape so the top of the pull will engage the teeth on both sides of the tape and run the pull up the zipper to close it. Bind the altered bottom edge to prevent the pull from coming off the track.

Dress zippers are nonseparating zippers which are open at the top and are most frequently used in theatrical costumes. A supply of 22 in. (55 cm) long, metal dress zippers in black and white should be kept on hand; white zippers can be dyed to match a costume. Zippers of this length are sufficient for long closings in the back of costumes. They can also be shortened for other uses. A simple method of shortening a metal zipper is to cut the zipper to the desired length plus seam allowance and remove the excess metal teeth of the zipper with pliers. Bind the new end with thread to make a stop for the zipper pull.

Jacket or *separating zippers* which open at the bottom as well as at the top are used in waist-length garments.

Placket zippers are connected at the top and the bottom. These zippers are commonly used in underarm seams.

three

basic costume construction techniques

Although costumes need to be designed, patterned, and cut before the assembly can begin, a solid foundation in the various construction techniques is necessary in order to pattern and cut the costumes. Therefore, familiarity with the techniques involved and learning the skills required to execute them are fundamental to the costuming process.

The terminology used in the construction of theatrical costumes is a combination of standard sewing terms and theatrical jargon. Since the function of the theatrical garment differs from the normal street garment, the construction approach also differs to a degree. This does not mean the theatrical garment is sloppily thrown together with shoddy construction; construction details must be accurate and precise in order to create an effective costume that fits the actor well and realizes the design.

The terms in the following Glossary of Costume Construction Terms are defined according to how to execute them and when they are typically used. The assumption is that once these methods and uses are understood separately, they can be applied when needed and in the appropriate combination required for the construction of any specific garment. The necessary methods will tend to make themselves evident as the construction process is analyzed and planned.

A simple exercise for becoming familiar with the techniques and to acquire the skills required for the construction of costumes is to prepare samples of the techniques cited in the glossary. These samples should be compiled in a notebook as a reference guide for future use since the construction of a single costume is not likely to require the use of all the techniques cited. Preparation of the examples of the techniques not only helps identify the terminology and learn the skills, but it also provides an excellent means of becoming familiar with the workshop and its equipment.

The glossary is divided into: Basic Hand Stitches, Basic Machine Stitching, and General Construction and Finishing Terms. The terms discussed in each section range from very basic to complex construction techniques; they are entered according to their primary usages. Instructions for executing the methods involved are included in most entries. However, in some cases, more detailed instructions can be found in other chapters which deal with major applications of the techniques.

Basic Hand Stitches

The instructions for each hand stitch, both the descriptions and the diagrams, are applicable to right- or left-handed individuals. Basically, the difference between the right- and left-handed orientation is the sewing direction employed in executing the stitch. The right-handed individual sews from right to left for most hand stitches; those who are left-handed sew from left to right. In those instances where this general rule is not applicable, instructions for both approaches are included in the discussion.

The stitching diagrams use the letter A to show the start of the stitch and B to show the end of the stitch. The arrow indicates the direction of the stitch; the dash line indicates the unseen portion of the stitch on the underside, and the solid line shows the stitch on the top, or working side, of the garment.

BASTING STITCHES. Temporary stitches that can be done by hand or on a machine, these stitches are longer than permanent stitches and have several uses that range from holding fabric in place for permanent stitching to gathering the fabric into smaller dimensions. There are four basic hand-basting stitches.

Hand-basting (running stitch). The sim-plest hand stitch, the needle runs in and out through the fabric on a straight line; the stitch length varies from about ¼ in. to ½ in. (0.6 cm to 1.3 cm). This stitch is used to hold garments together for fittings, to gather fabrics, to mark the centerline of a garment, and the like. The stitch can be removed easily since it is not tied off at either end of the row of stitching and is not intended to be a permanent stitch.

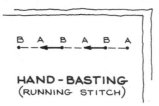

HAND-BASTING
(RUNNING STITCH)

Slant-basting. A stitch that counteracts strains in various directions, this stitch is used to hold slippery fabrics together for sewing and to hold interfacings in place for the permanent stitching. To execute this stitch, the first part of the stitch is parallel to one edge of the cloth, the second part is at a slant to the edge as shown.

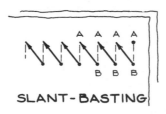

SLANT-BASTING

Slip-basting. Used to help shape the fabric, this stitch is especially important when draping a pattern or reshaping a garment in fittings. It is used to hold a draped or fitted fold, dart, or seam in position until it can be marked and permanently stitched. As shown, the needle is slipped through the single layer of the fold, then through the single layer of the other side of the fold. If the fabric is folded over on itself with a single rather than a double fold, for something like a dart or pleat, the needle is slipped through the single layer of the fabric and then through the fold edge. The thread should not be angled but should be carried straight across from the end of one stitch to begin the next. This stitch, when completed, will not be visible on the outside and will look like a hand-basting stitch on the inside. (Straight pins can also be used in this manner, if necessary.) Slip-basting can also be used to add collars, sleeves, or other pieces to the garment temporarily and to match plaids and stripes when cutting the fabric.

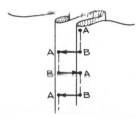

SLIP-BASTING

Gathering stitch. This is a running stitch done by hand on heavy or bulky fabrics to pull (gather) the fabric into a smaller size (see Cartridge Pleats, Chap. 9); the length of the stitch controls the depth of the gathers. A short stitch creates shallow gathering and longer stitches deeper gathering. Two rows of parallel stitching are standard for the gathering stitch, using a heavyweight thread; three or more parallel rows are used for shirring. This stitch may be done on a machine if the fabric is not too heavy—see Machine Gathering.

BACK STITCH. A strong hand stitch, this is most commonly used for quick hand-sewn repairs. Take one full stitch; then move the needle back to start the next stitch. Complete the length of the second stitch beyond the end of the first stitch;

repeat. This stitch shows twice as much length on the underside as on the top side.

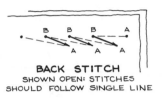

BACK STITCH
SHOWN OPEN: STITCHES
SHOULD FOLLOW SINGLE LINE

CROSS STITCH (Catch Stitch). A strong stitch which is good for hems and helps prevent fraying; it is also a good stitch on stretch fabrics and knits.

Right-handed: Hold the needle facing left and stitch from left to right. Take a small stitch through a single layer of the hem parallel to the edge, cross to the right above the hem edge and catch a small amount of fabric parallel to the hem edge; then cross back to the hem fabric and repeat.

Left-handed: Hold the needle facing right and stitch from right to left.

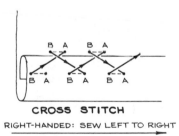

CROSS STITCH
RIGHT-HANDED: SEW LEFT TO RIGHT

GATHERING STITCH. See Basting Stitches.

OVERCASTING STITCH. A common stitch used to keep a raw edge from raveling, the needle carries the thread through the fabric, over the edge, and back through the fabric. This stitch is also a popular hemstitch; the needle catches the hem fold, moves over to the garment fabric for a tiny stitch, then goes back under and through the hem fold.

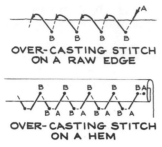

OVER-CASTING STITCH
ON A RAW EDGE

OVER-CASTING STITCH
ON A HEM

PADDING STITCH. Used to control rolled shapes such as collars, lapels, shoulder pads, and other padding pieces, this stitch is done in the same manner as the slant-basting stitch. Working toward yourself and holding the piece in the desired rolled position, slant-stitch along the roll line through the interfacing and catch the garment fabric with the stitch. Make as many rows of stitching as necessary to hold the desired shape; work from the inside of the curvature and keep the thread as taut as necessary to hold the desired amount of roll in the unit. To control the degree of roll always hold the piece in the proper shape and stitch in the direction of the roll (also see Chap. 16).

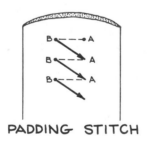

PADDING STITCH

RUNNING STITCH. See Basting Stitches.

STAB STITCH. A strong, nearly invisible stitch with the needle working in a vertical plane; the thread is not pulled at an angle on the good side of the fabric. The needle literally "stabs" through the fabric on a straight line, leaving only a very tiny stitch visible on the good side; con-

sequently, this stitch is the same for both right- and left-handed individuals. It is used for appliqués and for attaching such items as hooks and eyes or snaps.

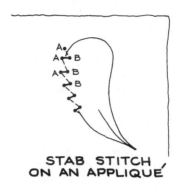

STAB STITCH
ON AN APPLIQUÉ

Basic Machine Stitching

BACK STITCH OR LOCK STITCH. Used at the end of a row of stitching, it prevents stitching from coming undone. Use the reverse stitch control on the machine and stitch back over four or five stitches at each end of the stitching line. A simple reverse and forward stitching is quite sufficient; more back stitching only creates more bulk.

BASTING (Machine Baste). The longest stitch length on the machine, it is used to baste garments together for fittings, to gather or shirr the fabric, to ease a seam, and for stay-stitching. This stitch is not locked (back stitched) and is not meant to be a permanent stitch.

BLIND-HEM STITCH. A method of hemming by machine. On some zigzag machines, there is a specific stitch for hemming which makes one zigzag stitch to every four straight stitches. A regular zigzag stitch can also be used for blind hemming; the sewing machine manual usually describes the process for the specific machine. Also see Blind-Stitch Machine in Chap. 2.

EDGE STITCH.   See Top Stitch.

MACHINE GATHERING (Shirring).   Parallel rows of the basting stitch about ¼ in. (0.6 cm) apart along the edge to be gathered or eased; four rows of machine basting are generally used for shirring. To gather the fabric after stitching, the bottom (bobbin) threads are pulled gently while the fabric is slid to the side. If the fabric is heavy, altering the tension on the machine so the bobbin thread floats will simplify the gathering process. Do not lock the stitch or tie it in a knot. After the fabric has been gathered, wrap the thread in a figure eight around a pin which is set perpendicular to the stitch line (see Fig. 9–8). This holds the gather in place and allows for flexibility in the gather.

MERROWING.   See Merrowed Seam under General Construction and Finishing Terms.

PERMANENT STITCH.   This is the basic stitch for finished work. Generally a medium-length stitch, the exact setting on different machines may vary; review the machine manual for recommended settings.

PIQUÉ STITCH.   This is a method of overcasting edges with a tight decorative stitch such as is seen on many gloves. A popular method of hemming in the late 1920s and early 1930s, it can be done on a zigzag machine with a very tight zigzag stitch to finish hems.

SHIRRING STITCH.   See Machine Gathering.

STAY STITCH.   (1) The baste-length machine stitch is used around curved edges and on bias edges about ¼ in. (0.6 cm) from the edge to hold the shape and to prevent stretching. (2) The term is also used when stitching lining fabric to the good fabric all the way around the piece ¼ in. (0.6 cm) from the edge, making the lining and good fabric workable as one piece.

TOP STITCH.   This is a line of stitching visible on the good side of the fabric or garment; it is used as reinforcement or as decoration that is visible on the good side.

Edge stitch.   This is top stitching that is done very close to the seam line or edge of the garment piece and is frequently used on collars and lapels.

UNDERSTITCHING.   This is a means of controlling seam allowance so that it does not slip or bunch into unsightly thickness at a finished seam. All of the seam allowance edges are folded to the same side and secured to the garment fabric with a line of stitches placed close to the seam line. On a collar, the allowances are stitched to the under-collar piece so that only the upper-collar fabric forms the edge of the collar, but this must be done inside the collar after it has been turned right side out. The technique is also used to hold facing seams in place; the seam allowances are stitched to the facing, which is then turned inside the garment where it is not seen.

General Construction and Finishing Terms

BALANCE LINES.   These are lines drawn at junctions of the drafted patterns to show where to align the pattern pieces; commercial patterns use notches to show how the pattern pieces line up. These lines are particularly useful on curved seams. Balance lines are also used to mark the alignment of pleats.

BINDING.   Usually a decorative method of finishing raw edges, the unfinished edge is sandwiched between the sides of a folded strip of fabric. The strip may be tape (bias tape is necessary for curved edges) or either matching or decorative fabric. Bindings are used to finish edges of garments such as necklines, armholes, and hems. They serve the same function as facings but are decorative since they are visible; facings also finish an edge but are not visible on the good side of the garment. A common example of the use of bindings is found on blankets.

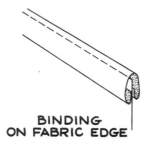

BINDING ON FABRIC EDGE

BUTTONHOLE.   There are various methods for making buttonholes. The specifics of how to make them on a sewing machine are generally included in the machine manual. Two basic methods for making buttonholes are described here: the Piquéd or Worked Buttonhole and the Patched Buttonhole. Both of these methods require accurate markings to show the length of the finished hole.

This length is determined by the diameter and thickness of the button to be used on the garment. Consequently, the buttons that are to be used must be selected before the buttonhole can be made. The standard guideline for what length to make the buttonhole is: ⅛ in. (0.3 cm) longer than the diameter of a thin button, ¼ in. (0.6 cm) longer than the diameter of a thick button. In any case, always make a sample buttonhole on a scrap of the good fabric to check and finalize the length required for the button; duplicate the layers of fabric at the edge of the garment for accuracy.

The ends of the buttonhole can be marked with tailor's chalk or straight pins with the centerline marked in chalk or whatever can be seen. The centerline for holes placed parallel to the edge, as in shirts or blouses, should follow the warp (lengthwise) thread of the fabric; those on the horizontal should follow the filling (crosswise) thread. The placement and length of each hole should be measured and marked before the actual sewing is begun. Mark the good side for the Piquéd Buttonhole, the wrong side for the Patched Buttonhole.

Piquéd or *Worked Buttonholes* can be made on a machine with a buttonhole attachment (see Chap. 2) or on a zigzag machine without an attachment; the process is usually fully described in the machine manual. Briefly, set the zigzag stitch length for a very close, tight stitch. A buttonhole requires two widths of zigzag stitches; usually one is twice as wide as the other. For purposes of description, assume the width settings on the machine to be 2 and 4. If the needle position on the machine can be shifted—that is, moved from center to the left and right—set the needle left of center and on a number 2 width. Stitch down one side of the centerline of the hole to the end of the line; set the stitch width at number 4 and stitch across the end of the line; then turn the fabric, reset the stitch width to number 2, and stitch up the other side of the centerline; reset the stitch width to number 4 and stitch across the end of the buttonhole. Slash through the centerline but do not cut the stitching at the sides or the ends.

Using a clear plastic zigzag presser foot makes the process easier because you can see the work through the foot.

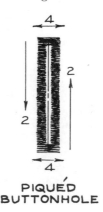

PIQUÉD BUTTONHOLE

Patched buttonholes finish the holes as slashed openings (see Placket). Cut a strip of the garment fabric or a contrasting fabric, if desired. Cut the strip 2 in. (5 cm) wide and 1 in. (2.5 cm) longer than the buttonhole; roll-hemming or overcasting the edges will guard against raveling. Mark the buttonhole centerline on the wrong side of the garment fabric and pin the patch to the right side but centered on the marking.

Stitch all around the marking, allowing ⅛ in. (0.3 cm) on each side of the centerline; if the fabric ravels easily, allow ¼ in. (0.6 cm). Slash the buttonhole centerline and clip diagonally at each corner of the stitching. Turn the patch inside through the slashed opening and press. Stitch the edges of the patch in place using a cross-stitch in the manner of securing a hem.

The patched buttonhole is more time-consuming and creates a bulkier buttonhole than the piquéd method; therefore, it is rarely used in theatrical costumes.

may be added after the edge is finished. In either instance, an opening must be left to thread the drawstring or elastic through the casing, and the width of the casing must be slightly wider than the drawstring or elastic. If the method of drawing the garment up is to be concealed, the casing and opening are placed inside the garment. If the ties are to be revealed and/or decorative, the opening is on the outside of the garment. In either case, the edges of the opening must be finished to prevent raveling.

To create a ruffled edge with the casing, set the casing away from the edge according to the desired width of the ruffle. In other words, if the ruffle is to be 1 in. (2.5 cm) long, the bottom of the casing is placed 1 in. away from the edge. In all instances, the casing must be stitched at both the top and bottom to create a complete housing for the drawstrings; it must also be stitched through all the layers of fabric which are to be drawn in.

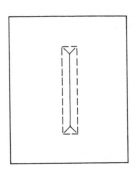

PATCHED BUTTONHOLE
STITCHED ONTO GOOD
SIDE OF FABRIC
BEFORE TURNING

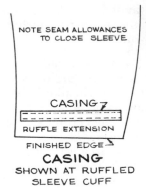

NOTE SEAM ALLOWANCES
TO CLOSE SLEEVE

CASING
RUFFLE EXTENSION
FINISHED EDGE

CASING
SHOWN AT RUFFLED
SLEEVE CUFF

CASING. A method of controlling a drawstring or elastic in a garment, it is typically found in a "peasant" blouse or pajama bottoms. Casings may be made as part of the facing construction, or tape

CLIP. A cut in the seam allowance on curved edges and at corners, clips are cuts made at angles to the seam to allow the seam allowance to lie flat and smooth with the garment. Clips are made after the stitching is completed; never cut through the stitching in the seam. If the enclosed seam allowance fabric makes the finished

seam bulky, make the clips as notches to remove the overlapping fabric.

CLIPS IN NECKLINE SEAM ALLOWANCE BEFORE TURNING THE FACING

DART. Used to control fabric and to shape the garment to the body, a dart tapers to nothing at the tip and may be defined as a tapered seam.

Fitting darts are used to take in fabric where the body is narrow, such as at the waist, and taper to the tip to allow for the wider portions of the body, such as the chest or bust.

Decorative darts may be placed almost anywhere on a garment for appearance detailing. As such they may or may not contribute to the fitting of the garment to the body; however, since they are made in the same way as fitting darts, the additional fabric for them must be included in the pattern layout.

EASE. (1) A slight gathering to shape or pull fabric into the desired size or shape, easing is used for shrinking extra fullness in one seam edge to match the size of another. No puckering or pleating is visible with easing because it is worked evenly over the area with one or two rows of basting stitches and drawn, or eased, up to the proper size. Curved seams for something like a princess-line bodice (see Chap. 13) are often eased for a better fit. Easing the hem allowance on a flared skirt simplifies the hemming process and eliminates puckers in the hem. Perhaps the most typical use of easing is found in working with set-in sleeves which appear to have no pleats or gathers at the armhole. If a curved or bias edge has stretched out of shape, it can often be shrunk into its proper shape by easing.

(2) The term *ease* is also used to refer to the extra fabric provided in a fitted garment in order to allow for the expansion and movement of the body inside the garment.

FACING. Facing is a method used to finish cut edges such as armholes in a sleeveless garment, necklines in collarless garments, or slashed openings. A facing is stitched to the right (good) side of the garment and turned to the inside of the garment to conceal the seam and the facing. Facings for straight edges may be cut-in-one with the garment, such as jacket front openings, and folded inside to finish the edges. Facings for curved edges may be narrow strips of bias cut from matching fabric or bias tape. The seam allowance on any curved edge must be clipped before the facing is turned inside. Facings can also be cut to match the shape of the garment; this process is discussed in Chap. 11.

Self-facing. This is a facing cut-in-one with the garment as an extension for something like a jacket lapel.

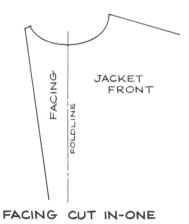

FACING CUT IN-ONE

GATHER. Used to pull in excess fabric to a desired size, gathering is used primar-

ily for puffy sleeves and full skirts with a gathered waist. Two or three rows of basting stitches are required. The finished gather will have the appearance of small pleats or puckers; see Basting Stitches.

INTERFACING. A stiffened fabric, cut slightly smaller than the facing, which is sandwiched between the garment and the facing, interfacing is used to stiffen, reinforce, or shape sections of the garment such as collars and cuffs, to reinforce openings in tailored garments, and to reinforce closings, including those which require cutting through the fabric for buttonholes, grommets, or eyelets. The interfacing is not visible on a finished garment on either side. Interfacing materials are discussed in Chap. 4; patterns are discussed in Chap. 11.

LAYERING. Also referred to as *staggering* or *grading,* layering is a method of trimming excess fabric to alleviate bulk where several seams come together as may occur with collars, full sleeves, or interfaced edges. The seam allowances are trimmed away separately so that some layers are narrower than others.

PIN BASTE. This is using pins instead of stitching with thread to secure seams, darts, and hems for permanent stitching or for preliminary fittings. Pin basting may cause problems in the fitting process since pins fall out easily and the sharp points may be uncomfortable or dangerous to both actor and costumer.

PIPING. See Welting.

PIQUÉ. A method of overcasting edges for hems, buttonholes, and the like, the piquéd edge is an effective means of preventing the fabric from raveling. The simplest method of piquéing an edge is with a tight zigzag stitch (see Machine Stitching terms and also refer to Merrowed Seam under Seams).

PLACKET. A method of finishing a slashed opening in the edge of a garment, the placket allows the garment to go on and off the body easily and is most commonly located at the neckline, waistline, and wrists of sleeves. A simple method for creating the slashed and faced placket is to cut a rectangle of fabric that matches the garment. This facing piece should be at least 4 in. (10 cm) wide and 2 in. (5 cm) longer than the slash line in the garment. Locate and mark a slash line on the facing 1 in. (2.5 cm) from the lengthwise edge of the rectangle. Setting this slash line off-center creates allowance for an extension of the facing to cover the space created by the opening and can be used for snaps or hooks and eyes to close the space.

Piqué or roll-hem the edge of the rectangle before pinning the facing to the garment with right sides together. Match the slash lines of the garment and the facing. Permanently stitch, as close as possible to the slash line, around three sides, leaving the seam allowance edge of the garment unstitched. Cut the slash line through both layers and clip diagonally at each corner of the stitched end of the line. If the fabric ravels easily, piqué the edges of the cut opening. Turn the facing through the opening, and press and pin it in place.

To make the cover extension behind the placket opening, fold the wrong side of the facing toward the opening, leaving enough of the folded facing to cover the seam allowance of the slash line. Press the folded facing and top stitch around the slash to reinforce the opening. If the extension is to support snaps or hooks and eyes, it must be a double rather than a single layer of fabric. Usually, there is enough in the placket facing to fold back on itself to make the double layer. The facing is secured when the seam allowance edge of the garment is finished and by tacking the other edges in place.

The same technique is often used in period garments to finish decorative openings like slashed and puffed sleeves or hose. These openings, however, are usually closed at both ends and can be treated in a manner similar to that described under Patched Buttonholes.

The term *placket* is also sometimes used to refer to zippered openings.

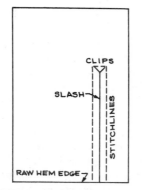

PLACKET STITCHED TO GOOD SIDE BEFORE TURNING THROUGH SLASH

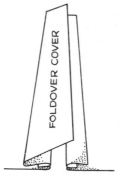

PLACKET TURNED THROUGH SLASH TO WRONG SIDE

PLEAT.   A method of controlling fullness in a garment, the fabric is doubled back upon itself to adjust the fullness to the desired size. Types of pleating include knife pleats, box pleats, and cartridge pleats. See Chap. 9 for a more complete discussion of pleating methods and their functions.

ROLL HEM.   This is a method of finishing raw edges, using a minimum of fabric for the hem, as is often found on handkerchiefs. Using the roll hemmer foot (see Chap. 2) on the sewing machine makes roll-hemming a one-step operation.

RUCHING.   Generally used as a decorative finishing detail, ruching is a narrow strip of pleated cloth which can be made up into long lengths in advance. The fabric can be lace, muslin, or any lightweight fabric and is generally white for strong contrast. Ruching is quite useful for finishing off cuffs or necklines in many period costumes. A long strip of fabric 4 in. (10 cm) wide is cut and folded in half along the length and pressed. This creates one finished edge; the raw edge is overcast to control raveling. The strip is then pleated into narrow pleats; a pleater foot (see Chap. 2) works very well for this. Lengths of ruching made up in advance can be kept in stock to be used when necessary.

RUCHING

SEAMS.   There are several types of seams, the following six are the most commonly used for costumes.

Standard or plain seam.   The right sides of the fabric are placed together and stitched with a ½ in. to ⅝ in. (1.3 cm to 1.8 cm) seam allowance or on the marked stitching lines. A basted seam is stitched together with a basting stitch; a permanent seam is stitched with a medium-length stitch (see Basic Machine Stitching). If the stitching is too tight, the stitching may pucker; if it is too loose, there will not be enough strength to hold the seam together when worn.

STANDARD SEAM

Eased seam. This seam is used when one side of the seam edge is slightly longer than the other as is often the case when setting in sleeves or attaching a curved edge to a straight or less curved edge, as in a princess-line garment. Use a gathering stitch to ease the longer seam edge to the desired length (see Ease). No pleat or pucker should be visible in an eased seam. Steam pressing an eased seam helps to shrink and control any puckering that may occur.

French seam. This is essentially two standard seams in one. First, stitch the wrong sides together with a narrow ¼ in. (0.6 cm) seam allowance; trim the allowance close to the stitching line and press the fabric open with the seam allowance pressed to one side; then press a fold into the fabric at the stitching line with the right sides together. Next stitch the fabric, with right sides together, to enclose the trimmed seam. This seam is used to conceal the seam allowance and to prevent raveling; it also makes a very strong seam. The french seam does not necessarily re-

quire more seam allowance than a regular seam.

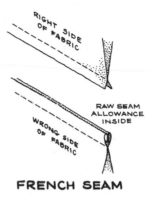

FRENCH SEAM

Flat-felled seams. Often seen on shirts or jeans, these seams are very strong and can be used as decoration. The simplest method of making flat-felled seams for theatrical use is to make a reversed french seam so that the encased seam allowance is on the outside of the garment. The encased seam is pressed to one side and edge-stitched flat to the garment with matching or contrasting thread, depending on the effect desired. To make a reversed french seam, stitch the garment with right sides of the fabric together; trim, turn, and press the same way as for a regular french seam, and then stitch the seam with the insides of the fabric together. This stitching can be done with matching or contrasting thread, depending on the desired appearance. This method is effective for creating strong seams, but it can be a problem on bulky fabrics where it may create a very thick seam.

The traditional method of constructing a flat-felled seam is to make a standard seam with ⅝ in. to ¾ in. (1.8 cm to 2 cm) seam allowance on the right side of the garment. One edge of the seam allowance is trimmed close to the stitch line, and the other edge is folded over the cut edge (with the raw edge turned under), pressed flat, and edge-stitched. This method is less bulky than the method described above but is also more time-consuming, and the felled seam can stretch and pull off grain unless done very carefully.

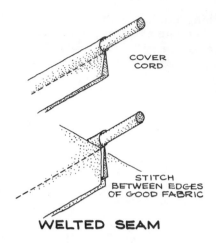

COVER CORD

STITCH BETWEEN EDGES OF GOOD FABRIC

WELTED SEAM

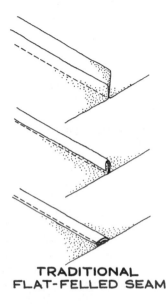

TRADITIONAL FLAT-FELLED SEAM

Merrowed or lockstitched seam. This seam is done on a special machine (see Chap. 2). The machine trims the seam allowance while overcasting the edges and chain-stitching the stitchline. The seam is strong and especially good on jerseys or other stretch fabrics as well as for seams in corsets. There is very little seam allowance when the seam is completed; consequently, the garment cannot be let out to enlarge it.

Welted or corded seams. Commonly used in upholstery for edges of cushions, welting is used to decorate or define seams in costumes. The welting can be made of matching or contrasting fabric (see Welting). It is sandwiched in a regular seam, right sides together, and stitched as a regular seam with a cording or zipper foot (see Chap. 2). Stitch the seam as close to the cord as possible.

SHIRRING. A decorative detail for garments, shirring is a multiple gathering and is used for decorative detail on blouses, sleeves, or other garment items. Shirring requires even stitch lengths in several parallel lines. The fabric is then shirred (gathered) to the desired size, and the stitching is wrapped around a pin (see Gathering) until it is finalized, at which time it can be tied off.

SLASH. (1) A cut in the garment used to provide an opening where there is no seam (see Placket). (2) A cut in a pattern to alter the pattern shape (see Chap. 13).

TACK. A hand stitch used to hold one section of a garment to another with a few, somewhat loose stitches for control; commonly used to hold facings in place, cuffs in position, or to secure other loose edges without stitching them all around.

Swing tack or *chain tack.* This is a hand stitch used to hold a section of the garment in control but which allows some movement and space between the pieces. It is commonly used to hold coat linings at hemlines, to control large falling collars, and to control drapery in a garment. A swing tack can be a single chain crochet stitch or half hitches tied over several strands of thread; the length of the tack varies from about ¼ in. to 1 in. (0.6 cm to 2.5 cm) between the sections to be controlled.

TRIM. (1) To cut away excess fabric which creates bulk at seams, collars, armholes, or the like; less trimming of this sort is done in theatrical costuming than in street-wear, since the garment may be altered many times for different actors in various productions. (2) The term is also used to refer to decorative finishing on the good side of the garment.

WELTING (Piping). A covered cording used to decorate edges of garments or to define seams; welting for costumes is usually made by covering cording with the desired fabric. Welt cording can be a solid cord or a core of soft cotton encased with a soft mesh; both are available at fabric and upholstery shops. The soft welt cord is more pliable than the solid cord; therefore, it is more adaptable to costumes. The diameter of the cord ranges from ⅛ in. to 1 in. (0.3 cm to 2.5 cm); the size selected depends on the scale and proportions in the costume.

To cover the cord, cut strips of the fabric on the bias; they should be wide enough to cover the cord plus about ½ in. (1.3 cm) seam allowance. Use a cording or zipper foot (see Chap. 2) to stitch the fabric as close to the cord as possible. Ready-made welting is also available; however, it is generally too small for theatrical use.

COSTUME CONSTRUCTION GUIDELINES

The actual process of assembling a costume depends on the type of garment, the phase of construction it is in, and what the completed outfit is to look like. The phase of construction and type of garment dictate the degree of completeness used in assembling the garment. For example, fitted garments (those that conform to the contours of the body) are machine-basted together, with no back stitching, and the seams and darts are not pressed for the first fitting, since adjustments in these may be necessary in the fitting. Garments for this first fitting generally have the related units, such as collars, sleeves, and the like, prepared but unattached. This is to allow for adjustments at the neckline, armhole, and so forth, during the fitting.

Loose or nonfitted garments, such as robes, full skirts, or full sleeves, can have the seams permanently stitched with back stitching, since these seams will not be subject to adjustments in the first fitting.

There are additional rules of thumb that are applicable when preparing a garment for the first fitting, and specific details for preparing costume units are discussed with each pattern draft. Each pattern piece should be pressed before it is sewn, for better control and freedom from unwanted wrinkles. If the garment is to be lined, determine whether it is to be flatlined or to have a separate but matching lining. Garments with seams that will not be seen by the audience, or those that are lined to alter the "body" of the fabric, are usually flat-lined. This means that the lining is pressed and stay-stitched to the good fabric so that they can be worked with as one piece.

Garments which may allow seams to be revealed, such as an open sleeve or a robe, are usually set up with a separate but matching lining. In such a case, both the lining and the good fabric are pressed, and then darts and seams are joined together before the lining and good fabric are put together. Often, when the lining is separate, the lining alone is prepared for the first fitting and then used as the final pattern for the good fabric. These separate linings are also often used to finish off edges. In an open sleeve, for example, the underarm seams of both the lining and the good fabric are permanently stitched, put together with the right sides together, stitched at the bottom (wrist) end, and turned inside out so that the wrong sides of the fabrics are together with all the seam allowances concealed and the bottom edge finished with no raw edges.

The processes for assembling costumes after the first fitting are determined by the specific requirements of each garment. One aspect of the process which is consistent for all costumes and cannot be overstressed is the need for pressing the garment as the work progresses. Pressing is crucial for maintaining control of the fabric and the garment as a whole. This is true even if the costume is for a character like the windblown mad King Lear since the costume must first be constructed well to ensure manageability and a comfortable fit on the actor before it is distressed and made to look old and worn.

A primary guideline for putting a costume together is based on the concept of preparing the individual units of a garment before they are joined together. The darts in the bodice front and back, for example, should be permanently stitched and pressed before the side seams and shoulder seams are joined and then pressed. Some finishing details also need to be completed before units are attached. For instance, the placket opening at the wrist of a full sleeve (detailed in Chap. 8) should be finished and pressed before a cuff is added and before the underarm seam is stitched together. In some instances, like the double puff sleeve discussed in Chap. 13, adding the decorative trim should also be considered part of the preparation process.

Another guideline to consider when the individual pieces are ready to be attached to each other is the handling of the whole costume. In other words, it may be simpler to add the sleeves before a long, heavy skirt is attached to the bodice. Essentially, the specific order of when to finish and decorate a unit, and when to attach it, depends on how heavy or bulky the items are.

Additional criteria for assembling a costume are established by the requirements of the design and the fitting process as discussed in Chap. 12. The step-by-step details for each costume need to be thought through, and the costumer often needs to prepare worksheets outlining the process to be followed by the people working on the costume. These worksheets serve the same function as the instruction sheets in commercial patterns in that they provide an outline of the sequence of operations and techniques needed in completing the specific garment.

Essentially, the construction of costumes is governed by the premise of "don't paint yourself into a corner." The process for each costume needs to be thought through logically so that individual units can be prepared and then joined together in a manner that is manageable and so that the costume is well finished, fits the actor, and looks like the designer's sketch.

four

fabrics

The proper selection of fabrics for stage costumes is as essential as good design is for character delineation and production requirements. Improper or poor selection of fabrics can ruin even the best designs. While the designer usually selects the fabrics, it is vital that the costumer gain a working knowledge of the fabrics, their characteristics, and their theatrical applicability.

The ever-increasing development of man-made fibers and blends, which are abundantly available, offers the costumer a large variety of fabrics and fabric names from which to select. Not only has the number and type of synthetic fabrics increased, but the manufacturers of synthetics each have trademark names for the fibers used. To further increase the variety available, there are a number of finishing processes and techniques which are used to complete the cloth and give it its final appearance. All these factors combine to provide a wide range of fabrics with various characteristics to meet the demands of the commercial market.

THEATRICAL CONSIDERATIONS FOR FABRIC SELECTION

Theatrically, the selection of fabrics is governed by the design and the requirements of the costume. The fabrics must be bold enough to project over a distance under strong lighting, must be adaptable to various treatments (such as dyeing and painting) to create specific effects, and must be strong enough to withstand the rigors of performance.

In order to make appropriate selections from the wide variety of fabrics available, let us first look at the criteria applied to

59

selecting fabrics for costumes and then consider the factors which are involved in creating the variety of fabrics, their composition and finishes. Use of the Glossary of Fabrics which is included in this chapter will provide the foundation for gaining familiarity with the terminology applied to fabrics and learning how to identify fabrics by name. But, since there are so many factors involved and because new products and manufacturing techniques continue to come onto the market, the study of fabrics must always be an ongoing process.

For theatrical purposes, there are three primary categories into which a fabric's characteristics fall: appearance, practicability, and historical applicability.

Appearance

The appearance of the fabric encompasses what you see and what you feel. What you see includes color, texture, and textile design. What you feel is the amount of stiffness and weight of the fabric, called the "hand" of the fabric.

COLOR. The fabric can be colored in several ways—the fibers can be colored before the cloth is woven or the entire fabric can be colored after it has been woven. The color can saturate the cloth or be printed on the surface; it can be treated to be permanent (color-fast), or it can be less color-fast, in which case it may fade and "run" when the cloth is washed.

Color is often the most influential factor in fabric selection, but many other aspects should also be considered. Actually the color is often the easiest feature to change or adjust with dyes, paints, and other means discussed in Chap. 15.

Color is influenced by light. For instance, fluorescent light distorts color. Since stage lighting is incandescent, colors should be selected under incandescent lighting or natural daylight, either of which distorts color less than fluorescent lighting. Our concern is with what the color will look like on stage under stage lighting.

TEXTURE. Texture can be defined by how the fabric responds to light. Satin, for example, has a hard, shiny texture; therefore, it reflects light. Most velvets absorb light, creating a soft, matte texture. A rough, coarse fabric, such as burlap, has an uneven surface which creates shadows for an uneven texture. In general, the texture of the cloth is created by a combination of the types and weights of the fibers used and the manner in which they are put together to make up the fabric. The texture can also be the result of a finishing process which may be permanent or nonpermanent.

TEXTILE DESIGN. The textile design of the fabric, such as plaids, stripes, patterns, or prints can be created by the way the cloth is made or by the way it is finished. With the finishing process, the design may or may not be permanent. Textile design incorporates the use of color and texture to create a fabric's appearance and is a primary factor in suggesting a particular era. An ornate floral pattern of the 1970s, for example, looks quite different from a rococo floral pattern of the eighteenth century.

HAND. The "hand" of the fabric includes the feel of the cloth and its "body," the degree of stiffness of the fabric, which influences how the fabric will drape or fall. A sheer lightweight fabric such as chiffon will fall into a soft drapery, while an equally sheer lightweight fabric such as organdy will feel stiffer. The organdy has more body than the chiffon, and it will hold a shape more readily but will not fall into a soft drape. It is important to note that there can be a great deal of variability in the draping qualities of the same type of cloth. Corduroy, for example, can range from soft and supple to stiff and firm depending on the thread count (number of warp and filling threads per square inch) and the amount of sizing and/or the type of finish used in processing the cloth.

To assess the appearance of the fabric, pull some yardage from the bolt and let it drape over the edge of the bolt. Observe it from a distance for a better idea of how the color, texture, design, and hand will look and work on stage.

Practicability

The fabric's practicability must often include the expense of the cloth as well as its serviceability. There are many inexpensive fabrics on the market which have a variety of theatrical uses; however, there are many fabrics for which there simply are not satisfactory substitutes. When considering the expense of a piece of fabric, it is necessary to consider not only the price per yard, but the design requirements, the fabric's texture, its degree of drapability, and the width of the fabric, since fabric is sold by the running yard rather than by the square yard. The characteristics of a good wool broadcloth, for example, can seldom be substituted for effectively, but since the fabric can be purchased in widths up to sixty inches, the cost per yard is modified. When all elements of such a fabric are considered, the final results in the appearance of the costume usually will more than compensate for the additional cost, and the costume will also be extremely durable and reusable.

Another consideration is any special treatment the fabric will need to undergo in order to create the costume. If the fabric will need to be dyed or if the costume will need to be aged, fabrics of all-natural fibers should be selected because they pro-

duce the most predictable results in creating these effects. On the other hand, if the show is to tour, and the primary concern is to keep the costumes as maintenance-free as possible, permanent press blends may well be the most appropriate fabrics to select. The practicability of fabrics, then, is determined by the qualities required in the costume, the cost per yard, and the serviceability of the cloth.

Historical Applicability

The third and equally important consideration when selecting fabrics is historical applicability. It is often impossible to use the fabrics which were common during a given period; many are no longer produced, and the few that are may be priced far beyond most theatrical budgets. However, the textures, colors, and designs can be approximated to create the feeling of period. Research will be necessary to determine what is and what is not appropriate.

It is essential to consider the color palette, the popular textile styles, and the predominant textures of the fabrics of the given period which the costumes are to reflect. For instance, the Rococo period with its lightness and buoyancy can hardly be captured if the costumes are constructed of inexpensive heavy canvas or even expensive heavy velvets or brocades. By the same token, most of the fabrics selected for Shaw's *The Devil's Disciple* (set in the New England of 1777) would not be appropriate for Goldsmith's *She Stoops to Conquer,* set in eighteenth-century England (see Fig. 4–1). Although in the same time period, the environments and motivations for the characters are entirely different. Therefore, period styles, environments, and character analyses are all part of the research for historical applicability of fabrics.

Figure 4–1 An example of fabrics used to reflect the lightness and bouyancy of the Rococo period in a costume for the character of "Miss Neville" in *She Stoops to Conquer* as produced at The Ohio State University. From the author's collection.

FIBERS

Cloth is made from fibers which are spun into a strand, called yarn. Fibers are fine, pliable, and hairlike units which are joined (spun) into long threads or yarns. These may be *staple* fiber yarns which are composed of short fibers, or *filament* yarns which are long continuous strands. Silk is the only natural filament fiber and that is the reason silk has a luster that other natural fibers lack. The fibers in a yarn can be seen by unraveling and then untwisting a yarn from a piece of cloth. The tiny hairs in the yarn are fibers.

There are two major categories of fibers: natural fibers and man-made, or synthetic, fibers. Natural fibers most commonly used for fabrics are cotton, flax, wool, and silk. Synthetic fibers, introduced in the early part of the twentieth century,

have become increasingly important in the fabric industry in recent years.

All natural fibers must go through a series of processes to remove the "impurities," the unwanted natural particles, from the fibers. How completely the impurities are removed is an indication of the quality and therefore the cost of the cloth. A fine cotton batiste, for example, has all the impurities removed; consequently, it is more expensive than an unbleached muslin which has many impurities left in the fibers. For theatrical use, fabrics which have some impurities left in are often more interesting and valuable. Synthetic fibers are made without impurities in the fibers; consequently, there is no processing necessary for removal of impurities so the cost of the fabric is not affected.

Natural Fibers

Prior to the twentieth century, all fabrics were made from natural fibers derived from plants or animals. The cotton and flax plants are typical sources for vegetable, or *cellulose,* fibers. These fibers have good absorbency and can be subjected to high temperatures. Sheep, goats, and the cocoon of the silkworm are typical sources for animal, or *protein,* fibers. These fibers characteristically resist wrinkles, but they can be harmed by heat.

VEGETABLE FIBERS

Cotton. The fibers come from the cotton plant's seed pods, called "cotton bolls." Cotton is durable and has good absorbency; it can be bleached at low temperatures without injuring the fibers, and it takes dye well, although not as well as wool or silk. Mercerized cotton has had the fiber treated to make it more absorbent and will take and hold dyes more readily and permanently than unmercerized cotton. "Slack Mercerization" is the process used to create stretch fabric of 100 percent cotton. Cotton fibers can be made into a wide variety of fabrics with numerous surface effects; the cost of cotton goods ranges from inexpensive to very expensive.

Linen. The fibers are taken from the stalk of the flax plant and are characterized by their body, great strength, and thick and thin fiber bundles which give texture to the fabric. Linen wrinkles easily, but this also means it will press into folds and creases and will hold the pressed shape. In recent years, finishes have been used to make fabrics which imitate the surface appearance of linen. "Irish" linen is the term which specifies that the fabric is made of flax. It is available in a range of quality from fine to rough.

ANIMAL FIBERS

Wool. The fibers are taken from the fleece of a sheep or from a goat; in the textile industry, wool also includes fibers from the angora goat, Kashmir goat, camel, alpaca, llama, and vicuña. The Federal Trade Commission has established three categories of woolens: wool or new wool, which has not been processed before; reprocessed wool, which is obtained from scraps of newly processed wool and treated to return it to its fibrous state; and reused wool, sometimes called "shoddy," which is taken from rags or old clothing and returned to its fibrous state and generally blended with new wool before it is used in fabrics. Reused wool is a utility fabric, a mackinaw-type fabric. There are numerous variations in yarns and weaves for wool which produce a wide variety of fabrics. Wool is strong, elastic, and takes dyes well if it has been treated to prevent shrinkage or is dyed in cool water. Wool is made into a variety of fabrics of various weights and textures. It ranges in price from moderate to very expensive.

Silk. The fibers come from the cocoon of the silkworm; as many as 3000 cocoons may be required to make one yard of silk. Silk is the only natural filament fiber; this gives the fabric its characteristic lustrous quality, lightness of weight, elasticity, and drapability. There are two varieties of silk: cultivated silk, which is obtained by carefully controlling the silkworm and its cocoon, and wild silk, which is not controlled so the cocoon is produced under natural circumstances. Several terms are used to describe the various kinds of silk: *Silk* refers to cultivated silk; *wild silk* or *tussah* refers to the uncultivated silk, which, in its natural state, is a tan-colored fiber that produces a heavily textured fabric. *Shantung, Pongee,* and *Honan* are fabrics from wild silk; *Duppioni Silk* comes from two silkworms that spin their cocoons together and produce an uneven, irregular yarn. *Raw silk* refers to cultivated "silk-in-the-gum," which is silk that has not been degummed by washing. Silk takes dyes well and is soft and pliable. It is luxurious and consequently generally expensive to very expensive.

Man-Made Fibers

In 1958 the Federal Trade Commission established sixteen generic names for man-made fibers. Within each of these generic categories, there are numerous brand names for fibers which are used in fabrics. These synthetic fibers are also blended with each other and/or with natural fibers to create additional fabrics. The result is an abundance of various types of fabrics.[1]

ACETATE. Made from a combination of chemicals, this fiber requires special dyes and treatments. Acetate is made in various degrees of luster; it retains crispness and is supple and shrink-resistant. It is blended with other fibers to make a wide range of fabrics. It is susceptible to acetone and other organic solvents such as those found in nail polish remover and perfumes; these solvents will dissolve the fabric.

Triacetate is a variation of acetate that is wrinkle-resistant, and fabrics made from these fibers are wash and wear; fabrics made from acetate fibers normally need to be dry-cleaned.

Selected Trade Names: Arnel (triacetate), Celanese, Chromespun, Estron.

ACRYLIC. These fibers are made in many modifications to provide special properties. The fibers are susceptible to heat and should be dried at low temperatures and pressed with a warm, not hot, iron. Acrylic fibers must be treated to ac-

cept dyes; the processes require commercial treatment. These fibers are often blended with other fibers to meet particular requirements.

Some Trade Names: Acrilan, Chemstrand, Orlon, Spectran.

NYLON. A chemically based fiber, nylon is exceptionally strong, easy to wash, quick drying, and difficult to dye. Fabric made from it is strong and not very absorbent, which means it can be very warm to wear. It is often blended with other fibers for fabric variations.

Some Trade Names: Actionwear, Cantrece, Chemstrand, Celanese, Qiana.

POLYESTER. The fibers are made from elements derived from coal, air, water, and petroleum. Polyester is strong, shrink- and stretch-resistant, quick drying, and retains heat-set pleats and creases. It is a basic element in most permanent press material and is often blended with other fibers and used in numerous ways.

Some Trade Names: Chemstrand, Dacron, Fortrel, Kodel, Spectran.

RAYON. Rayon is the oldest man-made fiber and was first produced commercially in 1910. It was called artificial silk until 1924 and has many of the characteristics of silk. Rayon is produced from cellulose, a fibrous substance in all forms of plant life; therefore, it is relatively easy to dye. It drapes well and has a luster which is often harsher than silk. The term *viscose rayon* refers to the process of manufacturing the fibers. Viscose fibers are easy to dye; other types of rayon fibers, which have not been given separate, distinctive names are less easy to dye. Rayon is a widely used synthetic and is moderately priced.

Some Trade Names: Avril, Colorray, Dy-lok, Rayflex.

SPANDEX. The fiber was developed to create an elastic yarn which could be

---

[1]The information on synthetic fibers and fabrics is taken from the *Man-Made Fiber Fact Book* which is published by the Man-Made Fiber Producers Association, Inc. and is available from: Education Department, 1150 Seventeenth Street, N.W., Washington, D.C. 20036.

stretched repeatedly and returned to its original shape and strength. It is lightweight, soft, and smooth. Spandex is used to create stretch fabrics. It is susceptible to chlorine bleach, which can cause deterioration of the fabric.

Trade Name: Lycra.

BASIC FABRIC TERMINOLOGY

Before reviewing the typical costuming fabrics listed in the Glossary of Fabrics, here are some terms which are part of the basic fabric vocabulary. A working knowledge of these terms is essential for working with and identifying the characteristics of fabrics.

BIAS. This is any direction or line away from the lengthwise or crosswise grain.

True bias is the line which cuts diagonally across the straight grain and is found by folding the fabric so the crosswise threads run the same direction as the lengthwise threads. Fabric folded on the true bias will stretch in both directions, on the fold and across the fold.

GRAIN. This refers to the direction of the fibers in the fabric; the lengthwise grain follows the warp yarns (those which parallel the selvage); the crosswise grain follows the filling or weft yarns (those which run at right angles to the warp yarns). *Straight grain* generally refers to the lengthwise grain. Great care should always be observed when placing patterns on the fabric or when drafting a pattern. Proper placement on or across the grain line is essential in determining how the garment will fall when worn.

NAP. Nap is often confused with "pile"; napped fabrics have a fuzzy surface on the face of the fabric made by a finishing process which lifts fiber ends from the ground of the cloth. The amount of napping varies from a slight fuzz to a thick nap, as in imitation furs. Some napped fabrics have an up and down direction as do most pile fabrics. Napped fabrics include flannel, suede cloth, and duvetyn. The latter is a popular inexpensive fabric sometimes used for theatrical drapes.

NAP AND PILE. Both nap and pile fabrics can be made with the surface going in one direction which can be tested by passing your hand lightly over the surface of the fabric. If the fabric feels smooth, the nap or pile is going in the direction of your hand; if it feels rough, it is going in the opposite direction. The reflectivity of the fabric is altered by the direction of the nap or pile, and the color will seem to change. If the nap or pile is going down (feels smooth) the color will be lighter; if it is going up (feels rough) the color will be darker. When cutting a garment, the nap or pile should always go in the same direction on all pieces for even coloration. For a darker, richer color, the nap or pile should go up. Because the direction of nap or pile fabrics must be consistent, more yardage is required for cutting a garment.

PILE. Often confused with and used synonymously with the term *nap*, pile is a three-dimensional fabric with loops of fibers standing up from the ground of the cloth. Piled fabrics can be woven (see Pile Weaves) or knitted, as in many fur cloths. The loops (or floats) can be cut, as in corduroy, or uncut, as in terry cloth. The pile can be overall and even on the ground as terry cloth, woven into wales such as corduroy, or cut with the pile in different lengths to create a pattern as in cut velvets.

This last process is also commonly used in carpet designs.

SELVAGE. This is the lengthwise edge of the fabric woven to interlock the fibers. On some fabrics the selvage is woven tighter than the rest of the piece, causing a pucker along the selvage edge. In this instance the selvage should be trimmed away and not included in the pattern piece.

WALE. This is the rib or ridge on the surface of the fabric generally associated with corduroy, such as the wide-wale or the pinwale; the term also refers to ribs created by thicker or heavier fibers in the weave, as in grosgrain ribbon, or patterns created by the weave, as in the twill weave. Wales in fabric can influence color, so the wale should run the same way in the pieces of a garment and be treated much like piled fabrics.

Fabric Morgue

Fabrics are a primary medium in executing costumes and are utilized by both designer and costumer to realize the design. Fabrics have individual characteristics which make them suitable for some types of garments and unsuitable for others. Learning to recognize the characteristics and identifying them with specific fabrics is fundamental in costuming.

We have found that using the information in the following glossary and assembling a collection of fabric swatches in a fabric morgue is a valuable method for becoming familiar with fabrics and their characteristics. Each swatch should be identified by name and its characteristics (such as stiff or soft, good or poor drapability, has pile or nap, reflective or nonreflective) noted next to the swatch. Additional information should include suggested uses in costuming (garments, period, character type, and the like) and estimated cost per yard.

Scrap boxes in any costume shop usually contain a wide variety of fabrics for starting a collection that can be assembled in a notebook or file card collection as shown in Fig. 4–2. Visits to fabric shops will provide additional swatches and more accurate (although temporary) information on fabric prices. The process of developing a fabric morgue is a continuous one that provides a valuable source of information for future use and should not be limited to those fabrics entered in the glossary.

GLOSSARY OF FABRICS

The following listing contains many of the fabrics commonly used in a shop. It is not intended to be all-inclusive; however, many of the common fabrics which have standard names have been included. No attempt has been made to describe or identify the fabrics but rather to indicate the fabrics' properties for theatrical use. Above all, it is important to become familiar with the appearance, hand, and performance qualities of the various fabrics in order to develop a working fabric vocabulary. The ability to identify the special properties of fabrics and to utilize them on stage is an absolute necessity for costuming. The Glossary of Fabrics is set up according to major usage. While these fabrics can be used in many ways, the following categories have been selected for general clarification: Basic Lining Fabrics, General Fabrics, Sheer Fabrics, Napped and Pile Fabrics, Upholstery Fabrics, Specialty Fabrics, and Interfacing Fabrics. See Appendix A for metric equivalents of fabric widths as approved by the Pattern Fashion Industry.

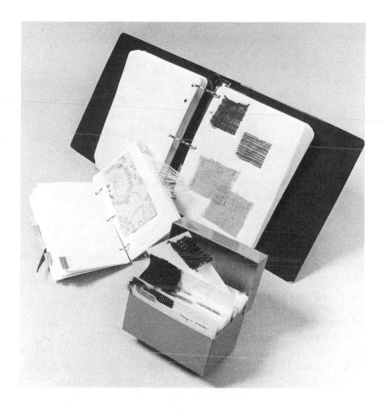

Figure 4-2 Examples of student fabric morgues. Photo by Robert Izzo.

Basic Lining Fabrics

CANVAS.   Available in several weights, 8 oz works well; a variety of widths is available, 72 in. wide works very well, but less than 45 in. is seldom useful; will shrink when washed; takes dye and paint easily; is inexpensive when bought in bulk.

Uses: lining garments, heavy undergarments, costumes.

LINING TAFFETA.   Generally 45 in. wide, can shrink and lose sheen and crisp finish when washed; due to its hard finish, it will not cling to other fabrics or to tights; it is inexpensive and comes in a wide range of colors.

Uses: lining garments, especially when the lining is to be visible; undergarments; decorative ruffles.

Note: Sheath lining is unsatisfactory for costumes; it is flimsy and will tear easily.

UNBLEACHED MUSLIN.   Varies in weight, 128 thread count is a good weight for general use; available in 36 in. to 120 in. widths, we use 72 in. to 90 in. widths; it will shrink when washed, and the finish is not permanent; it takes dye easily but usually unevenly; it is inexpensive, especially when bought in bulk. See Appendix B for bulk sources.

Uses: lining garments; undergarments, petticoats, and rehearsal skirts; patterns.

General Fabrics

BROCADE.   A heavy, multicolored, pattern-weave fabric, it is characterized by satin floats on a plain, ribbed, or satin ground. It drapes in heavy folds, has a rich texture, and is expensive.

Uses: Renaissance costumes and rich garments.

BURLAP. A coarse-textured, plain-weave fabric, it is available in 36 in. to 54 in. widths in a range of colors, often called Art Burlap. It is fairly stiff and inexpensive, but it is rough and scratchy and should not be worn next to the skin.

Uses: peasant costumes and for rough, textured effects.

COTTON. Name refers to the fiber content; consequently, it is available in a wide range of fabrics. It varies in weight from sheer to opaque in fabrics from cotton voile to duck or sailcloth. Textures, which vary according to weave and finish, can be as smooth as percale or as coarse as homespun and hopsacking; some textures are created by special weaves as with cotton piqués, eyelet, and marquisette; other textures are created by leaving impurities in the fibers; 100 percent cottons are preferable to blends for durability and easy dyeing, but they are not always easy to find.

Uses: basic garments such as shirts, undergarments, linings, and the like; any garments depending on texture and finish of the particular fabric.

Basic Cottons include:

Bark cloth. A heavy cotton fabric with an uneven horizontal rib creating an uneven texture like tree bark, it is fairly stiff and falls in long folds. It comes in assorted colors, which are dull and tend to lack life, but it dyes easily.

Uses: textured garments which fall in heavy folds and lower-class garments.

Crash. A textured fabric with thick and thin yarns to create an uneven, nubby look, it is fairly stiff but softens when washed; it also shrinks. It takes dyes easily.

Uses: textured garments, peasant and lower-class garments.

Egyptian cotton (Calcutta cloth). A soft, lightweight cotton with impurities left in the fibers, it has an irregular, crinkled effect lengthwise on the fabric. The color is similar to unbleached muslin, and it takes dye well. It falls in a soft drape.

Uses: period undergarments which are revealed; peasant garments.

Percale. A tight, plain weave, combed cotton or blend, it is often used as a substitute for muslin if colors are required. It is available in a range of colors and is inexpensive.

Uses: undergarments, linings.

BUTCHER CLOTH. A textured fabric with thick and thin yarns, it is similar to crash but is usually made of rayon or rayon-acetate blends. The 100 percent rayon is easy to dye, and the fabric has little shrinkage. Heavyweight butcher cloth looks like linen suiting.

Uses: textured garments, tailored garments, peasant and lower-class garments.

CREPE. A "crinkled" fabric of varying weights from sheer to heavy, the crinkled effect can be achieved by the weave, the finish, or by textured yarns; fabrics made with the textured or high-twist yarns create a permanent crepe effect and will drape well but can stretch and shrink. Some typical fabrics are French Crepe, Wool Crepe, Matelassé, and Crepe-de-Chine. Crepe fabrics created by weave have less drapability and less stretch and shrinkage. Typical fabrics include Sand Crepe, Seersucker, and Cotton Georgette. Crepe effects by finish can wash out or diminish with use; otherwise they will react much as crepe by weaving. Typical fabrics include Plissé and Embossed Crepe. Crepe is made from silk, wool, cotton, or synthetics. Price ranges from moderate to expensive.

Uses: multiple, from undergarments to flowing garments with soft folds.

DENIM. A twill weave cotton or blend, it is available in a range of colors, in some patterns, and with "brushed" surfaces for a nap finish. It is durable and easy to work with and to dye.

Uses: lower-class garments, peasant dress, breeches, and others.

JERSEY. A knitted fabric of cotton, wool, rayon, or nylon which varies in weight from very light to heavy. It is often made in tubular form in a wide variety of colors. It has extremely good drapability, or it can be fitted snugly to the body since it stretches. It can be difficult to work with since it will pucker and stretch. It is moderately expensive.

Uses: lightweight to medium-weight draped garments; snug, fitted garments.

MONK'S CLOTH. A basket-weave fabric, it is available in tight or loose weaves in limited colors. It is usually 50 in. wide and in its natural tan color it dyes easily but will shrink. It drapes well but will stretch and sag. The price is moderate.

Uses: heavy draped garments; peasant costumes and monk's robes.

PIQUÉ. A pattern weave that makes textured cloth, the word comes from the French, meaning "quilted." It features cords or wales that usually run lengthwise and has a right and wrong side to the fabric. It is fairly stiff and is available in a number of patterns. The piqué effect can also be the result of the finishing process.

Uses: accessory pieces such as collars, cuffs, and shirt fronts; also complete dresses.

SATIN. Fabric is made with a satin weave from silk, rayon, nylon, or other synthetic fibers. It comes in a wide range of colors and weights. It is lustrous and has a reflective surface; it falls in stiff folds.

Uses: lustrous gowns and other light-reflective garments.

TAFFETA. A plain weave fabric often made of rayon, it is available in a variety of colors, stripes, and prints and is generally stiff with a sheen and drapes in crisp folds. It is available in various weights but is always heavier than *lining taffeta* and often has a fine rib in the weave.

Uses: vests and breeches for seventeenth, eighteenth, and nineteenth centuries; gowns and undergarments.

WOOL. Refers to the fiber and is available in a wide range of colors, weaves, and textures. It comes in 54 in. to 60 in. widths and is excellent for heavy draped lines. It is moderately expensive.

Uses: suits, medieval costumes, and rich, draped garments.

Sheer Fabrics

CHIFFON. A transparent, lightweight, filmy fabric made of rayon, nylon, or silk (silk is very expensive), it comes in a variety of colors and drapes very well in soft, clinging folds. (Nylon chiffon builds up static and can be too clinging.) It is often difficult to work with.

Uses: soft, sheer garments and veils.

ORGANDY. Crisp, sheer, and lightweight, it is made of cotton or synthetics in a variety of colors. It holds its shape well since stiffness does not wash out.

Uses: stiff veils, starched collars; millinery.

ORGANZA. Similar to organdy but made of rayon or silk, it is not quite as stiff and does not hold shape as well.

Uses: veils, lightweight garments; millinery.

VOILE. A sheer, lightweight fabric of cotton, wool, or a variety of synthetics, it is available in colors and prints. The degree of stiffness depends on the finish; it is semitransparent and relatively inexpensive.

Uses: lightweight garments, veils, and special effects.

Napped and Pile Fabrics

CORDUROY. A pile fabric usually of cotton fibers, it is characterized by lengthwise wales which vary from pinwale, a fine wale with 16 to 21 wales per inch, to wide wale, 5 to 8 wales per inch; no-wale corduroy has an overall pile (no wale visible). Corduroy is available with plain and twill weave ground; the latter has a thicker pile and better durability. It is available in a wide range of colors and prints and has generally good drapability. It dyes easily.

Uses: multiple uses due to wide range of weights and textures.

SUEDE CLOTH.   A napped fabric made to simulate suede, the fibers can be cotton, a blend, or synthetic. It is available in plain or twill weave and in a wide range of colors; the weights and quality vary.

Uses: simulated suede, although a good quality is necessary; breeches, servants' outfits.

VELOUR.   A pile knit fabric of heavy weight and deep pile, it is available in a limited range of colors. It falls in deep folds and is very durable but expensive.

Uses: generally used for stage drapes and heavy, rich garments.

VELVETEEN.   A pile fabric often made with cotton fibers, sometimes difficult to distinguish from velvet, it generally has more body and less drapability than velvet; pile is generally shorter with less sheen than velvet. In moderately priced velvets and velveteens, the difference can sometimes be seen when the fabric is folded; the pile in velvet breaks in crosswise rows, in velveteen it breaks in lengthwise rows.

Uses: as with velvet, but velveteen is generally somewhat less expensive.

VELVET. ˙ A pile fabric made of silk, cotton, rayon, acetate, or nylon, it is closely woven with a short pile, $1/16$ in. high or shorter. Various weights and qualities are available in a wide range of colors and prints. It has generally good drapability but is expensive, and the pile crushes and flattens with wear.

Brocade velvet.   The pile is cut in different heights to create a textured pattern.

Nacré velvet.   This is a changeable fabric with ground of one color, pile of another.

Panne velvet.   This is a lightweight fabric with pile pressed flat giving a smooth, lustrous surface.

Uses: multiple uses for rich, heavy-looking garments and trimmings.

Upholstery Fabrics

A generic term, *upholstery fabrics* covers a wide range of fabrics, generally in pattern weaves characterized by heavy weights and stiffness which falls in deep folds or is stiff enough to hold its own shape. Some fabrics have a laminated rubberized backing and should not be used for costumes. Upholstery fabrics are usually fairly wide, 54 in. to 60 in. and offer good texture, variety in appearance, and a good period look.

BROCATELLE.   A tapestry-type fabric imitating brocade with designs raised to create a brocade look, it often has good drapability. The puffed or blistered texture can be flattened if quality is poor. Price ranges from moderate to expensive.

Uses: excellent for several periods, but the textile design should relate to the desired period.

MATELASSÉ.   A double fabric, it has regular warp and filling fibers and crepe warp and filling threads woven together to create a quilted effect. It is usually a rayon-acetate combination which gives the fabric a matte-sheen look. Occasionally, one set of threads will shrink when pressed, distorting the grain of the fabric, but it has good variety and often has good drapability. Prices range from moderate to expensive.

Uses: as with brocatelle, excellent for several periods when patterned fabrics of heavy body are required.

Specialty Fabrics

BUCKRAM. A stiff open-weave fabric which has been heavily sized with starch, it is available in black and white and in light, medium, and heavy weights. The last is the most useful.

Uses: millinery and stiffening parts of costumes.

Note: The starch will dissolve if the buckram gets too wet, and the fabric will lose stiffness.

CRINOLINE. Similar to buckram but much lighter in weight, it is available in black and white with a stiff finish that is more durable than starch, but it will still lose some stiffness in washing.

Uses: undergarments such as stiff petticoats and bustles; stiff interfacings for collars, cuffs, and sleeves, and so forth.

FAKE FUR. A napped or pile fabric made of various fibers, it is available in many textures and colors to simulate real fur. The wide widths can minimize the expense factor. It is easier to cut and sew than real fur and will have less deterioration.

Uses: decorative detail and trims; hats.

FELT. Generally 72 in. wide, it will shrink and warp if it gets wet; does not fray; will take paint, available in a wide range of color.

Uses: appliqués, trims, and shoe coverings.

INDUSTRIAL-WEIGHT FELT. A heavier, thicker felt, it comes in several thicknesses and weights. It is available in a limited range of colors and is expensive. Felt can be made from a blend of fibers; however, 100 percent wool felt works best for most theatrical uses since wool is easier to mold for something like blocking hats. Felt that has as much as 70 percent wool is somewhat less expensive and is still usable for blocking a shape. (See Appendix B for sources and sample books.)

Uses: special effects, footgear, armor, and millinery.

LACE. Open-work fabric or mesh textile, the threads are knotted, interlaced, or interlooped to create a design in the fabric. It is often made of cotton, silk, or synthetics, and the texture and quality vary greatly. It is available in 36 in. to 45 in. widths as well as in trimming widths. A heavy or strong texture is needed if the lace effect is to carry to the audience. Cotton lace dyes easily. The price of lace varies greatly depending on fiber content, type of manufacture, and quality.

Uses: multiple uses as trim, for lace garments, and for special effects.

LAMÉ. A fabric woven with metallic or metallic-like threads, it can be interwoven with other fibers or be all metallic. It is available in gold, silver, copper, and a range of other colors. A variation of lamé is Eyelash Fabric, which is a pile weave, metallic fabric. Originally lamés were made of pure metal but now are made of anodized aluminum or mylar polyester coated with metallics. It can give a rich appearance to the garment, but solid single-color lamés lack texture and depth. The fabrics are stiff and generally lack drapability, and prices range from cheap to expensive.

Uses: multiple uses as trims and rich-looking garments. A word of caution: Too much lamé can give a cheap, tinsel look.

LEATHER. From animal skins and hides that have been cleaned and tanned, it varies in size, thickness, grain, and uniformity. Various treatments, such as the type of tanning substances used, alter its characteristics and drapability. Additional processes alter the strength and appearance of the leather. Suedes are napped on the flesh side. Leather is available in various weights, colors, and qualities; cost ranges from moderate to expensive.

Uses: for periods which require leather

garments; footwear, trim, and special effects.

MILLISKIN. A stretch fabric that is relatively lightweight, it stretches on both the lengthwise and crosswise grains. It is available in a wide range of colors and takes dyes easily. A popular fabric for dance costumes, it is easy to work with (seams need to be merrowed or sewn with a stretch stitch) and has a warm sheen. See Appendix B for sources.

Uses: leotards, tights, unitards, and other fitted garments.

NET. A stiff, open fabric, available in 45 in. to 72 in. widths, it is made of cotton, rayon, or nylon. Nylon net is inexpensive, holds its shape, and is available in a wide range of colors.

Uses: ballet skirts, stiff veils, Elizabethan ruffs, and overlays to mute colors or modify other fabrics.

VINYL (Imitation Leather). Plastic film is laminated to fabric, and a leather grain is pressed into the film to create a leatherlike look. It is available in various thicknesses, finishes, and colors. Plastic lamination does not allow ventilation; consequently, it is very warm to wear, and it can be difficult to work with. However, it is less expensive than leather.

Uses: as with leather; cost factor allows more freedom in use.

Interfacings

There are numerous types of interfacings on the market, many of which contain their own adhesive for iron-on application. For costumes, the iron-on fabrics are generally not dependable and should be stitched in place where necessary. There are two typical types of interfacings.

HAIR CANVAS. Available in three weights: light, medium, and heavy, it is a woven fabric with a grain. It should be dry-cleaned only. Its trade names include Armo and Hymo.

Uses: shaping and tailoring garments; adding body for other fabrics.

PELLON (brand name). A nonwoven fabric available in "regular" and "all-bias," the former is available in three weights: light, medium, and heavy; the latter in lightweight only. It comes in white and black, and it can be washed or dry-cleaned; it does not ravel.

Uses: to stiffen and give body to pieces that need to hold shape and stand out such as peplums, puffed sleeves, collars, and so on. Also used to aid stiff appearance of corseted bodice (not to be used in lieu of a corset).

FABRIC TESTING

There are certain fabric characteristics which cannot be determined by what you see or feel in the cloth. For example, it is difficult, if not impossible at times, to determine what the fiber content of a piece of fabric is. It may be all natural fibers, all synthetic, or a blend of two or more of these. Also, it is not always possible to know if the fabric is going to shrink or how it will react to heat. Therefore, further identification of fabrics is often necessary before

final selection for a specific costume can be made. We generally run several tests on matching fabric swatches to include with the original swatch in the fabric morgue so the test results are available when we need them to make final selections.

The Burn Test

The burn test is a simple means of generally identifying the fiber content in fabric.

It is a limited test because, although it is useful for distinguishing natural fibers from synthetics (the latter melt rather than burn), it will not reveal the percentages of the fibers that are in blends. However, the information derived from the test usually provides sufficient information for most costuming problems. Testing for the fiber content is typically used for fabrics that need to be dyed, since natural fibers have a better affinity for dyes; dyes on natural-fiber fabrics produce more predictable results than dyes used on synthetics or blends of synthetics and natural fibers. Occasionally, the content information is indicated on the bolt of fabric, but even then it may have to be determined or verified by the burn test.

To test fabrics by burning, ravel out a few yarns, both warp and filling. A difference in luster, twist, or color of the yarns can indicate two or more fibers in the fabric. Ignite the yarns in a match flame and watch the results. More than one burning may be necessary.

Additional characteristics to be tested before the fabric is used in a costume include: (1) the washability of the fabric to determine if the colors and finish are permanent and if the fabric shrinks; (2) the fabric's reaction to heat and steam to determine if the cloth shrinks, puckers, or melts; and (3) the fabric's reaction to pattern and fitting marks to determine if the tailor's chalk leaves a stain or if other markings will show through the cloth.

The Wash and Shrink Test

To test the fabric's washability, cut a small rectangle of fabric and trace an outline of the shape onto a piece of paper. Wash the fabric sample in hot water and soap and rinse it thoroughly; the sample can be hand-washed in the sink. Dry the sample and then place it in the outlined drawing to test for shrinkage. The fabric should be placed in the same position on the paper to determine if the warp and/or the filling yarns have shrunk. Loosely woven fabrics tend to shrink the most and will usually become tighter and stiffer in the process; wool will shrink less in cool water than in hot; synthetics tend to shrink very little.

This test will also tell you whether the finish of the fabric is permanent and if the color is fast. If the sample has shrunk and/or if the finish or color has altered, the fabric should be washed before it is cut if the fabric is to be modified and if the

Fiber	Characteristics When Ignited
Cotton Linen Rayon	Burns rapidly and steadily, has a yellow-orange flame; leaves a fine feathery, greyish ash; smells like burning paper or leaves.
Wool Silk	Burns slowly, often with a sputtering flame, sometimes self-extinguishing; leaves irregular black bead which crushes easily to a gritty black powder; smells like burning hair.
Acetate	Burns and melts, not self-extinguishing; leaves a brittle black bead; smells like a combination of burning paper and vinegar.
Acrylic	Similar to acetate but has an odor similar to broiled fish.
Nylon	Burns slowly with melting, generally self-extinguishing; leaves a hard grey bead; smells like celery.
Polyester	Burns slowly with melting and gives off black smoke; generally self-extinguishing; leaves hard, dark bead and has a sweetish odor.

finished costume is to be washed. If the results of the water test are not satisfactory, the finished garment must be dry-cleaned and not treated with water at all.

The Iron Test

To test the fabric's reaction to heat and steam, press a sample with an iron. To test the reaction to tailor's chalk, press the markings with the iron; the wax compound may leave a wax stain on the cloth, or the pigment from the colored chalks may impregnate the cloth permanently.

Fabrics selected for costumes must often be modified (changed or adjusted) to realize the design. Chapter 15 elaborates on the modification processes and techniques such as dyeing, bleaching, and painting. Therefore, the fabric selection process needs to incorporate knowledge of what the final costume is to look like, and the selected fabrics should be tested prior to use in the actual garment.

In general, immediate response to the visual qualities of fabrics is only one aspect of selecting appropriate fabrics which will effectively realize the costume design. The nature and composition of fabrics must also be considered. This requires becoming familiar with what the fabrics, as discussed earlier in the chapter, learning how they are made, and how they are finished. All these elements combine to determine the characteristics of a given piece of cloth.

Fabric Processes

Fabrics made from fibers by one of the following methods are known as textile fabrics. Leather, for example, is not a textile fabric.

WEAVING. This is the interlacing of two sets of yarns, the warp yarns and the filling (also called weft or woof) yarns. The warp yarn runs lengthwise, and filling yarn runs at right angles to the warp across the fabric; woven fabrics are identified by raveling yarns from adjacent sides.

KNITTING. This is the looping of yarns together to form a fabric.

Filling knit. A single yarn travels across from needle to needle creating lengthwise

FABRIC PROCESSES AND FINISHES

ribs on the right side and wavy courses on the wrong side; this knit will stretch both ways and will run if snagged or torn.

Warp knit. This knit has numerous threads forming vertical ribs on the right side and chevron courses across on the wrong side; there is not much stretch lengthwise, but the knit will resist runs.

Double knit. Made with two sets of needles, the right and wrong sides are almost identical; this knit has more body than single knits; it does not stretch much or sag as readily, and the edges do not curl when the fabric is cut as many single knits will.

CROCHETING. A single yarn is used to create a series of loops; a hook is used to create a chain of the loops which combine to form the fabric.

BRAIDING. Yarns are interlaced at angles of less than 90 degrees to form a flat tubular fabric.

KNOTTING. This is a mesh or openwork fabric with the yarns knotted together in a pattern.

FELTING. Fibers are matted together by heat, steam, and pressure, creating a nonwoven fabric which has no grain and will not fray or ravel; the fabric will separate under stress.

BONDING OR LAMINATING. Two fabrics are adhered together by adhesive or the addition of a chemical foam backing; these have little advantage for theatrical use since the adhesive often does not hold up, the backing fabric can often be off-grain, and the lining or backing is often not strong enough for theatrical purposes.

Woven Fabrics

Weaving is an ancient art form. People learned very early how to take the short fibers and twist them into yarn or thread and then to form the yarns into fabric. Of course, methods and machinery for forming fabric have been developed over the centuries, and many of today's machines that are used to manufacture cloth are much more complex than the early looms. However, the processes are still basically the same. Variations in woven fabrics are achieved through the pattern of interlacing (identified by weave name), the thread count, and the balance.

The *plain weave*, the *twill weave*, and the *satin weave* are the three basic weaves. All woven fabrics are made in one of these three basic weaves or a variation thereof. The variations include such weaves as the *pile weave*, the *pattern weave*, and the *gauze (leno) weave*. Woven fabrics can be made of any fiber or a combination of fibers.

The *thread count* is the number of warp and filling yarns per square inch of fabric as it comes from the loom; it should not be confused with the number of yarns in a square inch of the finished fabric since that may be changed by shrinkage or other effects of the finishing processes. The thread count is an indication of the quality of fabric: the higher the count, the better the quality, since there is less potential for shrinkage and less raveling of cut edges. Thread count is written with the warp number first, for example: 80 × 76, or it may be written as a total of the two: 156. Mail-order catalogs often give the thread count to assist the customer in judging the quality of the fabric, since the fabric cannot be seen.

Balance is the ratio of warp yarns to filling yarns and indicates a possibility of slippage (twisting of the fabric). A well-balanced fabric, for example, has a 1:1 ratio or approximately one warp yarn to every filling yarn, such as is found in percale fabrics, and has little possibility of slippage. Examples of unbalanced fabrics include cotton broadcloth which has approximately a 2:1 ratio (thread count 144 × 76) or satin with approximately a 3:1 ratio (thread count 200 × 64). Balance is not always related to quality, but balance and thread count are helpful in predicting slippage; a low thread count in unbalanced fabrics suggests a greater possibility of slippage.

When used theatrically, woven fabrics which are unbalanced, or which have variety in the yarns (thick and thin), or impurities left in the fibers are much more interesting because they have more texture and/or variety; however, if the thread count is low (a loose weave), the fabric will have a tendency to twist or sag. But even this tendency can be used to advantage for such things as aged or ragged costumes.

Basic Weaves

The *plain weave* is the simplest weave and is made by passing the filling (weft or woof) yarn over and under each warp yarn, alternating in each row as shown in Fig. 4-3. The regular interlacing of the warp and filling yarns can be woven tightly or loosely (high or low thread count). Burlap is an example of a loosely woven plain weave; Percale is a tightly woven plain weave. For theatrical purposes, the plain weave is a good all-purpose weave. It is generally inexpensive, strong, and in a tight weave it

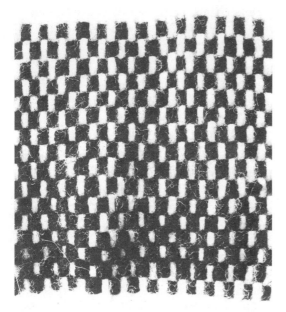

Figure 4–3 An example of the plain weave; in this sample, the warp yarns are white and the filling yarns are black. The weave sample was made by Constance Meiklejohn. Photo by Robert Izzo.

popular fabrics of this weave include Faille, Bengaline, and Ottoman. The last has the heaviest of the horizontal ribs. The rib weave provides individuality and interesting textures, and it is fairly strong; however, the slippage of the threads can be a problem because it may cause the fabric to twist off-grain, particularly when washed in hot water. Generally, there is also a high percentage of shrinkage in many ribbed fabrics.

The *twill weave* (Fig. 4–5) is the second basic weave. Each warp or filling yarn floats over two or more filling or warp yarns. (A *float* is that portion of a yarn that crosses over two or more yarns.) The next row is offset by one and repeats the pattern, forming the characteristic diagonal ridges, called wales, of the twill weave. A popular variation of this weave is the *herringbone* or *chevron weave*. Common characteristics of twill weave fabrics include a right and wrong side of the fabric; if the twill wale goes up to the right on one side, it will go up to the left on the other side. The diagonals may be even or uneven, or

holds its shape well, since it does not stretch or sag easily. However, the plain weave generally lacks individuality and texture.

Two common varieties of the plain weave are the *basket weave* and the *rib weave*. The basket weave (see Fig. 4–4) has two or more filling yarns passing alternately over and under two or more warp threads and often creates a coarse textured look. Monk's Cloth and Oxford Cloth are woven in the basket weave; the former is a looser weave than the latter. This weave is fairly inexpensive and provides good ventilation, but it can stretch and sag, depending on the thread count and balance.

The *rib weave* is made by increasing the number or thickness of either the warp or filling yarns to create a rib in the fabric. Perhaps the most familiar example of this type of weave is Grosgrain Ribbon, which has the rib in the filling thread. Other

Figure 4–4 An example of the basket weave; in this sample, the warp yarns are white and the filling yarns are black. The weave sample was made by Constance Meiklejohn. Photo by Robert Izzo.

Figure 4–5 An example of the twill weave; in this sample, the warp yarns are white and the filling yarns are black. The weave sample was made by Constance Meiklejohn. Photo by Robert Izzo.

they may reverse direction at regular intervals as in the herringbone weave.

The twill weave is decorative, durable, and has texture. Denim is an example of a twill weave in which the warp yarns are dark, and the filling yarns are light. Drill, Gabardine, and Serge are other examples of twill weaves, and so is Twill Tape (cited in Chap. 2). Wool, cotton, and synthetic fibers are all typically used in twills.

The *satin weave* (Fig. 4–6) has every warp yarn floating over a number of filling yarns, interlacing with the filling yarn, and then floating over more yarns with the interlacing offset in a regular progression. The float in the satin weave gives the fabric the characteristic luster of satin since the interlacings of yarns are placed farther apart than in the twill weave to avoid forming wales. Satin fabrics have a right and wrong side and vary greatly in thread count and balance. The weave can have the warp yarns floating over the filling, called *warp-faced satin,* or the filling yarns floating over the warp, called *filling-faced satin* or *sateen.* In a loosely woven low-thread-count satin, the floats can snag easily or the fabric can twist. Satin woven fabrics are available in a variety of fibers and weights.

Variations on Basic Weaves

The *pile weave* (Fig. 4–7) creates three-dimensional fabrics with yarns creating a cover over the ground fabric. A third, or extra, yarn is woven into the basic weave structure, called the ground, which may be either a plain or twill weave. With the twill weave, it is possible to have more yarns per inch which creates a thicker or denser pile.

The additional, or pile-forming, yarn is classified as a filling pile when it is woven in with the filling yarn. It is classified as a

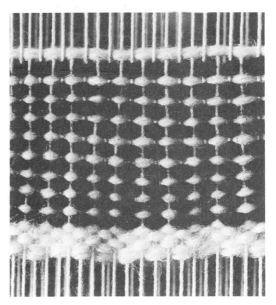

Figure 4–6 An example of the satin weave; in this sample, the warp yarns are white and the filling yarns are black. The weave sample was made by Constance Meiklejohn. Photo by Robert Izzo.

Figure 4–7 An example of the pile weave; in this sample, the ground is light and the third yarn is dark. This is a cut-pile and is not very dense. Photo by Robert Izzo.

color is richer and deeper if the fabric is used so that the pile is directed up. Garments cut from piled fabric should be cut with the pile going in the same direction on all pieces of the fabric; otherwise, the light will not be reflected the same way, and the colors will not look the same.

Piled fabrics must be steamed or brushed and not pressed flat with an iron; many of the fabrics must be dry-cleaned. The fabric can be tested as suggested under Fabric Testing to determine whether the fabric can be washed. The pile weave is an interesting weave with many variations and has multiple uses for theatrical costumes.

Pattern weaves require either special looms or special attachments for the simple loom used for the three basic weaves. Pat-

warp pile when it is woven with the warp yarn. The third yarn can be woven as loops: Uncut loops create the *terry weave;* cut loops create a *cut-pile weave.* It can also be woven as a float across the ground, which is then cut and pressed to stand up and create the pile. In Corduroy, for example, the ribs are created when the floats are woven in lengthwise rows and then cut and pressed; in Velveteen, which has no ribs, the floats are woven in a scattered fashion on the ground, cut, and pressed. Interesting effects in the fabric can be created by the use of cut and uncut float combinations, by variations in the height of the pile or combinations of high- and low-twist yarns, by woven sections of pile forming floats in an over-all pattern, or by printing, curling, or crushing the pile.

Many pile fabrics are finished by pressing the cut floats to where they stand up from the ground, giving a direction, up and down, to the pile; this influences the appearance of the color of the fabric. The

Figure 4–8 An example of the gauze or leno weave; in this sample, the two white warp threads form a loop and the black filling yarn is passed through. The weave sample was made by Constance Meiklejohn. Photo by Robert Izzo.

tern weaves, as the name implies, are used to weave a pattern into the fabric as seen in Piqué, Brocade, and Brocatelle. Many upholstery fabrics are pattern weaves and are of great value in costuming certain periods because of their weight, widths, and texture. Although they tend to be somewhat expensive, these fabrics can provide a very effective period costume.

The *gauze* or *leno weave* also requires either a special loom or special attachments. In this weave, two warp threads are crossed over each other, and the filling thread passes through the loop created by the crossover as shown in Fig. 4–8. This weave makes up into a strong, sheer fabric such as Marquisette or even Mosquito Netting.

Fabric Finishes

If, in a fabric store, your eyes start to burn or water, you are probably experiencing an allergic reaction to some of the finishes that are used on fabrics. A finish is anything that is done to the fiber, yarn, or fabric before or after the weaving or knitting process. The appearance, the hand, and the performance of any fabric are affected by the finish. As with the development of synthetics, numerous developments in finishing processes have been introduced in recent years so that now fiber properties can be altered so completely that the finished fabric bears little resemblence to the original. Fabrics have always been finished; however, the earlier finishing techniques were only done for the appearance and the hand of the fabric. These finishes were generally not permanent and were lost after the first washing; the techniques included adding starch, china clay, and dyes to the fabrics. Today, many of the finishes are treated to withstand cleaning, wear, and sunlight in order to make the finish more permanent and the fabric more durable.

Woven fabrics that have received no finishing are called gray goods (greige or loom state) regardless of color. Before the gray goods receive finishing treatments, they go through initial cleaning processes. These processes include one or more of the following:

> Desizing: the removal of a stiffening agent on the warp yarns
> Degumming: the removal of the gum from silk yarns by boiling-off or washing
> Washing: the removal of oil, dirt, sizing, and grease from wool
> Scouring: the removal of oil, dirt, sizing, and grease from wool
> Singeing: the burning-off of projecting fiber ends from the surface of the cloth

After the fabric is cleaned, it is ready for further treatment. However, the order of application and the kind of finish applied will vary with the fiber content of the fabric and will be governed by what the fabric is to look like, how it should feel, and how it is to be used. Finishing treatments are categorized as mechanical, additive, and chemical.

MECHANICAL FINISHES. Mechanical finishes are those which cause a physical change in the cloth and include the following:

Beetling flattens yarns by pounding, to make the weave appear less open than it really is. The process is used on linen and a few fabrics resembling linen to increase the luster, absorbency, and smoothness of the fabric.

Brushing cleans the surface of the fabric after shearing. When combined with steam, this process will lay nap or pile in a direction and fix it in position giving the "up-and-down" direction on nap or pile fabrics.

Calendering is a process which presses the fabric in a manner similar to household ironers. There are several types of calendering processes.

Embossing calendering produces either flat or raised designs on fabric. The advent of heat-sensitive fibers, such as nylon, acetate, acrylic, and polyester, has made the process more popular because the finish can now be permanent.

Friction calendering gives a highly glazed surface to the cloth by saturating it with starch and waxes. The finish is permanent only if resin finishes are used; otherwise, the glazed finish will wash out.

Moiré calendering produces a "water-marked" design on ribbed silk and wool fabrics. Ribbed fabrics such as taffeta and faille are required to make a "true moiré."

Schreiner calendering produces a "deep-seated" luster rather than a shine. This finish was not permanent until the advent of resins and thermoplastic fibers. It is now used on nylon and polyester tricot jersey as a *satinette* finish which is permanent.

Decantizing is comparable to steam-ironing and produces a smooth wrinkle-free finish and a lofty hand on woolen and worsted fabrics and on synthetic and wool blends. The process is done either wet or dry; wet decantizing is a more permanent finish.

Loop drying serves the same drying function as tentering but does not dry the fabric under tension. This process is used on fabrics with a soft finish and on stretchy fabrics.

Pleating, a variation on the embossing process, is an ancient finishing process. The advent of the heat-sensitive fibers has made this finish more permanent; however, the degree of permanence depends on fiber content and care.

Shearing is used to remove loose fiber or yarn ends, knots, and so on, and to control the length of the pile or nap on the surface; it can be used to create a design or a smooth surface. A shearing machine is similar to a lawn mower.

Tentering is one of the final finishing processes that performs the double process of straightening and drying fabrics. In principle, tentering machines are similar to the old-fashioned curtain stretchers.

ADDITIVE FINISHES.   The additive finishes are those in which a compound or a substance is mechanically held on the fiber or fabric and include:

Sizing, also called *dressing,* is used to give body, strength, weight, stiffness and/or smoothness to the fabric. Some sizings are temporary, such as starch, gelatin, and softeners; others are permanent, such as resin and cellulose solutions. A typical use of these solutions is on permanent press and wash-and-wear fabrics.

Surface coating finishes are used to give luster, to waterproof, to act as a binder, and to increase abrasion resistance. Glazing, or polishing, is a popular surface coating finish.

CHEMICAL FINISHES.   Chemical finishes are those which bring about a change in the fiber through chemical reaction and are some of the oldest finishes used. These include natural dyes, iron rust dyeing, bleaching by the sun, and caustics from ashes and urine. Some of the most common chemical finishes include the following:

Bleaching is used by the finisher to clean and whiten gray goods in preparation for dyeing and other finishing. Bleaches may be either acid or alkaline in nature, and most are oxidizing agents. Not all fibers are suitable to all bleaches.

Liquid chlorine bleach is safe for cotton and rayon but will cause such fabrics as nylon and acetate to yellow, and it can dissolve wool and silk. Other synthetics are not affected by the bleach.

Peroxide bleaches are common factory bleaches and are sold commercially as powder bleaches (sodium perborate). When water is added, they become hydrogen peroxide which is a safe cleaning bleach for all kinds of fabric.

Reducing bleaches are used to strip color from dyed cloth and are available in the market as color removers.

Mercerization is a process using caustic soda to increase luster, softness, strength, and affinity to dye on cotton and linen.

The finishes are used in combinations to produce the desired effect in the cloth. A piece of organdy, for example, starts as sheer fabric of combed cotton. The goods are singed, desized, bleached, and mercerized before going into an acid treatment. This treatment adds strong sulphuric acid to produce a transparent, or parchment, effect. The goods are then dyed or printed with colors that resist acid damage, after which the cloth is immersed in an acid solution which reacts to the surface to give permanent crispness and transparency to the dried cloth. The fabric is then mercerized again, washed, tentered, and calendered before it is ready for the market as organdy.

Finishes are used to enhance the quality, appearance, and feel of the fabric. Some finishes are readily visible, such as glazing or polishing cotton or moiré (watermarking) on taffetas; others are easily recognized by feel, such as starch sizing used to stiffen fabrics—in this instance, the fabric feels sticky to the touch. However, it is often difficult to determine how the fabric is finished and whether or not the finish is permanent. Therefore, it is advisable to test the fabric prior to use to determine the permanence of the finish.

There are many variables involved when working with fabrics, and the increase of synthetics and the blends of these and natural fibers provide a wide range of fabrics to select from. It is important to develop a working vocabulary of fabric terminology and a means of identifying various fabrics and their characteristics. Compiling a collection of fabric swatches and identifying them as thoroughly as possible is an effective way of developing the vocabulary and recognizing fabric characteristics.

ADDITIONAL SOURCES

The following sources provide an in-depth study of fabrics and weaves.

HOLLEN, NORMA, AND JANE SADDLER, *Textiles* (3rd ed.). New York: The Macmillan Co., 1968.

Man-Made Fiber Fact Book. Washington, D.C.: Man-Made Fiber Producers Association, Inc.

TOVEY, JOHN, *Weaves and Pattern Drafting.* New York: Reinhold Book Corporation, 1969.

WINGATE, ISABEL, ed. *Fairchild's Dictionary of Textiles.* New York: Charles Scribner's Sons, 1975.

WINGATE, ISABEL, *Textile Fabrics and Their Selection* (5th ed.). Englewood Cliffs, N.J.: Prentice-Hall, 1964.

measurements

An accurate and comprehensive set of measurements for each actor in a production is essential to assure the proper fit of the costumes. A complete set of measurements, carefully recorded, provides necessary information for realizing the costume, whether it is to be constructed in the shop, purchased, or rented.

The use of standardized measurement forms to record all the information simplifies the process of taking the measurements and helps to ensure that the information will be complete. Typical forms are shown in Figs. 5-1 and 5-2 (pp. 85-86). These blank forms should be duplicated and kept in stock for future use; we duplicate our forms on two colors of paper, one for male and one for female, for quick identifica-

tion of the forms. In situations where the acting company is more or less permanent, completed forms should be kept on file for future shows.

Taking measurements requires practice in order to produce an accurate set; therefore, it is necessary to get experience by taking measurements of several people. The simplest way to test the accuracy of the measurements is to draft a basic pattern such as those detailed in Chaps. 7-10 and then fit the garment on the individual. This type of project clarifies and reinforces how and where to take measurements, how the measurements are used in pattern drafting, and how patterns work on the body.

BASIC RULES IN MEASURING THE ACTOR

Taking an accurate set of measurements requires time and concentration. There are two important rules to observe in your

own behavior when taking any measurements. First, do not be timid. A light, tentative contact with the body can be disconcerting to anyone, especially if the individual is ticklish, and it does not instill a feeling of confidence toward the person taking the measurements. Secondly, be businesslike. Everyone is sensitive about the size and shape of his or her body; therefore, comments regarding any of the measurements are out of order. For the same reason, the information on the form should be considered confidential, for use only in providing a properly fitting costume, not for gossip.

FACTORS TO REMEMBER IN MEASURING THE ACTOR

The body is a mobile, flexible unit; portions of it expand and contract with different movements and postures. Each of us has experienced garments which seemed to fit when the body was standing in a relaxed state but which did not fit comfortably when we moved or even sat. A sleeve may become too short when the arm is moved, or pant legs may become uncomfortably tight around the thighs when seated. Too tight a fit can be uncomfortable and inhibit movement. At one point in the eighteenth century, gentlemen intentionally had pants made only for standing and other pants made for sitting, but in the modern theatre, costumes usually have to give actors full freedom of movement.

Allowance for the flexibility of the body is called *ease*. Providing the proper ease in a garment is part of the cutting process; however, certain information to guide that process is acquired when the measurements are taken. The chest, for example, should be measured when it is expanded rather than relaxed; the arm should be bent rather than straight when it is measured. Additional measurements which provide information to determine ease are cited in the discussion of individual measurements.

The body is round and three-dimensional. While each body is unique to some degree, there are certain constants which are universally applicable. The neck, for example, is lower in the front than in the back. Therefore, the measurement from the neck to the waist in the front will be shorter than the neck to waist measurement in the back. The back side of the body is fuller than the front, especially at the hips and legs. The distance across the shoulders in the back is usually ½ in. to 1 in. greater than across the front. A greater variation than this generally indicates rounded or beefy shoulders, or it may mean inaccurate measurements.

Proportions within the body frame differ. The right and left sides of the body are not identical; one side is smaller than the other. Generally, this difference is not noticeable, but occasionally the difference may be great enough to interfere with a comfortable fit. A typical occurrence of this is in the foot size where, for some people, the difference may be great enough to require wearing shoes of two different sizes.

However, if differences in body proportions are enough to affect the fit of garments, the actor will usually be aware of them and will inform the person taking measurements. Needless to say, information of this nature should be noted on the forms.

Any assumptions on body proportions should be avoided. For instance, the height of an individual does not determine the torso and leg length. Some individuals who are 6 ft tall will take a 32 in. inseam, while others of the same height may take a 29 in. inseam. In the first instance, the height is more in the legs; in the second instance, the height is more in the torso.

Since there are individual variations between bodies, a complete set of measurements must be taken. To create costumes that fit well, it is necessary to have the information available when it is needed.

An awareness of the common factors which are applicable simplifies the measuring process and aids in understanding what measurements are needed and why. To take the measurements you must have a good, clean tape measure (the plastic tapes ½ in. to ¾ in. wide with large numbers work best). There should be ample space to move around the actor, a place in which to fill in the form, and a straight-back wooden chair. It is also helpful to have someone with you to write down the measurements to make the process faster and more efficient.

The measurement forms, Figs. 5-1 and 5-2, are set up to identify the actor, production, and the character. These forms are organized so that the measuring process begins at the head and moves down and around the body, but the method of organizing the form can vary according to individual preferences. The concern is to set up a form that provides the necessary information quickly and easily.

Measurements, such as crotch, girth, tights and leotard sizes may not be required for all productions. However, if the acting company is fairly consistent, these measurements should be taken and kept on file. If an actor's measurements are over six months old, retake the chest or bust, waist, and hip measurements. All other measurements should remain the same unless the actor has gained or lost considerable weight or has grown in height.

The actor can usually fill out the first four lines of the form, including the information on height, weight, and dress or suit size. To begin, have the actor remove bulky clothing such as a heavy sweater or a thick belt; bulky items should also be removed from pockets. High-heeled or thick-soled shoes should be removed, since the length measurements are taken to the floor.

When taking the measurements, hold the tape firmly, placing it around the body smoothly. Watch for twists in the tape and make sure that it is placed where it should be on the body. Do not take measurements by "cinching-in" the tape or by leaving space between it and the body. The tape should rest easily on the body.

The following discussion indicates how and where to take the measurements to get the information necessary for the forms.

A common problem when taking measurements is in determining the specific point at which to start and end the measurement. The most problematic areas are those which have no precise point of definition, such as the location points on the shoulders. The rule of thumb is to take measurements of these areas by starting at the points of juncture—that is, where the arm joins the torso and where the neck joins the shoulder or torso. The important thing is to establish identifiable points and then to use them consistently for each set of measurements. The natural waistline is pertinent to several measurements; a piece of cord tied around the waist is helpful in specifying its precise location.

In the following list, a single asterisk before an entry indicates a measurement used for buying ready-made items; the double asterisk is for measurements which are also necessary for renting costumes. (M) indicates measurements for males

MEN

Date _____

Name _____ Phone _____

Production _____

Character _____

Height __ _____ Weight _____ Suit size _____

Head _____ Shoulder (front) _____ Shoulder (back) _____

Neck _____ Shoulder (neck to armhole) _____

Chest _____ Arm bent:
                        to elbow _____ to wrist _____ Sleeve length _____

Waist _____ Underarm length:
                        to wrist _____ to waist __ _____

Hips __ _____ __ Back (seam to seam) _____

Neck to waist (front) _____ Neck to waist (back) _____

Neck to floor (front) __ _____ __ Neck to floor (back) _____

Shoulder to waist _____

Waist
to below knee _____ to mid-calf _____ to floor _____

Inseam
to below knee _____ to floor _____

Crotch _____ Rise _____

Girth _____ Thigh circumference _____ Calf circumference _____

Tights size _____ Leotard size _____ Ballet slipper _____

Hat size _____ Glove size _____ Shoe size _____

Comments: _____
_____
_____

Figure 5-1 Measurement form for men. Form should be duplicated on an identifying colored paper and kept in stock for future use.

WOMEN

Date _____

Name _____ Phone _____

Production _____

Character _____

Height _____ Weight _____ Dress size _____

Head _____ Shoulder (front) _____ Shoulder (back) _____

Neck _____ Shoulder (neck to armhole) _____

Bust _____ Arm bent:
to elbow _____ to wrist _____

Waist _____ Underarm length:
to wrist _____ to waist _____

Hips _____ Back (seam to seam) _____

Neck to waist (front) _____ Neck to waist (back) _____

Neck to floor (front) _____ Neck to floor (back) _____

Shoulder to tip of bust _____ Bra size _____

Waist
to below knee _____ to mid-calf _____ to floor _____

Inseam
to below knee _____ to floor _____

Crotch _____ Rise _____

Girth _____ Thigh circumference _____ Calf circumference _____

Tights size _____ Leotard size _____ Ballet slipper _____

Hat size _____ Glove size _____ Shoe size _____

Comments: _____
_____
_____

Figure 5-2 Measurement form for women. Form should be duplicated on an identifying colored paper and kept in stock for future use.

only; (F) for females only. Figures 5–3 and 5–4 illustrate the placement for measurements.

*/** *Head*: the circumference above the ears, for hat sizes. (Also see Wig Measurements.)

Shoulder (front): across the shoulders just below the collarbone between the normal armhole seam lines.

Shoulder (back): across the shoulders about 3 in. below the neckline to the normal armhole seam lines. (This measurement is usually ½ in. to 1 in. greater than across the shoulder front.)

*/** *Neck*: circumference of the neck, dropping in the front to just above the indentation of the collar bone (the position of a normal garment neckline). Men can often give their neck sizes, since it is the collar size of ready-made shirts.

Shoulder (neck to armhole): from the base of the neck to the armhole seam line at the top of the shoulder. This line is the normal seam line in modern garments.

*/** *Chest (M), Bust (F)*: circumference around the fullest part of the chest. Have the men expand their chests for this measurement. This measurement indicates suit size, see Fig. 5–6.

*/** *Waist*: circumference of the natural waistline. In addition, ask the men what size they normally buy in trousers. If the measurement is different, write the trouser size in parentheses next to the waist measurement, but remember that certain styles in pants have a low waistline, located below the natural waist, that is, larger than the natural waist measurement.

*/** *Hips*: circumference of the hips at the widest part, normally about 8 in. below the waist.

Arm bent (to elbow, to wrist): length of the arm when it is bent and held in front of the actor, as shown in Fig. 5–3, taken from where the arm joins the shoulder in the back along the back or outside of the arm to the center of the elbow and then to the wrist.

*/** *Sleeve length (M)*: taken from the center of the back, at the spine, along the length of the bent arm to the wrist. This measurement is the sleeve size of ready-made shirts, and men can often provide the size they buy. Men's shirts are sized by neck and sleeve length; a ready-made shirt size 15/32 indicates a 15 in. neck and a 32 in. sleeve.

** *Underarm length*: taken from the armpit to the wrist with the arm outstretched.

Wrist: circumference of the wrist; taken on the wrist of the dominant hand—that is, of a right-handed or left-handed person.

Underarm to waist: taken at the side of the body from the armpit to the natural waist.

Back (seam to seam): taken across the fullest part of the back from the center of the armpit on each side across the shoulder blades. The tape should curve upward slightly to catch the fullness of the back, as shown in Fig. 5–3. This is an important measurement for case since the area fluctuates a good deal in movement.

** *Neck to waist (front)*: taken from the indentation at the collarbone to the natural waistline.

** *Neck to floor (front)*: taken from the collarbone indentation to the floor.

** *Neck to waist (back)*: taken from the large bone at the base of the neck to the natural waistline in the back.

** *Neck to floor (back)*: taken from the base of the neck to the floor in back.

Shoulder to waist (M): taken from the base of the neck at the top of the shoulder to the natural waist.

Shoulder to tip of bust (F): taken from the base of the neck at the top of the shoulder to the nipple of the breast. It is important to note if the actress is wearing a bra; the measurement will vary depending on the amount of support and lift provided by the bra. An accurate measurement, with appropriate support, is important since the front fitting darts on women's garments radiate from the nipple.

Crotch: taken from the natural waistline

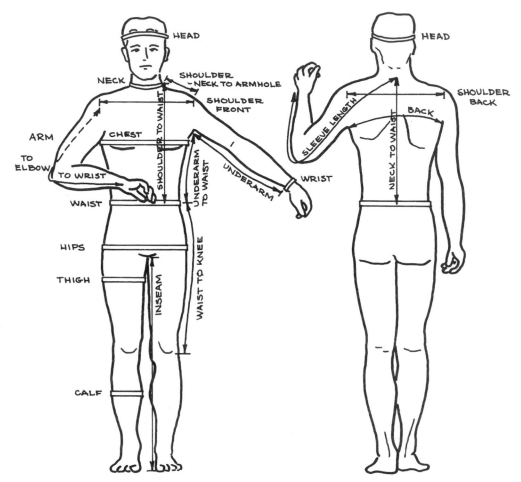

Figure 5-3 Selected measurement placement and locations showing where to start and end the measurements.

in front through the crotch to the back waistline.

Rise: seat the actor in a solid straight-back chair and measure from the waist to the top of the chair at the side of the body.

Waist to below kneecap: taken from the natural waistline at the side of the leg to below the kneecap.

Waist to mid-calf: taken at the side of the leg from the natural waistline to the middle of the calf.

Waist to floor: taken at the side of the leg from the natural waistline to the floor. Heeled shoes should be removed.

Inseam to knee: taken along the inside of the leg from the crotch to below the kneecap. A useful measurement if knee-length pants are required. If this length is required, the circumference of the leg below the knee is also necessary.

*/** *Inseam to floor*: taken along the inside of the leg from the crotch to the floor to give the maximum length that may be required. Men can often give the inseam size they normally buy; this information should be written in parentheses.

* *Bra size (F)*: this information can sometimes be supplied by the actress. If she

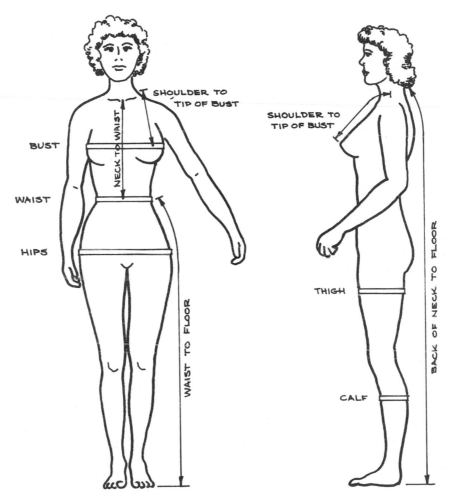

Figure 5–4 Additional measurement placement and locations.

does not know the size, measure the rib cage under the bust and add 5 in. Since bra sizes are designated in even numbers, add up to 1 in. to the total (rib cage plus 5) to determine the correct size. Generally, the cup size is determined by comparing the bust measurement with the bra size: 1 in. difference indicates an A cup, 2 in. a B cup, 3 in. a C cup, and 4 in. a D cup. While this formula is not applicable to all manufacturers, it can be used as a guideline for selecting the proper bra size. When buying a bra, it is advisable to have the actress present to try on the vari-

ous styles in order to select the best fit and appearance.

Girth: taken from the base of the neck at the top of the shoulder through the crotch and back up to the starting point. This measurement is used when making leotards and the like.

Thigh circumference: taken around the fullest part of the thigh.

Calf circumference: taken around the fullest part of the calf. Both of these measurements are used when making fitted pants or tights.

Tights size, leotard size, and ballet slipper size: the actor can often supply this information; if not, see Dancewear Sizes, or check size information in dance catalogs.

*/** *Hat size*: this can occasionally be supplied by the actor. Women's hat sizes are the same as the head measurement. Men's sizes are designated by hat manufacturers in increments ranging from sizes 6 to 8. See Fig. 5-7 for the men's hat size chart.

*/** *Glove size*: occasionally the actor can supply this information. One method of determining a glove size is to measure the circumference of the hand at the palm, excluding the thumb; for example, if the hand measures 8 in. around, the glove size is 8.

*/** *Shoe size*: the actor should be able to provide this information. Be sure to get the width of the shoe size as well. The shoe width is designated by a letter after the size number; the basic range is AAA (very narrow) through E (very wide). If the shoe size is not known, or if the shoes are to be made, trace around the stockinged feet while the actor is standing. Some mail-order houses, such as Sears, have foot sizing charts available which are useful in determining shoe sizes. If possible, when buying shoes, have the actor with you to try them on; if that is not possible, make arrangements with the vendor to return the shoes if they do not fit properly.

Comments: this space on the form is used for any special information concerning the actor or the production. For example, entries might note if the actor has allergies to certain fabrics, or will be padded and therefore require additional measurements with the padding completed, or has personal items which can be used for the production.

Wig Measurements

Special measurements are required when buying or renting a wig. In addition to the head measurement, measure over the top of the head from the front hairline at the

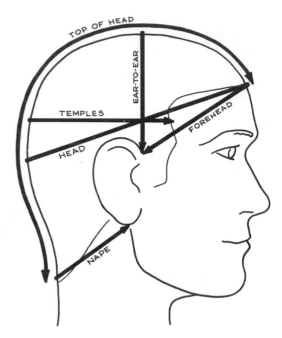

Figure 5-5 Wig measurement placement and locations.

forehead to the nape of the neck, from ear to ear over the top of the head, from temple to temple around the back of the head, from ear to ear across the forehead, and across the full width of the hairline at the nape of the neck as shown in Fig. 5-5.

Ready-Made Sizes

Basic information for sizes of ready-made items is included on the measurement forms. For men, the shirt size is provided by the neck measurement and sleeve length; trouser size information is provided by waist and inseam; and suit sizes are indicated by the chest measurement. Suit sizes are also proportioned in Short, Regular, and Long according to the height of the individual. Figure 5-6 provides a guideline for chest and waist proportions used by many manufacturers. Big and Tall sizes are also available, usually in shops

Chest/Suit Size		Waist	
Inches	Centimeters	Inches	Centimeters
36	92	30	76
38	97	32	81
40	102	34	87
42	107	36	92
44	112	39	99
46	117	42	107
48	122	44	112

Short designates height of 5 ft 8 in. or less.
Regular designates height of 5 ft 8 in. to 6 ft 1 in.
Long designates height over 6 ft 1 in., sleeve
  length is 34 in. or longer.

Figure 5–6 Men's suit sizing guidelines used by some, but not all, men's clothing manufacturers. Metric as approved by the Measurement Standard Committee of the Pattern Fashion Industry.

Head Measurement		
Inches	Hat Size	Centimeters
19½	6¼	49
20	6½	50
21	6¾	53
21½	6⅞	54
22	7	56
22½	7¼	57
23	7⅜	58
23½	7½	59
24	7⅝	61
24½	7¾	62
25	8	63

Figure 5–7 Men's hat sizing guidelines used by some, but not all, hat manufacturers. The metric is rounded for convenience.

which specialize in these size ranges. Information for men's hat sizes, which are based on the head circumference measurement, is shown in Fig. 5–7.

Women's clothing manufacturers use various methods for sizing garments. However, there are guidelines which can be utilized if the actress is uncertain about her sizes and if the necessary information is on the measurement form. Women's sizes for ready-made items are included on the form under dress size, bra size, and shoe size. The bust measurement generally corresponds to blouse sizes.

Two of the basic types of sizing women's ready-made garments are Junior and Misses.[1] The Junior sizes are primarily for figures with small, defined waists and high bust lines; they are designated for a youthful figure and are indicated by odd number sizes. Misses sizes are for the more

[1] It should be noted that the dimensions standardized by the clothing industry are not the same dimensions used by commercial pattern manufacturers. Measurement charts used by the Pattern Fashion Industry can be found in commercial pattern books and on the pattern package.

mature figure with less defined waists and fuller, lower bust lines. Age is not necessarily a factor in this sizing process, and many women can wear either Junior or Misses sizes, depending on the manufacturer. Figure 5–8 gives basic guidelines for selecting sizes for both Junior and Misses. It is always advisable to have the actress try on the clothing before it is purchased to assure proper fit.

Measurements for Rental Houses

Accurate measurements are essential when renting costumes. All rental houses supply data sheets indicating the measurements they need to fill a rental order. The specific measurements requested vary from company to company; however, the information on the sample measurement forms (Figs. 5–1 and 5–2) will supply all information that might be requested.

When renting costumes, be sure to supply accurate information for everything that is requested; otherwise, the rental house will not be able to supply costumes that fit the actor.

Junior Sizes

	Imperial (in inches)			Metric (in centimeters)		
Size	Bust	Waist	Hips	Bust	Waist	Hips
3	30	22	33	76	56	84
5	31	23	34	78.5	58.5	86.5
7	32	24	35	81.5	61	89
9	33	25	36	84	63.5	91.5
11	34/35	26/27	37	86/89	66/68	94
13	36	28	38/39	91.5	71	96/99
15	37/38	29/30	40/41	94/96	73/76	102/104

Misses Sizes

	Imperial (in inches)			Metric (in centimeters)		
Size	Bust	Waist	Hips	Bust	Waist	Hips
6	32	23	34	81.5	58.5	86.5
8	33	24	35	84	61	89
10	34	25	36	86.5	63.5	91.5
12	35	26	37	89	66	94
14	36/37	27/28	38/39	91/94	68/71	96/99
16	38	29	40	96.5	73.5	102
18	40	30/31	41/42	102	76/78.5	104/107

Figure 5–8 Ready-made sizing guidelines for women in Junior and Misses sizes used by some, but not all, manufacturers. The metric is rounded for convenience.

Dancewear Sizes

Leotards for women come in four sizes: Small (size 8–10), Medium (size 12–14), Large (size 16–18), Extra Large (size 20). Women's tights are also available in four sizes, designated as Small or AA (4ft 9 in.–5 ft), Medium or A (5 ft–5 ft 4 in.), Large or B (5 ft 5 in.–5 ft 7 in.), Extra Large or C (5 ft 8 in. and up) and E (Extra Stout 5 ft 8 in. and up). Men's tights are available in four sizes: Medium or A (5 ft 2 in.–5 ft 5 in.), Large or B (5 ft 6 in.–5 ft 9 in.), Extra

Large or C (over 5 ft 8 in.), and D (over 6 ft). Ballet slippers and other soft dance shoes generally are bought one size smaller than the normal shoe size. Check with the actor on sizes for dancewear; vendors can also provide information if measurements are available.

Creating well-fitting costumes is dependent upon a complete and exact set of measurements taken and recorded in a standardized order. The information on the measurement forms is sufficient for drafting patterns or for procuring ready-made items.

basic pattern drafting and fitting

part 2

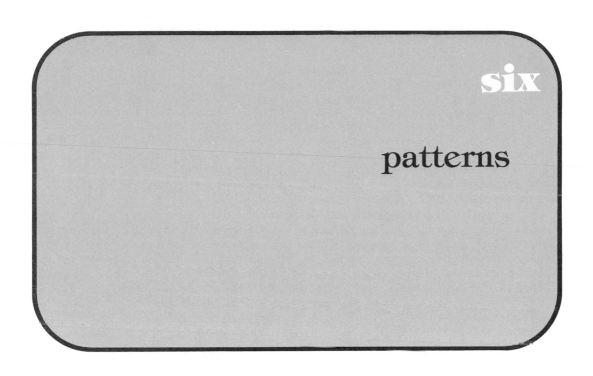

six

patterns

There are three approaches to creating a theatrical costume: using the commercial, flat paper pattern; draping the fabric on a dress form or the body; and drafting patterns from a set of measurements. All three approaches are used in costuming. Depending on the design, a single costume may be cut using only one approach, but in some cases any or all three may be necessary to achieve the best possible results.

COMMERCIAL PATTERNS

Commercial flat patterns can be of value to the costumer when preparing a modern dress show. They provide a wide variety in current female fashions and basic patterns for male and children's fashions. These patterns are especially helpful when the costumer cannot find, or in many cases cannot afford to buy, the right ready-made garment.

Present-day commercial patterns are sold in sizes with a sizing chart on the back of the envelope along with information on the types and amount of fabric and notions required for the garment. Each piece of the pattern is identified and includes seam allowance, instructions for placing the pattern on the correct grain of the fabric, and markings to match with other sections of the pattern. The packet also includes detailed instructions for assembling the garment.

Commercial patterns from other decades are also valuable, although the information may not be as detailed. It is wise to collect and keep patterns intact and to develop a library of patterns for future use.

Anyone who has ever used commercial patterns knows that it is very difficult to refold and return them to their original packages. In addition, pattern pieces get lost, and the tissue-paper pieces are easily torn. Transferring patterns to heavy brown paper along with the size and other identifying information preserves the pattern. Use a large manila envelope for easy storage and tape the original package on the outside of the envelope for easy identification.

Many pattern manufacturers also make a number of "costume" patterns for garments supposedly for historical periods. Generally, these are of very little value for theatrical use since they have a definite modern flavor that is inappropriate in creating the illusion of the period.

Another commonly suggested approach for obtaining period costumes, especially men's garments, is the use of basic pajama patterns which can be altered to the necessary torso and leg shape of a given period. While these patterns do offer a viable method of patterning certain loose-fitting garments, they are not appropriate for most costume requirements because they do not reflect a period pattern cut or the appropriate use of the grain of the fabric to capture the illusion of a period costume.

Using modifications of commercial patterns is really only practical for men's garments after the 1840s and after 1900 for women's garments. Costumes that are to reflect earlier periods should be drafted from patterns that are taken from authentic garments. Many patterns of this nature are available in scaled drawings in the period pattern books, some of which are cited in the bibliographies. Patterns for period garments can also be drafted by combining the principles of modern drafting techniques with period pattern styles and techniques. An introduction to this process is detailed in Chaps. 13 and 14.

DRAPING

Draping is the process of working with fabric on a three-dimensional form—either a dress form or directly on the body. The process is used to develop patterns for a garment or to make the garment by carefully stitching the cloth as it has been draped.

Draping is an exciting method for creating costumes and for finding solutions to patterning problems. The process can be used to achieve various results: to create fitted garments by shaping the fabric with seams and darts to conform to the body; to create soft flowing garments; or to control folds in a garment.

The basic principles of draping include working with the proper fabric, either the actual fabric or fabric that has similar draping qualities. For draping fitted patterns, muslin is effective; for a soft flowing garment, the actual fabric should be used. Essentially, the draping process requires keen observation of the fabric as it is being worked, with very careful attention to the grain of the fabric.

Dress forms (male and female) are necessary for draping garments since they provide the contours of the human form as well as seam lines to identify the body centerlines, top of the shoulders, neckline, armholes, and waistlines. These lines provide guides for establishing proper balance in a garment and aid in controlling the grain of the fabric. A garment that is to mold the human body, such as a bodice for a corseted figure, should be draped on a dress form that is smaller than the actor's size. The form should be padded with layers of thin foam or other pliable materials to the correct size before the draping is begun. This approach allows for the pliability of the human body that an unpadded form does not have. Other garments that do not mold the figure can be draped on a dress form that matches the actor's measurements as shown in Fig. 6–1.

Marking the centerline on draped items is an added aid to keeping the draped pieces in proper balance and to controlling the proper grain of the fabric. The centerline of the bodice front in Fig. 6-1 is marked with a hand baste or running stitch; this line is matched to the centerline seam on the dress form; the natural waistline is identified with a cord tied around the waist of the form.

The principles of draping are used in the fitting process of flat patterns (see Chap. 12). One method of developing the refined techniques required for draping is to gain experience and to sharpen thoughtful observation through drafting and fitting flat patterns. Although the specific details on the draping process are beyond the scope of this book, the basic principles are part of working with fabrics to create costumes. In actuality, draping is an integral part of costuming, since draping is used to achieve three-dimensional effects with cloth. Draping is much like working with sculpture; the medium of the sculpture in this case is fabric.

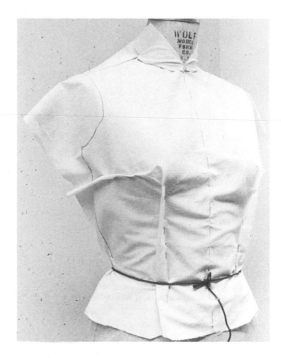

Figure 6-1 Example of a draped bodice front on a dress form. Notice the centerline of the bodice. Photo by Robert Izzo.

DRAFTING PATTERNS FROM MEASUREMENTS

Drafting patterns requires more time and consideration for the beginner than the use of commercial patterns. However, with practice, drafting modern and period patterns is often faster and more efficient, and the results are far more satisfactory and exciting than those achieved by relying on commercial patterns.

In order to draft a pattern, it is necessary to have an accurate set of body measurements, an understanding of basic pattern shapes, plus a willingness to experiment.

Since, in effect, each stage costume is custom-built to fit a particular actor, each piece of the pattern for the costume must be laid out according to the dimensions of that actor's body. The measurements

suggested in Chap. 5 will provide all the information needed to lay out pattern pieces. Chapters 7 through 11 cover the techniques for using those measurements to draft basic pattern pieces. Figure 6-2 shows an example of a drafted bodice front that is described in Chap. 7. These drafting skills can then be utilized to draft patterns for many costumes.

The specific shapes of patterns can be obtained from a variety of sources. In addition to the basic patterns included here, several of the books cited in the bibliographies contain scaled-down patterns for period garments. Patterns may also be taken from actual garments when they are available.

However, even with sources readily

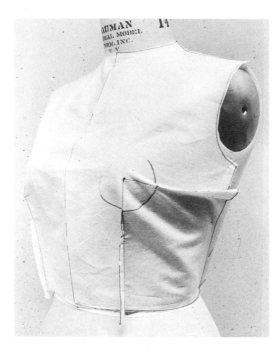

Figure 6–2 Example of a flat-patterned bodice front on a dress form; fitting darts have been basted together. Notice the bust circle and bodice centerline. Photo by Robert Izzo.

available, it is almost always necessary to make adaptations or modifications in a pattern piece in order to meet the requirements of a specific costume or to fit a particular actor. Experience and thoughtful analysis will lead to skill in determining and in making the necessary changes, but flexibility in thinking and a willingness to experiment and, if need be, try again will always be required to solve the problems of pieces that do not quite fit or of creating the pieces for which a pattern is missing.

Too often, a person will be stopped or delayed by such problems if there is too much reliance on patterns from other sources when what is really needed is confidence in one's own knowledge of the human body, of the appearance to be achieved with the garment, and of what can be done with a piece of fabric. With

that confidence and a willingness to try, virtually any pattern problem can be solved.

When learning how to draft patterns, it is advisable for several reasons to start with modern pattern shapes. The principal reason is that modern garments are more familiar to us than those of other periods. Consequently, it is easier to see how the separate pieces of a garment are made to fit together and how the pieces are shaped to fit the body.

Since the human body has remained relatively unchanged over the ages, the same basic methods of pattern making apply; only the silhouette of garments has altered from period to period. The proper silhouette for any period, therefore, can be achieved largely through the cut and construction of the garments and the proper support from appropriate undergarments. Once the fundamental techniques of drafting modern patterns are mastered, it is a relatively simple matter to draft patterns which reflect cuts from other periods.

Drafted patterns are *flat patterns;* they are drawn up on paper or fabric but always on a flat surface. The body they are to go onto is round; therefore, the drafting process includes learning how to cope with transferring the flat to the round.

Determining the shapes of pattern pieces that wrap around the curves of the body, locating points where the fabric must be taken up or where pieces must be joined in order to conform to curves, and how to take advantage of the grain of the fabric are all parts of the process. The principle of *ease* was discussed in Chap. 5 when considering measurements and movement in a garment; ease is also fundamental in shifting from flat to round. Understanding these principles is intrinsic to making modern patterns, just as it is in period patterns, but there are many more modern garments at hand to study and from which the principles can be learned.

The purpose of the study of modern

patterns is to develop an "eye," a sense of the proportions within garments. This awareness is important when analyzing period silhouettes and the patterns that create those shapes. The key to creating exciting patterns that accentuate the appropriate body shapes and garment lines is to learn how to manipulate the cloth and to identify what the shifts in the grain of the fabric can do in order to capture the sense of the period silhouette while "nudging" the body into the appropriate posture. Beginning with the modern basic pattern provides an effective means for mastering the drafting skills required for manipulating the fabric; fitting those patterns introduces the skills required for manipulating the fabric on the body.

Basic Pattern Pieces

In flat patterns, whether commercial or drafted, there are basic pattern pieces which are utilized in most periods.

The *bodice* is a female garment fitted to conform to the upper torso from the neck to the waist or hips. The number of pieces in a bodice pattern can range from three to ten. Closings for the bodice are generally located in the back or front.

The *jacket* is the male counterpart of the bodice, generally consisting of three to eight pieces with closings in the front or back.

The *sleeve* is the arm covering and can be of any length or fullness. A great deal of garment variety and a strong indication of period are suggested by the sleeve. Modern versions generally have one or two pieces in the pattern. Period sleeves can have numerous pieces and several variations in closings.

The *gusset* is a piece of fabric cut on the bias and set into seams which are stress points in movement. It provides an ease and enables the stress point to expand. General areas for placement of the gusset are at the underarm between the sleeve and torso garment and in the crotch of trousers where the four seams meet. The shape of the gusset varies; a square of fabric set in the crotch is very effective just as is the football shape which is often set under the arm (see Fig. 8–5 for details).

The *skirt* in period garments can be for both male and female. It is the garment or part of the garment which falls from the torso to anywhere from the thigh to the floor or longer. The waistline location varies from just below the bust to the hipline. The skirt may be cut-in-one with the torso garment or cut separately and joined at the waistline. Generally, the skirt is cut from three to eight or more pieces. The skirt may be rectangular in shape and controlled by darts or pleats to shape the garment at the waist, or it may be shaped with the narrowness for the waist cut into the garment. This narrowed shaping is accomplished with *gores*. A gore is a tapered piece of cloth used to vary the width of the garment; it is narrow at the top and wide at the hem, and a number of gores may be used to make up a skirt.

The *trousers* or *pants* covering the lower torso and legs can be of any length and vary from a snug fit to a very full, loose fit. As with sleeves, the number of pattern pieces varies according to the period; modern patterns consist of two pattern pieces with seams at the sides of the legs. Other periods may use either fewer or more pieces.

Supplementary Patterns

Important supplementary pattern pieces include collars, yokes, facings, and interfacings.

The *collar* is a decorative neck finishing which has many variations and can utilize several pattern pieces of numerous shapes. The length of the collar is determined by the neck size. The style is determined by the use of the grain of the fabric, the shape of the inside and outside edges, the width of the collar, and length of the outside edge. Collars can be classified into four general types: the standing collar, full-roll collars, partial-roll collars, and flat collars.

The *yoke* is a shaped piece which fits about the neck and shoulders or over the waist and hips and to which the rest of the garment is attached. Generally the yoke is no more than eight to ten inches; it is used to give a smooth fit over the shoulder or hip area and to support additional fullness in attached pieces of the garment such as a shirt back or skirt.

Facings are finishings for openings in the garment such as the neck on collarless garments or the armhole in sleeveless garments. They can be cut from the good fabric or from a complementary lining. Facings finish off raw seams neatly and must be shaped to lie smoothly.

Interfacings are cut in the same manner as facings, but they are somewhat smaller and sewn between the facing and the good fabric. They are used to give more body or crispness to the opening of the garment. Interfacings are also used to add body to collars, cuffs, lapels, and areas of openings fastened with buttons or hooks and eyes.

These basic pattern pieces form the foundation for all types of stage garments of any period. Specific shapes and details in cutting will alter with the different periods, but these variations are relatively simple once the basic pattern principles have been mastered.

Shaping Patterns to the Body

Shaping the flat pattern to fit the curvatures of the body can be achieved with fitting darts, tucks, pleats, gathers, and seams, or a combination of these.

Fitting darts are used to take up extra fullness where the body narrows, such as at the waist, and to provide fullness where the body is fuller, such as bust or chest and hip areas. A fitting dart tapers to nothing at the area fullness while shaping the fabric

to follow the contours of the body. In modern patterns, darts are directed toward the highest point of a bulge and can be placed at various points along the outside edge of the pattern. The highest point of a bulge is a pivot point for darts, which means that the placement of the darts can be changed without changing the fit of the garment. This feature of fitting darts is discussed and illustrated in Chap. 13.

Darts taper to nothing at the tip of the dart so that no puckering is created by the dart stitching. Fitting darts that do not go to the outside edge of the pattern, such as a waist-fitting dart in a dress with no waistline seam, are tapered to a point at both ends (see Fig. 13–9). Darts that end at a seam are triangular in shape, and the tip of the dart is either at a pivot point or on a line with the pivot point, as is the case with bust-fitting darts. The tips of those darts (see Fig. 7–3) do not extend to the pivot point and, therefore, create more fullness in the garment for the bust.

The stitching lines of a dart may be straight or curved lines. All drafted darts have straight lines; darts adjusted in fittings or draped darts may have curved seamlines due to the curvature of the body. Either dart is satisfactory. However, in either case the darts must taper to nothing so there is no bubble or pucker at the tapered end.

Darts require extra seam allowance at the outside edge of the pattern, and the stitching lines must be equal in length with the centerline of the dart at least ½ in. longer than the stitching lines. Always check a dart before it is stitched to be sure there is ample seam allowance and that the fabric is not twisting or pulling. If twisting does occur, the grain of the fabric is off, and the centerline of the dart needs to be adjusted to correct the problem.

Tucks, also called *tuck darts*, give both fullness and shape to fabric, but they have a softer, less molded effect than darts. Tucks are not stitched closed to a point;

the stitching lines can be drawn in as for a regular dart, but the actual stitching stops before the tip is reached. As with a regular dart, the stitching lines are brought together and stitched from the seam edge, but the stitching is only about 1 in. to 2 in. long. The unstitched portion then becomes an intentional pucker or soft pleat. Tucks are often used in bloused or pleated pants or skirts.

Pleats are flat double folds of fabric used to control fullness. They may be stitched flat at the seam line for soft fullness or stitched in place for less softness. The various types of pleats and pleating methods are discussed in Chap. 9.

Gathers are used to create soft fullness and are formed by drawing up fabric on lines of stitching. Gathering techniques are discussed in Chap. 3.

Seams are the means by which two pieces of fabric or two parts of a garment are held together. Seams are also used to mold nonstretch fabric to the body since they can be used to follow contours. A bodice with six or more seams in the normal dart locations will give a smoother fit than a bodice with just darts and side seams. The angle of the seams also helps mold the body and influences posture. Moving the shoulder seam back from the top of the shoulder, for example, tends to pull the shoulders back slightly. Adding and/or changing seam positions is discussed in Chap. 13.

The design of the costume and the period it represents will determine what method or methods will be needed to shape the garment to the body. Whatever method is used, it must be planned and drafted into the pattern.

Tools for Pattern Drafting

These tools plus an accurate set of the actor's measurements provide the necessities for drafting a costume. Generally the pattern is laid out on unbleached muslin or on paper.

Tool	Description	Use
Tape measure	Plastic, ½ in. wide, with large numbers, should be clean and unbroken	Taking actor's measurements; transcribing them to pattern
Tailor's square	A wide, rectangular plastic rule; generally 15 in. long and 4 in. wide	To lay in right angles on cloth; straight edges
Triangle	A large, clear plastic right triangle	To lay in right angle lines
French curve	Plastic dressmaker's curves with measurement guides	To lay in curves at neck, armhole, etc.
Straight edges	A yardstick and a longer board	Laying long straight lines
Pencils	No. 2 with erasers	General notations and laying out pattern lines
Tailor's chalk	Wax compound type that will not brush off; remove with hot iron	To lay in pattern lines and fitting lines
Paper scissors	One old pair	Cutting paper only
Sharp dressmaker's scissors	Large size is recommended (use for fabric only)	Cutting a muslin pattern once it has been drafted
Trace wheel	Looks like a small pizza cutter with teeth around the edge	Transferring pattern markings, such as darts, etc., to other side of fabric and to other fabrics
Tracing paper	Heavy paper with a waxed, colored surface; assorted colors	Transferring pattern markings

Drafting Guidelines

Before drafting any pattern, consider the following guidelines. To begin, have ample, clear space to draft and cut. The drafting tools should be close at hand, and the measurements should be set up for reference.

When you lay out the fabric or paper, make sure there is a sufficient amount for the pattern piece. The basic patterns detailed in the subsequent chapters are for half of the body, since only one of the matching sides of a garment is drafted and two are cut. Each basic pattern draft also suggests how large a piece of fabric or paper will be required to draft the half pattern. These directions include allowances for ease in the garment and seam allowances for assembling the pattern pieces.

Always allow enough for the pattern to be drafted, but do not waste fabric. Do not cut a pattern piece out of the middle of the fabric, leaving only small scraps. If the pattern piece is placed on the fold, the fabric does not necessarily have to be folded in half. Fold the fabric so there is enough width for the pattern, leaving excess width in the fabric in one large piece rather than in two small pieces.

Determine the straight lengthwise grain of the fabric. Many patterns are laid out with the centerlines of the pieces on the straight grain; others are laid out at angles to the straight grain. Lay out the fabric so you know the direction of the straight grain. All the basic patterns in the subsequent chapters call for a line drawn across the straight grain at the top of the pattern; this line is called the "right-angle line," and it forms a reference line for the layout of the rest of the pattern piece.

Always allow for the seam allowance and hems in the pattern pieces. Many patterns include seam allowance; if they do not, there is a notation reminding the drafter to add the seam allowance. The seam allowance should be no less than ½ in. and usually no more than 1 in. The exception to this is a 2 in. allowance at the closing line of torso garments. The pattern drafts here call for a ½ in. seam allowance with a 2 in. allowance at the closing for the torso-fitting garments. Plan to allow about 3 in. for hems on skirts and robes and about 2 in. for hems on sleeves.

Keep the markings on the pattern simple and clear to avoid confusion when cutting or putting the pieces together. There should be enough information to identify the pattern, the grain line, the dart stitching lines, seam allowance, and centerline. Additional markings can quickly become confusing.

Finally, there are two cardinal principles to keep in mind: (1) You can always cut off excess length; it is very difficult to add length once something is cut. (2) You can always cut a hole larger, but you cannot cut it smaller after the hole has been cut out.

ENLARGING A PATTERN TO SCALE. Patterns drawn to scale can be enlarged by using an opaque projector and tracing the outline or by laying out a full-size grid and locating the points on it. These methods are relatively easy and are particularly useful if the original scale is unusual. However, the pattern, once drawn to full scale, still needs to be adapted to the actor's measurements.

Another simple method of enlarging a scaled-down pattern is illustrated in Fig. 6–3. This method of enlargement extends lines from a single point on the pattern through the key points on the pattern. The length of the extending lines is determined by the scale of the drawing. If the scale is ⅛ in. equals 1 in., the lines are extended 8 times the original length; if the scale is 1/16 in. equals 1 in., the lines are extended 16 times the original, and so forth. Enough points must be established to retain the original cut. Patterns enlarged in this manner also need to be adapted to the actor's measurements.

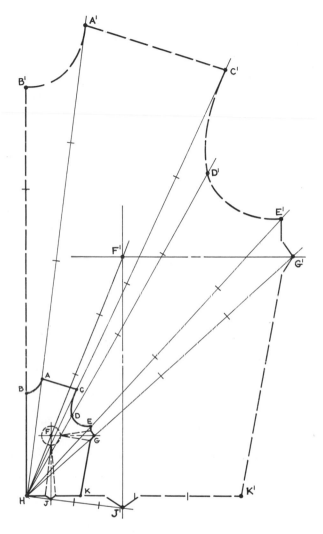

Figure 6–3 One method of enlarging a scaled-down pattern. The length of the extending lines is determined by the scale of the drawing; if the scale is ⅛ in. to 1 in., the lines are 8 times the original length.

USING THE BASIC PATTERNS. The pattern drafting process described in the following chapters combines two of the steps involved in the traditional sloper method. A *sloper* is a template of a basic pattern shape that is drafted from average body proportions without ease or seam allowances. The sloper method requires drafting the template before making the necessary adjustments of adding ease and seam allowances to complete the pattern, which then needs to be adjusted to the actor.

The pattern drafting method described in the following chapters uses a combination of some standard body proportions and the actor's measurements; the drafts also include ease and seam allowances. Essentially, the process of making the sloper, or template, is eliminated. Once the pattern is drafted and basted together, it is finalized on the actor in a fitting. This process allows for individual figure variations and produces a pattern for a specific actor.

The fitting process also utilizes many of the basic principles of draping. While the pattern draft includes seams and darts, adjusting the pattern to the irregularities of the body requires determining if these are in the correct position on the body as well as requiring careful observation of the

grain of the fabric. These are fundamental principles of draping that are crucial in developing any pattern.

We have found this drafting and fitting system is fast and results in producing patterns which fit well. Adaptation of these patterns for other styles of clothing is simple and effective for achieving silhouettes that are appropriate for making many period patterns. The knowledge and skill gained by mastering the basic drafts combined with the use of period patterns from the various sources cited throughout the book provide a solid foundation for patterning and cutting costumes.

ADDITIONAL SOURCES

There are several systems for drafting basic modern patterns, primarily for women's garments. These tend to be complex, but a study of these patterning approaches does offer insights into the methods used for making contemporary street-wear, and the principles involved can be applied to costuming. Sources for methods of draping clothes are also cited.

HOLLEN, NORMA, *Flat Pattern Methods* (4th ed.). Minneapolis, Minn.: Burgess Publishing Co., 1975.

JAFFE, HILDE, AND NURIE RELIS, *Draping for Fashion Design*. Englewood Cliffs, N.J.: Reston Publishing Co., Inc., distributed by Prentice-Hall, Inc., 1975.

MOULTON, BERTHA, *Garment Cutting and Tailoring for* Students (rev. ed.). New York: Theatre Arts Books, 1968.

PRISK, BERNEICE, *Stage Costume Handbook*. New York: Harper & Row, 1966.

ROHR, M., *Pattern Drafting and Grading: Women's and Misses' Garment Design* (rev. ed.). Fort Worth, Tex.: Texas Christian University, 1965.

SHAW, WILLIAM HARLAN, *Basic Pattern Drafting for the Theatrical Costume Designer*. New York: Drama Book Specialists/Publishers, 1974.

SHELDON, M. GENE, *Design Through Draping* (2nd ed.). Long Island City, N.Y.: Burgess Publishing Co., distributed by Eliot Books, 1974.

SIMPLICITY PATTERN CO., INC., *Simplicity Sewing Book*. New York: Simplicity Pattern Co., Inc., published annually.

seven

basic bodice/jacket patterns

This is a basic pattern with two fitting darts for the female bodice and one fitting dart for the male jacket. The closing for this sample pattern is in the center back since many theatrical garments close in the back for a better fit; note the layout change in step 2 if the garment is to close in front.

The pattern pieces will be cut on the fold of the fabric (Fig. 7–1) so that only one-half of the bodice/jacket will be drafted. The fitting darts will be traced through to the other side of the garment. Unless otherwise specified, the seam allowance is included in the instructions. The metric system notations are the standard equivalents as approved by the Pattern Fashion Industry.

Study Fig. 7–1 carefully for the overall shape and layout of the pattern. Figures 7–2 through 7–4 illustrate the developmental steps in the drafting process.

THE BODICE/JACKET FRONT

1. As shown in Fig. 7–1, fold fabric in half on the straight grain; width from the fold needs to be one-quarter of the "chest/bust" measurement plus 3 in. (7.5 cm) for fullness and seam allowance.

2. Establish the center-front line on the fold (if the garment is to close in the front, add 5 in. [12.5 cm] to the "chest/bust" measurement and establish the center-front line 2 in. [5 cm] away from the fold). At the top of the fabric, use a tailor's square to draw a line at a right angle to the center-front. This right-angle line will be the basis for drafting the neckline, shoulder line, and armhole.

3. To establish the neckline curve (Fig. 7–2), measure 2½ in. (6.3 cm)[1] across

[1]Set point A 2½ in. from the center-front if the neck measurement is under 15 in. (38 cm); if the neck

107

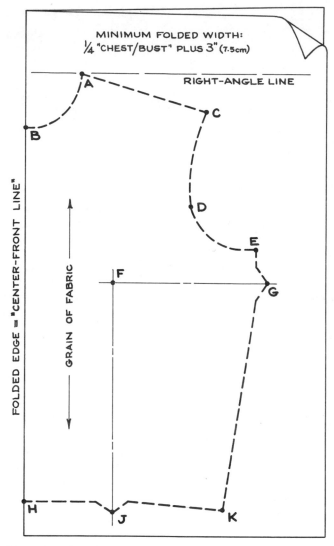

MINIMUM FOLDED WIDTH:
¼ "CHEST/BUST" PLUS 3" (7.5cm)

RIGHT-ANGLE LINE

FOLDED EDGE = "CENTER-FRONT LINE"

GRAIN OF FABRIC

Figure 7–1   Basic bodice/jacket pattern draft showing layout on fabric.

from the center-front line along the right-angle line and set point A. (For the male jacket pattern, set point A 3 in. [7.5 cm][1] from the center-front line.) Measure 2½

in. (6.3 cm) down from the right-angle line and set point B. Scribe a curve between points A and B; the curve should be oval in shape rather than circular.

4.   The length of the bodice at the center-front is determined by the "front-neck-to-waist" measurement. To locate point H on the center-front line, take the

measurement is 15 in. or over, set point A 3 in. from the center-front line. The final size and shape of the neckline will be determined in the fitting.

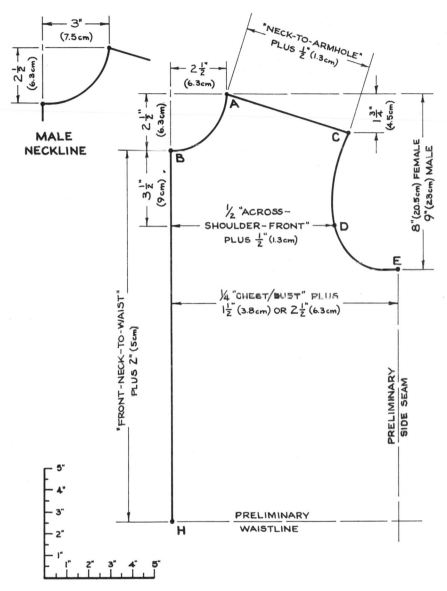

Figure 7–2 Basic bodice/jacket-front pattern draft showing initial layout steps.

"front-neck-to-waist" measurement from point B down the center-front line, add 2 in. (5 cm) for seam allowance and fitting convenience, and set point H.

5. To establish the length of the shoulder seam, take the "shoulder-neck-to-armhole" measurement plus ½ in. (1.3 cm) seam allowance and measure that distance from point A; bring the end of that measurement down from the right-angle line 1¾ in. (4.5 cm) to locate point C.

Connect points A and C for the line of the shoulder seam.

6. To establish the armhole curve, take one-half of the "across-shoulder-front" measurement and measure that distance across the bodice/jacket from a point $3\frac{1}{2}$ in. (9 cm) below point B. Add $\frac{1}{2}$ in. (1.3 cm) seam allowance and set point D.

7. To find point E, the lower point of the armhole, measure down from the right-angle line—8 in. (20.5 cm) for female or 9 in. (23 cm) for male—and intersect with a measurement from the center-front line that is one-quarter of the "chest/bust" measurement plus $1\frac{1}{2}$ in. (3.8 cm) for ease and seam allowance (for a female with a bra cup size C or D, add $2\frac{1}{2}$ in. [6.3 cm] rather than $1\frac{1}{2}$ in.).

The point of intersection is point E. Connect points C, D, and E with a line that can be shaped with the french curve. The front armhole is cut in a fairly deep curve, but remember that a curved opening can be cut larger in the fitting if necessary, but it cannot be cut smaller.

8. Establish the preliminary side seam by dropping a line from point E. This line should be equal in length to the "underarm-to-waist" measurement plus 2 in. (5 cm). Connect the bottom end of this line with point H to form a preliminary waistline. These are guidelines only; the final shapes of the side seam and waistline will be determined after the darts are placed.

9. *(Omit this step for the male jacket.)* To locate the bust dart (Fig. 7–3), drop a line from the right-angle line the length of the "shoulder-to-tip-of-bust" measurement plus $\frac{1}{2}$ in. (1.3 cm) for seam allowance and set point F 4 in. (10 cm) across from the center-front line. This is the pivot point for the fitting darts of the bodice.

10. *(Omit this step for the male jacket.)* Scribe a circle around point F $1\frac{1}{2}$ in. (3.8

cm) in radius for bra cup sizes A and B, $2\frac{1}{2}$ in. (6.3 cm) for bra cup sizes C and D. The radius of the circle will determine the angle and the length of the dart because point F^1 (the actual apex point of the dart) will be located on the circumference.

11. Bust fitting darts (*omit this step for the male jacket*):

a. Draw a line at a right angle to the center-front line which intersects point F and crosses the preliminary side seam. Set point F^1 on the circumference of the circle where this line intersects. Set point G $\frac{1}{2}$ in. (1.3 cm) beyond the preliminary side seam. Line F^1–G should duplicate the crosswise grain of the fabric as much as possible and will become the centerline (foldline) of the dart.

b. Locate point G^1 $\frac{3}{4}$ in. (2 cm) above point G and on the side seam line. Connect G^1 with F^1 for the top stitchline of the dart.

c. Locate point G^2 $\frac{3}{4}$ in. (2 cm) below point G and on the side seam line. Connect points G^2 and F^1 for the bottom stitchline of the dart. It is essential that lines F^1–G^1 and F^1–G^2 be of equal length. The center foldline (F^1–G) should be $\frac{1}{2}$ in. (1.3 cm) longer and should extend beyond the side seam line to allow ample seam allowance.

d. Alternate placement of the dart: placing the center foldline of the dart on the crosswise grain line is a standard practice; however, an alternative arrangement (Fig. 7–3) would be to drop the dart so that the top stitchline falls on the crosswise grain with the center foldline and the bottom stitchline measured into place below it. This lower placement of the dart will alter the grain line slightly and thereby increase the fullness in the bodice and accentuate the bust line more. The drafting sequence is:

1. Locate F^1–G^1 on the crosswise grain line
2. Measure down on the preliminary side seam $1\frac{1}{2}$ in. (3.8 cm) to locate G^2

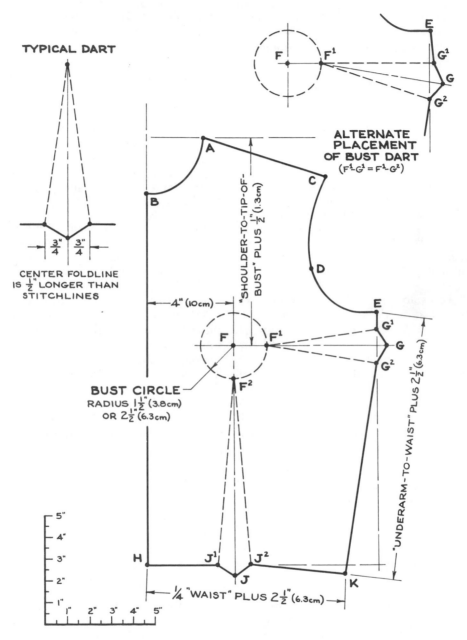

TYPICAL DART

CENTER FOLDLINE
IS $\frac{1}{2}$" LONGER THAN
STITCHLINES

$\frac{3"}{4}$ $\frac{3"}{4}$

**ALTERNATE
PLACEMENT
OF BUST DART**
$(F^1 G^1 = F^1 G^2)$

"SHOULDER-TO-TIP-OF-
BUST" PLUS $\frac{1}{2}$" (1.3cm)

4" (10cm)

BUST CIRCLE
RADIUS $1\frac{1}{2}$" (3.8cm)
OR $2\frac{1}{2}$" (6.3cm)

"UNDERARM-TO-WAIST" PLUS $2\frac{1}{2}$" (6.3cm)

5"
4"
3"
2"
1"
1"   2"   3"   4"   5"

$\frac{1}{4}$ "WAIST" PLUS $2\frac{1}{2}$" (6.3cm)

Figure 7-3   Complete bodice-front pattern draft including alternate placement of bust dart.

111

3. Extend F^1–G^1 to equal the length of F^1–G^2

4. Center F^1–G between the stitchlines and extend it to ½ in. (1.3 cm) longer than the stitchlines

5. Connect the points for the final outline of the dart.

12. Waist fitting darts (for the male jacket set point F 11 in. (28 cm) below the right-angle line and 4 in. (10 cm) across from the center-front line as shown in Fig. 7–4):

a. Locate point J 4 in. (10 cm) from point H and ½ in. (1.3 cm) below the preliminary waistline and connect points F and J. Line F–J is the centerline (foldline) of the waist fitting dart. For the female bodice, locate F^2 on the circumference of the bust circle where line F–J intersects as shown in Fig. 7–3.

b. To establish the dart stitchlines, set points J^1 and J^2 on the preliminary waistline and ¾ in. (2 cm) to either side of line F–J. Connect them with point F^2 for the female or point F for the male for the stitchlines. These stitchlines must be equal in length to each other with the centerline F–J ½ in. (1.3 cm) longer to shape the cutting edge of the dart. This 1½ in. width of the dart is for the average figure; any necessary alterations can be accomplished in the fitting.

13. The locating of point K to complete the side seam and the waistline seam varies slightly between the female and male patterns.

a. For the female pattern (Fig. 7–3), take one-quarter of the "waist" measurement plus 1½ in. (3.8 cm) for the dart plus 1 in. (2.5 cm) for extra allowance and measure across from point H. To locate point K, take the "underarm-to-waist" measurement plus 1½ in. (3.8 cm) for the dart plus 1 in. (2.5 cm) for extra allowance and measure down from point E.

b. For the male jacket (Fig. 7–4), take the "underarm-to-waist" measurement plus 2 in. (5 cm) and measure down directly from point E. Measure the waistline in the same way as that indicated for the female pattern.

c. Where the horizontal and the vertical measurements meet is point K. To obtain the final shapes of the side seams, connect points G^2 and K for the female and points E and K for the male. To complete the shape of the waistlines, connect points J^2 and K on both patterns. Note that the waistline and the side seam are not square to each other. This is to allow for the body shape and for ease in the pattern. The side seam should slant slightly toward the center; however, if the slant is too severe, add more seam allowance to the side seam at the waist. The side seam can be adjusted in the fitting. If the slant is too great, the garment will be pulled off grain and the side seam will not be straight on the body.

14. For final preparation and cutting, see instructions following Bodice/Jacket Back.

THE BODICE/JACKET BACK

1. Fold the fabric as the bodice front was folded. The maximum width of the back is one-half of the "back-seam-to-seam" measurement plus 3 in. (7.5 cm) for ease and seam allowance.

2. Establish the center-back line 2 in. (5 cm) away from the fold as shown in Fig. 7–5 (this sample pattern assumes a back closing; if the garment is to close in the front, establish the center-back line on the

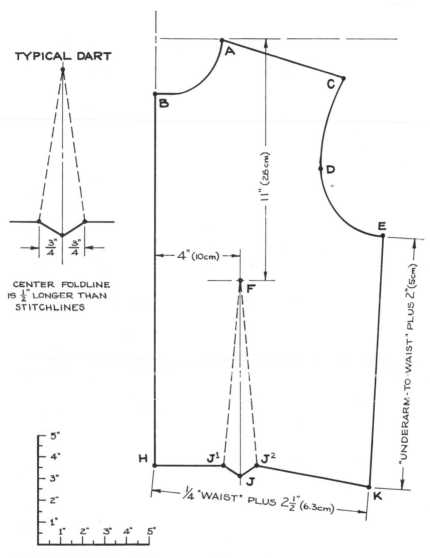

TYPICAL DART

CENTER FOLDLINE
IS ½" LONGER THAN
STITCHLINES

Figure 7–4 Complete jacket-front pattern draft.

fold). At the top of the fabric, use a tailor's square to draw a right-angle line to the center-back. This right-angle line will be the basis for drafting the neckline, shoulder line, and armhole.

3. To establish the neckline curve (Fig.

7–5), measure 2½ in. (6.3 cm) for the female, 3 in. (7.5 cm) for the male, across from the center-back line along the right-angle line and set point A. (See earlier footnote for size variations.) On the center-back line, measure 1 in. (2.5 cm) down from the right-angle line and set

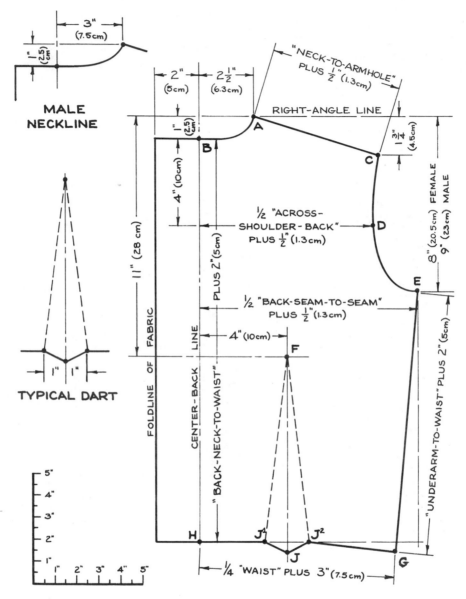

Figure 7-5 Complete bodice/jacket-back pattern draft.

point B. Scribe a curve between points A and B. Note that with the closing in the back, the center-back line is not a cutting line. Extend the neck-line into the 2 in. (5 cm) seam allowance beyond the center-back line.

4. The length at the center-back is determined by the "back-neck-to-waist" measurement. To locate point H on the center-back line, take the "back-neck-to-waist" measurement from point B down the center-back line, add 2 in. (5 cm) for

114

seam allowance and fitting convenience, and set point H.

5. To establish the length of the shoulder seam, take the "shoulder-neck-to-armhole" measurement plus ½ in. (1.3 cm) seam allowance and measure that distance from point A; bring the end of that measurement down from the right-angle line 1¾ in. (4.5 cm) to locate point C. Connect points A and C for the line of the shoulder seam.

6. To establish the armhole curve, take one-half of the "across-shoulder-back" measurement and measure that distance across the bodice/jacket from a point 4 in. (10 cm) below point B. Add ½ in. (1.3 cm) seam allowance and set point D.

7. To find point E, the lower point of the armhole, measure down from the right-angle line—8 in. (20.5 cm) for female or 9 in. (23 cm) for male—and intersect with a measurement from the center-back line that is one-half the "back-seam-to-seam" measurement plus ½ in. (1.3 cm). The point of intersection is point E. Connect points C, D, and E with a line that can be shaped with a french curve. The back armhole is a less deep curve than the front. Remember that a curved opening can be cut larger in the fitting if necessary; it cannot be cut smaller.

8. Establish the preliminary side seam by dropping a line from point E. This line should be equal in length to the "underarm-to-waist" measurement plus 2 in. (5 cm). Connect the bottom end of this line with point H to form the preliminary waistline. These are guidelines only; the

final shapes of the side seam and waistline will be determined after the darts are placed.

9. Waist fitting darts (set point F 11 in. [28 cm] below the right-angle line and 4 in. [10 cm] across from the center-back line as shown in Fig. 7–5):

a. Locate point J 4 in. (10 cm) from point H and ½ in. (1.3 cm) below the preliminary waistline and connect points F and J. Line F–J is the centerline (foldline) of the waist fitting dart.

b. To establish the dart stitchlines, set J^1 and J^2 on the preliminary waistline and 1 in. (2.5 cm) to either side of line F–J. Connect them with point F for the stitchlines. These stitchlines must be equal in length to each other with the centerline F–J ½ in. (1.3 cm) longer to shape the cutting edge of the dart. This 2 in. (5 cm) width of the dart is for the average figure; any necessary alterations can be accomplished in the fitting.

10. To finalize the waistline and side seam line, take one-quarter of the "waist" measurement plus 2 in. (5 cm) for the dart plus 1 in. (2.5 cm) for extra allowance and measure across from point H. To locate point G, take the "underarm-to-waist" measurement plus 2 in. (5 cm) and measure down from point E. Set point G where the horizontal and vertical measurements meet. As with the front pattern (step 13c), if the angle of the side seam looks too severe, add more seam allowance at the waistline and adjust the seam in the fitting; any excess length can be trimmed after the fitting.

CUTTING AND PREPARATION FOR FITTING

Before cutting out the bodice/jacket pattern, check the shape; if it looks distorted, check the measurements again and make any necessary corrections. Then trace all

the dart stitching lines and centerlines onto the other half of the bodice with tracing paper and a trace wheel. The tracing paper is placed face up under all of the fabric to transfer marks to the other half of the bodice. After all these markings have been made, cut the pattern. Be sure to cut on the cutting lines, not on centerlines or stitching lines.

The muslin pattern should be machine-basted together prior to the fitting. First hand-baste a centerline in the front, then machine-baste all the darts together, taking care to match the stitching lines and to maintain the grain line of the fabric so that the fabric does not twist. Next stitch the bodice front to the bodice back at the shoulder seams and the side seams. Do not stitch the center-back (or center-front if the garment closes in the front) together. This should be left unstitched so the actor can get into the garment for the fitting. Fitting procedures are discussed in Chap. 12.

eight

basic set-in sleeve patterns

The size, shape, cut, and detailing of sleeves are distinguishing features in establishing the illusion of period in the theatrical garment. Patterns for sleeves from different periods vary in size and shape; however, there are several characteristics for set-in sleeves which remain constant.

Set-in sleeves are sleeves which are cut separately from the garment and are joined to it at the armhole. Characteristically, sleeves are made for the right and left arm and are, therefore, mirror images of each other. This means that there is a front and back of each sleeve to allow for the forward movement of the arm and for comfort. The shape of the sleeve cap is instrumental in determining the front and back of a sleeve; the back of the sleeve cap is fuller to correspond with the fullness of the back of the arm.

The sleeve cap also corresponds to the armhole of the garment. Modern sleeves, for example, are cut with a sharper curve in the front than in the back, just as the armhole in the bodice/jacket has a deeper curve in the front and a less sharp curve in the back. The distance around the sleeve cap must also be equal to or larger than the armhole if the sleeve is to fit properly. Additionally, when the sleeve cap is larger than the armhole, the fullness is controlled on the upper portion of the armhole, never at the underarm section. The underarm is always kept smooth for a comfortable fit.

There are two types of basic, modern, set-in sleeves: the single-piece sleeve and the two-piece sleeve. The single-piece sleeve is characterized by a sharply curved sleeve cap and forms a tube when closed at the underarm seam. This sleeve may be a fitted sleeve (one which is shaped to the arm) or a full "blousy" sleeve. The two-piece sleeve has a less sharply curved sleeve cap and the tubular shape is created by seams at the front (inside) and back (outside or elbow line) of the arm. This type of sleeve is typical in a man's suit coat. These basic sleeves can be adapted to various sleeve patterns for both modern and period garments; standard adaptations are discussed under Sleeve Variations.

It is possible to use commercial sleeve patterns; they can be handy in that they have markings to indicate the front and back of the sleeve, how to position the pattern on the fabric, and also how to lengthen and shorten the sleeve. It is also possible to make your own variations of the basic patterns to fit many period and modern designs. Therefore, a selection of fitted and two-piece sleeve patterns, transferred onto heavy paper, are basic items in a pattern library.

Whether you are using a commercial pattern or an original drafted sleeve with a drafted bodice/jacket, always measure around the top of the sleeve cap to be sure that the cap is large enough to fit the arm-hole (adjusting the cap size is discussed under Adding Fullness).

Also, check the length of the sleeve pattern against the actor's measurements. On fitted sleeves, for example, the distance from the top of the sleeve cap to the middle elbow dart should match the "arm-bent-to-elbow" measurement plus seam allowance. The distance from the top of the cap to the wrist should match the "arm-bent-to-wrist" measurement plus allowances for the seam and hem.

Check and adjust the length of the sleeve according to the measurements but only above and/or below the elbow darts. An elbow dart is a fitting dart used to form a bulge or pocket for the elbow and to provide room for the arm to bend. Do not be tempted to add length just at the wrist; this will distort the sleeve line and the fit of the sleeve on the arm.

DRAFTING A BASIC SLEEVE

The following sections cover the two most commonly used basic sleeve patterns: the single-piece, single-seam pattern and the two-piece, two-seam pattern. The pattern drafts shown are for average arm measurements and can be laid out on a piece of fabric approximately 22 in. (56 cm) wide by the "arm-bent-to-wrist" measurement plus 5 in. (12.5 cm). Be sure to place the patterns on the fabric with the centerlines aligned with the grainline as indicated.

The Fitted Single-Piece Sleeve

This draft is for a basic pattern with one elbow fitting dart. As shown, it is a full-length sleeve that would be finished with a hem (see Sleeve Finishings for the use of a cuff). Study Fig. 8–1 carefully for the overall shape and layout of the pattern; ½ in. (1.3 cm) seam allowance and 1½ in. (3.8 cm) hem allowance are included in the draft. Draft the pattern on paper or muslin that is at least 20 in. (51 cm) wide by the "arm-bent-to-wrist" measurement plus 4 in. (10 cm) long.

1. As shown in Fig. 8–1, draw a line 20 in. (51 cm) long at the top of the fabric using a tailor's square to place it at a right-angle to the edge of the fabric. Set point A at the center of this right-angle line, 10 in. (25.5 cm) from the edge.

2. To establish the centerline of the sleeve, take the "arm-bent-to-wrist" measurement plus 4 in. (10 cm) and draw the centerline perpendicular to the right-angle line at point A. The centerline is on the straight (lengthwise) grain of the fabric and is 10 in. (25.5 cm) from the edge of the cloth.

3. To locate the capline, as shown in Fig. 8–1, measure down 6 in. (15 cm) from point A on the centerline and set point C.

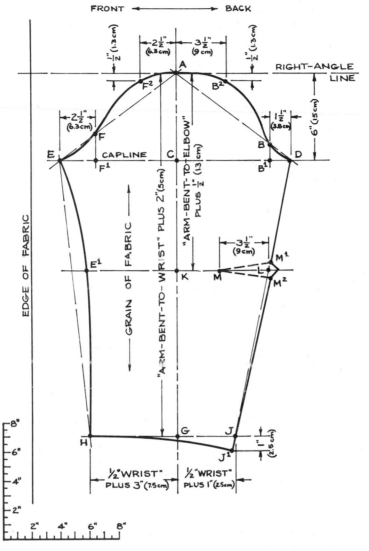

Figure 8-1 Complete basic set-in sleeve pattern layout.

Through point C, draw a line parallel to the right-angle line; this will become the capline. From point C, determine the length of the capline by measuring—8 in. (20.5 cm) for female, 9 in. (23 cm) for male—to each side of point C on the capline. Set point D at the back seam edge, and set point E at the front seam edge. Line D–C–E is the capline, 16 in. (40.5 cm)

long for female, 18 in. (46 cm) long for male.[1] One-half inch (1.3 cm) seam

[1]This is an average size: For female sizes 6 to 10 the capline should be 14 in. (35.5 cm) long, sizes 16 to 20, 18 in. (46 cm) long; for male sizes 36 to 40, 16 in. (40.5 cm), and sizes 44 to 48, 20 in. (51 cm) long. If the arms seem heavy, it is advisable to measure the biceps around the fullest part of the upper arm to determine the length of the capline.

allowance is included. The capline should be on the crosswise grain on the fabric.

4. To establish the sleeve cap curve, connect points A–D and A–E with straight lines. To locate the points for the curve:

a. From point D, measure across on the capline 1½ in. (3.8 cm) and set point B¹, draw a line straight up to line A–D and set point B where the lines intersect.

b. From point A, measure 3½ in. (9 cm) over on the right-angle line and then ½ in. (1.3 cm) down and set point B². Connect the points with a curve that can be shaped with a french curve. This is the back of the sleeve cap curve.

c. From point E, measure across on the capline 2½ in. (6.3 cm) and set point F¹, draw a line straight up to line A–E and set point F where the lines intersect.

d. From point A, measure 2½ in. (6.3 cm) over on the right-angle line and then down ½ in. (1.3 cm) and set point F². Connect those points with a curve that can be shaped with a french curve. This is the front of the sleeve cap curve; notice that the curves are not as full as those at the back of the arm.

5. To determine the length of the sleeve, take the "arm-bent-to-wrist" measurement plus 2 in. (5 cm) from point A and measure that distance down the centerline and set point G.

a. For the front underarm seam, on a line through G that is parallel to the right-angle line, take one-half of the "wrist" measurement plus 3 in. (7.5 cm) and measure across to the front from point G and set point H as shown in Fig. 8–1. Connect points E–H with a preliminary line.

b. For the back underarm seam, take one-half of the "wrist" measurement plus 1 in. (2.5 cm) and set point J. This point is a preliminary point; connect points D–J with a preliminary line. Notice that in this sleeve intended to be hemmed at the wrist, the wrist opening must be large enough to allow the hand to pass through.

6. To locate the elbow fitting dart, take the "arm-bent-to-elbow" measurement plus ½ in. (1.3 cm) for seam allowance and measure down on the centerline and set point K. Draw a line parallel to the right-angle line from the line D–J through point K to line E–H. Set point L where the parallel line intersects line D–J. This line will be the centerline of the dart.

7. To establish the dart stitching lines:

a. Measure 3½ in. (9 cm) over from point L on line L–K and set point M.

b. On line D–J, measure ½ in. (1.3 cm) on either side of point L. Set points M¹ and M² on line D–J. Connect points M–M¹ and M–M² for the dart stitch lines. The stitch lines should be equal in length and the centerline should be ½ in. (1.3 cm) longer than the stitch lines; make the length adjustments outside line D–J as shown.

8. To finalize the underarm seams, set point J¹ down 1 in. (2.5 cm) from point J on an extension of line D–J to allow for the take up of the elbow dart and connect points D–M¹ and M²–J¹. To determine the curve of the front underarm seam (line E–H), set point E¹ 1 in. (2.5 cm) over toward center on line through points L–M–K. Connect points E–E¹–H with a gradual curve as shown in Fig. 8–1.

9. To finalize the pattern, connect points J¹–H for the wrist curve. Check the length of the underarm seams against the "underarm" measurements; line E–E¹–H should be at least 1½ in. (3.8 cm) longer than the measurement to allow for ease and hem, and line D–J¹ should be 2½ in. (6.3 cm) longer for seam allowances and the dart.

CUTTING AND PREPARATION FOR FITTING.   Before cutting the pattern, check the shape of the pattern against the arm measurements and make any necessary corrections. When cutting the sleeve, we like to cut out the front half of the sleeve and fold it over to compare the underarm seam length, sleeve cap curves, and the grain of the fabric before cutting the back. If the fabric pulls or shows signs of twisting, the sleeve is off grain; that is, the capline is not on the crosswise grain or the centerline is not on the lengthwise grain. If the sleeve does twist, the pattern must be corrected before the good sleeves are cut.

After the sleeve is cut, machine-baste the dart. Bring points D and E together with the good sides of the fabric inside; machine-baste the underarm seam, and turn the sleeve tube right side out. A discussion of joining sleeves to the garment armholes is under Setting-in Sleeves.

Variations in a Single-Piece Sleeve

The basic single-piece sleeve pattern can be altered to create many different sleeves. The fullness, length, and finish of the sleeve are determined by the pattern and cut. Alterations in the basic sleeve are simple and create a variety of sleeve designs. Some of the basic means for varying the sleeve are illustrated in Figs. 8-2 and 8-3.

The shape of the sleeve cap controls the amount of fullness or "easing" of the sleeve. The height of the sleeve cap (line A–C) does not influence the amount of fullness; it influences the height of the sleeve puff above the shoulder line. The width of the sleeve cap (line D–E) controls the fullness. To lessen the amount of fullness in the sleeve cap, the curve can be trimmed, but the height of the sleeve cap must be retained for comfort and movement of the arm. Reshaping of the curve to lessen fullness is indicated by line X–Y in Fig. 8-2A.

ADDING FULLNESS. Fullness may be added to the basic sleeve at the top and/or at the bottom, depending on the design of the sleeve. When adding fullness to a sleeve, lengthen the sleeve 1 in. (2.5 cm) to 3 in. (7.5 cm) as needed to create "blouse" in the sleeve length. To add fullness at the top of the sleeve cap, line D–C–E is lengthened (see Fig. 8-2C); the sleeve cap is enlarged, but the proportions for the shape at the underarm front and back remain the same.

The length of the capline is determined by the amount of fullness desired. Adding 50 percent of the capline length creates a moderate puff. In other words, if line D–C–E is 16 in. (40.5 cm) long, adding 8 in. (20.5 cm) to make the capline a total of 24 in. (61 cm) long results in a moderate puff. Many theatrical garments require 100 percent fullness or more; a 16 in. (40.5 cm) capline must be increased to 32 in. (81.5 cm) for 100 percent fullness. Of course, the type of fabric used for the sleeves influences the percentage needed; lightweight fabrics need more fullness than heavyweight fabrics.

Maintaining the proportions for the sleeve-cap curve can be done by drawing a right-angle line the required length at the top of the fabric and then placing the top of the fitted sleeve pattern on the line. Trace around the curve E–F–F^2–A, and then slide the pattern across the fabric along the right-angle line and trace around curve D–B–B^2–A. The right-angle line connects the underarm curves and forms the top of the sleeve cap.

If the sleeve design calls for a high puff at the top of the sleeve, extending above the shoulder line, the height of the sleeve cap, line A–C, is extended (see Fig. 8-2B). Since the proportions within the sleeve cap influence how the fullness of the sleeve will be distributed around the arm, many variations are possible. When adding to the height of the sleeve cap, experiment with a number of shapes and sizes in mock-ups to develop patterns.

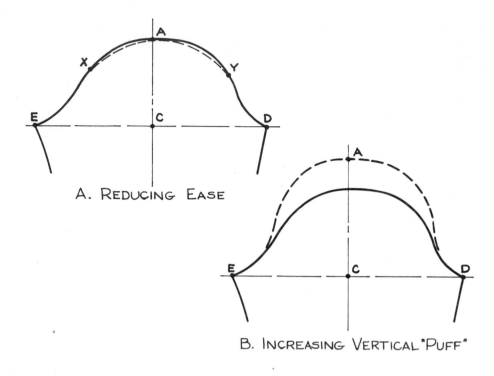

A. Reducing Ease

B. Increasing Vertical "Puff"

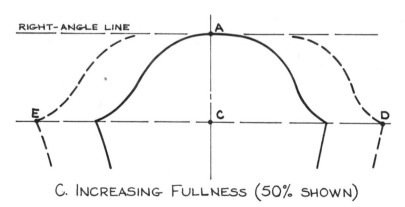

C. Increasing Fullness (50% shown)

Figure 8–2 Example variations in the fullness of the fitted sleeve cap.

To add fullness to the wrist, the width of the wrist line is extended. The underarm seams lose the curve and fall vertically or diagonally from the capline, depending on the design of the lower sleeve. Adding 50 percent of the wrist to the wrist line creates a very moderate puff, 100 percent, a moderate puff, 150 percent or more creates an ample puff. Figure 8–3C shows fullness added at the wrist only; Fig. 8–3D shows fullness at both the sleeve cap and the wrist.

oom for movement and makes up into a
ery graceful sleeve. This principle holds
rue whatever the length of the sleeve: a
hort puff sleeve, a three-quarter sleeve, or
full-length sleeve. The fullness at the bot-
om of the sleeve can be controlled by elas-
c or set into a cuff. Finishing methods are
iscussed under Sleeve Finishings.

If the full-length sleeve is to be finished
ith a cuff, a line to designate the opening
eeds to be located on the pattern. Since
ffs close on the outside of the arm rather
an at the underarm seam, this "cut" line
located at the back of the sleeve as shown
Figs. 8–3C and D. The exact location
ries depending on the fullness of the
eve; however, a general rule is to place
e line about 4 in. (10 cm) from the back
derarm seam. The cut line should be 3
(7 5 cm) long, but it should not be cut
til later when the sleeve is being
ished.

SLEEVE LENGTHS. Essentially, there are
ee basic sleeve lengths: the short sleeve
h the hem above the elbow (Fig. 8–3B),
three-quarter sleeve with the hem
w the elbow, and the full-length sleeve
the hem at the wrist or below. To pat-
a short or three-quarter sleeve, de-
nine the length required from the
m-bent-to-elbow" measurement and
sure that length plus seam and hem
wance from point A on the sleeve cap
set a point. Measure from point C to
new point and use that measurement
the capline to determine the under-
length. For a short fitted sleeve, add 1
2.5 cm) of width at the hem edge for
Fullness may be added to any sleeve
h by the methods described for add-
ullness to a basic sleeve.

wo-Piece Sleeve

draft is a basic pattern with an "up-
and an "under" sleeve. Two-piece
s provide control in the curve of
leeve. This pattern is appropriate

for late–nineteenth- and twentieth-century
men's coats.

Alterations in fullness and length of the
two-piece sleeve can be made from commercial patterns as well as from an original
drafted pattern. The principles for these
alterations are the same as for the single-
piece sleeve.

Study Fig. 8–4 carefully for the overall
shape and layout of the pattern; ½ in. (1.3
cm) seam allowance and 2 in. (5 cm) hem
allowance are included in the draft. Draft
the pattern on paper or muslin that is at
least 22 in. (56 cm) wide by the "arm-bent-
to-wrist" measurement plus 4 in. (10 cm)
long.

1. As shown in Fig. 8–4, draw a right-
angle line at the top of the fabric. Allow 2
in. from the edge of the fabric and set
points A and B on the line, 18 in. (46 cm)
apart for a female sleeve, 20 in. (51 cm)
apart for a male sleeve.[2]

2. Locate the center of line A–B and
set point C. Drop a perpendicular line
from point C the length of the "arm-bent-
to-wrist" measurement plus 4 in. (10 cm)
for allowance and set point D.

3. Take the same length of the "arm-
bent-to-wrist" measurement plus 4 in. (10
cm) and drop perpendicular lines from
points A and B parallel to line C–D; set
points E and F respectively as shown. Lines
A–E, C–D, and B–F are equal in length
and must be on the lengthwise grain of the
fabric.

4. To locate the top of the sleeve cap,
take one-half of the distance between
points A–C and measure that distance over
on the right-angle line from point A; set
point G.

[2]This is an average size: For female sizes 6 to 10
the capline should be 16 in. (40.5 cm) long, sizes 16 to
20, 20 in. (51 cm) long; for male sizes 36 to 40, 18 in.
(46 cm), and sizes 44 to 48, 22 in. (56 cm) long. If the
arms seem heavy, it is advisable to measure the biceps
around the fullest part of the upper arm to determine
the length of the capline.

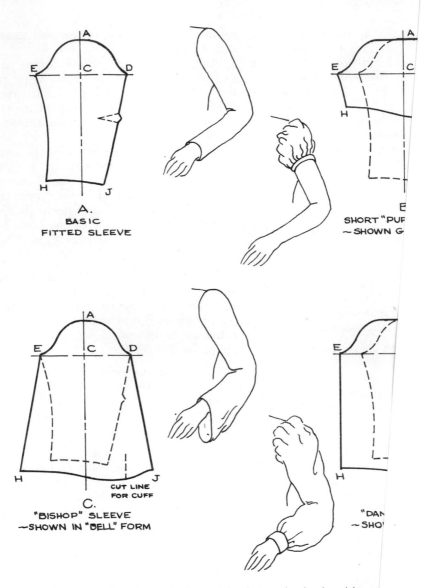

A.
BASIC
FITTED SLEEVE

SHORT "PUF
~SHOWN G

C.
"BISHOP" SLEEVE
~SHOWN IN "BELL" FORM

CUT LINE
FOR CUFF

"DAN
~SHO

Figure 8-3 Example variations in sleeve styles that can be developed from t

When creating fullness at the wrist of a sleeve, the wrist line must be shaped by giving greater length at the back of the arm. To shape the wrist line of a full sleeve, lengthen the front underarm seam 1½ in. (3.8 cm) and make the back seam the same length. Using the sleeve-cap

curve as a guide, sh
The lowest point o
(5 cm) longer thar
should line up with
of the arm curve,
and D.

Shaping the bo

w
n
c
tł
is
in
va
sle
th
ur
in.
un
fir

thr
wit
the
bel
witl
tern
tern
"ar
mea
allo
and
the
fron
arm.
in. (
ease
leng
ing

The

This
per"
sleev
the

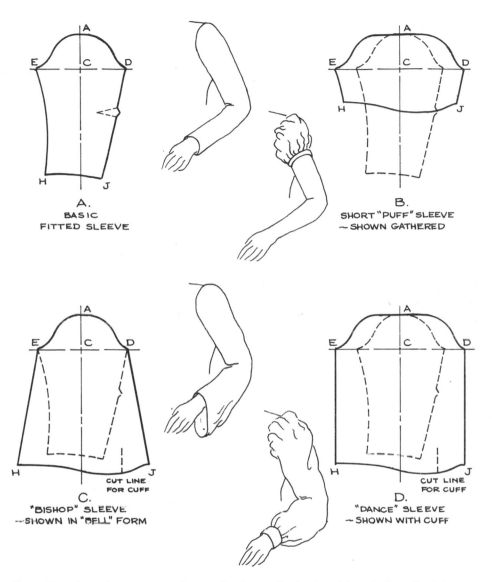

A.
BASIC
FITTED SLEEVE

B.
SHORT "PUFF" SLEEVE
~SHOWN GATHERED

C.
"BISHOP" SLEEVE
--SHOWN IN "BELL" FORM

D.
"DANCE" SLEEVE
~SHOWN WITH CUFF

Figure 8-3 Example variations in sleeve styles that can be developed from the basic fitted sleeve.

When creating fullness at the wrist of a sleeve, the wrist line must be shaped by giving greater length at the back of the arm. To shape the wrist line of a full sleeve, lengthen the front undercrarm seam 1½ in. (3.8 cm) and make the back seam the same length. Using the sleeve-cap curve as a guide, shape a curve at the wrist. The lowest point of the curve, about 2 in. (5 cm) longer than the underarm seams, should line up with the height of the back of the arm curve, as shown in Figs. 8–3C and D.

Shaping the bottom of the sleeve allows

123

room for movement and makes up into a very graceful sleeve. This principle holds true whatever the length of the sleeve: a short puff sleeve, a three-quarter sleeve, or a full-length sleeve. The fullness at the bottom of the sleeve can be controlled by elastic or set into a cuff. Finishing methods are discussed under Sleeve Finishings.

If the full-length sleeve is to be finished with a cuff, a line to designate the opening needs to be located on the pattern. Since cuffs close on the outside of the arm rather than at the underarm seam, this "cut" line is located at the back of the sleeve as shown in Figs. 8–3C and D. The exact location varies depending on the fullness of the sleeve; however, a general rule is to place the line about 4 in. (10 cm) from the back underarm seam. The cut line should be 3 in. (7.5 cm) long, but it should not be cut until later when the sleeve is being finished.

SLEEVE LENGTHS.   Essentially, there are three basic sleeve lengths: the short sleeve with the hem above the elbow (Fig. 8–3B), the three-quarter sleeve with the hem below the elbow, and the full-length sleeve with the hem at the wrist or below. To pattern a short or three-quarter sleeve, determine the length required from the "arm-bent-to-elbow" measurement and measure that length plus seam and hem allowance from point A on the sleeve cap and set a point. Measure from point C to the new point and use that measurement from the capline to determine the underarm length. For a short fitted sleeve, add 1 in. (2.5 cm) of width at the hem edge for ease. Fullness may be added to any sleeve length by the methods described for adding fullness to a basic sleeve.

The Two-Piece Sleeve

This draft is a basic pattern with an "upper" and an "under" sleeve. Two-piece sleeves provide control in the curve of the sleeve. This pattern is appropriate for late–nineteenth- and twentieth-century men's coats.

Alterations in fullness and length of the two-piece sleeve can be made from commercial patterns as well as from an original drafted pattern. The principles for these alterations are the same as for the single-piece sleeve.

Study Fig. 8–4 carefully for the overall shape and layout of the pattern; ½ in. (1.3 cm) seam allowance and 2 in. (5 cm) hem allowance are included in the draft. Draft the pattern on paper or muslin that is at least 22 in. (56 cm) wide by the "arm-bent-to-wrist" measurement plus 4 in. (10 cm) long.

1.   As shown in Fig. 8–4, draw a right-angle line at the top of the fabric. Allow 2 in. from the edge of the fabric and set points A and B on the line, 18 in. (46 cm) apart for a female sleeve, 20 in. (51 cm) apart for a male sleeve.[2]

2.   Locate the center of line A–B and set point C. Drop a perpendicular line from point C the length of the "arm-bent-to-wrist" measurement plus 4 in. (10 cm) for allowance and set point D.

3.   Take the same length of the "arm-bent-to-wrist" measurement plus 4 in. (10 cm) and drop perpendicular lines from points A and B parallel to line C–D; set points E and F respectively as shown. Lines A–E, C–D, and B–F are equal in length and must be on the lengthwise grain of the fabric.

4.   To locate the top of the sleeve cap, take one-half of the distance between points A–C and measure that distance over on the right-angle line from point A; set point G.

[2]This is an average size: For female sizes 6 to 10 the capline should be 16 in. (40.5 cm) long, sizes 16 to 20, 20 in. (51 cm) long; for male sizes 36 to 40, 18 in. (46 cm), and sizes 44 to 48, 22 in. (56 cm) long. If the arms seem heavy, it is advisable to measure the biceps around the fullest part of the upper arm to determine the length of the capline.

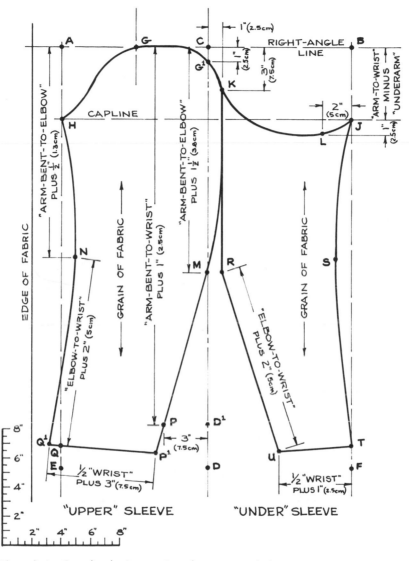

Figure 8–4 Complete basic two-piece sleeve pattern draft.

5. To locate the points of the capline, subtract the "underarm" measurement from the "arm-bent-to-wrist" measurement. On line A–E, measure this distance down from point A and set point H. Repeat this step on line B–F from point B and set point J. Connect points J–H with a straight line which becomes the capline.

6. To establish the "under" sleeve cap curve, locate point G¹ on line C–D 1 in. (2.5 cm) below point C.

a. On line C–B, measure over 1 in. (2.5 cm) from C toward B and then down 3 in. (7.5 cm) to set point K.

b. From point J, measure over 2 in. (5

cm) on the capline and then down 1 in. (2.5 cm) to set point L.

7. Connect points H–G–G¹–K–L–J using a french curve and draw in the curves of the sleeve cap.

8. To establish the back arm seams, take the "arm-bent-to-elbow" measurement plus 1½ in. (3.8 cm) from right-angle line through point G¹ on line C–D and set point M; connect points K–M, using a slight curve as shown in Fig. 8–4.

a. Measure down from the right-angle line on line C–D the length of the "arm-bent-to-wrist" measurement plus 1 in. (2.5 cm) and set point D¹. Measure over 3 in. (7.5 cm) toward line A–E and set point P.

b. Subtract the "arm-bent-to-elbow" measurement from the "arm-bent-to-wrist" measurement to obtain what can be called the "elbow-to-wrist" dimension. Take this figure plus 2 in. (5 cm) and measure down from point M through point P to set point P¹. Line K–M–P¹ is the back seam line of the upper sleeve.

c. Take the "arm-bent-to-elbow" measurement plus 1½ in. (3.8 cm) and measure down from the right-angle line through point G¹ on line C–D and then over 1 in. (2.5 cm) toward line B–F to set point R.

d. Take one-half of the "wrist" measurement plus 1 in. (2.5 cm) and measure across from line B–F; take the "elbow-to-wrist" measurement plus 2 in. (5 cm) and measure from point R; set point U where the two measurements intersect. Connect points K–R–U for the back seam of the under sleeve.

9. To establish the front arm seams, take the "arm-bent-to-elbow" measurement plus ½ in. (1.3 cm) down on line A–F from the right-angle line and over 1 in. (2.5 cm) toward line C–D and set point N.

a. Take the "elbow-to-wrist" figure plus 2 in. (5 cm) and measure from point N to set point Q on line A–E.

b. Take one-half of the "wrist" measurement plus 3 in. (7.5 cm) and measure over from point P¹ through Q to set point Q¹. Connect points H–N–Q¹ for the front seam of the upper sleeve; use a gradual curve as shown.

c. On line B–F, take the "arm-bent-to-elbow" measurement plus ½ in. (1.3 cm) and measure down on line B–F from the right-angle line and then measure over 1 in. (2.5 cm) toward line C–D to set point S.

d. Take the "elbow-to-wrist" figure plus 2 in. (5 cm) and measure from point S to set point T on line B–F. With a gradual curve, connect points J–S–T for the front seam of the under sleeve.

10. To complete the sleeve pattern, connect points P¹–Q¹ and points T–U with straight lines for the wrists.

CUTTING AND PREPARATION FOR FITTING. Check the pattern shape against Fig. 8–4 and the measurements; the front sleeve seams, lines H–N–Q¹ and J–S–T, should be equal in length as should the back seams, lines K–M–P¹ and K–R–U.

After the pattern is cut out, machine-baste the seams together for the fitting as with the single-piece sleeve.

SLEEVE FINISHINGS

The lower edge of the sleeve may be finished in one of three ways: with a cuff, a hem or facing, or a casing for elastic or drawstring. The method of finishing is determined by the design of the sleeve.

CUFFS. The cuff may be a fold-back type or an extension of the sleeve fitted to the wrist. In either case, the cuff is set onto the sleeve with the opening at the outside (elbow line) of the sleeve rather than at the underarm seam. For sleeves fitted to the wrist, this necessitates cutting and finishing an opening (called a *placket*) in the sleeve at the elbow line to allow the hand to pass through the finished sleeve.

To finish this type of opening, cut a rectangle of cloth that is 4 in. (10 cm) wide and 2 in. (5 cm) longer than the cut line on the sleeve. Roll-hem three sides of the rectangle leaving one short side of this "facing" rectangle unfinished. Mark the centerline on the length of the facing. With right sides together and the raw edge of the facing at the wrist, match the centerline to the cut line of the sleeve. Stitch around the cut line, ⅜ in. (1 cm) to each side and across the top, leaving 1½ in. (3.8 cm) of the facing at the top. Cut through the centerline (cut line) to below the top stitching line; clip the top corners as far as the stitching. Turn the facing inside the sleeve and press the opening. See Chap. 3 under Placket for details on finishing the opening.

To make cuffs, draw a rectangle that is the length of the wrist measurement plus 2½ in. (6.3 cm) and double the finished width plus 1 in. (2.5 cm). For example, if the cuff is to be finished at 2 in. (5 cm) wide, cut the rectangle 5 in. (12.5 cm) wide and "wrist" plus 2½ in. (6.3 cm) long. If the cuff is to be wider than 2 in. (6.3 cm), add 3½ in. (9 cm) to the "wrist" measurement. If the fabric is lightweight, interface the rectangle.

To set the cuff onto the sleeve, first run two rows of gathering stitches at the bottom edge of the sleeve and gather it to the "wrist" measurement plus 1 in. (2.5 cm) for seam allowance. Then stitch the cuff onto the sleeve, right sides together, lining up the edge of the cuff, plus seam allowance, with the back edge (opening) of the sleeve; leave 1½ in. (3.8 cm) for cuff overlap and seam allowance at the front edge. Press the cuff; then turn it in half over the edge of the sleeve and stitch around the inside with the seam allowances sandwiched between the layers of the cuff.

The fold-back cuff may be cut as an extension (cut-in-one) with the sleeve or cut as a separate piece. In either case, the shape must be flared to allow for the tapered shape of the arm, and it must be lined or faced with matching or contrasting fabric so that the wrong side of the cuff fabric is hidden and the raw edges are finished. The widely flared turn-back cuff must be cut separately and on the bias to allow for the proper fullness. There are commercial patterns which will give numerous variations on cuff patterns.

HEMS.   The sleeve that requires no cuff can simply be hemmed by turning the fabric up and either folding the raw edge under or by top-stitching hem binding tape onto the raw edge and stitching the hem in place by hand. The hemming stitch should be as invisible as possible on the outside of the sleeve.

If the bottom of the sleeve is wide and open enough around the arm to reveal the inside, the sleeve should be faced so as not to show the inside seam(s). The facing piece is cut on the same pattern as the sleeve (see Chap. 11) and as long as necessary to finish the inside of the sleeve. An easy method of attaching the facing to the sleeve is to first stitch the facing into a tube and then slip it over the lower edge of the sleeve, right sides together. The facing and the sleeve are stitched together at the bottom and the facing is turned into the sleeve with wrong sides together. The facing is pressed and then stitched into place as a normal hem.

CASINGS.   A casing is a narrow band used to hold elastic or a drawstring in order to control fullness at the bottom edge of the sleeve when a cuff is not being used. This method of finishing a sleeve is generally used for peasant blouses and some period shirts.

The casing may be cut as a narrow facing piece, or cloth tape may be used. In either case, an opening must be left to insert the elastic or drawstring. One-half inch wide elastic is the most comfortable width to use, and the casing must be wide enough to allow the elastic or drawstring to pass through freely.

A casing may be top-stitched onto the sleeve at the bottom edge in the same manner as the hem binding, or it may be set back from the edge ½ inch or more to create a ruffle at the bottom of the sleeve. If ruffles are included in the sleeve, the raw edge must be finished with a facing or hemming.

The design of the sleeve will indicate which method should be used to finish the sleeve. The final construction technique will be determined by the cut and by the weight of the fabric. It is important to avoid bulk in the seams. If, for example, the fabric is heavy, it is advisable to finish the hem with hem binding rather than turning the raw edge under, thereby avoiding three layers of heavy material at the hem.

SLEEVE GUSSETS

A *sleeve gusset* is a piece of fabric set into the juncture of sleeve and torso garment to improve the fit and flexibility under the arm. The function of a sleeve gusset is to allow the arm to move freely without pulling up the garment; it is most typically used in dance costumes but is equally important in theatrical costumes.

A simple and effective gusset for set-in sleeves is a football-shaped piece that is cut on true bias. Generally, this gusset, including ½ in. (1.3 cm) seam allowance, is 6 in. (15 cm) long and 4 in. (10 cm) wide. These dimensions vary somewhat with the size of the sleeve. For example, a sleeve with a 14 in. (35.5 cm) capline takes a smaller gusset than a sleeve with a 20 in. (51 cm) capline. The shape is easy to adjust by trimming away excess.

To cut a gusset: Fold a square of fabric, approximately 5 in. by 5 in. (12.5 cm), on the bias to form a triangle as in Fig. 8–5. Then fold a smaller triangle from the center of line D–D^1, point C. Locate point B

2 in. (5 cm) down on the second foldline, and point A 3 in. (7.5 cm) along the double-foldline. Scribe a curve between points A and B; this is the cutting line. Cut a notch at point B to show the center of the gusset; these will match up with the side seam of the garment and the underarm seam location of the sleeve. Open the triangle and press; be sure that the gusset is cut on the true bias, to stretch two ways, between points A–A^1 and B–B^1.

Setting the gusset into the garment is a simple process. First, pin notch B to the true underarm of the sleeve: the seam itself on the single-piece sleeve, or the underarm point (L) on the two-piece sleeve. Pin one side of the curve onto the curve of the closed sleeve, right sides together, and stitch into place. The sleeve with the gusset stitched into place can then be treated as one unit to be set into the armhole of the garment, as shown in Fig. 8–5.

SETTING-IN SLEEVES

The sleeve should be carefully pinned into the garment right sides together, prior to stitching. Be sure that the left sleeve is in the left armhole and the right sleeve is in the right armhole. The cap of the sleeve is cut higher in the back than in the front, so it is easy to determine which sleeve goes into which armhole.

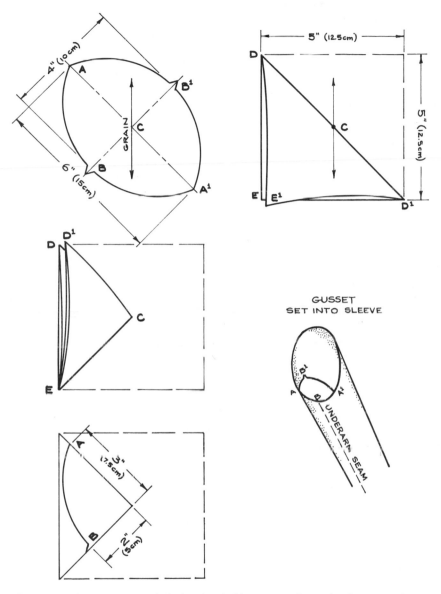

Figure 8–5 A gusset pattern draft showing drafting steps and completed gusset set into a sleeve.

The pins should be perpendicular to the raw edge to allow the sewing machine to stitch over the pins. Starting at the underarm, pin the sleeve (point B¹ of the gusset) smoothly into position. Work first one side of the gusset from point B¹ to point A and then the other side, point B¹ to A¹, setting the sleeve in smoothly under the arm. There should be no easing or pleating under the arm. If required, all fullness is

129

eased or pleated at the top portion of the sleeve (between points F and B on the basic pattern). The greater amount of fullness should be placed toward the back of the sleeve.

After the underarm section is pinned into place, the rest of the sleeve is pinned and then machine-basted in position. Both the pinning and stitching should be done from the inside of the sleeve with the sleeve inside the garment so that the right sides are together. Prior to stitching the sleeve permanently, check the garment on the good side to assure a good fit in the garment. There should be no puckers, pleats, or easing around the armhole on the bodice/jacket. If possible, it is advisable to fit the garment on the actor before the sleeves are stitched permanently to assure an accurate, easy fit.

After the sleeve is correctly basted in and fitted, it should be stitched permanently with two rows of stitching. The first row of stitching is on the seam line and the second just outside the seam line on the seam allowance. Trim away excess seam allowance leaving ⅜ in. to ½ in. seam allowance if the fabric is not too bulky (for bulky fabric, see Layering in Chap. 3). Clip the seam allowance as far as the stitching. Do not clip through the stitching itself.

Common Errors

1. Gathering the sleeve all the way around, including the underarm section
2. Gathering or puckering the armhole of the garment, making the armholes small, unsightly, and uncomfortable
3. Basting the sleeve into the armhole and gathering both the armhole and sleeve cap simultaneously
4. Failure to check the positioning of the sleeve (seams not properly placed so that the sleeve hangs awkwardly)
5. Failure to clip the seam allowance
6. Setting the left sleeve in the right armhole and vice versa.

As stated earlier, the cut and style of the sleeve are important features in establishing the illusion of period. The cut and addition of the sleeve to the garment is an important factor in the fit of the garment and to the comfort of the actor. The cut of the sleeve and armhole will begin to suggest the manner of both posture and gesture to the actor; consequently, it is a feature of the costume which should not be minimized. The addition of the gusset in most costumes will allow freer arm movement without distorting the period line or causing the garment to ride up and create unsightly wrinkles.

basic skirt patterns

For theatrical costumes, skirts can be required for both male and female garments, and the lengths vary from hip length to floor length or longer. A skirt needs to have enough fullness to go around the hips and to provide room at the hem so the wearer can walk, unless the skirt is a "hobble" skirt of the 1910s which literally had a hobbling effect on the wearer. The skirt must also be fitted at the waist to stay in place on the body; there are several methods of controlling the fit at the waist.

The appearance of the skirt is determined by the cut, the use of grain, the kind of fabric used, and the method of controlling the fit at the waist and hips. The skirt may be cut separately, or it may be cut-in-one with the garment as a continuation of the bodice/jacket. Garments which have the skirts cut-in-one are included in Chap. 13.

Skirts which are cut separately can be grouped in four basic classifications: the fitted or straight skirt, the gored skirt, the circle skirt, and the pleated skirt. Basically, each of these describes how the skirt is controlled at the waist or hips. The fitted skirt is shaped over the figure and has a narrow hem. The gored skirt is shaped by seams over the waist and hips and has a wide hem. The circle skirt is cut to fit the waist and has a wide hem, and the pleated skirt is fitted to the waist by a series of pleats and has a wide hemline.

Commercial patterns for each of these skirt types are readily available for women and can be adapted to men's period garments. A collection of these patterns is valuable in a pattern library. Each of these skirts, and variations on them, can also be drafted easily and with good success.

The fitted skirt is a straight, narrow skirt which has the fit at the waist controlled by fitting darts with additional control in the shaping of the side seams. The pattern consists of two pattern pieces with seams at the sides and center-back.

The pattern pieces will be cut on the fold of the fabric so that only one-half of the skirt will be drafted. The fitting darts will be traced through to the other side of the garment.

This draft is for a narrow hemline; if the skirt is to go below the mid-calf, flare, or fullness, must be added to the hemline to allow for movement. Steps 1 and 8 for the skirt front pattern draft show how to add the flare to the pattern.

Fitted Skirt—Front

1. As shown in Fig. 9–1, fold the fabric in half on the straight grain; the foldline will be the center-front line of the pattern. For a straight skirt, the width of the fabric from the fold needs to be one-quarter of the "hip" measurement plus 3 in. (7.5 cm) for seam allowance and ease. More width, up to 9 in. (23 cm), will be needed if flare is to be added to the pattern. The length of the fabric needs to be long enough to accommodate the designed length plus 4 in. (10 cm).

2. Draw in a right-angle line at least 1 in. (2.5 cm) below the top of the fabric and set point A at the fold. Measure across on the right-angle line one-quarter of the "hip" measurement plus 2 in. (5 cm) to set point C.

3. To establish the waistline curve, take one-quarter of the "waist" measurement plus 2 in. (5 cm) and measure across on the right-angle line from point A. Then measure up ½ in. (1.3 cm) above the line to set point B. Connect points A and B; this slightly curved line is a preliminary line.

4. To establish the hipline position, take the "rise" measurement and measure down from point C; take one-quarter of the "hip" measurement plus 2 in. (5 cm) and measure across from the center-front line; set point D where the measurements intersect. To form the line of the upper side seam, connect points B–D with a line that can be shaped with a french curve.

5. To locate the waist fitting dart, measure 4 in. (10 cm) over from point A on the right-angle line and set point G. Drop a line from point G that is perpendicular to the right-angle line; measure down 3½ in. (9 cm) to set point H. Connect points G–H for the centerline of the dart.

a. Measure ½ in. (1.3 cm) to each side of point G on the right-angle line and set points J and K as shown. Connect points J–H and K–H for the dart stitching lines; these lines should be equal in length.

b. Extend line G–H ½ in. (1.3 cm) beyond the right-angle line and connect points A–J–K–B to finalize the waistline as shown in Fig. 9–1.

6. The skirt length is determined by the design; therefore, to locate point F, measure down the center-front line from point A the skirt length called for by the design plus ½ in. (1.3 cm) for seam allowance plus 2 in. (5 cm) for hem allowance; set point F on the center-front line.

7. To locate the side seam, take one-quarter of the "hip" measurement plus 2 in. (5 cm) and measure across from point F; take the skirt length plus allowances and measure down from point B around the side-seam curve and through point D; set point E where the measurements intersect. Connect points D–E to complete the side seam; connect points F–E to complete the hem edge. The line of the hem edge will be slightly curved as shown.

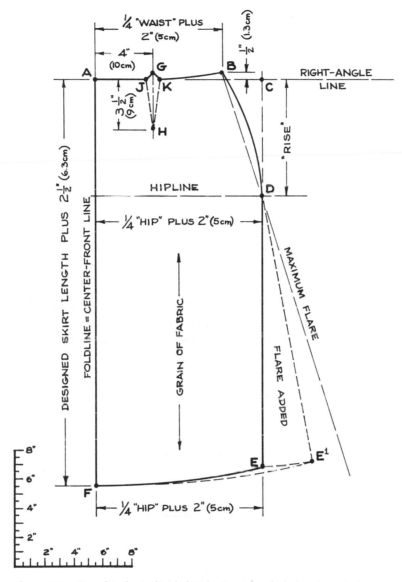

Figure 9-1 Complete basic fitted skirt front pattern draft showing a technique for adding flare.

8. To add flare to the skirt hemline, use point D as the pivot point and swing the length of line D–E outward from point E. Set point E¹ where the desired flare is reached.

a. The maximum amount of flare is determined by a line from point B though point D as shown. This line must go through point D to allow for ease at the hips because if it goes outside point D, the grainline of the skirt will be distorted, and the skirt will not hang properly.

b. Connect points D–E[1] for the flared side seam. Connect points E–E[1] for the edge of the hem; this line needs to be curved to keep the hemline even on the body, but the final hem will be determined in the fitting.

Fitted Skirt—Back

1. As shown in Fig. 9–2, fold the fabric in half on the straight grain. For a straight skirt, the width of the fabric from the fold needs to be one-quarter of the "hip" measurement plus 6 in. (15 cm) for seam allowance and ease. More width, up to 12 in. (30.5 cm) will be needed if flare is to be added to the pattern. The length of the fabric needs to be long enough to accommodate the designed length plus 4 in. (10 cm).

2. Draw the center-back line 2 in. (5 cm) from the fold and the entire length of the skirt.

3. Draw in a right-angle line at least 1 in. (2.5 cm) below the top of the fabric and set point A where the right-angle line intersects the center-back line. From point A, measure across on the right-angle line one-quarter of the "hip" measurement plus 3 in. (7.5 cm) to set point C.

4. To establish the waistline curve, take one-quarter of the "waist" measurement plus 2½ in. (6.3 cm) and measure across on the right-angle line from point A. Then measure up ½ in. (1.3 cm) above the line to set point B. Connect points A and B; this slightly curved line is a preliminary line.

5. To establish the hipline position, take the "rise" measurement and measure down from point C; take one-quarter of the "hip" measurement plus 3 in. (7.5 cm) and measure across from the center-back line; set point D where the measurements

intersect. To form the line of the upper side seam, connect points B–D with a line that can be shaped with a french curve.

6. To locate the waist fitting dart, measure 4 in. (10 cm) over from point A on the right-angle line and set point G. Drop a line from point G that is perpendicular to the right-angle line; measure down 6 in. (15 cm) to set point H. Connect points G–H for the centerline of the dart.

a. Measure ½ in. (1.3 cm) to each side of point G on the right-angle line and set points J and K as shown. Connect points J–H and K–H for the dart stitching lines; these lines should be equal in length.

b. Extend line G–H ½ in. (1.3 cm) beyond the right-angle line and connect points A–J–K–B to finalize the waistline as shown in Fig. 9–2.

7. To determine the length of the skirt back, and to complete the side seam, follow the instructions in steps 6 and 7 under Skirt Front.

8. To add flare to the skirt hemline, follow the instructions in step 8 under Skirt Front.

Kick Pleat

A *kick pleat* is a necessary addition to a narrow fitted skirt. It adds flexibility to the hemline so the legs can move without being bound by the narrowness of the skirt. There are variations possible in the form of the kick pleat, but a simple one can be added directly to the draft of the basic skirt pattern.

As shown in Fig. 9–2, measure 10 in. (25.5 cm) up from point F on the center-back line to set point X. Mark straight across from point X to set point Y at the foldline; line X–Y is a cutline and the top of the pleat. Point F[1] at the foldline on an extension of line E–F completes the kick-pleat addition to the skirt pattern.

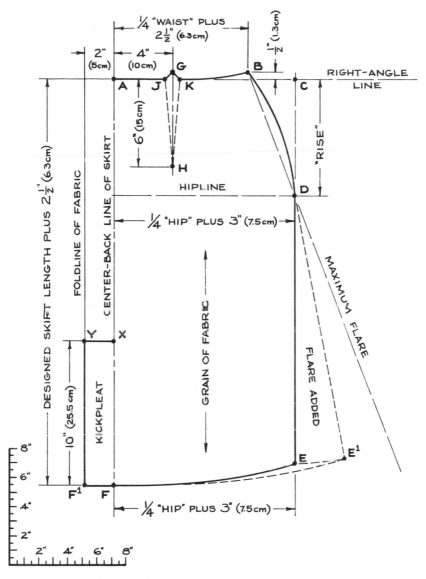

Figure 9-2 Complete basic fitted skirt back pattern draft showing a technique for adding flare.

Since line Y–F¹ is on the foldline, it may be left as a solid connection between the two halves when the skirt back is cut from the good fabric. But we have found that this connection can easily be damaged in handling, so we prefer to cut through line Y–F¹ when the pattern is cut out. It can be reassembled into the desired kick-pleat configuration as the skirt is being finished.

When the skirt is assembled, the center-back seam is stitched to below point X in order to cover the top of the kick pleat. The remainder down to point F is left unstitched.

The kick-pleat fabric is folded inside the skirt to form either a knife pleat or an inverted box pleat. The pleat is held in place with stitching across the top; this stitching can also become a form of decoration.

CUTTING AND PREPARATION FOR FITTING. Transfer the dart stitchlines with a trace wheel and tracing paper between the folded fabric surfaces. Since seam allowances have been included in the pattern draft, cut on the marked outlines. Be careful not to trim off the extension of the dart centerline and do not cut off the kick-pleat addition when cutting the center-back line.

Baste the darts together. Baste the center-back seam to below the top of the kick pleat, but leave a 10 in. (25.5 cm) opening at the top of the skirt for a zipper to be added later. Baste the edges of the kick-pleat additions if needed, but do not stitch the pleat into place before the fitting.

Place the good sides of the skirt front and the assembled back together and baste the side seams. Turn it right side out, and the skirt is ready for fitting.

CREATING FULLNESS AT THE HEM

The basic fitted-skirt pattern can be adapted to make a skirt with more fullness at the hem. The amount of fullness that is needed to make up a flared skirt is governed by the hip circumference, the length of the skirt, and the placement of the grain in the skirt panels. The following is a basic premise for deciding how many inches around the hem there should be for a knee to mid-calf length skirt:

> 100 in. to 130 in. (250 cm to 325 cm) for full flare
> 50 in. to 100 in. (125 cm to 250 cm) for moderate flare.

Floor-length period skirts and pleated skirts often require more fullness. The amount of fullness in these skirts is determined by the design and by the specific period to be depicted.

As can be seen in the pattern draft for the basic fitted skirt, the maximum amount of fullness that can be added to the hem of the fitted skirt is dictated by the hipline (point D in Fig. 9–1). To further increase the fullness in a skirt, the basic pattern must be altered to make a moderate or full flare skirt. This is done by increasing the number of seams in the skirt, since additional fullness is added at the seams.

THE USE OF GORES. Increasing the number of seams in the pattern creates panels or gores. A *gore* is a tapered panel of cloth which is narrow at the top (waist) and wider at the bottom (hem). The gored skirt is made up of a number of panels and is named according to the number of gores involved: A four-gore skirt has four gores, a six-gore skirt has six gores, and so on. Generally, gored skirts are used to allow fullness at the hem with a neat fitted look at the hips and waist; however, gores can also be used to add interest to the skirt through the addition of the seam lines without adding much fullness at the hem.

THE USE OF GRAIN IN A GORED SKIRT. When fullness is added, the use of the grain in the fabric increases in importance in the appearance of the skirt. Usually, the pattern is placed on the lengthwise, straight grain of the fabric since it has greater strength with less tendency to stretch; it also has better drapability than the crosswise grain. Placement of the pattern on the crosswise grain is generally only done on particular fabrics to

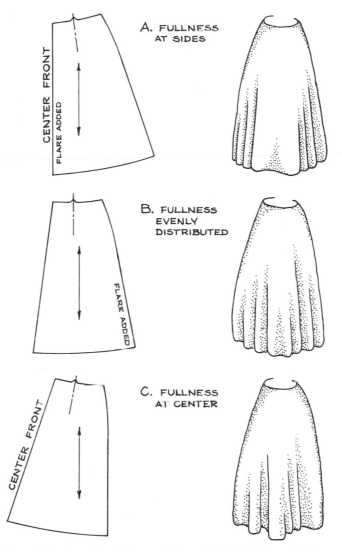

Figure 9-3 Examples of the use of the grain of the fabric to distribute skirt fullness.

achieve design effects with stripes or to take advantage of borders along the length of the cloth.

For gored skirts, the straight grain line can be placed in one of three major locations: parallel to the center-front and center-back, straight on the center of the gore, or parallel to the side seam of the gore. Locating the straight grain parallel to the center-front and center-back seam lines places the side seams on the bias so that the fullness is at the sides while the front and back hang straight as shown in Fig. 9–3A. Locating the straight grain in the center of the gore places both the side and center seams on the bias so the fullness is distributed evenly around the hemline as shown in Fig. 9–3B. Locating the straight grain at the side seams places the center seams on the bias so the fullness is at the front and back and the sides hang straight as shown in Fig. 9–3C.

The principle for the use of the grain line in gores as illustrated in Fig. 9–3 is derived from a four-gore skirt. However, the number of gores involved does not alter this basic principle for the placement of grain in the gore. The gore pattern pieces can be placed with the straight grain in any of the positions described regardless of the number of gores in the skirt. The

use of grain in the gores, however, must be consistent. For example, an eight-gore skirt with the straight grain centered on each gore will create a skirt with the fullness distributed evenly at the hem. The same skirt, cut with the left side of the gore on the straight grain and the right side on the bias, and stitched with bias seams connected to straight seams, makes up into a "trumpet" skirt of the 1900s which Charles Dana Gibson illustrated so handsomely. The placement of the grain in both instances is consistent; it is the appearance of the skirt that is different.

DRAFTING A GORED SKIRT

Four-, six-, and eight-gore skirts can all be drafted as alterations of the basic fitted-skirt pattern. The number of seams depends on where the basic pattern is cut to divide it into gore panels. The amount of fullness in this type of gored skirt depends on how much flare is added to the seam lines.

How the flare is added to this type of gored skirt also provides a choice in the appearance treatment of the upper part of the skirt between the waist and hipline. If flare is added from the hipline as shown in Figs. 9–1 and 9–2, the skirt will retain a fitted look with the fullness all below the hipline. However, flare can also be added from the waistline, and the appearance will be soft folds folding from the waist level that fit neatly but softly over the hips.

When a large number of gores—eight, ten, or more—are used, the intention is usually to create an appearance of considerable fullness while maintaining a smooth fit over the hips. When that is the intention, a simpler tapered-gore pattern can be used to good advantage (see Fig. 9–5B).

For either approach, it is best to develop the gored skirt pattern on paper rather

than on fabric. For patterns that are alterations of the basic fitted skirt, it is necessary to cut and relocate parts of the original pattern; this can be done easily with heavy paper, and the resulting final pattern can then be drawn on either paper or muslin. For skirts that use the tapered gore, several duplicates of the gore pattern must be traced in outline onto the good fabric, and paper works well for that process.

The Four-Gore Skirt Pattern

This alteration of the basic fitted-skirt pattern assumes that each pattern piece will be cut separately, not on the fold as is possible with the straight skirt. Therefore, two each of the front and back pieces will have to be cut in reverse image from the good fabric. Only the alterations to the skirt front are shown in Fig. 9–4, but the techniques can be applied in the same way to the skirt-back pattern pieces.

1. On heavy paper, lay out the basic fitted skirt pattern. Allow several inches of space on both sides of the pattern so that flare can be added.

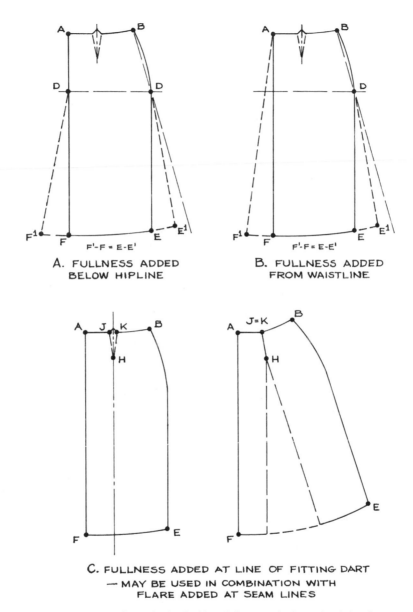

A. FULLNESS ADDED BELOW HIPLINE

B. FULLNESS ADDED FROM WAISTLINE

C. FULLNESS ADDED AT LINE OF FITTING DART — MAY BE USED IN COMBINATION WITH FLARE ADDED AT SEAM LINES

Figure 9-4 Sample methods of adding fullness to the basic fitted skirt front.

2. Add the flare to the side seam as shown in Fig. 9-1; remember that a line through points B and D determines the maximum amount that can be added to the side seam.

3. To add more fullness to the skirt, flare can also be added to the center seam. The amount of flare added should be no greater than the amount added to the side seam, but the center-seam flare can be added from either the hipline or the waist-line (see Fig. 9–4).

a. To add flare below the hips, draw in the hipline through point D and parallel to the right-angle line; set point D^1 at the intersection with the centerline. Take the length of line $E–E^1$ and measure out from point F; take the hip-to-hem length of line $D–E^1$ and measure down from point D^1. Set point F^1 where the measurements intersect to complete the flare addition.

b. To add flare from the waist level, take the "waist-to-hem" length measured from point B through point D to point E^1 and measure down from point A to intersect with the length of line $E–E^1$ measured out from point F. Set point F^1 to complete the flare addition.

ADDING FULLNESS AT THE DART LINE. This technique for adding fullness to the hemline may be used by itself or in combination with flare added to the original seams.

1. On heavy paper, lay out the Basic Fitted Skirt pattern. Draw a line as an extension of the centerline from the tip of the dart, point H, to the bottom of the pattern.

2. Cut out the dart on the stitching lines (J–H and K–H) and slash the pattern on the straight line from point H to the hemline.

3. With point H as the pivot, swing the side-seam section out until the cutout stitchlines of the dart come together as shown in Fig. 9–4C. Tape the dart edges together so that the altered pattern piece can be handled as a single piece.

4. The hemline has now been expanded for additional fullness, and the waistline curve has been adjusted to the same shape that it would have when the dart is stitched closed; therefore, the pattern is ready to use. This altered pattern

may be transferred either to other paper or to muslin so that the slashed opening can be filled in as a solid piece, or this paper pattern may be used directly on the good fabric, but, of course, cut only on the outline and do not cut either the slash lines or the line of the dart.

Notice that this technique of cutting through the skirt panel on the centerline of the fitting dart is also the basis for separating the basic fitted skirt pattern into six gores or even eight gores. Figure 9–5A shows the separations that would be typical for those patterns. Closures on any of these gored skirts may be either at the center-back or at the side seam, but notice also that a center-back closure on the six-gore skirt must be cut into the center panel of the skirt back since there is no construction seam in that position.

COMPLETING THE FOUR-GORE SKIRT PATTERN. Mark each pattern piece to show center-front or center-back, hipline, and waist. Also indicate waist and hip circumferences to show pattern size information.

Determine and mark where the straight grain of the good fabric is to be located on each gore. The straight grain can be maintained at the center seam, or it may be altered as indicated in the previous discussion on the Use of Grain in a Gored Skirt.

Cut out the altered paper pattern pieces for transfer to the fabric. Cut only on the altered outline and do not trim off any additions.

**Alternate Pattern Draft
for Eight or More Gores**

This draft is for a single tapered gore pattern that will be used for all the gores in the skirt. In this instance, the instructions are for a floor-length skirt; however, the draft can be used for any length specified by the design. The fullness of the gore is

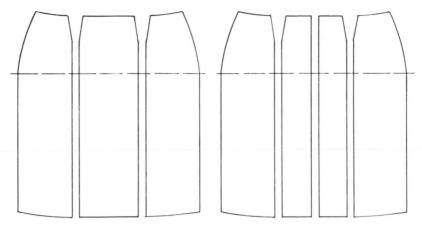

A. 6-GORE AND 8-GORE SKIRT FRONTS
— FLARE MAY BE ADDED AT ANY SEAMS

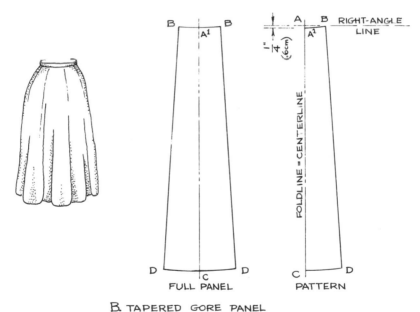

FULL PANEL   PATTERN

B. TAPERED GORE PANEL

Figure 9–5 A. an example of creating 6- and 8-gore patterns from the basic fitted skirt front pattern; B. an example of a basic multigore panel pattern.

determined by the design and by the hip circumference. Step 5 gives a basic guideline for determining the fullness in skirts made up of tapered gores. The illustration in Fig. 9–5B is based on an eight-gore skirt with a 100 in (254 cm) hemline for moderate fullness; the straight grain of the fabric is assumed to be on the centerline of the gore for even fullness around the skirt.

Draft the gore on heavy paper and mark the waist and hip circumference; also indicate the number of gores in the pattern for the skirt, such as eight- or ten-gored skirt.

1. Fold the paper in half, lengthwise; the fold is the centerline of the gore. Draw a right-angle line across the top of the paper from the centerline. Set point A on the fold at the right-angle line.

2. Divide the "waist" measurement by the number of gores to be in the skirt—8, 10, 12, etc. This figure will be the gore measurement at the waistline. Take one-half of this figure plus ½ in. (1.3 cm) for seam allowance and measure over on the right-angle line from point A to set point B.

3. On the centerline, measure down ¼ in. (0.6 cm) from point A and set point A¹; connect B–A¹ with a slightly curved line using a french curve.

4. To establish the length of the gore, take the "waist-to-floor" measurement plus hem allowance (or the length specified by the particular design) and measure down that length from point A¹ on the centerline; set point C.

5. To determine the amount of flare for the gore, take the amount of fullness needed for the hem and divide that di-

mension by the number of gores in the skirt. Take one-half of this figure plus ½ in. (1.3 cm) and measure across from point C; take the skirt length (line A¹–C) and measure down from point B. Set point D where the measurements intersect. Connect points B–D for the gore sides and D–C for the hem line. Line D–C will curve.

6. Cut out the gore on lines A¹–B, B–D, D–C. Make sure that all necessary information, such as number of gores and waist and hip circumferences, is marked on the gore.

CUTTING AND PREPARATION FOR FITTING. After the paper patterns are completed and marked, cut the skirt out of the fabric. Pay careful attention to the placement of the straight grain for each gore. Mark the center-front and the center-back of the skirt on the appropriate pieces and mark the seams so the gores will be joined together properly.

Baste the gores together, leaving a 10-in. (25.5 cm) opening at the center-back, or side, so the skirt can go on over the actor's head for the fitting, and a zipper or other closing can be added later.

The skirt is ready for fitting; adjustments in the waist and hem curves and the waist and hip seams will be made in the fitting.

DRAFTING A CIRCLE SKIRT

Full-circle skirts are cut from a square of cloth, the sides of which must be double the length of the waist-to-hem measurement plus 12 in. (30.5 cm). If the fabric is not wide enough to allow for a square that is large enough, add the necessary width by stitching additional fabric on the straight grain at the selvage. Adding fabric on the straight grain allows the seam to fall

in with the line of the skirt so that it is practically invisible.

1. Fold the square of fabric in half on the crosswise grain; then fold the fabric in half again on the lengthwise grain creating a square one-quarter the size of the original square. One side of the square will have a single fold following the lengthwise

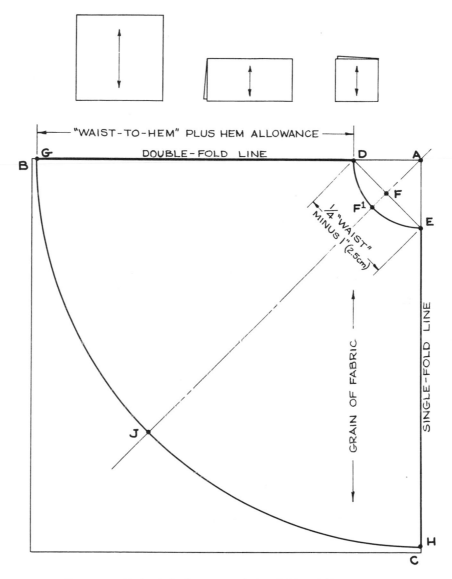

Figure 9-6 Basic circle skirt pattern draft with fabric folding method.

grain; the adjacent edge will have a double fold following the crosswise grain. Locate point A at the corner of the folded edges as shown in Fig. 9–6. For reference, set point B at the end of the double foldline, set point C at the end of the single foldline.

2. To establish the waistline take one-quarter of the "waist" measurement less 1 in. (2.5 cm); measure that distance across below point A, intersecting lines A–B and A–C. Set point D where the line intersects A–B, set point E where the line intersects

A–C. Points D and E *must* be equidistant from point A.

3. To finalize the waistline curve locate point F on the center of line D–E and draw a centerline through points A and F. Take the length from A to E and measure that distance from point A on the A–F centerline to set point F[1]. Lines A–D, A–E, and A–F[1] are equal in length since they are all radii of the same circle. Connect points D–F[1]–E with a circular curve for the waistline.

4. To establish the hemline, take the "waist-to-hem" measurement plus only a narrow hem allowance and measure down from point D on line A–D–B and set point G; on line A–E–C measure down the same distance from point E and set point H; repeat the step from point F[1] and set point J on an extension of the A–F centerline. Continue this process measuring down from the waist, line D–F[1]–E, to set additional points to mark the curve for the bottom of the skirt (a large compass technique can also be used, if available).

5. The skirt opening can be placed at the center-back or at the side, depending on the garment's requirements. Line A–E–H is the center-front and the center-back if the straight grain is to be in the front and back. If the center-front and center-back are to be on the bias, line A–F–J is the center of the skirt pattern.

6. Draw an 8 in. (20.5 cm) slash line at the desired location for the closing.

Cutting and Preparation for Fitting

To cut out the full-circle skirt, cut the waistline, line D–F[1]–E, and the hemline, G–J–H. Then stay-stitch the waistline and around the slash line. This stitching is a machine baste ¼ in. (0.6 cm) from the line. Cut on the slash line, but do not cut through the stitching at the bottom, to allow the skirt to go on over the actor's head.

The bottom of a full-circle skirt will tend to stretch in the bias areas. Before the hem is finalized in the fitting, it is best to hang the skirt on a skirt hanger for a period of time to allow it to stretch.

PLEATED SKIRTS AND PLEATING

Pleating is a common method for controlling fullness in skirts, as well as for creating interesting detail. For instance, the design may call for a few pleats at the center-front and center-back, primarily as a decorative feature; it may call for fullness controlled in pressed pleats as in an accordion-pleated skirt, or it may call for a large amount of fullness controlled with unpressed pleats at the waist (see Fig. 12–1).

Since there are several methods for pleating fabric, a careful selection should be made of the most appropriate method to use for pleating a skirt for a particular costume. The appearance is specified by the design, but the weight and thickness (bulk) of the fabric will influence the method of pleating as much as will the intended appearance. An accordion-pleated skirt, for example, must have pressed knife pleats which lie smoothly closed over the hips. A wide, full-length period skirt, such as the one shown in the Isabella plate (see Fig. 1–8), needs cartridge pleats to control fullness, to accommodate the weight of the fabric, and to fulfill the appearance of the design.

Working with the pleating of fabric can be rather time-consuming, but when it is done with patience and accuracy, the results are well worth the effort. For the preliminary layout and folding, it is usually most convenient to work on a large flat surface so that the measuring, marking, and pinning of each pleat into place can be done efficiently. An experienced person may be able to do an effective job of pleating with a minimum of measuring and marking by "eyeing" in the pleats; however, in most instances, careful planning, calculating the number and sizes of the pleats, and clear and precise marking will lead to the best results.

Since so much of the layout and marking, as well as the folding itself, is done from the wrong side of the fabric, it is important to develop a consciousness of working both sides of the fabric at the same time. Markings are put on the wrong side to keep the good side clean and neat, but it is necessary to remember that the good side is what will be seen and that the pleats must be put in so that they will look right and function correctly from the good side. There is little that is quite as frustrating as a row of pleats that has to be redone simply because they were folded in backwards.

Knife Pleating

The knife pleat is a single fold of cloth turned over on itself either to the right or left (see Fig. 9–7). These pleats may be pressed flat or left unpressed; they are held in place by stitching at the waistline. Two common variations of the knife pleat are the box pleat and the inverted box pleat as shown in Fig. 9–7. The *box pleat* is two knife pleats turned away from each other on the good side of the fabric with the inner folds meeting at the inside of the garment; the *inverted box pleat* has two knife pleats turned toward each other on the good side and the inner folds turned away from the center on the inside of the skirt—the reverse of the box pleat.

Knife-pleated skirts can be evenly pleated; that is, the exposed surface and the depth of each pleat are made equal, and the pleats are usually distributed evenly around the body. These pleats may be unpressed for a soft appearance or pressed for a crisp appearance. Pressed pleats are time-consuming, since each pleat must be on the straight grain of the fabric to fall properly. Each pleat must be carefully marked, pinned, and ironed before the pleats are basted to hold them in position while the construction of the skirt is finished; therefore, it is often advisable to buy fabric already pleated or to have the fabric pleated commercially if the budget allows. If pressed pleating is done in the costume shop, it is unlikely that the typical shop ironing equipment can set the pleats sharply enough or hard enough for the durability desired. If possible, then, the pleated fabric, with the control basting in place, should also be steamed commercially.

Knife pleats can also be folded so that the pleat depth is greater than the distance between pleats on the outside; this is referred to as overlap pleating (see Fig. 9–7). Overlap pleating is necessary when the circumference of the hem is too large to be evenly pleated to the waist measurement, a situation that is determined by the design and the amount of fullness required, as discussed under Creating Fullness at the Hem. Since pressed pleats are made to lie smoothly over the hips, they also need to be overlapped slightly at the waist to fit properly at both points.

An additional factor that must be considered in all knife-pleated skirts is the way the grain of the fabric falls when the skirt is on the body. Preliminary pleating is done on a flat surface; however, the body is round, and some of the pleats will pucker or puff out when taken around the body. This is corrected by "swinging" the pleats to adjust the grain. The effect of swinging pleats is to create a curve for the waistline as the other skirt patterns have. The pro-

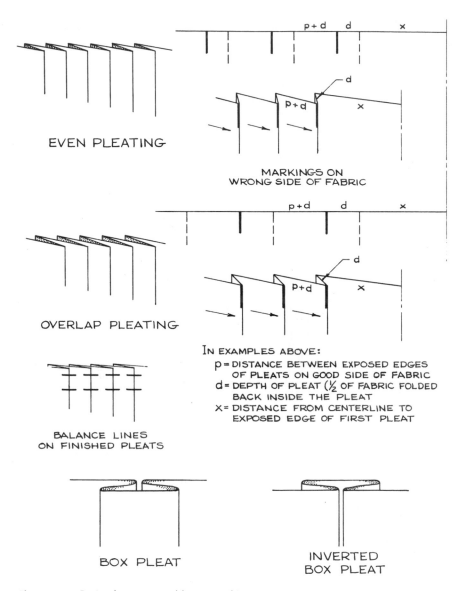

EVEN PLEATING

MARKINGS ON
WRONG SIDE OF FABRIC

OVERLAP PLEATING

IN EXAMPLES ABOVE:

p = DISTANCE BETWEEN EXPOSED EDGES
OF PLEATS ON GOOD SIDE OF FABRIC
d = DEPTH OF PLEAT (½ OF FABRIC FOLDED
BACK INSIDE THE PLEAT
x = DISTANCE FROM CENTERLINE TO
EXPOSED EDGE OF FIRST PLEAT

BALANCE LINES
ON FINISHED PLEATS

BOX PLEAT

INVERTED
BOX PLEAT

Figure 9-7 Basic pleat types and layout markings.

cess for swinging pleats is discussed later in the chapter.

CALCULATING THE NUMBER AND SIZES OF PLEATS. Knife pleats for evenly pleated skirts can vary in pleat depth and number in a garment; however, the ratio of 3 to 1

for each pleat remains constant. In other words, a knife pleat 1 in. (2.5 cm) deep requires an additional 2 in. (5 cm) of fabric for a total of 3 in. (7.5 cm) to create a 1 in. pleat. A ¾ in. (2 cm) deep pleat requires 2¼ in. (5.6 cm) of fabric; 1½ in. (3.8 cm) deep pleat requires 4½ in. (11.5 cm) of

fabric; 2 in. (5 cm) deep pleat, 6 in. (15 cm) of fabric, and so on.

The minimum amount of fabric required for an evenly pleated skirt can be determined by using the 3:1 ratio and applying it to the waist measurement if the pleats are to be unpressed or to the hip measurement if the pleats are to be pressed.

The formula for determining the amount of fabric required for a skirt with *unpressed pleats* is: "waist" measurement plus 1 in. for ease times 3. For example, add 1 in. to the waist measurement, 1 plus 27 = 28, for the working circumference. Take this figure and multiply it by 3 to determine the total width of fabric required for the skirt:

28 times 3 = 84 in. of width required.

Since 84 in. is not a typical fabric width, two or more widths of fabric will need to be stitched together to make a total of 84. Add ½ in. seam allowance to each fabric edge for each seam in the skirt; these seams will probably be hidden in the pleats.

The number of pleats in the skirt is determined by dividing the working circumference ("waist" plus 1 in.) by the depth of the pleat. If the pleat depth is 1 in., the number of pleats will be the same as the working circumference. If the pleat depth is more or less than 1 in., the number of pleats is computed by dividing the pleat depth into the working circumference.

Examples: 28 divided by 0.75 (¾ in.) = 37.33 pleats

28 divided by 2 in. = 14 pleats

In the first instance, the number of pleats is not a whole number; therefore, the pleat depth can be changed to equal a whole number, or some of the pleats can be slightly deeper to accommodate the waist with 37 pleats. If this adjustment is done, the deeper pleats should be located at the back of the skirt for a better appearance. If the number of pleats is a whole number, no adjustment in the pleat depth is necessary.

Since the box pleat and the inverted box pleat are knife pleats facing in different directions, the amount of fabric required and the number of pleats is the same as that computed for straight knife pleats.

For *pressed pleat skirts,* the amount of fabric and number of pleats is determined in the same manner. However, the "hip" measurement is used instead of the "waist" measurement with 1 in. added to the "hip" measurement for ease. In pressed pleated skirts, the depth of the pleats at the waist must be increased since the waist is smaller than the hips.

To determine the amount of fabric, take the "hip" measurement plus 1 times 3 for the amount of fabric; then determine the number of pleats by dividing the working circumference by the pleat depth.

Examples: 39 plus 1 = 40 times 3 = 120 in. of fabric

40 divided by 0.75 in. = 53.33 pleats

40 divided by 2 in. = 20 pleats

To make the adjustments in the pleats at the waist, the distance between pleated edges will be smaller than at the hips, and the depth of the pleats will be greater, so the pleats will overlap each other inside the skirt. To determine the approximate distance between pleats on the exposed surface, divide the working circumference of the waist by the number of pleats at the hips.

Examples: 28 divided by 53.33 = 0.525 as the distance between the exposed edges of the pleats; the pleat depth

will be approximately ⅞ in. 28 divided by 20 = 1.4 distance; the pleat depth will be approximately 2¼ in.

Since the amount of fabric in each pleat is the same at the waist as it is at the hips, the depth of the pleat is determined by subtracting the exposed surface dimension from the total fabric in the pleat and using half of that result as the pleat depth, since the fabric is folded back on itself behind the exposed surface. Therefore, in the first example, the surface distance of the pleats would be approximately ½ in.; since this is based on a pleat that is intended to be ¾ in. deep at the hipline, it contains 2¼ in. of fabric. Subtracting the ½ in. from the 2¼ in. leaves 1¾ in. to be folded in half for the ⅞ in. pleat depth at the waist. In the second example, the approximately 1½ in. surface is subtracted from the 6 in. of fabric in the 2 in. pleat for a waist pleat depth of 2¼ in.

OVERLAP PLEATING.   If fullness greater than regular pleating is required in the skirt, the ratio must be changed, the pleats will overlap, and the depth of the pleat will be greater than the exposed surface of the pleat. Full skirts for many period garments, for example, often require more fullness than the 3:1 ratio of the evenly pleated skirt.

These full pleated skirts are often made by joining several widths of fabric together and then pleating that to fit the waist. Consequently, the width of the fabric is often a factor in the fullness of the skirt. Most full-length pleated skirts need at least 130 in. (325 cm) or more at the hem. Three lengths of 44 in. or 45 in. fabric will give about 132 in. (330 cm) of width after seam allowances have been taken; four lengths of the same fabric will give a total of about 176 in. (440 cm) after seam allowance.

There are two methods of knife pleating to distribute the fullness at the waist.

One method is to take the width of the fabric, stitched together as a rectangle, and pleat one-half of the fabric to one-half of the working circumference of the waist by eye. That is, pin the pleats in position by trial and error on half of the skirt and then duplicate the pleating on the other half. With a little experience, this method can be executed quickly.

The second method involves computing the amount of fabric in each pleat. This figure does not always make a precise dimension to work with; therefore, the figure needs to be rounded to the nearest fraction for easy pleating. The excess which results is added to the pleats in the back of the skirt. Another variable when computing pleats is the type of fabric being pleated. This is accounted for and adjusted when working with the cloth and setting in the pleats.

The second method requires determining the number of pleats for the skirt. This is accomplished by arbitrarily determining what the distance between the pleats on the surface will be and dividing that dimension into the waist. If the distance is 1 in. between, the number of pleats will equal the waist (waist divided by pleat distance = number of pleats).

Next divide the hem circumference by the number of pleats to determine the amount of fabric in each pleat (hem divided by the number of pleats = fabric in pleat).

Subtract the distance between the surface edges of the pleats from the fabric in each pleat; the result is twice the pleat depth, so divide by 2 to determine the pleat depth (fabric in pleat minus pleat distance = twice pleat depth; one-half of which equals the depth of each pleat).

Examples: A. 28 divided by 1 = 28 pleats

168 divided by 28 = 6 in. of fabric per pleat

6 minus 1 = 5; ½ of 5 = 2½ in. pleat depth.

B.   28 divided by 0.5 (½ in.) = 56 pleats
168 divided by 56 = 3 in. of fabric per pleat
3 minus 0.5 = 2½; ½ of 2½ = 1¼ in. pleat depth

Many period garments for women often feature no pleating across the abdomen; this section is usually about 8 in. (20.5 cm) wide to coincide with the fitting darts or seams of the bodice. To determine the number of pleats for this style of skirt, subtract the length of the unpleated section from the hem circumference of the skirt as well as from the waist. Use the formula for overlap pleating to determine the number of pleats, the fabric in each pleat, and the pleat depth.

Examples: A.   1 in. between pleats; 28 in. working circumference
28 minus 8 = 20, the adjusted waist to be pleated
168 minus 8 = 160, the adjusted hem
20 divided by 1 = 20 pleats
160 divided by 20 = 8 in. of fabric per pleat
8 minus 1 = 7; one-half of 7 = 3.5 in. deep pleats

B.   ½ in. between pleats
20 divided by 0.5 = 40 pleats
160 divided by 40 = 4 in. of fabric per pleat
4 minus 0.5 = 3.5; one-half of 3.5 = 1.75 in. deep pleats

PRELIMINARY PLEATING—UNPRESSED PLEATS.   Normally, the pleats are folded away from the center-front on the good side of the skirt for a more flattering line. Marking for the pleats will be done on the inside of the skirt so the lines will not be visible on the outside. This means that the pleating on the inside will be reversed, folded toward the center (see Fig. 9–7).

1.   Stitch the lengths of fabric together at the selvages, leaving one seam open which will be the center-back. This allows the fabric to be laid out flat as one large rectangle for easier pleating.

2.   Working on the wrong side of the skirt at the waistline, mark the center-front line with a hand-basting stitch 8 in. to 10 in. long. If the center-front of the skirt is to be left unpleated, draw a broken line, about 1 in. long, at each side of the center where the pleating is to begin, usually 4 in. (10 cm) from the centerline.

3.   To mark the pleating for half of the skirt, start at the broken line which locates the edge of the first pleat; from the broken line, measure the pleat depth and mark it with a solid line about 1 in. long. Take the pleat depth plus the distance between pleats and measure over from the solid line and draw another broken line as shown in Fig. 9–7. Then take the pleat depth and measure over from the broken line and draw a solid line; repeat the process to the end of the waist. The pattern should end with the pleat depth plus the distance between pleats to provide an overlap for the closing.

4.   Repeat step 3 on the other half of the skirt.

5.   Working on the wrong side of the skirt fabric, fold the pleats toward center, as indicated by the arrows in Fig. 9–7; the broken line is a foldline for the edge of the pleat that will be exposed on the outside of the skirt; the solid line is the foldline at the depth of the pleat. The pleats on the wrong side of the skirt will be folded toward the center and away from center on the good side. Note that the center-front and center-back pleats will be box pleats.

6. Pin each pleat on both folds, to hold the pleats in position.

The skirt is now ready to be put on a form so that the pleats can be swung to complete the pleating preparation for the fitting.

PRELIMINARY PLEATING-PRESSED PLEATS. The process is the same as for unpressed pleats; however, the markings for the pleats are located on the hipline rather than at the waist since the pleat depth will be greater at the waist than at the hips. The markings should also be located at the hem and at intervals between hips and hem.

The most efficient method of making pressed pleats is to work on an ironing board with the iron. Each pleat should be carefully pinned or basted and pressed from the hipline to the hem, then the waist portion of the pleat, which is deeper, is pinned and pressed. It is essential to observe and maintain the straight grain of the fabric.

Skirts with pressed pleats should be checked on the dress form to make sure that the use of the grain is correct. If there are puckers or pulls, the pleats need to be shifted and re-pressed.

After the skirt has been fitted and finished, the pleats should be pressed commercially for longer lasting and sharper pleats.

SWINGING PLEATS. All pleated skirts should be checked on a dress form before the pleats are stitched in place to make sure the pleats will fall properly. Maintaining the proper grain in the pleating is very important to the appearance of the garment. Since the skirt is made up of unshaped rectangles which are stitched together and pleated into a circle at the waist, it is often necessary to "swing" the pleats to prevent the folds from buckling and sagging. The straight-cut skirt pattern illustrated in Fig. 9-1 has a slightly curved waistline; the pleated skirt will also have a slightly curved waistline after the pleats have been properly swung.

It is easy to identify the pleats which need to be adjusted when the skirt is on the dress form. These pleats will pucker, puff out, or tend to fall toward the front or back of the skirt rather than fall on a straight line. The center-front and center-back pleats generally do not need to be swung; the pleats at the sides and over the full part of the hips do need some adjustment. The pleats are swung with the skirt on the dress form.

To adjust the pleats, the angle of the folds at the waist is shifted until the pleat falls in a smooth, straight line from the waist. Experimenting with the pleats and watching the fabric carefully will quickly reveal how the swinging of the pleats improves the appearance of the skirt.

The angle of the folds of pleats which have been swung is shown on printed patterns and period patterns with "balance lines." These lines are drawn perpendicular to the pleat foldlines and are matched up when the pleat is folded into its proper position. Balance lines can also be drawn on the drafted skirt, with the pleats folded in the proper angles, by drawing two straight lines across each pleat at the fold as shown in Fig. 9-7. One line is not really sufficient because the pleat could still twist. If the pleats are opened up for any reason, merely bringing the balance lines back together will realign the pleat in its correct position.

Once the pleats have been swung and carefully pinned to hold each pleat securely, remove the skirt from the form and draw the balance lines on the inside of the garment. Machine-baste the pleats in place for the fitting. Some additional adjustment may be needed in the fitting, since the dress form is not likely to have the same configurations as the actor.

All knife-pleated skirts need to have some pleats swung to get the best appearance. Cartridge-pleated skirts do not require swung pleats because the construction and appearance of the skirt is different from knife pleating.

Cartridge Pleats

Essentially, *cartridge pleating* is controlled, even gathering used to condense fullness into a small dimension. The fabric is gathered into a series of loops as shown in Fig. 9–8. Cartridge pleats are usually attached perpendicularly to the bodice or waistband; in other words, they are placed butt-ended to the waist so the skirt is held out slightly from the body. This method of pleating is often used with sixteenth-century skirt supports such as the bum-roll (see Chap. 16), or it may be used simply to condense a great deal of fabric into a small waist while providing fullness at the hips and hem.

To make cartridge pleats, the top edge of the fabric must be finished to conceal the cut edge, since these pleats will not be flattened and stitched to the bodice or waistband in the conventional manner. The finished edge must also be marked in regular increments for even gathering, which, in turn, must be done by hand. Two rows of gathering stitches are required to control the pleats. After the stitching is complete, the fabric is gathered into the required measurement and each pleat is hand-stitched to the bodice or waistband.

This process is somewhat involved, but the results are worth the effort, for no other technique will provide the same appearance.

PREPARATION FOR CARTRIDGE PLEAT-ING. Since a function of this method of pleating is to have the skirt stand out from the waist, the top edge is usually interfaced with a medium weight or heavyweight interfacing material. We also usually make a matching skirt of lining taffeta, which serves as a petticoat, and attach it to the good skirt as part of the finishing at the waist. The skirt should be pleated before it is stitched closed at the final seam.

1. Cut a strip of interfacing 3 in. (7.5 cm) wide and long enough to match the full length of the top of the skirt fabric.

2. Pin the taffeta petticoat to the right side of the skirt at the top; then pin the interfacing to the skirt over the taffeta and machine-stitch the layers together.

3. Turn the interfacing and taffeta inside and press the seam.

4. With matching thread, topstitch the layers together at the seam and bottom edge of the interfacing to control the three layers.

5. Determine the depth of the pleat; we often grade the pleats from ¾ in. (2 cm) at the front to 1 in. or 1½ in. (2.5 or 3.8 cm) in the back. As with other period skirts, the front section is often left unpleated over the abdomen.

6. On the inside of the skirt, mark the center-front of the skirt with a basting stitch about 10 in. long on the lengthwise grain. Then measure and mark the increments determined for the pleated depth (see Fig. 9–8). These marks should be about 1 in. long and perpendicular to the edge.

7. Measure down ¼ in. (0.6 cm) from the top edge and draw a line parallel to the edge; measure down 1 in. (2.5 cm) from the top and draw a line parallel to the edge. Where these lines intersect, the increment mark specifies where the hand-stitching goes. Both the parallel lines and the increments are necessary for the even gather required for cartridge pleating.

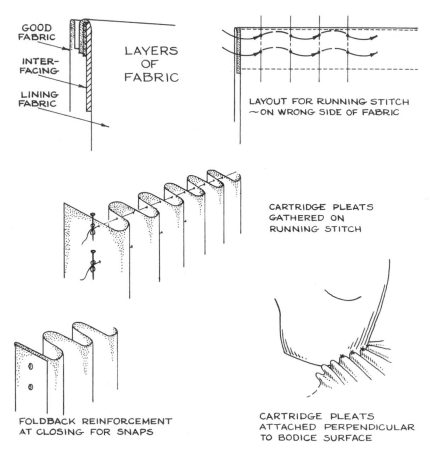

GOOD FABRIC

INTER-FACING

LINING FABRIC

LAYERS OF FABRIC

LAYOUT FOR RUNNING STITCH ~ON WRONG SIDE OF FABRIC

CARTRIDGE PLEATS GATHERED ON RUNNING STITCH

FOLDBACK REINFORCEMENT AT CLOSING FOR SNAPS

CARTRIDGE PLEATS ATTACHED PERPENDICULAR TO BODICE SURFACE

Figure 9–8   Process of making cartridge pleats.

8. Thread two needles with button thread and do a running stitch where the marks intersect as shown in Fig. 9–8. Both needles should be advanced evenly in the stitching, and the ends of the thread should not be knotted. As with any gathering stitch, the ends of the threads are wrapped in a figure 8 around a straight pin so the gathering can be adjusted easily.

9. Complete the stitching to the closing on each side of the centerline. The last stitch should have the needles coming through the marks from the good side so that the last small portion to the seam edge can be folded back onto the pleat to be-

come a self-facing reinforcement for the closing. Since the skirt will be attached to the bodice, which has its own secure closing device, there is usually little strain on the closing of the pleated fabric, so snaps are generally sufficient to hold the skirt pleats closed and to blend the closing into the other pleats.

10. Gather the skirt to the waist measurement. Do not tie-off or cut the gathering threads; wrap them around a straight pin which is perpendicular to the edge. These threads are not tied and cut until after the skirt is attached to the bodice or waistband.

152

ATTACHING CARTRIDGE PLEATS. Using a heavyweight thread, stitch the top of each loop to the outside of the bodice or waistband with a cross stitch as described in Chap. 3. Repeat the process at the bottom of each loop. Since cartridge-pleated skirts are heavy due to the amount of fabric in the skirt, they are usually used mounted on pieces that are interfaced and lined, or on boned bodices. Otherwise the weight will pull the pieces and create wrinkles or pull lines.

THE WAISTBAND

The waistband is essentially a finishing or binding for the top edge of a skirt, slacks, or other waist-supported garments. In its simplest form, it is a strip of fabric cut in a long rectangle and folded along its length to sandwich the raw top edges of the garment between its two sides.

The waistband can be cut on either the crosswise or lengthwise grain unless the pattern on the fabric requires a specific direction of the grain. The width of the band should be double the desired finished width plus seam allowance. In other words, if the band is to be 1½ in. (3.8 cm) finished, cut the band 4 in. (10 cm) wide: 3 in. (7.5 cm) for the finished band and ½ in. (1.3 cm) for seam allowance on each edge. The length of the band should be 3 in. (7.5 cm) longer than the waist measurement to allow for ease, overlap, and seam allowance.

If a fitted skirt or other garment fits well over the top of the hips, there will not be much strain on the waistband from the weight of the garment. However, if the fabric of the garment is heavy, or if the garment, such as a skirt of unpressed pleats, has a loose fit over the hips, it may be worthwhile to include an interfacing in the waistband for reinforcement. Interfacing can also be valuable as stiffening if the fabric is lightweight or has little body of its own.

An interfacing is usually necessary also if the finished waistband is to be wider than about 1½ inches (3.8 cm). A wider waistband is cut as two pieces, stitched together along the length, and turned to form the sides which sandwich the garment fabric. A wider waistband may also have to be cut in a curve to conform to the body, and in some cases it may have to be cut on the bias to provide a certain amount of give as it wraps around the body.

The waistband may be attached before the first fitting, but usually—and especially with pleated skirts—it is better to wait until all the seam and pleat adjustments have been made in the fitting before adding the waistband.

To attach the waistband to a skirt, match the center-front of the waistband to the center-front of the skirt with right sides together. Stitch the waistband to the skirt; fold the band up and press the seam. Next, fold the band to its finished width and press the band. Turn the inside seam allowance under with the skirt waistline sandwiched between the sides of the band and stitch it in place by hand or machine. Slacks or other garments may take the alignment from the center-back, but otherwise the attachment process is the same.

When attaching the waistband, be very careful of the grain of the waistband fabric. If the grain is not aligned, or if the two sides of the waistband are not aligned with each other, the fabric can twist or draw into creases at the seam.

ten

basic slacks patterns

Over the centuries, this garment has had many names, some of which are utilitarian such as *trousers, pants,* or *slacks;* others are descriptive terms such as *slops, baggies, melon-hose*, or "unmentionables." The size, shape, and length of this garment have altered many times in the course of fashion history. Decorum has also been very much a part of the history; Roman men considered pants to be "barbaric" and would not wear them, but there was quite an uproar from men in the early twentieth century when women appeared in public in pants.

However, regardless of the individual name or style given to the garment, slacks are a basic part of the wardrobe, and many variations are possible from a basic pattern. This is as true for women's styles as men's, since women have worn some version of pants in several periods.

The modern basic pair of slacks is generally cut from two pattern pieces with the back section wider than the front to allow for the roundness of the hips and the backs of the legs. To accommodate the fullness of the hips, the back crotch-curve is cut higher in the back to allow for ease when sitting. If the crotch is not cut full enough or deeper than the front, the pants ride down below the waist when sitting or bending.

The crotch-curve and the grain of the fabric are key factors in the fit of the slacks. Generally, the upper front section of the crotch is cut on the straight grain along with the leg of the slacks. The length and fullness of the slack leg is determined by the design requirements.

The "rise," which is the distance from the fork of the legs to the waist, is established by the crotch-curve and is important for style as well as for comfort. Normal rise indicates that the pants are fitted to the natural waist; low-rise pants such as hip-huggers are fitted below the natural waistline; and high-rise pants fit above the natural waist. Many dance pants feature a high-rise.

Slacks for theatrical costumes can be closed in the back, at the side seam, or in the center-front, depending on the style and period. This is true even of men's slacks, since the front "fly" closing was not in general use until after 1840. The typical closing for men's pants in the eighteenth and early nineteenth centuries was a flap, or "fall," such as one sees today in the traditional sailor pants.

Commercial patterns for modern slacks are available and work very well for contemporary clothing needs. The patterns for men's slacks include instructions for cutting and making the fly opening and, if contemporary slacks are needed, the commercial patterns are simple to use. Therefore, a selection of these patterns in various sizes is basic to a pattern library.

It is relatively simple to draft a basic pattern for slacks and to achieve a good, comfortable fit. The following instructions for drafting the basic slacks pattern are also adaptable for any period garments, and some standard variations are discussed later in this chapter.

The pattern is laid out on fabric or paper that is about 8 in. (20.5 cm) longer than the "waist-to-floor" measurement and 12 in. (30.5 cm) wider than one-half of the "hip measurement."

Basic Slacks—Front

1. As shown in Fig. 10-1, draw a right-angle line across the width of the fabric and at least 4 in. (10 cm) below the top edge. Draw another line on the straight grain and parallel to and about 4 in. (10 cm) from the side edge of the fabric to intersect the right-angle line. Set point A at the intersection of the lines.

2. To establish the hipline, from point A measure down 8 in. (20.5 cm) for female or 9 in. (23 cm) for male and set point B. Draw a line through point B parallel to the right-angle line.

3. On the hipline, from point B measure one-quarter of the "hip" measurement plus 1 in. (2.5 cm) to set point C. On the right-angle line, from point A measure one-quarter of the "waist" measurement plus 1½ in. (3.8 cm); then measure up ½ in. (1.3 cm) to set point D. Using a french curve to shape the lines, connect A–D for the front waistline and D–C for the upper-front side seam.

DRAFTING THE BASIC SLACKS PATTERN

4. To establish the front crotch-curve, measure 3 in. (7.5 cm) down from point B and 3½ in. (9 cm) over toward the edge of the fabric to set point E. Use a french curve to shape the line to connect A–E; notice that line A–E does not pass through point B.

5. To shape the front inseam below the crotch, measure from the right-angle line on an extension of line A–B the length of the "waist-to-knee" measurement and set point F. From point F, measure 1 in. (2.5 cm) toward the edge of the fabric to set point G. Use a french curve to shape the line to connect E–G.

6. To establish the length of the leg, draw a line through point C parallel to line A–F. Take the "waist-to-floor" measurement plus 2 in. (5 cm) and measure from point D through point C and down the new reference line to set point H.

7. To complete the front leg pattern, measure 1 in. (2.5 cm) across from point H to set point J; extend line G–F parallel to the right-angle line and on it measure from line C–H across 1 in. (2.5 cm) to set point K; extend line H–J as the location of the leg hem edge and transfer the length of line G–K to it by measuring across from J to set point L. Connect C–K with a

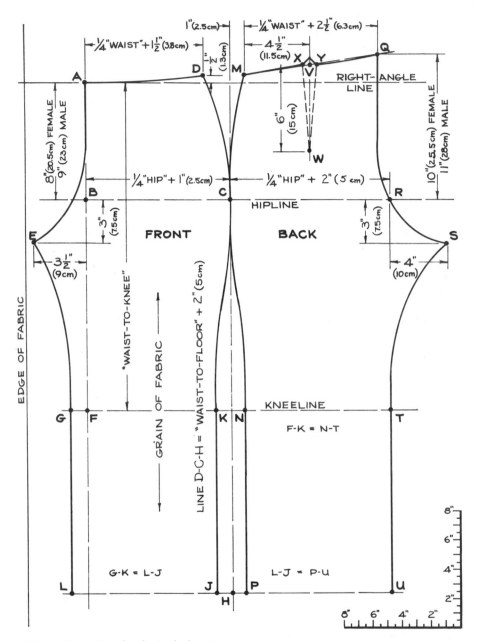

Figure 10-1 Complete basic slacks pattern.

156

slightly reversing curve and K–J with a straight line to complete the front side seam. Connect G–L to complete the front inseam, and connect L–J to complete the hem edge.

Basic Slacks—Back

1. On the right-angle line, measure 1 in. (2.5 cm) across from an extension of line H–C; then measure up ½ in. (1.3 cm) to set point M.

2. To complete the back side seam, measure 1 in. (2.5 cm) across from line H–C on the kneeline to set point N; on an extension of line L–H, measure 1 in. (2.5 cm) across from point H to set point P. Use a french curve to connect M–C–N and connect N–P with a straight line.

3. To establish the preliminary back waistline, measure across from point M one-quarter of the "waist" measurement plus 2½ in. (6.3 cm); measure up from the *hipline* 10 in. (25.5 cm) for female or 11 in. (28 cm) for male and set point Q where the measurements intersect. Connect M–Q with a straight preliminary line which will be altered when the fitting dart is added.

4. To complete the center-back line and the back crotch-curve, measure across on the hipline from point C one-quarter of the "hip" measurement plus 2 in. (5 cm) to set point R; from point R, measure down 3 in. (7.5 cm) and across 4 in. (10 cm) to set point S. Use a french curve to shape the line to connect Q–R–S.

5. To complete the back inseam and hem edge, set point T by measuring the length of line G–K across on the kneeline from point N; set point U on an extension of line L–P by measuring the length of line L–J across from point P. Connect S–T with a curved line and T–U with a straight line for the back inseam, and connect P–U with a straight line for the hem edge.

6. To locate the fitting dart, measure 4½ in. (11.5 cm) from point M and set point V on the preliminary back waistline.

a. Drop a centerline on the straight grain from point V; measure down 6 in. (15 cm) to set point W.

b. Measure ½ in. (1.3 cm) to each side of point V to set points X and Y. Connect X–W and Y–W as the stitching lines for the dart; lines X–W and Y–W must be equal in length.

c. Extend centerline W–V to ½ in. beyond the preliminary waistline and finalize the back waistline as shown in Fig. 10–1.

THE WAISTBAND. The waistband for slacks can be cut and attached in the same manner as the skirt waistband described in Chap. 9. The waistband can also be used as a casing for elastic or a drawstring.

A variation of the basic waistband that is often used on men's trousers is a split in the waistband at the center-back for a smoother fit at the small of the back and easy adjustment of the waist and center-back seams. Belt loops often have to be added to the waistband also; place them at the points of greatest downward strain and either attach them to the surface of the waistband after it is in place or hide the ends of the loops in the seams as the waistband is being assembled and attached.

When belt loops and a belt are used, or whenever the waistband fabric needs stiffening or reinforcing, include an interfacing that is equal to the width of the finished waistband. Secure the interfacing against slipping inside the band by stay-stitching it at the folded edge of a one-piece band and to the seam edge. Then attach the waistband to the slacks with the stay-stitching next to the body.

CUTTING AND PREPARATION FOR FITTING. Before cutting the pattern, check the draft against the measurements. The combined hipline for the two pieces should be 3 in. (7.5 cm) longer than one-half of the "hip" measurement, and the back hipline should be 1 in. (2.5 cm) longer than the front. Also check the length of the pants. The draft should be at least 2 in. (5 cm) longer than the "waist-to-floor" measurement. If the leg is not long enough, extend the inseams and side seams as needed. Cut two of each of the front and back pattern pieces; the draft is for one leg only.

After the pattern is cut, determine where the opening is to be and plan to start

the stitching on that seam 8 in. (20.5 cm) below the waist (line A–E is the center-front seam, and Q–S is the back seam). With the right sides of the two front pieces together, machine-baste the front crotch-curve; then stitch the back fitting darts and the back crotch-curve. Next join the back to the front with the right sides of the fabric together. Baste the inseams together, matching the crotch seams; then baste the side seams together and turn them right side out to complete the slacks for the fitting.

VARIATIONS IN THE BASIC SLACKS

The basic variations include altering the fullness in the legs of the slacks, changing the length, and altering the position of the waist on the body.

Low-Rise Slacks

As indicated, pants with a low rise do not reach the normal waistline, but stop near the top of the hips. Therefore, the distance from the hipline to the top of the pattern is shorter than indicated in the pattern draft. The measurement for the waistline is also altered, since the body widens from the waist to the hip, and the pattern must allow for this. At the same time, it is very important to keep the waistline curve at the back waist to allow for the fullness of the buttocks and for movement. If the back waistline shape is shortened too much, the pants will pull down when the actor sits or kneels, exposing more than is desired and making the garment uncomfortable. The tighter the pants at the hips and thighs, the greater the need for ease in the rise.

One method for obtaining low-rise slacks is to draft the pattern as outlined and alter it in the fitting to the desired style and fit. As with any garment, it is essential to have the actor move around to check the

ease in the costume. When fitting the pants, it is important to have the actor sit and kneel to make sure there is ample cut in the rise as well as sufficient fullness for the legs.

A second method of adapting the draft for a low rise is to shorten the distance from the hipline to the waistline on the pattern itself (see Fig. 10–2A). Keep in mind that the "waist" measurement will no longer be applicable as a working dimension.

The easiest technique is to lay out the complete basic slacks pattern, including the fitting dart, to determine the new rise dimension, and make the adjustments directly on the basic pattern layout. For the typical low-rise slacks that fit just at the top of the hips, this new rise dimension can be calculated by subtracting the "waist" measurement from the "hip" measurement and using half of that result for the "rise" above the hipline. This "rise" measurement should be applied only at the side seam, and the rest of the waistline curve should be kept in proper proportion to the body.

The "rise" can, of course, be higher or lower as called for by the design. But a general rule is that the point of the center-

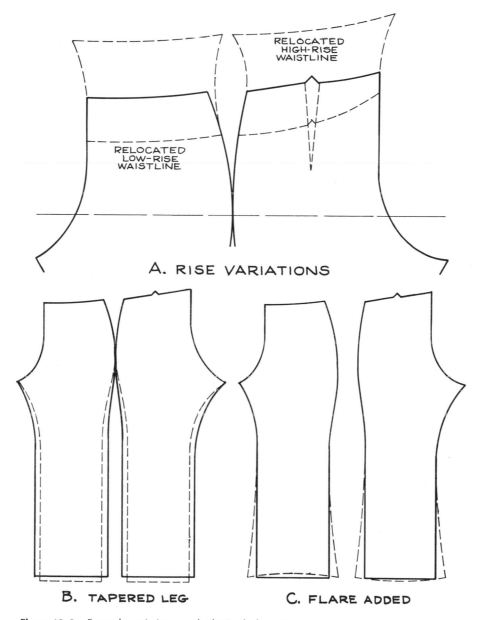

RELOCATED HIGH-RISE WAISTLINE

RELOCATED LOW-RISE WAISTLINE

A. RISE VARIATIONS

B. TAPERED LEG

C. FLARE ADDED

Figure 10-2 Example variations on the basic slacks pattern.

front should be ½ in. (1.3 cm) lower than the point of the side seam, and the center-back point should be enough higher to cover the body curves at the back (see Fig. 10-2A).

Do not change the drafted fitting dart

except in the actual fitting procedure. Allow the new waistline curve to cut across the fitting dart as it is laid out in the basic slacks pattern. This will allow the hip contours to conform properly to the body.

High-Rise Slacks

Pants with a high rise can be extended from the normal waistline to the rib cage or as high as the design specifies. The key aspect to allow for is the shaping of the lower portion of the upper torso, which is done with fitting darts tapered at both ends, and shaping the side seams to conform with the waist indentation. Pants with a very high rise are often made of stretch fabric to fit snugly. They can be supported with suspenders since the upper torso is wider than the waist, and gravity takes over to make the upper part of the pants roll down.

To extend the rise above the normal waistline, extend the pattern the desired number of inches above the hipline and add 2 in. (5 cm) to both the front and back waistline dimensions as shown in Fig. 10–2A. Final shaping of the seams and darts can be done in the fitting.

Adapting Leg Shapes

Several variations in the leg shapes are possible. The length can range from shorts to floor length, and the fullness of the leg can also be altered. When altering the shape of the leg on a commercial or drafted pattern, the grain line and the proportions of fullness between the front and back leg must be maintained to prevent the seams from twisting around the leg. The fullness at the hipline must also be maintained for proper fit; therefore, alteration in the leg starts at the hipline or below rather than at the waist.

The shape of the leg can be changed to a narrow or tapered leg, or to a wide or flared leg, by changing the dimensions at the leg hem and shaping the side and inseams to conform with the hem. As a general guideline, the finished hem circumference for an average straight leg is about 18 in. to 19 in. (46 cm to 48.5 cm), the average tapered leg is about 15 in. to 17 in. (38 cm to 43 cm), and the flared leg is about 20 in. to 25 in. (51 cm to 63.5 cm). The exact amount at the bottom is determined by the height and size of the actor and the proportions of the pants when they are on the actor. The dimensions of a flared leg will not have the same appearance on a short, heavy-set actor as on a tall, slender one.

TAPERING THE LEG. When taking the fullness out of the pant leg, be sure to allow for the fullness and expansion of the thigh and calf muscles. The tapering can be done in the fitting by taking in the side seam and the inseam simultaneously. Working with both seams is necessary in order to keep the proper balance.

The pant leg can also be tapered when the pattern is drafted. The side seam and the inseam can be set in at the knee and hem as shown in Fig. 10–2B. When tapering the pant leg, it is advisable to add some length to the leg to allow for ease since fitted pant legs tend to ride up when the actor is seated.

ADDING FLARE TO THE LEG. Depending on the design, fullness can be added to the legs of the pants from any point below the hipline as long as the crotch-curve is not altered. As with tapered legs, keeping the proper grain line and balance is important; therefore, an equal amount of fullness should be added to both the side seam and the inseam.

However, for a flared leg, the dimension of the back hem edge should be slightly longer, about 1 in. (2.5 cm), than the hem edge of the front pattern piece. Divide the flared-leg hem circumference accordingly and add equal amounts to each seam edge at the hem. Connect the ends of the new hem lengths to the original seams as shown in Fig. 10–2C; the exact points of connection to the original seams will vary according to the design.

Adapting the Length

As with sleeves, when adjusting the length of slacks, the changes must be kept in proportion with the leg. In other words, the pattern should not be lengthened or shortened just at the bottom. To check the proportions of the leg and determine where and how much to adjust the pattern length, compare the rise to the actor's "rise" measurement, the length from waist to knee to that measurement, and the knee to the floor to that dimension; adjust the pattern where necessary to fit the actor properly.

The slack pattern can be adapted to any length by determining the desired length plus hem allowance and cutting the pattern at that point. As a rule of thumb, leave some excess both in length and fullness which can be adjusted in the fitting and checked for necessary ease and movement. For example, if shorts are to be patterned, keep the side seams in line C–H (see Fig. 10–1), rather than tapering them in as you would for long pants. This is to allow for the fullness of the thigh, and the final shape of the side seams can be determined in the fitting.

KNEE-LENGTH SLACKS. The basic slacks pattern draft can be adapted in length to make simple knee-length breeches. Primarily the alteration requires additional allowance and shaping at the kneeline to get the proper fit and appearance. If the pants are to be worn below the knee, the front of the leg must be longer than the back, and some fullness (which can be eased or pleated into the circumference of the hem below the knee) is necessary for the pants to stay in place while the leg is bent. Knee pants that are fitted to the leg

below the knee must also have an opening at the side seam to allow the foot to go through the hem.

RESHAPING THE KNEE

1. As shown in Fig. 10–3, complete the layout of the basic slacks pattern draft to below the hipline and crotch-curves. Carry the layout down far enough on the leg to locate points G and K and points N and T on the kneeline as shown in Fig. 10–1; these points from the original draft will provide references for the adjustments to knee-length slacks.

2. Relocate the new kneeline by adding 2 in. (5 cm) to the "waist-to-knee" measurement represented by line D–C–K; draw a new kneeline across both front and back pattern layouts.

3. To establish the new width on the front kneeline, take one-half of the "below-knee" measurement plus 3 in. (7.5 cm) for seam allowance and ease, and center that length on the kneeline of the leg front. Set points G^1 and K^1 to locate the ends of the measurement.

4. To establish the new width on the back kneeline, take one-half of the "below-knee" measurement plus 2 in. (5 cm) and center that length on the kneeline of the leg back. Set points N^1 and T^1 to locate the ends of that measurement. Note that these new points may coincide with the original widths, but the new points will be 2 in. (5 cm) lower.

5. With curves similar to those in the original draft, connect E–G^1, C–K^1, C–N^1, and S–T^1.

6. To reshape the front hem edge, measure down 3 in. (7.5 cm) from the center of the new kneeline (line G^1–K^1) and set point *a*. Connect points G^1–*a*–K^1 with a curve as shown in Fig. 10–3. This shaping allows the knee to stay covered when the leg is bent.

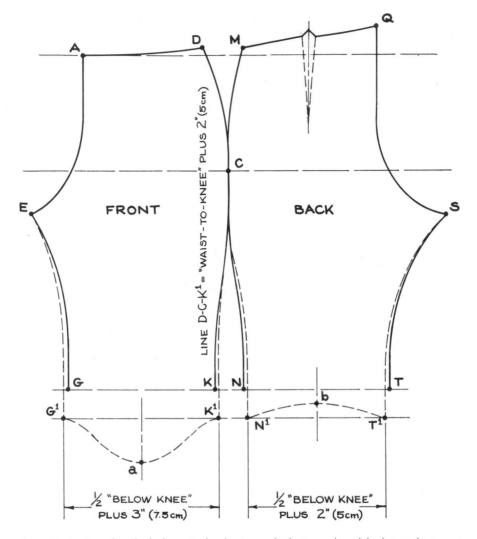

Figure 10-3 Knee-length slacks; note the shaping at the bottom edge of the leg on the pattern.

7. To reshape the back hem edge, measure up 1 in. (2.5 cm) from the center of the new kneeline (line N^1–T^1) and set point *b*. Connect points N^1–*b*–T^1 with a curve as shown. This shaping allows for flexibility at the back of the knee.

To prepare the knee-length slacks for fitting, assemble the pieces in the same manner as described for the basic slacks.

Leave a 3-in. (7.5 cm) opening in the side seam at the knee which will be finished as a placket (see Chap. 3).

To finish the hem edge, ease or pleat the edge into a band that is 3 in. (7.5 cm) longer than the "below-knee" measurement. Position the band to make an attachment overlap at the side-seam opening similar to cuffing a sleeve.

If the design specifies a bloused or full

bloomer type of garment that comes below the knee, this shaping of the kneeline is still necessary. To create the fullness, shift points K^1 and N^1 to line C–H; the side seam in this instance becomes a straight line down from point C. The hem can be finished with a band or with a casing as described for full sleeves in Chap. 8.

eleven

supplementary patterns

To complete a garment like the basic bodices, skirts, and slacks described in the preceding chapters, several additional pieces may be needed. It is not likely that all will be used on the same garment, nor will they always be necessary to fulfill the design of a particular garment. In some instances, they will not even be seen by the audience. However, when called for, they are necessary to complete the appearance of the costume.

The supplementary pieces are collars, yokes, facings, and interfacings, and each of them can be made from a basic drafted pattern. Facings and interfacings are used to finish and reinforce edges of a garment and are rarely visible; however, they may vary in shape and dimensions in different garments. Collars and yokes are, in many cases, as much a decorative feature as they are functional; consequently, they may have many variations in the details of their finished appearance. But the basic patterns from which the pieces are developed can be drafted as the foundation for any of the variations that may be required by a specific design.

In a sense, all of these supplementary patterns are derived from the basic pattern drafts for other garments. All of these pieces are attached to or made part of another garment for decorative, reinforcing, or finishing purposes. Collars must match and fit with the shape and size of the neckline on a bodice or jacket; yokes must conform to the shape of the body at the shoulders or hips in the same way that the basic fitted garments do. Interfacings and facings must follow the shapes in a garment in order to provide well-fitting reinforcement and to finish raw edges properly. Therefore, all of these pieces relate directly to the patterns for the whole garment with which they are to be used.

164

The classifications of the four basic collar styles are descriptive of their appearance, and they are referred to as standing, full-roll, partial-roll, and flat collars. The relationship of the collar to the neckline of the garment determines the style of the collar. In other words, the shape of the collar's neckline seam, the grain of the fabric, and the form and dimensions of the outer edge of the collar specify how the collar is to look.

The shape of the neckline curve of the collar is the key factor in whether the collar lies flat, rolls, or stands. The more closely the curve matches the curve of the garment neckline, the flatter the collar will lie. The greater the difference between the two curves, the more the collar will lift up from the garment. This principle is illustrated by the collar patterns in Fig. 11–1. All the collars illustrated are for a garment neckline fitted to the base of the neck, but, regardless of the type of neckline on the garment, the relationship of the curves will create the same effect. In all cases, the necklines of the garment and the collar are the same length.

The shape of the neckline seam also influences the grain of the fabric in the collar. The flat collar has straight grain at the center-back and sides; the partial-roll collar has straight grain at the center-back; and the full-roll and standing collar are cut on the bias.

The width of the collar from the neckline to the outside edge and the shape or the decoration of that edge form the third factor in the appearance of the collar. However, the dimensions and shape can be determined only by the specific design for the garment.

COLLAR PATTERN PIECES. Collar patterns consist of the upper-collar, the under-collar, and generally an interfacing. The under-collar matches the upper-collar but is cut slightly smaller so that it is hidden when the collar is finished, and the interfacing matches the under-collar. Basic commercial collar patterns are available, and a collection of collar styles for male and female, in various sizes, should be made up on sturdy paper and added to the pattern library. Each pattern should be identified by style, size, and grain line.

Flat collar patterns are cut to follow the curve of the garment neckline and fall close to the garment. The collar may be as small as the "Peter Pan" collar or as large as the traditional "sailor" collar.

Roll collars feature neckline curves that range from a modification of the garment neckline to little or no curve and even to a reverse curve. The degree and type of curve controls the amount of roll; the less the collar neckline conforms to the curvature of the neck, the greater the roll will be. The size and shape of the collars can also vary greatly, from the moderate "convertible" collar (a partial-roll style that can be worn open or closed) with its slightly convex curve (Fig. 11–1) to the larger shawl and circular roll collars with no curve. Those cut without a curve are cut on true bias to allow the collar to fit smoothly around the neck. While the style of the roll collar can be varied, all roll collars rise from the neckline seam, fold over on themselves and fall down to the garment. A "turtleneck" collar, for example, is only a full-roll collar, cut on the bias, that is double the width of the finished collar because it folds down over itself for its distinctive appearance.[1]

The standing collar is cut with no neckline curve and on the bias so that it will have enough give to conform to the body

[1]The front neckline curve on the garment should be raised ½ in. (1.3 cm) to allow the turtleneck collar to fall over the seam. If the curve is not raised, the seam will show.

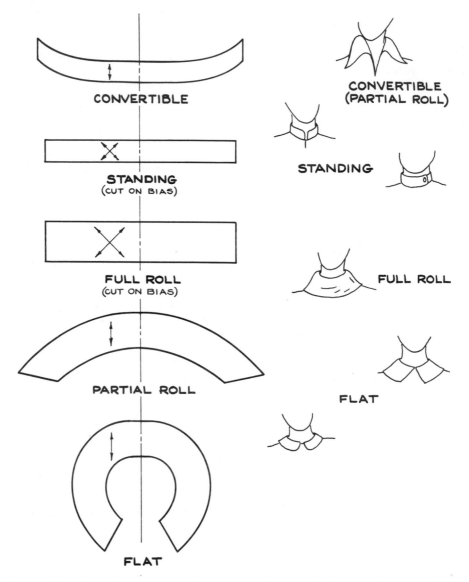

Figure 11-1 Basic collar patterns; the shape of the neck seam edge dictates whether the collar will be flat or if it will roll or stand at the neck opening.

curves and still stand up neatly from the garment neckline. Standing collars may be as discreet as a dainty "mandarin" collar on a girl's pajamas or as forthright and rigid as the wing collar on a fashionable male at the turn of the century, but the width and details of the collar will be determined by the design.

PATTERNING GUIDELINES FOR COLLARS. The process of making a pattern for a

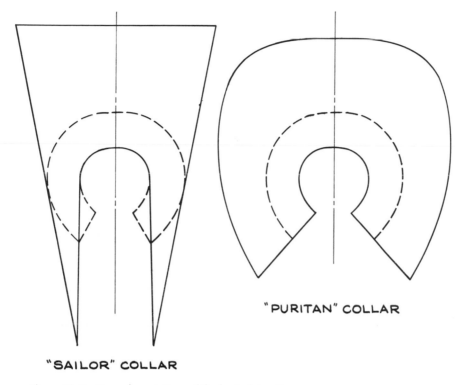

"PURITAN" COLLAR

"SAILOR" COLLAR

Figure 11-2 Example variations of the basic flat collar.

collar is not difficult; however, the variety that is possible (simply because of the numerous styles of collars and garment necklines) makes generalized basic pattern drafts impractical. The collars in Fig. 11-1 show shapes which can be adapted in a number of ways. For example, adding width to a basic flat-collar pattern and altering the shape of the outside seam will create a "puritan" collar, and yet merely adding lace to those same edges will turn it into a "cavalier" collar. The basic flat collar can also be made into a "sailor" collar by altering the seam line and neckline as shown in Fig. 11-2.

Combining features of the basic styles also adds to the variety in collars. The traditional collar for a man's dress shirt, for instance, combines the partial-roll collar (Fig. 11-1) with a narrow standing collar.

The partial roll is attached to the narrow band, and the resulting unit is attached to the neckline of the shirt. Adding a standing collar or band to other collar styles, such as the puritan collar, lifts the collar higher on the neck, which is appropriate for several styles. The standing collar can also be shaped so that it is higher in the back than in the front to tilt the collar to follow the slant of the jaw line. An interfaced, shaped band of this nature would be an appropriate base for an Elizabethan ruff similar to the one illustrated in Fig. 1-3. A lightweight fabric or lace over pellon can be cartridge pleated and attached to the band in the manner described in Chap. 9.

Using the basic principles which influence collar styles, apply the following guidelines to develop collar patterns.

1. A collar pattern is not usually drafted until after the size and shape of the garment neckline has been determined by the initial fitting process.

2. The length of the collar neckline equals the length of the garment neckline plus seam allowance; allow ½ in. (1.3 cm) for each seam and about 2 in. (5 cm) for overlap.

3. The type of collar is specified by its neckline curve (see Fig. 11–1).

4. The width of the collar is determined by the design, but the distance from the garment neckline to the armhole, compared to the design, is a guide in determining how wide a flat collar needs to be. The height of the neck is a guide for standing collars, and the amount of overfold on roll collars determines the width required in the patterns for these collars.

5. The collar opening must match the location of the opening in the garment. While this seems obvious, it is often overlooked (especially since many costumes open in the back) until after the collar has been cut and is ready to be attached.

6. Flat, partial-roll, and convertible collars can be cut on a fold; standing and full-roll collars are cut on the bias and therefore cannot be cut on a fold.

7. The tips of a collar can be rounded or pointed, as on a man's dress shirt, and the shaping of the outside edge can take almost any form specified by the design.

8. The under-collar and interfacing are cut slightly smaller than the upper-collar, about ¼ in. (0.6 cm) smaller all around, so that they are hidden when attached to the garment.

An alternative method to flat-patterning a collar is to drape it with the garment. Select the appropriate neckline shape for the collar style and draw a preliminary neckline on a piece of muslin that is larger than the desired final collar shape. Leaving ample seam allowance, cut out the neckline and mark the centerline of the piece. Place the garment on an appropriate dress form and pin the collar piece to the garment, matching the centerlines. Adjust the neckline curve and determine the outer shape of the collar to finalize the pattern. Experimentation with collars in this manner helps to create a wide variety of patterns as well as to create individuality in the costumes.

CUTTING AND PREPARATION FOR FITTING. First check the pattern with the garment to make sure the collar is long enough to go around the neckline with extra for seam allowance and overlap, if needed. Cut the upper-collar; then cut the under-collar and interfacing, both of which are slightly smaller than the upper-collar.

To prepare the collar requires several steps; the sewing terms in the following instructions for assembling the collar are explained in the Construction Glossary (Chap. 3). Before putting the collar together, check it with the garment for size and appearance.

To assemble the collar, *stay-stitch* the interfacing, if it is used, to the under-collar on the wrong side (inside); this stitching should be in the seam allowance so the stitches do not show when the collar is finished. Next join the upper-collar to the under-collar; with the right sides of the fabric together, stitch around the outer edge leaving the neckline seam unstitched. *Clip* the tips of the collar and the outside curves to the stitch lines and turn the collar so the right side is out. *Understitch* the under-collar and interfacing to sharpen the edge of the collar, *layering* the seam if there is too much bulk. Press the collar before attaching it to the garment.

To attach the collar to the garment for the fitting, pin the under-collar onto the garment, centering the collar on the garment neckline, and machine-baste the collar in place. Any adjustments can then be made in the fitting.

There are three methods typically used to make the final attachment of the collar to the garment. One simple method is similar to attaching a waistband. Fold the seam allowances inside the collar, sandwich the raw edge of the garment neckline between the upper-collar and under-collar edges, and stitch the three together.

The other two methods involve an additional step since part of the collar attachment is finished by hand. The collar may be joined to the garment (except in standing collars) by stitching the upper-collar to the inside of the garment neckline, with the right side of the upper-collar against the wrong side of the garment fabric. Then the collar is turned up over the stitching, pressed, and the seam allowances are clipped. The seam allowance of the under-collar is turned inside (clipped, if necessary) and hand-stitched to the garment. Handstitching with care allows the grain to be kept properly aligned while working the fabric with the curve of the neckline.

This process can also be reversed (except in standing collars). The under-collar is stitched to the good side of the garment fabric (right sides together), turned, pressed, and clipped. Then the upper-collar, with seam allowance folded in, is handstitched inside the garment.

BASIC YOKES

Patterning Yokes

Yokes are fitted sections of a garment normally used at the shoulders and upper hips since these areas expand less with movement than other sections of the body. A yoke is often used in a design to add interest and detail at the shoulders or hips as well as to support fullness in the body of the garment. Typical uses for a yoke are in the back of men's shirts, in the back of pants or jeans, in smocks, or in nightshirts. As examples, western-style shirts accentuate a design detail with both a front and back yoke, and choir robes have the fullness of the gown supported by the yoke.

Yokes also provide additional strength since they are usually made in two layers, an upper yoke and an under yoke. An interfacing is also often added. The body of the garment is attached with its raw edge sandwiched between the upper and under yokes, although in some periods robes have been attached with the body fabric on top of the yoke.

Commercial patterns for yokes are available and are valuable additions to the pattern library. They are also easy to draft. Essentially, the shoulder yoke is identical to the upper portion of the bodice/jacket pattern, the hip yoke is identical to the upper portion of the basic slacks pattern or of the basic fitted skirt. The vertical length of the yoke and the shape of the bottom edge are determined by the design, but since all yokes are abbreviations of other pattern drafts, those patterns can be used to draft a yoke pattern. The yoke can easily be adjusted to the desired length and shaped as called for by the design.

When the function of the yoke is to support extra fullness, it is drafted and cut separately from the body of the garment. The fullness of the body fabric, which is generally rectangular in shape, is gathered or pleated into the necessary dimensions and attached to the yoke. A typical example of this is found in a smock. In this instance, however, part of the armhole needs to be cut in the body of the garment, since the yoke usually does not come below the arm. To locate and cut out the lower armhole, assemble the garment first, and place it on a dress form to mark the location of the hole; then cut it out, leaving a seam allowance.

If the yoke is primarily decorative rather than a support for fullness, the pattern for the whole garment can be drafted; then the pattern can be cut apart at the bottom edge of the established yoke line. Balance lines should be placed on the pattern prior to cutting so the pieces can be aligned when they are put together. Seam allowances have to be added to each of the new pieces since the cutting line is the stitch line when the garment is assembled.

Finally, yokes can be used in both the front and back of a garment, or just in the back; they are rarely used only in the front. If the design calls for a yoke in the front and back, match the lengths of the yoke pieces at the armholes of the shoulder yoke and at the side seams of the hip yoke. Be-

fore drafting a yoke, determine if a closing will pass through it and where the closing will be. Also determine what the finished length of the yoke will be and what the final shape is to look like. Seam allowances will need to be added.

DRAFTING SHOULDER YOKES.   Yokes for the shoulders rarely extend under the arm; consequently, the yoke is cut to accommodate the upper part of the armhole while the remainder of the armhole is cut in the body of the garment. The shape of the bottom edge of the yoke is specified by the design. To begin the layout of the yoke pattern, follow the drafting procedures for the neck, shoulder, and armhole segments from the pattern draft of the basic bodice/jacket in Chap. 7.

1.   As shown in Fig. 11–3, to locate the position of the bottom edge of the yoke, take the designed length and measure down from point B on the pattern draft to set point X. This length is usually between 3 in. and 6 in. (7.5 cm to 15 cm) plus 1 in. (2.5 cm) for seam allowance. The 1 in. allowance in this instance is to provide flexibility in fitting unusual edges on the yoke

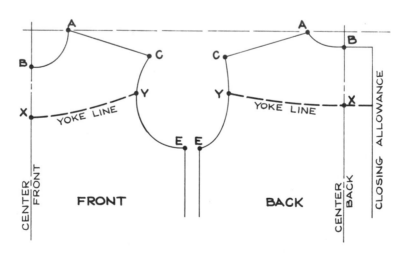

Figure 11–3   Example of a basic shoulder yoke pattern taken from the bodice/jacket pattern; add seam allowance to the yoke line.

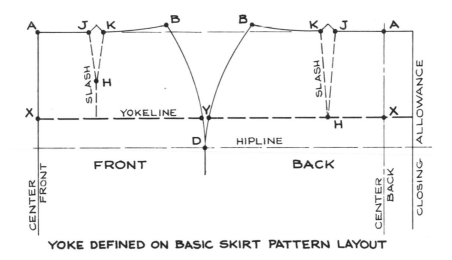

YOKE DEFINED ON BASIC SKIRT PATTERN LAYOUT

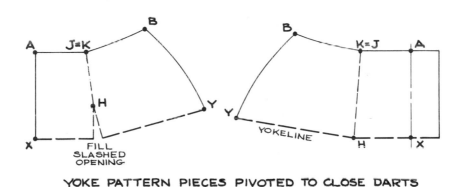

YOKE PATTERN PIECES PIVOTED TO CLOSE DARTS

Figure 11-4   Example of a basic hip yoke taken from the basic fitted skirt pattern; add seam allowance to the yoke line.

and the chest/bust body curves; the shoulder seam already has allowance added in the bodice/jacket pattern.

2.   Connect point X with the armhole with a line that scribes the desired shape of the yoke and set point Y. If both the front and back sections are used, the distance from point C on the draft to point Y should be the same on both pieces.

DRAFTING HIP YOKES FOR SKIRTS AND SLACKS.   Skirt hip yokes are usually used

to create a smooth line above the hips, so the upper portion of the basic fitted skirt pattern draft can be used to draft the yoke. The length of the yoke should not go below the hipline of the draft, and any fitting darts can be eliminated by cutting the dart centerline through the bottom edge of the yoke and matching the dart stitching lines. This procedure alters the waistline curve and the bottom edge of the pattern as shown in Fig. 11-4, but it keeps the correct size in the pattern and creates a

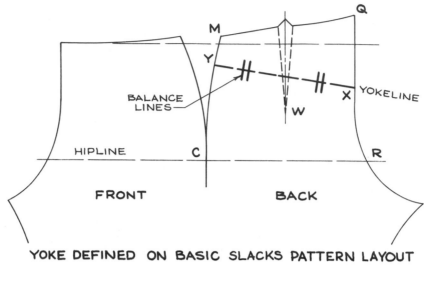

YOKE DEFINED ON BASIC SLACKS PATTERN LAYOUT

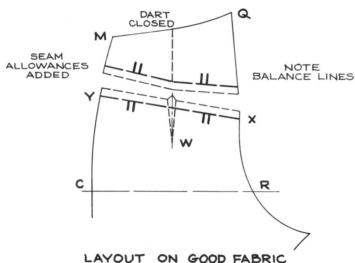

LAYOUT ON GOOD FABRIC

Figure 11–5 Example of a basic back hip yoke taken from the basic slacks pattern; add seam allowance to the yoke line.

smooth fit; any small increase in fullness that may occur below the point of the dart can be adjusted in the side seams during the fitting. Note that the straight grain remains at the center-back and center-front on both the yoke and the skirt body pattern pieces. (The procedure of eliminating darts is also discussed in Chap. 13.)

To draft the skirt yoke, follow the drafting instructions for the basic fitted skirt to lay out the waistline, hipline, side seams, and fitting darts.

1. As shown in Fig. 11–4, to locate the position of the bottom edge, take the designed length of the yoke and measure down from point A on the skirt draft to set point X; this is usually 3 in. to 6 in. (7.5 cm to 15 cm) plus 1 in. (2.5 cm) for seam allowance.

2. Connect point X to the side seam with a line that follows the desired shape of the yoke edge and set point Y. If both the front and back yokes are used, the distance between point B on the skirt draft and point Y should be the same for both pieces.

For slacks, the yoke is usually a decorative detail and is typically used only in the back. As such, there is no additional fullness in the rest of the garment for the yoke to support; therefore, the whole pattern for the slacks is drafted, the yoke dimen-sions are laid in, balance lines marked, and then the pattern is cut on the bottom edge of the yoke line as shown in Fig. 11–5. The back fitting dart in the yoke pattern is removed by using the method described for the skirt hip yoke, but the dart in the lower portion of the pants will be treated as a regular fitting dart to be stitched on the stitching lines.

To draft the pattern on the good fabric, lay out the pattern pieces leaving room for seam allowances to be added at the yoke cutting line. The straight grain of the pattern stays the same as the original pattern. Add ½ in. (1.3 cm) seam allowance at the bottom of the yoke and at the top of the pants; trace through the balance lines and the dart stitching lines for the lower portion of the pants, and then cut out the pieces.

FACINGS AND INTERFACINGS

Facings are used to finish off raw edges of a garment. The most typical uses for facings are at the neckline (if there is no collar), the armholes in a sleeveless garment, a waistline (if there is no waistband), and lapels.

Facings can be cut from matching fabric or from a contrasting fabric as a decorative feature of the garment. They can also be made out of lining fabric or bias tape. The selection of the material is based on the particular function of the facing. Lapel facings, for example, are cut from the good fabric or from contrasting fabrics as a decorative detail because they are meant to be seen. Neckline facings, on the other hand, are turned inside the garment and are not meant to be seen; therefore, the fabric is selected for its function rather than for decorative purposes.

PATTERNING GUIDELINES. A facing cut from the good fabric or lining can be a narrow strip (about 1½ in. [3.8 cm] wide) cut on true bias, or it can be cut to match the area to be faced. If the curves are sharp, or if the facing needs to be wider than 1 in. (2.5 cm) when finished, the facing must be cut to match the area since it must have enough ease to lie smoothly against the inside of the garment.

Since facings are part of the finishing of a garment, they are not attached until the garment has been fitted and the stitching lines at the openings have been marked. Therefore, they are often not patterned or cut until after the first, or even the second, fitting.

Facings are easy to pattern and cut. A simple method is to lay out the fitted pattern, or the actual garment, on the fabric so that the grain lines match and draw a line around the opening to be faced, including the seam allowance. Then remove the pattern from the fabric and measure over from the drawn line the desired width, and set points to mark the outer edge. Connect these points and cut the facing. Generally, facings are between 1½ and 2½ in. (3.8 and 6.3 cm) wide inside a garment opening or cut to the full width of the lapel. If the facing covers a dart, it can be cut after the dart in the garment has been stitched in place so the facing does not need to be darted to fit the area.

Interfacings are cut the same way facings are cut. However, since interfacing materials are stiffer than the facing fabrics, they are usually cut less wide so there will be less bulk in the turned seams. The pro-

cess for attaching interfacings is discussed under Collars.

ATTACHING FACINGS. After the facing is cut, the outside edge should be finished to prevent raveling with a zigzag stitch or with a rolled hem if the fabric is not too bulky. Then the facing is stitched to the garment with the right sides together. Curved seam allowances need to be clipped before the facing is turned inside the garment, pressed, and then tacked in place.

twelve

the fitting process

Fittings are generally done by the costumer and approved by the designer. The costumer is responsible for the cut and fit of the garment. The details and proportions of the costume on an actor, such as final necklines, hem lengths, trim placement, and other design concerns, are the designer's responsibilities. Therefore, both individuals must be present for all fittings.

The number of fittings required varies according to the number of pieces involved and the complexity of the costume. Three fittings, representing each of the costume's stages of development, are typical. Costumes that are dependent on padding, corseting, or other special units require additional fittings for those items as well. The purpose of the first fitting is to check and finalize the pattern; the second fitting is to finalize details of the fit of the actual costume; and the third is to check the completed costume and all the accessories. The appropriate undergarments should be worn for all fittings.

The initial fitting actually completes the patterns because this is when the patterns are adjusted to the exact shape of the actor's body. The patterns (bodice, sleeves, collars, skirts, and the like) are basted together as individual units, but they are not joined together to make up the complete garment for the first fitting since each of the items needs to be checked and adjusted as necessary on the actor.

Most costume patterns are initially developed in muslin since it is an inexpensive fabric and these pattern pieces can often be used as linings for the actual garment. These are, naturally enough, called *muslins,* and after adjustments in the first fitting they become the actual pattern from which to cut the good fabric that is to be used for the particular costume and actor. Obviously, muslins are more important for fitted garments than for non–form-fitting garments such as full skirts or capes. Fitting guidelines and methods of marking muslins to finalize the pattern are discussed later in this chapter.

For the second fitting, the costume, in

the good fabric, should be assembled with sleeves in place, waistbands on skirts or pants, and whatever else is appropriate for the particular costume. For this fitting, the closings are usually not finished because the closing line will shift after the sleeves are added, and the collar is not attached since the neckline and shoulder lines occasionally need adjustment. This fitting is to determine the specific details in the costume, such as hems, trims, and appliqués, and to finalize closings.

The final fitting brings the entire costume together—that is, the completed garment and all accessories. If the actor has more than one costume, the costume changes are gone through in the correct sequence to familiarize the actor with the changes. This fitting is to assure all concerned that everything is there and ready to be used.

If possible, the director should see the costumes in the second or third fitting. This gives the director the opportunity to consult with the designer and the costumer on the individual costumes prior to the dress rehearsals, thus avoiding surprises for anyone at the last minute.

THE FITTING AREA

A separate fitting area should be available in order to conduct the fittings with the least amount of distraction from the workshop activities. This space is intended to provide privacy for the fitting; an area partitioned off with walls or just curtains is all that is necessary, but the space should also provide ample room in which the actor, costumer, and designer can move freely. The costumer and designer need room to work around the actor, and the actor needs to move in the garment to check it for fit, ease, and freedom of movement. Movement in the garment is a very important aspect of costuming and should be checked during every fitting.

Ideally, the fitting space should be furnished with the following items. Those items marked with an asterisk are essential; the others are nice additions to the space.

Full-length mirror mounted on the wall or on wheels. A single panel is sufficient, but a threefold mirror, similar to those often found in department stores, is ideal to give an actor a full image of the total costume.

Clothing rack and hangers. The rack may be permanently installed or mounted on wheels; it provides a place to hang the costumes for the fitting as well as the actor's personal clothing.

Raised platform for the actor to stand on while the hem on long garments is being pinned.

Bulletin board. This provides a place to tack up the costume plate and other related information for reference during the fitting.

Chair for the actor to check ease in garments when seated and for trying on shoes.

Lights with "gel-frames." Small instruments with dimmers (baby spots, PARs with gel-frames, or strip lights with colored lenses) to light an actor in the costume will give the designer an idea of how the costume will look on stage under stage lighting.

Shelf or table for laying out working tools, small garment pieces, and accessories.

Drawers to hold fitting tools and small accessories when not in use.

Fitting tools:

Straight pins and safety pins in containers

Scissors, a small pair for snipping and trimming

Seam ripper to remove basting stitches when necessary

Figure 12-1 An example of a fitting-room arrangement off the costume shop at the University of Rhode Island. Notice the additional storage shelves and the use of the wall and door for additional storage. Photo by Robert Izzo.

Pencils and tailor's chalk to mark the garment

Tape measure for checking adjustments

Hem marker for marking hems on non–floor-length garments

Cord or string to lace garments closed or to tie around the waist.

The fitting space is also a useful storage area for small items that often need to be close at hand during a fitting. How many, and the types of items that can be stored in the area, are determined by the amount of space and personal preference (see example in Fig. 12-1).

The walls and doors of a fitting room provide useful storage space for items that get tangled up easily in boxes or drawers,

such as belts, ties, and long necklaces. For example, a series of nails driven into the wall provides hanging space for belts and simplifies finding the right color and size during the fitting. A cord stretched between nails makes a good hanging space for regular neckties and simplifies locating the appropriate tie for a costume.

Other items which are frequently stored in the fitting area include basic undergarments (such as T-shirts, slips, and hose); basic accessories (such as tights, neckties, gloves, garters, and belts), and specialty items (such as shoulder pads and innersoles).

While the walls may be used for many purposes, keeping the floor clean and clear for the fitting activities is a necessity. A smooth hard-surfaced floor of tile or linoleum is easier to keep clean than carpet. It also makes it easier to retrieve dropped pins before they are stepped on or knelt upon. Indeed, a small magnet can be a valuable addition to the fitting area as an aid in picking up pins.

Time, for everyone, is always at a premium when a production is being prepared. This is true for the actor as well as for the costumer and designer. Therefore, everything needed for a fitting should be ready beforehand so the fitting time can be used efficiently. This includes having the fitting area and tools ready for use. It also means that the appropriate costume pieces and accessories must be ready to be fitted; an inventory of the costumes, called a *costume plot* (see Chap. 20), will show what items should be dealt with in combination or in sequence.

In addition, this means making arrangements to have the necessary people available for the fitting. Ideally, the designer will be in close contact with the costumer and will be available for fittings. However, some production organizations may have differing means for scheduling the actors' time and, therefore, availability for fittings. In most professional and many noncommercial organizations, schedules are set through the stage manager. In some organizations, it may be necessary to go through the director. In others, it is up to the costumer alone to contact the individual actors and then hold them to their appointments. But, regardless of the means available, the method for communicating the fitting schedule should be established definitely and early in the rehearsal process so everyone knows the procedure.

When scheduling fittings, the costumer should allow enough time to fit the actor in all the necessary items. The schedule should also allow enough time between fit-

Finally, the fitting space should be well lit and as comfortable as possible. A great deal of work is done in this space; each fitting takes time and care if the costume is to fit properly and comfortably.

PREPARATION FOR THE FITTINGS

tings to collate and check the notes taken during the fitting as well as to prepare for the actor's next fitting.

Preparation for the first fitting includes having the muslins basted together, with any fitting darts basted in place and with the closings left open so the garment can go on the actor. The pattern should not be pressed for the first fitting. Pressed seam lines and darts are difficult to adjust. Since a purpose of the first fitting is to locate all the final stitching lines, the muslins should not have sleeves or other pieces stitched in place. These are to be attached after the stitching lines are marked on the pattern pieces. The Preparation for Fittings section following each pattern draft in Chaps. 7–11 indicates how to prepare each pattern for the first fitting.

Prior to the fitting, the items to be fitted should be set up in the fitting area in the order in which the actor is to put them on. Any special undergarments that are required should be included. The costume plate should also be available for the costumer and designer to refer to and to remind the actor what the finished costume will look like.

Sample Plan for a Fitting Sequence

Whether written down or merely maintained mentally by the experienced costumer, the sequence of what should be done at each fitting for each costume at its various stages of completion should be planned. The following breakdown is the plan which was followed for the fitting of the Isabella costume shown in Fig. 1–8. The first fitting was for the special undergarments, which needed to be completed as soon as possible since they were to be used as rehearsal garments so the actress could become familiar with the movement characteristics of the costume. They were also worn as part of the undergarments with the completed costume.

First Fitting:

Pattern Pieces	Object of the Fitting
Corset—basted together (see Chap. 16 for the construction process)	Finalize placement of seams and waistline (V-shaped over abdomen); locate and finalize placement and length of stays; locate back closing line
Bum-roll (see Chap. 16 for the construction process)	Check waist and hip size, check fullness proportions on actress (designer)
Muslin petticoat	Check and mark waist closing; mark hemline with bum-roll under the petticoat and use as pattern for the plaid petticoat

Due to the number and type of undergarments for this costume, the first fitting is to get the necessary information to complete them. The second fitting is used to finalize the over-garment muslin patterns since the finished corset will mold the torso and alter the bust and waistline somewhat.

Second Fitting (corset, bum-roll, and muslin petticoat complete):

Pattern Pieces	Object of the Fitting
Blouse body—neckline finished with casing, elastic in casing with ends pinned together	Check neckline; check and adjust armhole, mark stitchline for sleeve; check blouse length; finalize and pin elastic in neckline
Blouse sleeves—stitched together with puff and gusset	Check over-all fit and length, which needs to be 3 in. (7.5 cm) longer than the arm length to the wrist; check the fullness of the proportions (designer)
Over-gown bodice—muslin	Check placement of seams; locate and mark neckline and armhole; wing pieces at the top of the arm to be added later. Locate and mark preliminary back closing

For the next fitting, the blouse should be completed and the over-gown bodice, in the good fabric, should be assembled so the neckline, shoulder lines, and closing can be finalized. The crescent-wing pieces should be ready to pin in place during the fitting, and the plaid petticoat should be sufficiently assembled for the final swinging of the pleats. The over-gown skirt should also be ready with the cartridge pleats in place. The hems for the skirts cannot be finalized during this fitting; the waistband needs to be added to the plaid petticoat, and the over-skirt needs to be attached to the bodice.

In the final fitting, the assembly and fit of all pieces can be checked, and with all pieces worn together, the last hem positions can be marked for stitching. As with the previous fittings, all predicted movements by the actor in the costume should be reviewed.

With something like the Mr. Twinkle costume (see Fig. 1–10), the preparation for the fitting can be less extensive. For that costume the shirt body, the sleeves, and the pants will need to be prepared. The detachable collar is added in the second fitting after the other elements are stitched together. Simple costumes like this require less fitting time than the more complex ones and can be scheduled accordingly.

Basic Rules for Conducting Fittings

There are a number of constants for all fittings which are part of the process of achieving the proper fit.

1. Fit the garment with the wrong side next to the body. This rule is especially important if the garment is form-fitting. Some costumers prefer to fit with the wrong side of the costume out. This method of fitting simplifies the fitting process because the seams are on the outside. However, since the two sides of the body are not symmetrical, except in rare instances, this method can create problems in fit later when the garment is turned right side out. Fitting with the wrong side next to the body eliminates these problems.

2. Work with the actor standing in front of a full-length mirror so you can see what is happening with the whole garment. It is important, when making adjustments in the back of the garment, to know that the front of the garment is not being pulled out of balance or twisted, and vice versa.

3. Start each fitting with the undermost layer of the costume over the proper undergarments, and fit each layer in the costume. In other words, check the suit pants before the suit coat is added.

4. Before any adjustments are made, make sure the garment is placed properly on the body; that is, make sure that centerlines are on the center of the body, that the garment sits properly on the shoulders, and that the grain of the fabric is falling as it should.

5. Take time during each fitting to step back periodically from the garment to see how the garment is fitting. Watch the balance of the garment, the location of the seams, and observe the grain of the fabric to see what it is doing.

6. When pinning the garment, place the pins with the points down. Applying this rule saves a lot of pin-gashed fingers and arms for both costumer and actor. It also simplifies adherence to the unwritten rule: "Don't bleed on the costumes."

7. Remember to provide enough ease in the garment for movement and to leave ample seam allowance; ½ in. (1.3 cm) is the minimum seam allowance, but more will be necessary for the closings. This rule also refers to the necessity of checking the actor's movements in the costume against the posture and movement requirements of the historical period and the actor's performance in the production.

An exception to the rule of maintaining ease is for the body-support type of garment. A corset, for example, must fit very snugly if it is to be comfortable and support the torso.

A word of caution concerning the proper amount of ease is needed here; the line dividing "proper amount of ease" and "hanging loosely on the body" can be a fine one. The objective is to have a well-fitted garment with just the right amount of ease for appropriate movement.

8. Do not be tentative or uneasy about touching the actor. A firm, assured touch inspires confidence; a weak, tentative touch has quite the opposite effect and can even tickle the actor, which creates other problems.

9. Take notes on the adjustments in the costume that will need to be made after the fitting and on any special information concerning the requirements of the costume for performance, such as pocket size or placement. These notes should be complete and clear, since the only thing you can be absolutely sure of is that you will forget something.

There is no substitute for experience when fitting costumes. However, everyone must start somewhere, and while each fitting seems to introduce new problems, it also brings solutions to problems. All the basic rules apply to each fitting. The most important rule for every fitting, however, is the one that calls for stepping back and observing the garment and what it is doing on the body. The fabric will tell you if there is too much strain, if the fabric is off-grain, if it is pulling or twisting, or if there is too much fabric, causing the garment to pucker or bulge in the wrong places.

Avoid the temptation of immediately dealing with one area by tugging or pulling at the fabric. Take time to look at the whole garment in order to determine where to make the necessary adjustments. Work different areas to find the best solution, which may be found by making adjustments in more than one area. To achieve the best results, experiment with the pattern on the body. Keeping this in mind, study and practice the processes outlined in the following section.

FITTING SPECIFIC TYPES OF GARMENTS

The following processes are applicable to all the fittings used to complete a costume. However, the major emphasis in these descriptions is on working with the muslins in the first fitting, since the adjustments and markings made in that fitting establish the basis for proper fit in the finished garment.

The methods and fitting techniques described have been set up in a recommended sequence for ease and convenience. Each costumer will, of course, determine through experience and personal preference the sequence that works best.

Fitting Torso-Supported Garments

The following guidelines are drawn up for torso-fitting garments such as bodices and fitted jackets.

WHERE TO START

1. Put the garment, with the wrong side against the body, on the actor over the appropriate undergarments. For the first fitting, the garment does not have the sleeves, collar, or other pieces attached.

a. Make sure the garment is aligned correctly on the body and that the side seams and shoulder seams are in the appropriate locations.

b. When working with the muslin pattern, keep the thickness and weight of the good fabric in mind and make the necessary allowance in the snugness of the fit.

2. Start the fitting at the closing to hold the garment in place. The pin line of the closing will be a preliminary line which may need to be adjusted as the fitting is being completed. Pin the closing with the seam allowance sticking out from the body, not as you would for finishing, by overlapping the edges. Pinning with the seam allowance out makes it easier to keep the garment balanced and the closing on center.

a. Line up the closing so the neckline edges match and hold onto the fabric so the garment does not shift after it has been lined up.

b. Starting at the small of the back for a back closing, or at the waist for a front closing, pin the garment closed. Work up toward the neck, pinning as you go; then complete the closing by pinning any of the garment that extends below the waist. This method of pinning helps to distribute the weight of the garment and minimizes the possibility of the garment pulling down on the shoulders.

c. Watch the garment closely as you work with the closing, and in all other phases of the fitting. Watch to make sure that

> The centerlines are kept on center
> Any excess fabric is evenly distributed around the body at the side seams, darts, and closing
> The fabric is not forced, twisted, or pulled
> Seams and darts are in the proper location.

d. If the muslin is too snug, either the measurements or the pattern drafting is inaccurate. If the problem is not too severe, the waist fitting darts or side seams can be released and repinned. If there is not enough seam allowance for this, the measurements should be retaken and the pattern redrafted.

3. Observe the garment from all sides to determine where adjustments need to be made in the pattern. Watch for any loose creases in the pattern; vertical creases generally indicate too much width in the garment, horizontal creases indicate too much length, and diagonal creases, too much length and width. Strain lines or areas pulled taut mean there is not enough fabric in the pattern piece for a good fit.

a. Always work both sides of the front and/or the back simultaneously to keep the garment centered and balanced.

b. When making adjustments in the front, watch the back of the garment in the mirror, and vice versa, so as not to pull the garment out of alignment.

WHAT TO LOOK FOR. Once the garment is properly settled on the actor's body, use the following list of common problems encountered in fittings as a guide to determine what adjustments to make in order to eliminate problems with the fit. Solving a problem may involve reworking one or all of the mentioned areas.

1. Horizontal creases or pulling in the area between the mid-chest and the shoulders:

> Check the neck opening for size
> Check the shoulder seams for location and excess length.

2. Diagonal creases or puckers from the armhole to the mid-chest section, most typical in female garments:

> Check the armhole for size
> Check position and take-up of the darts
> Check the shoulder seams.

3. Horizontal and/or diagonal creases or puckers at the midsection:

> Check the length of the garment
> Check the fit of the garment over the hips
> Check the placement of the side seams and the ease across the front and back of the garment.

4. Side seams not vertical and/or in an incorrect position:

> Check the closing line and the other adjustments which have been made in the garment

Check the pattern front or back sections which may have been cut too small or with too severe an angle at the side seams (see basic bodice/jacket pattern draft).

WHAT ADJUSTMENTS TO MAKE. With the garment on properly and the problems in the fit noted, use the following checklist as a guide to determine how to make the appropriate adjustments to solve the problems. Make all the adjustments necessary to answer these questions.

1. *Are the seams in the proper location?* If not, pin them in the correct position; this may mean taking the garment in if it is too large or releasing the basting stitching and repinning if the garment is too snug.

2. *Are the darts in the proper location?* If the placement is correct but the dart is too short, pin the dart to the desired length. If the dart is too long, mark the new length and release the basting stitches to shorten the dart.

If the dart needs to be relocated, release the basting stitches and repin the dart in the proper location. Note that if the bust fitting darts need to be relocated, the side seams from the armhole down to the new dart locations as well as the darts will need to be opened and repinned.

Remember to keep the waist-fitting darts equidistant from the center and to keep the garment balanced.

3. *Is the neck-hole the proper size?* If the neck opening is too small, the shoulder seams may be opened slightly at the neck, or the opening can be carefully clipped with very short cuts to enlarge the opening; do not cut the hole bigger. Remember to leave the seam allowance, and do not cut through the stitching line.

If the neck opening is too large, mark the section to be made smaller with an arrow—the pattern will need to be recut since it is impossible to make a hole smaller once the fabric is cut away.

4. *Is the neckline to be reshaped?* If so, sketch the new shape on the pattern while the actor is in the garment. Check the new line with the designer before cutting away the excess. Leaving a seam allowance, trim away only one-half of the new shape, fold the trimmed-away piece over on the centerline to transfer the shape and balance the other side of the new neckline. Note: the new, larger neckline may create some extra fullness in the upper portion of the garment; this can be adjusted by taking up the shoulder seams.

5. *Are the armholes the proper size?* If they are too small, *carefully* trim away the excess; but remember to leave seam allowance.

If the armhole is too large, mark the section to be made smaller with an arrow—the pattern will then need to be recut: a hole can always be cut larger—it cannot be cut smaller.

6. *Is the garment too long and/or too snug over the hips?* If so, release the pinning at the closing line below the waist and the stitching below the waist at the side seams, as necessary, to allow the garment to sit properly on the torso. Repin the adjusted areas below the waist. If absolutely necessary, the excess length below the waist can be trimmed away. Remember to leave seam allowance and to check the movement requirements for the actor before cutting anything away. Remember that fitted torso garments can ride up when the arm is lifted, so allow for this before any excess is cut away.

7. *Are the shoulder seams in the proper location and/or do they need adjusting to control the grain of the fabric?* If the shoulder seams need to be adjusted, release the basting stitches and repin the seams in the proper location.

8. *Is the preliminary closing line still appropriate?* If not, repin the line, keeping the garment balanced and the closing on center.

Check the garment carefully to be sure it is fitting properly. If there are any problems, review the process again.

MARKING THE FITTING ADJUSTMENTS. After the garment has been fitted satisfactorily, mark all adjustments to be made while the garment is still on the actor's body; pins can drop out as the garment is removed. Be sure to include all markings that will be needed in the shop to complete the costume.

1. Use a pencil to mark the muslin garment, tailor's chalk to mark the good fabric (see discussion of tailor's chalk and fabrics in Chap. 2). All lines marked on the garment indicate stitching lines, not cut lines; assume that seam allowances will be provided with any cuts made.

2. Mark the neckline around the base of the neck or at the proper location specified by the design.

3. Mark the armhole; use the bones which protrude slightly at the shoulder joint at the top of the arm as a guide unless the design specifies otherwise. Allow some additional opening at the armpit for ease of movement.

Also remember the fullness and thickness of the sleeve which is to be set into the armhole when marking the armhole. Allow slightly more ease under the arm if the sleeve has extra fullness or thickness.

4. Mark the waistline; the position and shape will depend on the design. If the waist is to follow the natural waist, place a cord around the waist as a guide to the marking. If the garment is to be tucked into a skirt or pants, mark the waistline as a pattern guide.

5. Mark the closing line only after the rest of the garment has been fitted to the body. The marked closing line from the

first fitting will probably need to be adjusted when the garment is completely together with sleeves, collar, and other pieces in place. Therefore, this closing marking is preliminary and will not be finalized until the second fitting, when the garment is completely together.

6. Mark decorative detail placement as appropriate to the design.

ADDING PIECES TO THE BASIC TORSO GARMENT. In the first fitting, adding pieces that will be attached to the body of the garment gives the actor a better sense of what the costume will eventually look like and gives the costumer and the designer the opportunity to check the size, ease, and proportion. The typical pieces to be added include the sleeves, collar, and skirt or other units to be attached to the waist.

Sleeves. One or both sleeves can be slipped on the actor and carefully pinned with safety pins at the top, sides, and underarm of the armhole. This process should be approached carefully so as not to stick the actor with pins.

1. Check the sleeve for length: from sleeve cap to elbow and from sleeve cap to wrist. A preliminary sleeve length can be marked at this time; however, the length should not be finalized until the sleeves are stitched in place.
2. Check the sleeves for ease around the arm. Remember that the arm muscles expand when flexed.

Collar. The collar can be pinned carefully on the garment at the center point opposite the closing and at the shoulder seams to check for size, fit, and proportion. Depending on the pattern style, or on time available, it may be simpler to check the collar on the dress form as part of the preparation for the second fitting.

Attached Skirt or Waist Pieces. The type of item to be attached often influences whether or not these pieces will be included in the early fittings. The method of attaching the piece to the torso garment and the size and bulk of the unit usually determine when it should be brought into the fitting sequence.

The Isabella costume discussed earlier contains two examples of this. This pleated petticoat was easy to manage and finalize early because its pleats were controlled by a baste stitch at the waist. However, the over-gown skirt, with its cartridge pleats, was not as easy to manage nor was the attachment to the bodice easy to do properly. Therefore it was held out of the fittings until more of the total costume was complete and ready to accept the addition.

Fitting Waist- or Hip-Supported Garments

The same basic rules for torso-supported garments apply to garments which are supported by the waist or hips. However, there are generally fewer fitting contact points on the body with these garments. Consequently, the fitting process is somewhat less involved than the process for the torso-supported garment.

SKIRTS

1. The garment needs to be aligned properly on the body with the centerlines on center, darts and seams in the appropriate location, and with the proper undergarments and/or body supports in place.

a. If a waistband is to be added later, place the waistline of the garment slightly below the waistline designated by the design; the distance should equal that of the finished waistband less the skirt seam allowance at the waist. For example, for a 1½ in. waistband, drop the waist about 1 in. below the designated waistline.

b. If the waistline is gathered, the gathers may be tightened or loosened as necessary by reworking the gathering stitch as described under Machine Gathering in Chap. 3.

2. Match the top edges of the waistline at the closing and use a safety pin to fasten them together; carefully pin the rest of the closing together while watching seam locations and signs of improper snugness.

3. Observe the garment all around the actor. Check for ease over the hips and thighs. As with the torso-supported garments, creases and puckers over this area suggest problems in length and/or width as indicated under What to Look for.

a. If there are puckers or creases over the hips or thighs:

> Check to make sure the garment is closed properly and is sufficiently supported at the closing; one safety pin at the waist, for example, will not support the garment—the bulk of the weight will be on the pin rather than distributed over the waist and hips.

> Check to make sure there is enough ease over the fullness of the hips. If, for example, the puckers or creases in a gored skirt disappear when you raise the garment higher on the body, the skirt is too tight over the hips. Adjusting the seams to enlarge it over the hips will eliminate the puckers or, if there is enough length, the waistline can be adjusted by pulling the skirt up and removing the excess at the waist.

b. Watch the grain of the fabric and the placement of seams and/or darts.

> Check the waistline curve (see skirt and slacks pattern drafts). If the grain of the fabric or the seams twist off the proper line, the waistline curve may be cut too severely or may not be cut deeply enough.

c. Check the placement of the fitting darts. If the darts need to be relocated, release the stitching and re-pin the dart in the proper location. If the length of the dart needs to be adjusted, adjust the length in the same manner as for torso-supported garments. If additional darts are needed, pin them in at the appropriate locations.

d. Check the swing of the pleats (see Chap. 9) to make sure the grain of the fabric is falling properly.

4. After the waist and hip areas have been fitted, a preliminary length can be marked. This length cannot be finalized until the second fitting after the garment has been stitched together. The actor must be wearing the shoes that are to be worn with the costume.

a. Skirts cut on the bias of the fabric, such as circle skirts, will stretch on the bias. Therefore, they should be hung up by the waist to allow the fabric to stretch before the length is finished.

b. Any padding or skirt supports to be worn under the skirt must be complete and in place before the skirt can be fitted for length and the hem marked.

5. Fitting markings: Mark the skirt on the body after it has been fitted satisfactorily; be sure to include all the necessary information to complete the costume. Since there are fewer fitting points on skirts, there are fewer fitting markings. All markings are finishing or stitching lines rather than cut lines.

a. Mark any corrections or adjustments at the waistline.

b. Mark the closing and the stitching line for the waistband.

c. Mark or pin up the hem as appropriate.

SLACKS. There are additional fitting points for pants, regardless of length or degree of fullness.

1. The pants need to be properly aligned on the body with the centerlines on center, and with the darts and seams in the correct position. Adjust the waist and hip area as you would for a skirt.

a. Before finalizing the waist and hip areas, check the position of the crotch and the rise (see Chap. 10). If the crotch is too long, hanging lower between the legs than desired, the rise is too long. This may be corrected by raising the waistline on the body to the point where the crotch is in the correct position. The new waistline can then be marked and the excess trimmed away; but be sure to leave seam allowance.

Adjusting the crotch in this manner may shorten the length of the pant leg too much, or it may not allow enough ease for the thighs. However, since the fit at the hip and crotch area is what is most crucial in slacks, the fitting can be completed to get the necessary information, and the pattern can be recut with additional length and/or fullness.

b. If the crotch is too short or tight, the crotch-curve has not been cut deeply enough and the rise is too short. If the problem is not too severe, the waistline can be dropped slightly to correct the placement of the crotch. Otherwise, the pattern will have to be recut with a higher rise, as discussed in Chap. 10.

2. Check to see if the seams are in the proper position. If the seams need adjusting for a better fit, whether to be taken in or let out, work with both the inside and outside seams simultaneously to maintain the proper balance. If the seams tend to twist around the leg, it is generally an indication that the pant leg is not cut on the straight or proper grain of the fabric. Depending on the degree of the twist, the problem seams can be opened and re-pinned to make corrections. If the twisting cannot be corrected in this manner, the pattern will need to be recut on the correct grain line.

3. Check to be sure there is enough ease in the slacks for sitting and other movement. Have the actor sit, bend, and move in the fitted slacks. If they ride down in the back when the actor sits or bends over, it means that there is not enough fullness in the hips or there is not enough length from the crotch to the waist in the back. This can often be adjusted in the fitting by adding a strip of fabric, on the same grain as the pants, at the waistline in the back. This strip can be treated as part of the pants and be fitted in the normal fitting process for waist and hips. The pattern will have to be recut, but this approach assures that the fitting adjustments will be accurate.

Also check to see if there is enough ease in the thigh and calf area. The actor needs to sit and move to determine if there is

sufficient ease since the leg muscles expand when they are flexed.

4. After the waist, hip, and seams have been fitted, a preliminary length can be marked. This cannot be finalized until the second fitting, after everything is stitched together. The actor must also be wearing the appropriate shoes when length is marked.

Knee-length pants must be longer in the front than in the back if there is to be enough ease to cover the knees when the actor is sitting (see knee-length pattern draft).

5. Fitting markings: Mark the slacks on the body after the fitting is complete in the same manner as for skirts; see step 5 under Fitting Skirts.

COMPLETING THE FITTING

After all the necessary adjustments have been completed and marked and the garment has been checked for movement requirements and comfort, the garment is ready to come off the actor. In the first fitting, the additional pieces such as sleeves and collars may either be removed from the body of the garment or left pinned in place.

Before removing the garment, be sure that the separate pattern pieces on both sides of the closing line are marked. Remove the pins at the closing line and carefully remove the garment; watch for pins which can snag and gash, and make sure the opening is large enough for the actor to get in and out of the garment. At this point, the costumer may discover that the garment is pinned to the T-shirt or other garments and there is no way the actor can get out of what has been fitted. When this happens, there is no alternative but to pull

out the offending pins and to re-pin the garment carefully—but not through the T-shirt this time.

Before releasing the actor at the end of the fitting, review the notes taken during the fitting to make sure all the necessary information is noted. These notes will provide the basis for the work to be done on the costume through the subsequent stages of completion.

MARKING THE PATTERN AFTER THE FITTING. These comments are directed toward working with muslins after the first fitting. However, the methods are applicable to marking costumes after any fitting.

Because the garment was fitted with the wrong side next to the body, all the fitting marks and pinnings are on the outside and will need to be transferred to the inside. As indicated earlier, the two sides of the body are rarely symmetrical; therefore, the two sides of the fitted muslin will not necessarily be identical, but they must be balanced. You will also find that the adjusted fitting lines follow the curve of the body rather than the straight drafted lines.

When transferring the fitting markings, the balance of the garment and the grain of the fabric must be maintained for the garment to fit properly. To maintain the balance, the centerlines must be kept on center and the darts equidistant from center. To maintain the grain of the fabric, the two sides of the neck opening should match, armhole stitchlines and side seams should correspond with each other, and the grain of the good fabric should match the grain of the pattern.

Transferring the markings from the outside to the inside of the pattern is a simple process but must be done carefully. Pins have a nasty habit of falling out of fabric; therefore, the pin markings of the pattern should be transferred as soon as possible after the fitting has been completed. The tools required for this process include pencils, tailor's chalk, tracing wheel, and tracing paper.

Either of two methods for transferring the pin lines may be used. One method is to mark both sides of the pin line on the good side of the muslin with a pencil, or tailor's chalk if the fabric is too dark to show a pencil line. Remove the pins and lay the piece out flat over some tracing paper. Then transfer these lines with the trace wheel to the wrong side of the fabric.

Another method of marking the pin line is to work on the inside of the garment and mark the location of the pins on both sides of the pin line. If, for example, the side seam has been adjusted, mark the new seam line, which is held in place by the pins, on both the front and back pattern pieces, on the wrong side of the muslin. This method eliminates the process of tracing the new lines through to the wrong side; therefore, this is generally a faster means of transferring the pin lines. It also eliminates having fitting marks on both the good and wrong sides of the fabric.

After the pin lines have been marked, and the pins removed, trace the other lines, such as neckline, armholes, waistline, onto the wrong side of the muslin.

To avoid confusing the numerous markings which can accumulate on the muslins, use a different color tracing paper to indicate the markings which result from different fittings. For example, the drafted dart stitch lines may have been marked with blue lines during the drafting process. The fitted stitch lines need to be identifiable as the correct stitching lines when the garment is ready to be sewed together. Marking the correct lines with a different color helps avoid confusion over which lines to follow.

Check the garment carefully to make sure everything has been marked, including stitch lines which were not adjusted in the fitting. This is particularly necessary if the pattern was drafted and the seam allowance is not the standard ⅝-in. allowance used in commercial patterns. Balance lines at key points should also be marked on the pattern to maintain the alignment of the garment. These are particularly important on such things as curved seams and pleats.

If the garment is still basted together, remove the stitching and separate the muslin pieces. Mark each piece carefully so the piece can be identified and put back together properly. Each piece should be pressed before it is used as the lining or as a pattern for the good fabric. Be careful not to eliminate the markings made with tailor's chalk when pressing the pieces.

The fitted, marked muslin pieces are then ready to use as a pattern for the good fabric. If the acting pool is fairly constant, a paper copy of the fitted pattern should be made for the pattern library and identified with the actor's name and key measurements.

The attitudes and conduct of the people involved in the fitting process create the atmosphere for the fittings. The nature of this atmosphere is an all-important factor in the process. The first fitting can often be trying and tiresome for all concerned. It can be particularly so for an actor who finds unbleached muslins anything but exciting, attractive, or even flattering. That is why the costume plate should be where the actor can see it and thus get an idea of what is being developed by the costumer and designer; both of them should be able to describe what is happening with the muslins during the fitting and how the finished product will look.

It is equally important for those conducting the fitting to be confident in what they are doing, even if that confidence requires a bit of acting on their part. When working through the fitting and making the necessary adjustments, include the actor in the discussion when appropriate. Everyone resents being talked around as though they were not present, and an actor is no exception.

In addition, the type of movement and posture required by the costume should be discussed with the actor in the costume in front of the mirror. Many historical periods, as discussed earlier, have different movement and posture requirements. These variations from modern dress should be explained and discussed during the fittings. Experimenting with posture and movement in front of the mirror gives the actor a better sense of what the movements will look like and allows all concerned to check the comfort as well as the fit of the costume.

In the early fittings, particularly, the actor may be quite self-conscious. Putting the actor at ease as much as possible is one of the major reasons for setting up a private fitting area. Another is to avoid the natural desires of onlookers to kibitz while the fitting is in progress. The kibitzing can be intended as good fun, but it can often create problems. For instance, a lot of kidding and joking about what a costume looks like or what shapes it can suggest at different stages of its development occurs in a costume shop. If these jokes or comments are made to the actor in a fitting, they can be taken seriously or even personally, which is worse. This can strongly influence the actor's attitude toward the costume.

The costume is often the one tangible, concrete element in the whole production with which the actor has an immediate, personal contact. If an actor is insecure in the role, or if the atmosphere surrounding the production is tense, the actor will often complain of numerous problems with the costume that cannot be detected by the costumer, designer, or even the director. Responding with patience, consideration, and as much tolerance as possible is the key rule in these instances. If responses to an actor's performance are good, the problems with the costume usually dissipate very quickly. If the complaints continue, deal with the adjustments as much as possible. Do not develop the habit of brushing the complaints aside and run the risk of not dealing with the valid ones.

When preparing for a production, it is important to remember that everyone is ultimately working toward the same goal—an exciting, complete show. The fitting process is one of the elements which leads toward that goal. The objective of the fittings is to prepare the costume as effectively and efficiently as possible and to assist the actor in realizing the character being portrayed. To do this requires skill in the fitting process and, oftentimes, skill in dealing with people.

thirteen

pattern variations

The basic patterns described in the previous chapters are provided with the intention of helping the costumer gain skill in pattern drafting and to further comprehension of the principles of developing a pattern for a particular garment to fit a particular body. Obviously, each of the patterns described can be made up into a perfectly usable garment. But theatrical costumes for a given production are made to fulfill specific designs, and many of those designs are intended to capture the appearance effects of a wide variety of modern fashions and period styles. Many of those styles and fashions, in turn, require patterns or patterning techniques that are somewhat different from the basic patterns discussed so far.

These basic patterns can also be considered as starting points for variations that will capture the appearance of many garments of the present and the past. Many variations are possible. Some have been described in the chapters with the particular garment patterns; some others will be described in this chapter.

The premise is that once the basic patterns are understood, the practice of adjusting patterns to satisfy the appearance of a particular fashion or period silhouette is not difficult to master. The instructions given in this book describe how adjustment techniques can be applied. For the costumer who is willing to analyze the construction needs of a garment and who will continue to experiment with pattern variations beyond these instructions, almost any silhouette can be obtained.

Experimenting with the methods described on scaled-down paper patterns and then on full-scale muslins will provide comprehension of the principles of pattern variations. At the same time, the experiments will lead to solutions for patterning puzzles which may not be discussed directly in these chapters.

This chapter will deal with adjustment techniques involved in making variations in the basic patterns. Fitting darts, for example, can be altered in several ways to change the way in which the garment appears to mold the body. The patterns can be extended; seams can be relocated or eliminated; and pattern pieces can be combined to alter the shape and appearance of the garments themselves. The basic patterns can also be used as foundations upon which more elaborate garment shapes and decorative effects can be built up. These are fundamental techniques, but they can have many applications in a wide variety of garments.

ALTERING FITTING DARTS

Fitting darts are used to shape fabric to fit the contours of the body. These darts may be moved, combined, divided, or converted to seams to alter the appearance and shape of the garment. Altering the fitting darts is an effective means of expanding the versatility of the basic patterns and for fullfilling the costume design.

Before describing the actual process of reworking the darts, a brief review of the basic rules for fitting darts will establish some of the principles for altering darts.

BASIC FITTING DART RULES.   The first rule deals with the position, length, and pivot point of a dart. In the flat patterning process, these are determined by a series of measurements. The location of the fitting darts on the front of the basic bodice pattern, for example, is determined by the bust pivot point, point F on the draft (see Fig. 13-1). The bust circle around point F determines the length of the dart and both the point and the circle are located by measurements, as discussed in Chap. 7. Since there is no bust pivot point or circle on the back of the bodice or in the male jacket pattern, the pivot point for each dart is again located and marked on the pattern through standard measurements. If any adjustments are required in the placement of darts, they are made in the fitting. The pivot points of the darts, however, are the guides for reworking the darts of the basic patterns whether they are measured or fitted into place.

Secondly, ample seam allowance at the seam end of the dart must be included in the drafting of the dart. The dart stitching lines should always be equal in length, and the dart centerline should be at least ½ in. (1.3 cm) longer than the stitching lines. Darts which are placed on a diagonal to the side seam as in Fig. 13-2 (p. 194) should have extra allowance; the centerline should be at least 1 in. (2.5 cm) longer than the stitching lines. Remember that it is much easier to cut off excess than it is to add it on or to recut the pattern.

To assure enough seam allowance, match and pin the dart stitching lines in position and fold the dart in the direction it will lie when stitched. Mark the seam line, with seam allowance, prior to cutting the final pattern.

GUIDELINES FOR ALTERING DARTS.   A major point to keep in mind when reworking fitting darts on a full-scale pattern is to maintain the appropriate grain of the fabric. In practically all cases, this means maintaining the grain line of the original pattern even after it has been slashed and adjusted. This, of course, implies careful marking of the pattern as it is adjusted. If applicable, balance lines, stitching lines, and additional seam allowances required also need to be noted on the pattern piece as adjustments are made.

Notice that altering fitting darts will affect the way in which the grain of the fabric in the garment will fall at various points on the contours of the body. These subtle shifts in grain are an aspect that provides the authenticity of period or fashion to the garment. In some few cases, the necessary shift in grain may require a slightly different placement of the pattern on the grain lines of the garment fabric, so careful analysis should always be made.

The rules for dart length and pivot point need to be observed when reworking the darts. Briefly, the dart length is determined by the location of the pivot points on basic patterns and by the bust circle on the basic bodice front. When there are two or more darts in the bodice front pattern, the darts terminate at the bust circle; if there is only one fitting dart, it terminates at the bust point (see Fig. 13–2).

When reworking the pattern to alter darts, work with the pattern as flat and smooth as possible in order to maintain enough ease in the garment. Since slashing and closing darts and pivoting sections of the pattern may cause bulges to occur or seam lines to be temporarily distorted, it is essential that necessary shapes and dimensions be restored. If laying the adjusted pattern out flat alters a seam line, reshape it to the proper dimensions by adding and filling out the distorted line rather than by trimming away any of the original pattern material. This is illustrated in several of the figures in this chapter.

Darts which are drafted have straight stitch lines; darts which have been fitted generally have slightly curved stitch lines which conform to the rounded body contours. Those darts which have been established or altered in a fitting can also be reworked as easily as the drafted darts. The essential difference is that the stitching lines of the fitted darts are more curved and may therefore create a greater bulge at the end of the dart. If the bulge is strong, simply straighten the stitch lines on the pattern and readjust them, if necessary, in the fitting.

Finally, the appropriate alteration and reworking of fitting darts is dependent upon the design of the garment. Experimentation with the alteration process will reveal a wide range of variety which can be achieved from the basic pattern. Only a few of the possibilities can be mentioned here.

THE BODICE FRONT PATTERN.   All the pattern variations discussed here require relocating the darts as the first step. Typically, the relocation of darts is more common in women's garments since more darts are involved because of the shaping required to match the body contours created by the bust. Therefore, this discussion will focus on reworking the fitting darts in the bodice front.

Once the process of altering these darts is understood, reworking the darts for the bodice back, the male jacket, and fitting darts in other patterns is a simple procedure. To understand the steps involved more quickly, draft a basic pattern in half or quarter scale on paper. Make several copies of the small paper patterns and practice altering darts before working with the actual pattern pieces in full scale.

The following instructions involve adjusting the basic bodice/jacket pattern in Chap. 7, and all require a draft of that pattern. However, the methods described are applicable to all the basic patterns.

RELOCATING DARTS.   An easy method of altering fitting darts is to start with the basic bodice/jacket pattern and determine where the dart is to be relocated. Draw a line in the new location; then slash the pattern to the pivot points of the old dart and new dart locations to adjust the darts. The old dart is closed on the stitching lines causing the new position to spread apart to locate and show the dimensions of the new dart.

The locations of the waist and bust fitting darts on the basic pattern are already established. The adjusted locations of new darts will be determined by the design and

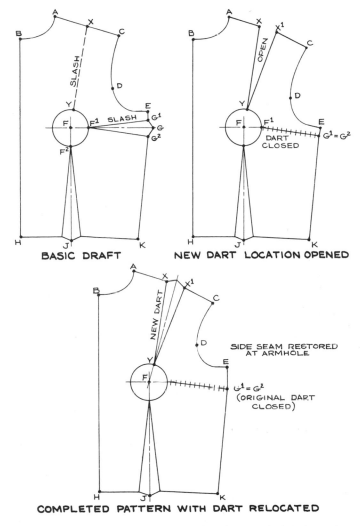

Figure 13-1 An example of the process for relocating the bust fitting dart to the shoulder seam.

the required silhouette of the garment, but determining where to place the new dart, and to what purpose, is the key to reworking the fitting darts; analyze carefully.

1. Take the bodice front pattern and determine the location of the new dart. Draw a line from the seam allowance to the bust pivot point (point F) in the new loca-

tion. Set point Y where this line crosses the bust circle and set point X at the seam allowance end of the line. Line X–Y is the relocated dart line as shown in Fig. 13–1.

2. Slash the top stitching line of the bust fitting dart, line G^1–F^1, to the bust circle.

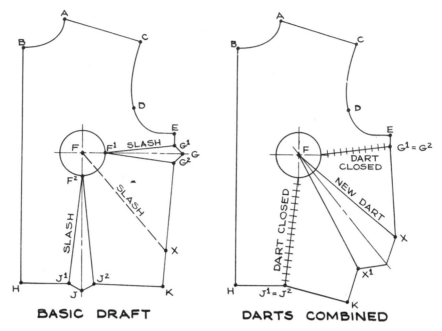

Figure 13-2   An example of combining the bust and waist fitting darts and relocating them on the side seam. The combined dart terminates at the bust pivot point.

3. Slash the relocated dart line, line X–Y, to the bust circle.

4. Match the stitching lines of the bust fitting dart, lines G^1–F^1 and G^2–F^1, and pin or tape them in position as shown in Fig. 13–1.

a. Matching the stitchlines of the original dart will cause the pattern to spread at the new dart location. There will be a slight puckering at the tip of the closed dart, and the side seam below the armhole will be distorted.

b. Smooth and flatten the pucker with the hand and adjust the side seam as shown to replace the ease taken up by the puckering at the bust.

5. Pin the adjusted pattern on muslin or paper; mark the new dart stitching lines, X–Y and X^1–Y, as shown. Locate the

center of the new dart and lay in a centerline. This line should be ½ in. (1.3 cm) longer than the stitching lines.

6. Shape the seam edge of the dart by connecting the ends of the stitching lines X–Y and X^1–Y and the centerline as shown. The pattern is now ready to mark and cut.

COMBINING DARTS. This technique is typically used for something like an A-line dress with one long diagonal fitting dart. In this instance, the combined dart terminates at the bust pivot point, rather than at the circle. It will also be as wide as the combined widths of the darts that it replaces.

1. On the bodice front pattern, draw a line from the seam to point F, and set point X at the seam allowance as shown in Fig. 13–2. Note that this line terminates at the bust pivot point.

2. Slash line G^1-F^1 of the bust dart and the stitching line of the waist fitting dart that is closest to the center fold (line J^1-F^2). These lines are slashed to the bust circle. Slash line X–F to the bust pivot point.

3. Match the waist dart stitching lines and pin them or tape them in place; match the bust dart stitching lines and pin or tape them in place to open the new dart position. Note: There will be a slight puckering at the bust circle. Flatten the pattern before continuing to the next step.

4. Pin the adjusted pattern on muslin or paper; mark the new dart stitching lines, lines X–F and X^1–F.

5. Locate and mark the centerline of the new dart. This line should be 1 in. (2.5 cm) longer than the stitching lines of the dart to provide ample seam allowance.

6. Shape the seam edge of the dart by connecting the end of the stitching lines X–F and X^1–F and the centerline as shown. The pattern is now ready to mark and cut.

CONVERTING DARTS TO SEAMS. A number of patterns use seams instead of darts to fit the configurations of the body. The location of these seams can be determined by altering the fitting darts. This technique is applicable to all basic fitted patterns, but the example here is for the upper torso pattern. The primary criterion for converting darts to seams is that the centerline of the waist fitting dart and the new seam line, regardless of location, go through the bust pivot point. The new seam line is, in a sense, a continuation of the centerline of the waist fitting dart.

1. Take the bodice front pattern and determine the location of the new seam line in the same manner as locating the position of a relocated dart; draw a line from the seam to the bust pivot point, line X–F in Fig. 13–3. This figure shows two examples, one with the new seam line running from the shoulder to the waist over the bust, and the other with the seam line running from the armhole to the waist over the bust.

2. Draw two balance lines across the new seam line, halfway between the seam and the bust pivot point, and draw two more across the waist fitting dart as shown; these balance lines will be matched when the garment is put together.

3. Slash the new seam line to the bust pivot point.

4. Cut the centerline of the waist fitting dart through the bust pivot point to separate the pattern pieces. Cut away the stitching lines of the waist dart from point F^2 to the waist.

5. Slash the top stitching lines of the bust dart, line G^1-F^1, to the bust circle. Match the bust dart stitching lines and pin them or tape them together as shown.

6. Lay out and pin the adjusted pattern pieces on paper or muslin, leaving space between the pieces for seam allowance as shown. The waist dart stitching lines and the cut edges are the stitching lines of the new seam.

7. Mark the stitching lines of the new seam and add seam allowance; trace through the balance lines.

8. Adjust the armhole and side seam at the closed bust dart as shown. The pattern is then ready to be marked and cut.

DIVIDING DARTS. Darts are usually divided as a design detail since dividing darts generally means that there will be two or more darts on the same seam line. Many variations are possible when dividing darts, although only four are illustrated here.

There are, however, some additional considerations to keep in mind which are dictated by the shape and size of the seam from which the dart originates. For exam-

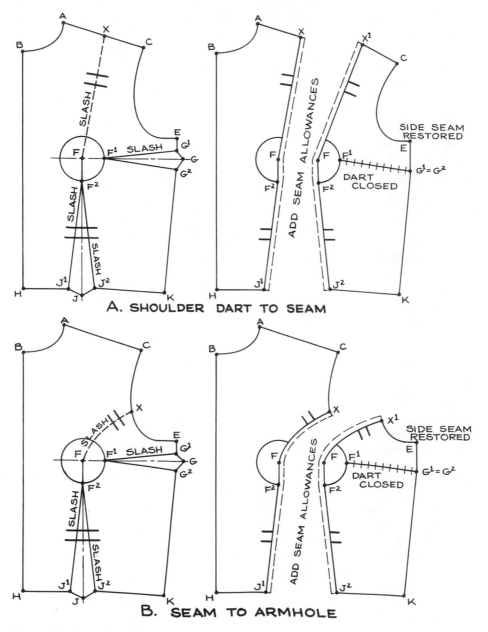

A. SHOULDER DART TO SEAM

B. SEAM TO ARMHOLE

Figure 13–3 Examples of converting fitting darts to seams; seam allowances must be added to the new seams. Note the use of balance lines on the new seams.

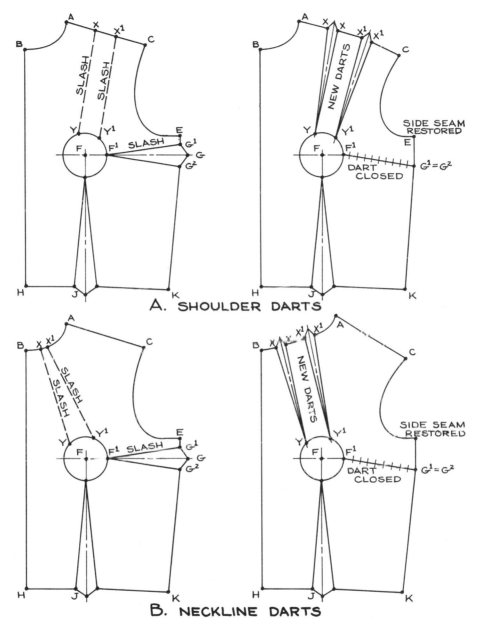

Figure 13-4 Examples of relocating and dividing bust fitting darts; the divided darts do not point to the bust pivot point, but they do terminate at the bust circle.

ple, shoulder darts which originate from a short seam are parallel to each other and terminate at the top of the bust circle as shown in Fig. 13–4A. The tips of the darts do not point at the bust pivot point but are located equidistant from the bust point by

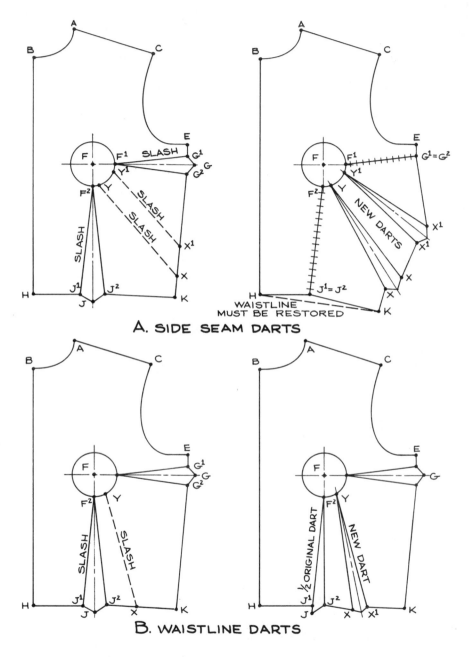

Figure 13-5 Examples of dividing darts: A. combined bust and waist dart relocated on the side seam and divided; B. waist fitting dart divided. All the new darts terminate at the bust circle.

terminating on the bust circle. These shoulder darts are relocated from the bust dart. Since the bust dart is being relocated and divided, the stitching lines are matched and pinned together; the amount of spread in the pattern at the shoulder is divided between the two new darts. The new divided darts may not be the same length; however, the stitching lines of each dart must be equal in length, with the centerline ½ in. (1.3 cm) longer than the stitching lines.

Neckline darts, which originate on a curved seam, fan out from the seam. They terminate at the bust circle and are, therefore, equidistant from the bust point as shown in Fig.13–4B. These darts can be converted from either the bust or waist fitting darts. The stitching lines of the darts must be equal in length, with the centerline ½ in. (1.3 cm) longer.

Divided darts which are in a diagonal position to a seam, as in Fig. 13–5A, are not the same length. They generally terminate at the bust circle and are equidistant from the bust pivot point. The darts in Fig. 13–5A are combined bust and waist darts which are divided. The stitching lines of the individual darts must be equal in length, with the centerline 1 in. (2.5 cm) longer.

If a dart is to be divided without a major relocation, as shown in the division of the waistline dart in Fig. 13–5B, only half the width of the dart is moved. The pattern is slashed on the line of the new dart location and on the stitching line of the original dart nearest the center-front. The original dart is closed halfway by matching that stitching line to the dart centerline. This opens the new dart; find the new centerline, lengthen it ½ in. (1.3 cm) beyond the length of the stitching lines X–Y and X¹–Y, and mark the new seam allowance as shown.

The general principles to keep in mind when dividing darts include:

1. The tips of the divided darts are equidistant from the bust point; terminating them at the bust circle automatically places them equidistant from the bust pivot point.

2. If a fitting dart is to be divided, the original dart is slashed on one stitch line and the line is matched to the dart centerline; if the fitting dart is to be relocated and then divided, the dart stitchlines are matched to each other.

3. Always provide extra seam allowance for the new darts to compensate for the bulge created at the bust circle when the original pattern is slashed and spread. This is particularly important for darts that are diagonal to the seam line.

The Bodice Back and Jacket Pattern

The same processes are followed for reworking fitting darts in the bodice back pattern and the jacket pattern. Generally, however, the variety of styles used in the bodice front is not required for either the bodice back or the jacket. Therefore, the typical treatment for these patterns is the conversion of darts to seams for additional control of fit and the achievement of proper silhouette.

The technique for converting darts to seams is essentially the same as the process described under Bodice Front. However, since there is no bust circle, all slashing is carried to the pivot point at the tip of the dart as shown in Fig. 13–6. Use balance lines to simplify the realignment of the pattern pieces on the new seam. Add seam allowances as shown before marking and cutting the new pattern pieces.

Altering Darts to Suggest Period Silhouettes

A great deal of variety can be achieved by reworking the fitting darts of a basic pattern as is evident from the preceding discussion. The process of reworking darts is

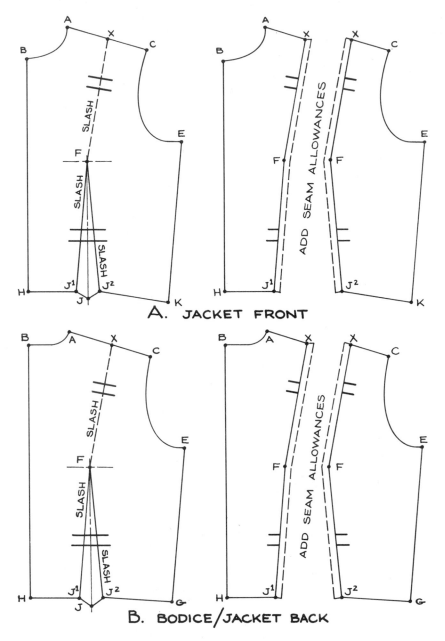

Figure 13–6 Examples of converting darts to seams: A. the jacket front; B. the bodice/jacket back. Seam allowances need to be added to the new seam; note the use of balance lines on the new seam.

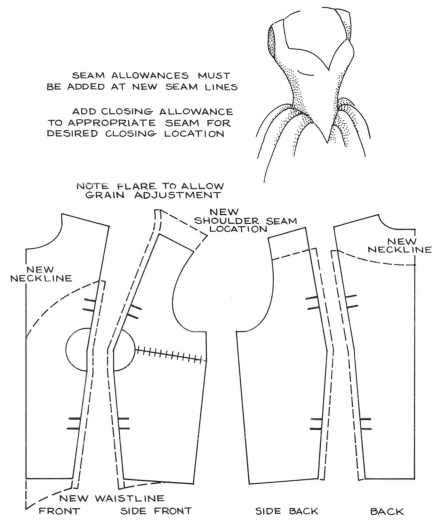

SEAM ALLOWANCES MUST
BE ADDED AT NEW SEAM LINES

ADD CLOSING ALLOWANCE
TO APPROPRIATE SEAM FOR
DESIRED CLOSING LOCATION

NOTE FLARE TO ALLOW
GRAIN ADJUSTMENT

NEW
SHOULDER SEAM
LOCATION

NEW
NECKLINE

NEW
NECKLINE

NEW
NECKLINE

NEW WAISTLINE

FRONT   SIDE FRONT   SIDE BACK   BACK

Figure 13-7 An example of converting the basic bodice pattern to a period silhouette showing a shift in the shoulder seam location and new shaping at the waistline.

also applicable to capturing various silhouette lines for period garments. For example, reshaping the waistline and lowering the neckline of the basic bodice pattern as shown in Fig. 13-7 creates a pattern suitable for the Isabella costume in Fig. 1-8, or a modified Elizabethan bodice.

Converting the waist fitting dart of the male jacket to a seam begins to suggest an Elizabethan doublet. Adding length at the center-front waistline, fullness for padding over the abdomen, and other minor adjustments in the basic pattern as shown in Fig. 13-8 creates a pattern for the "peascodded" doublet of the late sixteenth century.

The principles of lengthening seams and modifying patterns by other means are the subject of the following discussion. These can be applied to all basic patterns and can be combined with dart alterations for many other patterns that are appropriate to period silhouettes.

EXTENDING AND ELIMINATING SEAMS

Extending seams to reshape a waistline or shoulder line is illustrated in Fig. 13–7. The process is not difficult; the extensions originate from the original seams and are added with the contours of the body in mind. For example, the front shoulder extensions shown are curved to conform to an armhole; they are curved at the neckline to go around the neck and across the top of the seam to allow for the width at the back of the shoulders. An amount equal to the extension is removed from the shoulder seam of the bodice back. The final shape and position of the seam are determined in the fitting.

Eliminating seams is also illustrated in Fig. 13–8. In this instance, the underarm seam is eliminated and replaced by seams at the front and back to shape the torso in a different way. This requires matching the stitching lines at the underarm and pinning them together to make one pattern piece. As with all other pattern variations, final adjustments are made in the fitting.

The fundamental principles, then, for extending seams are to extend with the body contours in mind and to make the necessary adjustments in the joining seam to allow for the extension. When eliminating seams for a fitted garment, match stitching lines, but add seam allowance for any new seams that are created.

Altering the Basic
Bodice/Jacket Pattern

Several period costumes require a fitted look from the shoulders to the hips; this includes garments like the male jackets of the fourteenth century and the princess-line gowns of the late nineteenth century. Patterns for these and other fitted long-torso garments can be developed from the basic patterns.

The bodice/jacket pattern is part of the base, and the upper portion of the fitted skirt pattern can be used to complete the unit as shown in Fig. 13–9. If the bust fitting dart is to be relocated, establish the new dart location before adding the lower part of the pattern.

1. Place the bodice pattern on paper that is at least 15 in. (38 cm) longer by 6 in. (15 cm) wider than the pattern.

2. As shown in Fig. 13–9, to lay out the portion below the waist, take the "neck-to-waist" measurement plus 10 in. (25.5 cm) and measure down from the neckline (point B on the draft) on the center-front line and set point HH. Then draw a line at a right angle to the center-front to establish the hipline. This line is somewhat lower than the hipline on the basic skirt to allow for extra seam (or hem) allowance.

3. To establish the width for the hips, take one-quarter of the "hip" measurement plus 2 in. (5 cm) for the front (the same dimensions are used for the pattern back) and measure over from point HH on the right-angle line and set point KK. Connect this point with the side seam waist of the bodice (point K on the draft) with a slightly curved line similar to the upper-side seam of the basic fitted skirt.

4. To complete the fitting dart, measure down 3½ in. (9 cm) on the dart centerline from the waistline and set point JJ (this dimension would be 6 in. [15 cm]

Figure 14-5 "Coulmier's Wife and Daughter" in *Marat/Sade* as produced at the University of Rhode Island. The wife's over-gown is taken from the over-gown pattern in Fig. 14-4; the back measures 8 in. across the shoulders. From the author's collection.

Figure 15-15B Patchwork quilt ponchos on ensemble in Stravinsky's *L'Histoire du Soldat* as produced by the University of Rhode Island. From the author's collection.

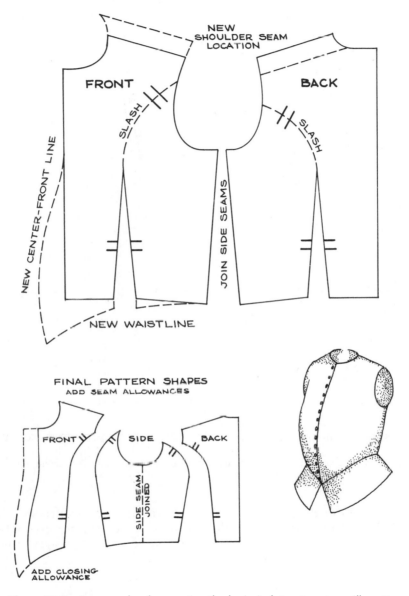

Figure 13-8 An example of converting the basic jacket pattern to a silhouette appropriate for the late sixteenth century. Darts are converted to seams, the original side seam is eliminated, and the shoulder seams, center-front seam, and waistline are extended and reshaped.

on the pattern back). Extend the centerline of the dart to that point; then connect the bottom of the dart stitching lines.

This pattern is cut as the regular bodice/jacket pattern and will need to be adjusted in a fitting to finalize the side seams and fitting darts.

The darts can be converted to seams by

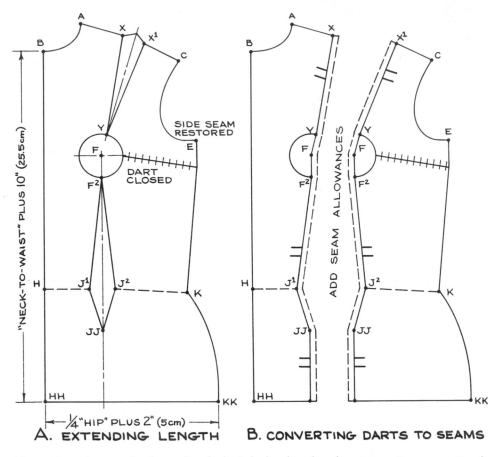

Figure 13-9 An example of extending the basic bodice front for a long-torso pattern; converting the darts to seams makes a princess-line pattern.

the same procedure detailed for the bodice. The slash line is extended to the bottom of the pattern on the dart centerline. After the pieces are separated, the necessary seam allowances need to be added for the new seams (see Fig. 13-9B).

ADDING LENGTH TO THE EXTENDED BODICE/JACKET. The lower portion of this pattern can be extended by dropping lines from points HH and KK to a desired hem length with flare added as needed by applying the methods for adding flare to a basic fitted skirt. Gored, gathered, pleated, or circle skirts can also be attached to this

pattern when appropriate. The drafting processes are the same except that the hip-line is the top of the skirt rather than the waistline.

Altering the Basic Slacks Pattern

The basic slacks pattern can be altered to a number of styles from different eras for such things as Elizabethan pumpkin hose, Restoration petticoat breeches, and women's bloomers. Methods for altering the length of the pants for shorts and knee-

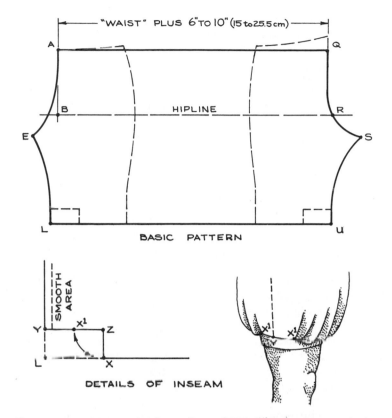

"WAIST" PLUS 6" TO 10" (15 to 25.5 cm)

HIPLINE

BASIC PATTERN

SMOOTH AREA

DETAILS OF INSEAM

Figure 13-10 An example of extending and eliminating the side seam in the basic slacks pattern for a "pumpkin hose" pattern appropriate for the late sixteenth century. Note the shaping of the bottom edge to enhance the "puff" around the leg.

length versions have been detailed in Chap. 10. Other adjustments can be made by extending and eliminating the side seams. To explore this process of altering the pattern, drafting pumpkin hose is used as an example.

The process is not difficult; it is done by enlarging the waistline and eliminating the side seam; the waistline is continued in a solid line from the front to the back crotch-curves, and the back fitting dart is eliminated. The bottom of the pattern is also connected with a solid line from inseam to inseam as shown in Fig. 13-10.

To create the fullness required for pumpkin hose, the pattern needs to be en-

larged. If the waistline in the finished pants is double the actor's "waist" measurement, the result will be only moderate fullness; a very full appearance will need an additional 12 in. to 20 in. (30.5 cm to 51 cm) to achieve that effect. This means that on the pattern draft, which is only one-half of the garment, the waistline dimension should equal the entire "waist" measurement with possibly another 6 in. to 10 in. (15 cm to 25.5 cm) added to that.

The average length of the pattern is about 24 in. (61 cm) from the waistline to the bottom of the leg. The garment, of course, is not worn at that length. The bottoms of the legs are usually gathered into bands that are worn pushed up on the leg to make the fullness puff out to the "pumpkin" shape of the garment's name.

The pattern is laid out on fabric that is at least 8 in. (20.5 cm) wider than the new waistline is to be. Use the layout of the basic slacks pattern; the enlarging of the layout is accomplished in the same manner as the technique used for adding fullness to a basic sleeve described in Chap. 8.

First, at one edge of the fabric, trace the front crotch-curve and inseam; then slide the pattern (keeping on the crosswise grain) across to the other end of the waistline and trace the back crotch-curve and inseam. Connect the waistline across the top; the curve for the waistline is not really necessary since there is plenty of ease. Finally, connect the inseams with a line for the bottom of the pants, and cut two copies of the pattern, one for each leg.

To help control the fullness around the leg, a variation can be made in the treatment of the inseam and bottom edge of the leg (see the detail in Fig. 13–10). Cut a rectangle out of the corner of the seam edges as shown. The dimensions are only approximate and can be adjusted for greater or lesser fullness. When the pattern is cut out, points X and X^1 are brought together and the edges are stitched to point Z to create a controlled fullness puff. The remainder of line Y–X^1 becomes a continuation of the bottom edge of the leg and is attached to the leg band; however, it should not be gathered into the band. The idea is to leave a flat area at the inseam so the actor's legs can move freely even though the pants appear to be pleated all around.

The fullness at the waist and legs can be controlled by overlap pleats or cartridge pleats. The amount of fullness in these pants is best controlled if they are mounted on a fitted undergarment; otherwise, they fall with their own weight and do not hold the round shape.

The amount of fullness at waist, hipline,

and legs can be varied to make several styles from the basic slacks pattern by extending the seams, eliminating the side seam, or by joining the inseams so that the side seams are open to work with. Analysis and experimentation will suggest many possibilities.

Altering the Basic Single-Piece Sleeve Pattern

The basic sleeve pattern can also go through a number of metamorphoses; several examples of these are discussed in Chap. 8. As mentioned in that chapter, sleeves are a distinguishing feature in establishing the illusion of period in a costume. The basic sleeve patterns can be used to develop patterns appropriate to a number of period styles; some examples are cited here to provide guidelines in this process.

ADDING LENGTH. The single-piece sleeve, for example, can be converted to a long, straight, hanging sleeve popular in the fourteenth and fifteenth centuries by simply extending straight lines from the sleeve cap, points D, A, and E in Fig. 13–11A. The length of the sleeve is determined by the design, but this sleeve should be at least 4 in. to 5 in. (10 cm to 12.5 cm) longer than the arm and hand combined. Since some of the sleeves of the period are depicted as knotted, to keep them from trailing in the dust, the maximum length is obviously arbitrary. An opening for the hand and arm to pass through the hanging sleeve is necessary. Whether it is circular or a slit, the opening is placed between the elbow and the wrist area of the arm for convenience. The bottom edge of the sleeve can be gathered or pleated into a cuff to make a "bag-sleeve" or hemmed as is for a straight hanging sleeve. Depending on the design specifications, additional fullness in this type of sleeve may be required; this is accomplished as described under Adding Fullness in Chap. 8.

The wide-mouth, open-hanging sleeves

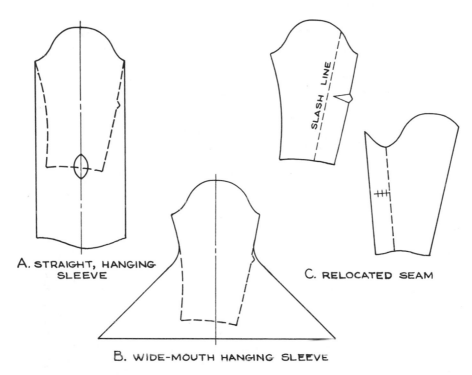

A. STRAIGHT, HANGING SLEEVE

C. RELOCATED SEAM

B. WIDE-MOUTH HANGING SLEEVE

Figure 13-11 Examples of variations on the basic sleeve pattern: A. hanging sleeve appropriate for fourteenth and fifteenth centuries; B. wide-mouth sleeve appropriate for the fourteenth and fifteenth centuries; C. relocating the underarm seam, a process appropriate for many eras.

of the Gothic era can also be created using the single-piece sleeve as a guide. By itself, this sleeve can also serve as the fitted under-sleeve with the hanging over-sleeve. As shown in Fig. 13–11B, the underarm seam edges are extended to the hem edge of the sleeve. If this extension starts at the elbow line rather than at the capline, the sleeve will be fitted over the upper arm. The extensions can also originate from other points on the sleeve, and they can be straight, as shown, or curved lines according to the design specifications. The length of the sleeve can also vary from wrist-length to longer if a fold-back cuff is part of the design. The hem edge can be scalloped (called *dagging*) or cut in any number of ways for decorative effects.

ALTERING SEAMS. Since several patterns for period silhouettes have the shoulder seams set toward the back rather than on top of the shoulder, the seam in the single-piece sleeve should also be shifted to conform with the new shaping of the shoulder of the garment. In many instances, the underarm is shifted forward as part of this shaping. This process is accomplished by slashing the sleeve pattern as shown in Fig. 13–11C, closing the fitting dart, and joining the old underarm seam so that the shape of the sleeve cap is altered as shown.

Altering the Basic Circle Skirt Pattern

A full-length circle cape can be drafted using the circle skirt pattern as a model. The opening is cut to match the bodice/jacket neckline rather than the waist, the

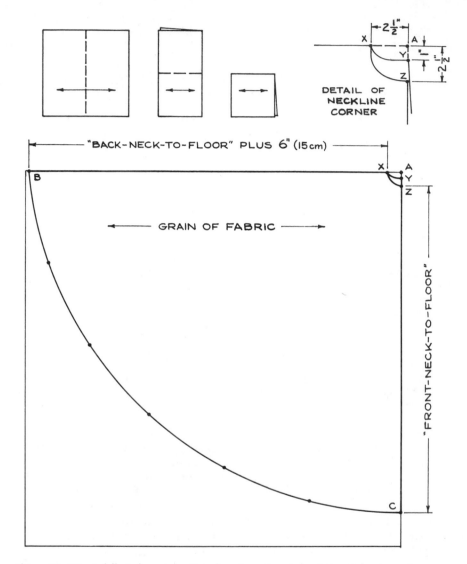

Figure 13-12 A full-circle cape pattern based on the circle skirt pattern; inset shows an enlarged detail of the neck shaping.

length is taken from the "back-neck-to-floor" measurement, and the area over the shoulder is extended about 6 in. (15 cm) to accommodate to width of the shoulders, as shown in Fig. 13–12. The sides of the square of fabric for the cape need to be double the "back-neck-to-floor" measurement plus an additional 18 in. (46 cm).

1. Lay out the pattern so that the center-front and center-back are on separate folds of the crosswise grain and set point A at the fold corners as shown.

2. To establish the neckline, measure over 2½ in. (6.3 cm) on the lengthwise grain fold and set point X; then measure

Check the similarities and then compare those that are dissimilar and make the necessary corrections on your pattern sketches. Finally, select those patterns on which you miscalculated and do muslin mock-ups to see how the actual pattern works and how it influences the posture and silhouette. Projects of this nature will help define the guidelines for determining what needs to be adjusted to the actor's measurements for the proper fit.

CONSTRUCTING AND FITTING PERIOD GARMENTS

The basic rules for constructing and fitting garments drafted from period patterns are essentially the same as those for modern garments. The construction process involves preparing everything for the initial fitting; fitted units are basted together, full units can be permanently stitched. As with modern garments, items like sleeves, collars, and the like are not attached to the body unit for this initial fitting.

It should be noted, however, that the pattern structures will not be the same as the modern basic drafts. For example, fitting darts to control a fitted garment were not traditionally used until the nineteenth century (and then they were called "bosom plaits"). Prior to that time, control in the fitted garments was achieved with seams and careful use of the grain and often involved stiffening or padding. Therefore, preparation of additional elements such as corsets, padded pieces, or the like may be necessary for the first fitting.

The notation and marking processes typical for fittings are also the same; however, the location of seams or darts may be quite different from those for modern garments (see Fig. 14–6). For example, the location of the shoulder seam for the gown in Fig. 14–5 is shifted quite far back from the normal modern position. The armhole for this garment is also cut much deeper in the back than is typical in modern garments, and the waistline is very high. The effect of these locations, combined with the narrow back, holds the shoulders back and raises the bustline so that the waistline is just under the normal nipple line.

Another example can be seen in Fig. 14–7 which has the waistline of the gown on the natural waist in the front and raised higher in the back. The effect of this line enhances the "pouter pigeon" look typical of turn-of-the-century female fashions. This effect and earlier Victorian silhouettes for women require that the fitting darts be doubled and angled to the outside of the nipple, which is quite different from

Figure 14–6 Example of the use of darts and seams to control a fitted bodice for a "Courtesan" in *Comedy of Errors* as produced by The Champlain Shakespeare Festival. From the author's collection.

Figure 14-7 An example of the "pouter pigeon" silhouette created by the angle of the fitting darts and the positioning of the waistline. The character is "Lucienne" in *A Flea in Her Ear* as produced by the University of Rhode Island Summer Theatre. From the author's collection.

the angle and placement of the modern fitting darts.

Determining the locations for the fitted markings and how to manipulate the grain of the fabric comes through study and analysis of period patterns. Working with and fitting the mock-ups made as part of the pattern analysis project clarifies where and how to adjust the period garments in fittings.

The construction phases after the initial fitting also follow the same guidelines as for modern garments. The planning and mapping out of the sequence of processes is as important for period garments as for modern ones, particularly since construction for many period garments is more complex than for most modern garments.

ADDITIONAL SOURCES

There are several books which have a compilation of patterns and illustrations of actual period garments. Patterns from these and other resources are invaluable in the study of period garments. They are easy to enlarge and work with for theatrical application. Of course any study of period patterns and garments will need to include some contact with the actual garments. Fortunately, most museums have costume collections available for study, and many costume shops have original items from previous decades which have been donated to the theatre. These are invaluable as study resources and for pattern sources.

The following is a selected bibliography; some of the Additional Sources cited in other chapters also contain authentic and adapted period patterns.

ARNOLD, JANET, *Patterns of Fashion, 1, 1660–1860; 2, 1860–1940*. New York: Drama Book Specialists/Publishers, 1972.

BRADFORD, NANCY, *Costume in Detail*. Boston: Plays, Inc., 1970.

BURNHAM, DOROTHY, *Cut My Cote*. Toronto, Canada: Textile Department, Royal Ontario Museum, 1973.

CROONBORG, FREDRICK, *The Blue Book of Men's Tailoring*. New York: Van Nostrand Reinhold Co., 1977.

EDSON, DORIS, and LUCY BARTON, *Period Patterns*. Boston: Walter H. Baker Co., 1970.

HILL, MARGOT HAMILTON, and PETER A. BUCKNELL, *The Evolution of Fashion: Pattern and Cut from 1066 to 1930*. New York: Van Nostrand Reinhold Co., 1970.

KOHLER, CARL, *A History of Costume*. Emma Von Sichart, ed., trans. by Alexander K. Dallas. New York: Dover Publications, Inc., 1963.

WAUGH, NORAH, *The Cut of Men's Clothes, 1600–1900*. New York: Theatre Arts Books, 1964.

———, *The Cut of Women's Clothes, 1600–1930*. New York: Theatre Arts Books, 1968.

the costumer's crafts
and techniques

part 3

fifteen

fabric modification

Fabric modification is used as a generic term incorporating a variety of materials and techniques that are used to change or adapt the appearance of a fabric or even an entire theatrical costume. It includes all the things that can be done with dyes, paints, glues, overlays, or whatever, to create special effects on costumes. It is used to enhance the texture and/or detail of fabrics, to change or tone the color(s), and to create the patina of aged and/or ragged costumes. Fabric modification is a broad area; essentially it includes any treatment of fabric which alters the appearance and is used to create a variety of interesting and exciting costumes.

The processes evolve through experimentation. The materials come from a variety of sources, many of which appear to have no relationship to fabrics. Hot-melt glue, for example, can be used to create a raised texture, and graphite added to glue can make a piece of felt look like plate metal for a handsome piece of armor.

Virtually anything can be used, so long as it is not toxic, to achieve the desired appearance.

There are no real rules for fabric modification processes, only guidelines. There are also typical materials, supplies, and methods which are standard to many of the processes. Experimenting with these and the actual fabrics is necessary to learn what will do the job to capture the special effect desired for the costume.

Typical processes include dyeing, painting, and appliquéing. Each requires specific tools and equipment; each must be tested on samples of the actual fabric to be treated, and each requires time to execute the process effectively.

Beyond these guidelines, the processes involved require gaining a working knowledge of typical modification methods, such as dyeing fabric. This knowledge provides the means for the experimentation that is necessary to fulfill the appearance requirements of the costume.

225

The elements involved in dyeing, painting, and appliquéing techniques need to be explored in order to gain the necessary background and to be able to proceed to the experimentation stages of fabric modification. The processes may be used separately or in combination and can be developed through experience with methods and materials.

DYEING

Typical uses for dyes in a costume shop include *dip-dyeing*, immersing the fabric in the dye bath to tone or change its color; *batiking*, using wax to resist the dye so that only areas free of wax take the dye to create a pattern; *tie-dyeing*, tieing, knotting, or stitching fabric tightly in order to repel dye in the tied areas and create a pattern in the cloth; and *texturing* fabrics by spraying, brushing, or applying dyes in other ways. These processes are discussed under Dyeing Guidelines.

There are a number of factors which determine how a dye will react with a piece of cloth. First, the fiber content of the fabric influences what a dye will do. As mentioned in Chap. 4, not every type of natural or synthetic fiber reacts to dyes in the same way. Finishes on fabrics also influence how a dye will color the fabric; for example, it is likely that two pieces of muslin cut from different bolts and immersed in the same dye bath will not come out exactly the same color.

Finally, the influx of synthetic fibers in recent years has considerably altered the dye industry since special dyes have had to be developed to color them. Consequently, a number of dyes with special characteristics are now on the market to meet the needs of coloring the variety of fabrics commonly used today.

Classifications of Dyes

From the earliest times people have been coloring fabrics; sources for the colorants have included plants, insects, land animals, and sea creatures. The dyes which were obtained from the roots, bark, leaves, or fruit of common plants were the most plentiful, but those from sea creatures were rare and therefore more expensive. A small sea snail was the source for a reddish-purple dye, which made that color very expensive. As a result, "purple" was reserved for rulers of state and church, and it still has that type of regal association today.

Such natural dyes provided the only methods of coloring cloth until the nineteenth century, when synthetic dyes were developed. Synthetic dyes provide many advantages over natural dyes in that they are easier and faster to work with, and they offer a range of colors at low cost for all types of fabrics.

The first synthetic dye was discovered accidentally by Sir Henry Perkins in 1856. He was working with a substance known as "aniline," and his experiments led to an artificial dyestuff that was named *mauvine*, or mauve, because of the color it produced. Aniline was originally derived from coal tar, but today various chemicals are used to create synthetic dyes. The term *aniline* has remained, however, and in its common usage refers to all synthetic dyes.

The synthetic dyes are divided into different classes according to their dyeing properties or according to how they react with different fibers. Since dyes will only be truly effective on the fibers they were developed to color, it is necessary to know the basic fiber content of the fabric and the dyeing process to be used in order to select an appropriate dye for a given project.

The principal means for classifying dyes

is to use the labels applied by the dyeing industry: *household* or *union* dyes, *fiber-reactive* dyes, *direct* dyes, *acid* dyes, *vat* dyes, and *naphthol* or *azoic* dyes. The following discussions are based on those classifications, and the chart in Fig. 15–1 will provide an overview of the classifications, specific brand names, and general instructions for use.

Another means of classifying a dye is by the type of *assistant* that is required when using the dye. All aniline dyes require an assistant (salt or acetic acid) mixed in the dye bath to help the dye molecules penetrate the fibers. Dyes which use common (noniodized) salt for an assistant are referred to as *basic dyes; acid dyes* require acetic acid or vinegar as the assistant.

Two other terms which may be encountered in connection with dyes are "unified" and "nonunified"; these refer to aniline dyes. The term *unified* covers essentially the union or all-purpose dye classification. *Nonunified* is a broader term that is applied to those classifications of dyes intended for use on specific types of fibers. They are usually designated for cotton (vegetable fibers) or for wool or silk (animal fibers), and they may be either basic (requiring a salt assistant) or acid dyes.

According to Dona Z. Meilach, author of *Contemporary Batik and Tie-Dye,* there are actually only about four manufacturers of all dyestuffs. Distributors buy from these companies and package the dye under their own label. There may be slight variations in the formulas used, but the dyestuffs and methods of working with them will be essentially the same.

Household or *union dye* is a combination of several dye classes to color most fabrics, including many synthetics, and usually consists of a mixture of direct, acid, and other dyes. Only the dyes that can be absorbed by the fibers in the particular fabric are taken into the cloth; the other dyes are sloughed off and not absorbed. The union dyes, which include Rit, Tintex, and Putnam, are most efficient in hot water (140°), but can be used in cool water (90°–100°) as well. Union dyes are the easiest to work with and have the broadest application for theatrical costumes. Some brands already have the salt assistant mixed in the formula; others require the addition of salt. Instructions on the package will indicate if salt will need to be added.

Fiber-reactive dyes actually form a bond with the fiber and are essentially cold-water dyes. These dyes have been on the market only since 1956, but they have become very popular for batik dyeing and for direct application such as painting on fabric. This type of dye is most effective on cotton, linen, and viscose rayon. Fiber-reactive dyes require several assistants to activate the dye, including salt, washing soda, and softened water, but they give excellent brilliant colors that are very fast. (The term *fast* refers to how well the dye holds to the cloth.) These dyes are more complex to work with than union dyes, but they are becoming popular for theatrical use because of the quality of the colors and the versatility of the dye. Methods for working with fiber-reactive dyes are discussed more fully under Dyeing Guidelines.

Direct dyes are used mainly for cotton, linen, and viscose rayon. They are most efficient in high-temperature dye baths but can be used at a cool temperature. These dyes are very effective with the fabrics cited in the chart but not for other fabrics or blends. They give good, clear colors which are generally fast.

Acid dyes are used for silk and wool and use acetic acid as an assistant. White vinegar is a common substitute for the acid; ½ cup of vinegar is the equivalent of 2 tablespoons of acetic acid. The colors produced by acid dyes are generally bright, clear shades. Since these dyes are for wool and silk, they tend to have less versatility than union or fiber-reactive dyes and have a somewhat limited use in a costume shop.

Dye Class	Brand or Distributor	Dyebath Temperature	Assistants	Rinsing Procedure	Finishing
Fiber reactive (*Procion*) For Cotton Linen Silk Viscose rayon	Dylon Fabdec Fibrec Hi-Dye Putnam Color Fast	For batik and tie-dye at temperature 90°–100° F. Short and long dye procedures	Salt Washing soda (sal soda) for the reactive agent	After dipping or after fabric has dried	Wash in hot soapy water Ironing Steam treatment for direct application
Direct For Cotton Linen Viscose rayon	Aljo Dick Blick Calcomine Craftool (red label) Deka-Type L Fezan Keco-Direct Miyako 7-K	Hot dyeing at simmer 140°F. Adapted to cool dyeing 90°–100° F. Dye time 20 to 60 minutes	Salt	After dipping After fabric dries After dipping After fabric dries After dipping	Wash in warm water Ironing
Acid For Silk Wool	Aljo Craftool (black label) Fezan Keco-Acid (Keystone) Kriegrocene 7-K Miyako	Hot dyeing at simmer 140°F. or boil 212°F. Adapted to cool dyeing 90°–100° F. Dye time 20 to 60 minutes	Acetic acid (white vinegar) Some also call for common salt or Glauber's salt	After dipping After fabric dries After dipping	Steaming (optional) Ironing
Vat For Cotton Linen Silk Rayon	Inkodye	Room temperature for dipping and direct application Dyeing time—a few seconds	None	Colors develop as fabric is exposed to heat and light	

Household (all purpose) For Cotton Linen Silk Wool Acetate Nylon Rayon and blends	Cushing's Perfection Dylon Multicolor Keystone Union Putnam all purpose Rit—liquid & powder Tintex	Hot but adapted to cool dyeing. Best for tie-dye at summer Temp. 140° F. Dyeing time 20 minutes. Can be used at cool temperature for batik but colors are not as bright as in hot dyeing	Salt Many have salt included so no added assistants necessary	After dipping	Iron while damp
Naphthol or azoic For Cotton Linen	American Hoechst GAF	For cool dyeing 85° F. Dyeing time 20–40 minutes	Naphthol caustic soda Monopol Oil Fast-color salts Salt	After dipping	Wash in detergent and iron

HOW TO USE THIS CHART

Consult any given package of dye and determine the class. Then follow general instructions for that particular group regarding fabric, assistant, temperature, amount of dye and time. If a dye does not have the class specified, consult the known factors such as assistants required and directions for mixing, then determine the class and use the general instructions for dyeing.

Figure 15-1 Dye class chart taken from *Contemporary Batik and Tie-Dye* by Dona Z. Meilach, © 1973 by Dona Z. Meilach. Used by permission of Crown Publishers, Inc.

Vat dyes are used for cotton, linen, silk, and viscose rayon. They require special preparation with lye and caustic soda additives, and when the solution is applied to the fabric, the final color of the dye cannot be identified. The color is developed through the use of heat in the drying process. Inkodye, which was developed for crafts purposes, is useful because it contains the necessary assistants in the dye mixture. But vat dyes have limited use in a costume shop unless a person is willing to obtain the advanced skills needed to use them.

Naphthol or *azoic dyes,* essentially used only for cotton, require a two-bath process; one bath is with naphthol, monopol oil (sulfonated castor oil), and caustic soda (sodium hydroxide), while the second bath requires water softener, salt, and fast-color salts (dyes). The complexity of the naphthol dyes limits their usefulness in a costume shop.

Dyeing Tools, Equipment, and Materials

The specific types of tools and equipment necessary for working with the different dyes vary somewhat, but there are certain essential items which are necessary for all dyeing. In addition to a supply of dye, which is cheaper to buy by the pound, and the necessary assistants, which are also cheaper when purchased in large quantities, appropriate containers for dye baths are needed. These should be large enough to allow the fabric to be completely covered and agitated freely. The dyeing containers should be enameled metal, glass, copper, plastic, or noncorrosive metal to avoid chemical reactions. Laundry tubs and top-loading washing machines can also be used.

Top-loading automatic washing machines are often recommended for dyeing large amounts of cloth. While they will do the job, there are definite drawbacks to using these machines, especially if the machine is also used for laundry. No matter how carefully the machine is cleaned after dyeing, there always seem to be some dye granules left which are guaranteed to appear when the white shirts are being washed. The automatic cycles also make it more difficult to control the timing for dyeing and rinsing.

An apartment-size, top-loading washing machine with a separate extractor is an excellent and inexpensive large dye receptacle. These machines provide automatic agitation for the fabric, but they do not have an automatic drain and rinse cycle, which means that you have greater control over the length of dyeing time (the dye solution does not suddenly disappear down the drain). The fabric can be rinsed in the extractor by continued flushing of water through the fabric. The dye solution can be saved and reused immediately if the shade of the rinsed fabric is too light. These machines, though smaller than the standard automatic machines, will dye a surprisingly large amount of fabric (up to ten yards), and they can be reserved for dyeing, leaving the other machine free of dye particles.

A collection of pots and pans, for small dye jobs, and hot plates to heat the dye solutions are valuable. Providing heat for larger receptacles is more problematic. Dye vats with heating units are very expensive; used industrial sterilizers, if they can be found, are less expensive and work very well, or industrial immersion-type heaters installed in laundry tubs (Fig. 15–2) can be used. Another method involves a large metal drum with a drain at the bottom that can be heated with an external heating element that wraps around the drum like a belt.[1] Most often, however, the costumer

---

[1]Acra Electric Corporation in Schiller Park, Illinois, manufactures "Wrap-it Heat" (type RX-1) that requires 230 volts but has two heating levels and works very well on a standard 55 gallon drum.

must rely on a good hot-water supply to provide the heat for a large dye bath.

Additional supplies necessary for working with dyes include *aprons* or *"lab" coats* to protect the clothing and *rubber gloves* to protect the hands. *Glass* or *plastic jars* for mixing dyes and preparing them in paste form are useful. These jars can also be used to store dyes that have been mixed with water, but only for a few days and only before the assistant is added. The shelf life of all dyes is limited, so check the instructions on the dye container before storing it after it has been mixed. *Wooden spoons* are valuable for stirring the fabric and lifting it from the hot dye bath and a *candy thermometer* should be used to keep track of the temperature of the dye bath.

Since soft water is preferable for dyeing, 2 to 4 teaspoonfuls of Calgon water softener per gallon of water can be added to the bath. Mild detergent, about 1 teaspoonful, added to the dye bath helps to further the even penetration of the dye into the fabric.

The amount of dye required for each dye job is determined by two factors: the amount of fabric and the desired intensity of color. Most of the packaged union dyes indicate in their instructions how much fabric, by yardage or weight, the contents will dye. To eliminate some of the guesswork, an infant scale (used to weigh babies) is valuable to weigh the fabric. Dona Meilach suggests the following general measures for the most economical and accurate use of union, direct, and acid dyes:

½ to 1½ teaspoonfuls of dyestuff per pound of cloth for a pale color strength

1½ to 4 teaspoonfuls of dyestuff per pound of cloth for a medium color strength

4 to 6 teaspoonfuls of dyestuff per pound of cloth for a deep color strength.

Assistants are also measured according to fabric weight:

3 tablespoonfuls of salt per pound of cloth (union and direct dyes)

4 tablespoonfuls of acetic acid (about 6 tablespoonfuls of white vinegar) per pound of cloth (acid dyes).

The water must cover the fabric, but you can roughly figure 2½ gallons of water per pound of fabric. Obviously, a collection of measuring spoons and cups is essential for measuring the dyestuff and assistants.

Recording the factors involved in preparing the dye solutions is essential in order to duplicate color and to keep track of the results of the dye experiments and testing. These factors include:

The actual fabric—a swatch of the fabric should be attached

The amount (weight and yardage) of the fabric

Type and amount of dyestuff(s)—when mixing colors keep careful records of the proportions used in the formula

Type and amount of assistant(s)—note proportions

Amount of water—note proportions

Temperature of the water

Length of dyeing time

Additional dye bath treatment—for example, addition of softener or mild soap

Special pretreatment of the fabric—for example, washed to remove size or other finishes

This information can be recorded (see Fig. 15-3) in a loose-leaf notebook, set up on 5 in. by 8 in. file cards, or by any other means which will permit accessibility to the information. Careful notation of dyeing results will ultimately save hours of time and eliminate a lot of trial and error.

Fabrics and Dyes

Natural fibers, primarily cotton, linen, silk, and wool, are the most receptive to dyes and the most predictable to work with; synthetics are the least predictable. An interesting means of studying the effects of dye on various fiber content fabrics is to run samples of a multifiber fabric.[2] This fabric is referred to as "test fabric" and consists of ¼ in. stripes of various fibers identified and woven into a unit of cloth. Each stripe is designated for fiber content, and it is fascinating to see how the different fibers react to the dye bath. The test fabric is also useful in helping to identify fiber content in a piece of cloth.

Generally, in a costume shop, the identification of fabric is limited to obtaining the information when the cloth is purchased (content is usually noted on the end of the bolt) and by the burning test (see Chap. 4). The burn test is a somewhat limited means of fabric identification, and it is often helpful to compare results with the test fabric to help confirm identification.

Quite often, an accurate identification of the fabric seems to mean little, since there are so many other factors which influence how the fabric will dye. The costumer needs to collect as much informa-

[2] Available from: Test Fabrics, P.O. Box 118, Blackford Avenue, Middlesex, N.Y. 08846; ask for Multi-Fabric #5.

Fabric	Dye Solution	Type	Amount
Swatches—original and dyed samples here	Dye color(s):		
	Assistant:		
	Water temperature:		
	Time in dye:		
	Additional dye bath treatment(s):		
Shrink test here	Pretreatment(s):		
	Other comments:		

Figure 15-3 Dyeing record chart used for keeping accurate, detailed records of the dyeing processes used for each fabric.

tion as possible about the nature and types of cloth and the properties of the various dyes in order to make a logical decision about the dyeing process to be used. Then it becomes a matter of testing and experimenting to achieve the best results.

Certain fabrics and finishes should be avoided as prospects for dyeing. Permanent-press fabrics are very difficult to dye; they can be tinted but will resist deep, or even medium, coloration. Water-repellent or water-proofed fabrics should be avoided for obvious reasons. Specific synthetics which resist strong coloration include acetates, nylons, and polyesters. The latter can sometimes be made more receptive to dye by boiling the fabric for about 30 minutes in salt water and vinegar

to break down the coating on the fiber. The formula for the solution is one part salt to two parts vinegar for about 2½ gallons of water per pound of fabric. For example, for 9 pounds of cloth, use ¼ cup of salt and ½ cup of vinegar in approximately 22 gallons of water.

All fabrics should be tested for fiber content, shrinkage, and the like, before samples with the dyes are prepared. The fabrics should be washed thoroughly with soap and water before dyeing to remove any fixative, starch, or dressing. It should be noted here that it is generally advisable to dye the fabric before it is cut for the garment. Occasionally, however, it may be necessary to cut the pattern before the fabric is dyed for such reasons as placing designs on the pattern pieces with dyes, but even then the fabric must be washed before it is cut. The raw edges of the pieces must then be zigzagged after they are cut to prevent raveling during the dyeing process.

At other times, a finished garment may need to be dyed; this is usually to alter the color of a ready-made garment, or the dyeing is used as a method of achieving a patina of age on a costume. In this instance, the garment must be fitted and finished, since the dye will not penetrate the seams or other double fabric areas evenly, making later alterations very difficult. Whether dyeing cloth or whole garments, some extra fabric should be dyed in the same dye bath at the same time in order to have extra matching fabric on hand.

After the fabric is washed, samples should be tested in a preliminary dye process which is used to establish the dye and the length of dyeing time needed for the precise color desired. This preliminary procedure is important in all cases but especially if colors are being mixed, unfamiliar types of dye are being explored, or dip-dyeing is to be done in an unheated vat. The samples should be thoroughly rinsed and dried and viewed under incandescent light, if gelled instruments are not available. Fluorescent light will distort the color and will not show what the fabric will look like under stage lights.

Since the samples are small, be aware that the enlarged formula may not produce the same results as the sample; take an additional sample in the full dye bath before the good yardage is added. Having a wet sample to compare with the fabric in the dye bath provides a fairly accurate guide for achieving satisfactory results.

DYEING GUIDELINES

Dyeing fabrics is an effective and inexpensive means of achieving a vast array of variations in the fabric and the completed costumes. The steps involved in *dip-dyeing* (completely immersing the fabric in a dye bath) follow an essentially simple format. (1) The dye is mixed or "pasted" with a few tablespoonfuls of cold water and then dissolved in a cup of hot water. (2) The dissolved dye is added to the dye bath; for best results the "pasted" solution is strained through several layers of cheesecloth to remove any dye granules. (3) The assistant, which helps the dye penetrate the fibers, is dissolved and added to the dye bath. (4) The fabric, which has been washed in soap and thoroughly rinsed but not dried, is added to the dye bath and stirred until the desired color is obtained. Remember that the color will be darker when wet. (5) The fabric is then removed from the dye bath and rinsed in cold water until the water runs clear. (6) The fabric is then dried and pressed and is ready to be cut. How effective the result of this procedure will be depends on the type of dye, the type of fabric and finish, and the care taken during the process.

Many of the effects created by dyeing require immersing all or part of the fabric or garment in a dye bath. For even coloration, the fabric should be washed, rinsed, and *wetted-out* (made thoroughly wet) before it is added to the solution. It is often suggested that the fabric should be wetted-out in cold water; however, if the dye solution must be hot and the vat is unheated, wet-out the fabric in warm or hot water so the dye temperature is not cooled when the fabric is added.

To mix the dye solution, paste the dye in a small amount of cold water and dissolve it in some hot water before straining it through cheesecloth. The assistant may be dissolved with the dye or added to the bath after the strained dye has been added. Note that if the dye is being prepared for samples, the assistant must be in the dye mixture. After the dye and assistant have been added to the bath, stir the solution well to mix the granules thoroughly. If the water is hard, add a water softener, such as Calgon (use 2 to 4 teaspoonfuls per gallon); this is especially important for fiber-reactive dyes. Mild soap or detergent is also added at this point, if necessary.

Add the wetted-out fabric to the solution; the fabric should be loose, free from twists and folds, to avoid uneven coloration in the fabric. The fabric should be stirred or agitated to provide an even flow of dye through the fabric. If, for some reason, more dye or assistant needs to be added to the bath, remove the fabric before making the addition, and stir the altered solution thoroughly before returning the fabric to the bath. Note that fiber-reactive dyes require that the fabric be removed from the dye after 10 minutes; pasted washing soda (1 tablespoonful per gallon) is added to the bath and stirred in well; then the fabric is returned to the dye bath for 15 or more minutes until the desired color is obtained.

With some types of dye—direct dye, for example—the dye bath may get lighter in color as the fabric gets darker. This is the result of the dye molecules' being "exhausted" (absorbed) into the fabric. Union dyes rarely do this because of the mixture of dye types, some of which will not be absorbed, but sloughed off and remain in the bath.

Once the appropriate shade has been achieved (remember the color is darker when wet), the fabric is removed from the bath and rinsed thoroughly in cold water to help fix the colors. The fabric should be rinsed until the rinse water runs clear to make sure all the excess dye is removed.

The fabric is then ready to be dried. Heat is also a method of fixing colors, so drying the fabric in a dryer is advisable except for fiber-reactive dyes.

Fabrics treated with fiber-reactive dyes must be slowly air-dried directly from the dye bath and before they are rinsed. After the fabric has been air-dried, it is rinsed, first in cool and then in warm water, and finally washed in a mild detergent to remove the excess dye and rinsed again. The fabric then may be dried in a dryer.

After the fabric is dry, it should be ironed, which also helps fix the color. For theatrical purposes, the small wrinkles in the fabric may often be left in the fabric to texture the cloth and create a more interesting visual effect.

That is the fundamental sequence for dip-dyeing. Union, direct, and acid dyes follow essentially the same procedures, but be sure to use the correct assistants. Fiber-reactive dyes also follow the sequence, but the two exceptions of adding washing soda and drying before rinsing must be included.

Dip-dyeing is, of course, a process in itself for altering or toning the color of a fabric. It is also a part of the processes of overdyeing, batiking, and tie-dyeing. But in order to use any of these processes effectively, it is worthwhile to review the basic principles of color theory.

BASIC COLOR THEORY. Since dyes are colorants, the principles of using and mixing them are essentially the same as those which apply to paints. The characteristics of color are termed *hue, intensity,* and *value*. These characteristics may be varied, separately and in combination, to obtain the color desired.

Hue refers to the basic or pure color which for our purposes can be illustrated in the standard color wheel, Fig. 15–4. There are twelve colors (hues) in the full color wheel: three primaries, three secon-

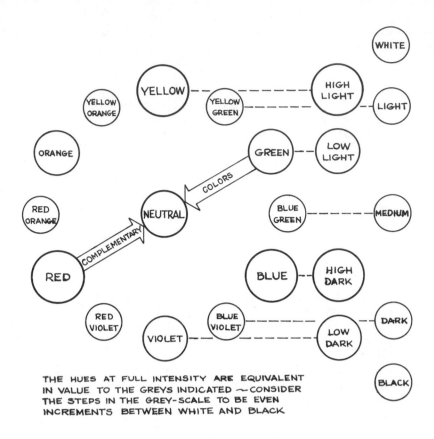

THE HUES AT FULL INTENSITY ARE EQUIVALENT
IN VALUE TO THE GREYS INDICATED ~CONSIDER
THE STEPS IN THE GREY-SCALE TO BE EVEN
INCREMENTS BETWEEN WHITE AND BLACK

Figure 15–4 Color wheel and value chart showing three relationships among colors: the wheel shows primary and derivative colors for mixing (hue) and neutralizing complements (intensity); the vertical chart shows relative values in a brilliance scale (value).

daries, and six tertiaries which are made by mixing a primary and secondary hue. The primary colors are yellow, red, and blue; the secondary colors are orange (mixture of yellow and red), green (mixture of yellow and blue), and violet (mixture of red and blue). The tertiary colors, which complete the wheel, are yellow-green, blue-green, blue-violet, red-violet, red-orange, and yellow-orange. Colors that are directly opposite each other on the wheel are called *complementary* colors, those that are next to each other are called *analogous*. The center of the wheel is *neutral* or grey; theoretically, if one mixes equal parts of two complementary colors the results will be neutral grey.

Intensity or *chroma* denotes the purity or saturation of a color. In theory, the red on the color wheel is pure and has full intensity. It loses intensity when it is mixed with another color. For example, mixing red with some of its complement, green, moves the color closer to the neutral or grey center, and the color loses intensity. The scale of the intensity depends on the ratio of the mixture: ¾ red to ¼ green neutralizes the red less than a mixture of ½ red to ½ green. Remember that this is theory, to be used to help gain an understanding of mixing colors; you cannot, in practice, mix equal volumes of red and green for a neutral grey, nor can you separate the pure red or green from the mixture. Once the intensity is neutralized in any way, the color cannot regain its original hue or intensity. Also remember that because of differences between the actual pigment materials, proportions in these theoretical mixtures cannot be measured by simple volumes.

Value refers to the lightness or darkness of a color. With opaque colors (those which you cannot see through) the value is heightened or lightened by adding white and lowered or darkened by adding black to the hue. The ratio of white or black to the hue relates to the position of the color on the scale illustrated in Fig. 15–4. A *tint* is the result of the addition of white to a color, lightening the hue; a *shade* is the result of darkening a color. Obviously, tinting or shading a color influences the intensity of the color, neutralizing it to some extent. Also obvious is the fact that a color can be lightened or darkened by the addition of colors other than white and black. But since that also changes the hue, it is not a tinting or shading process so much as a change to a different color that is lighter or darker than the original.

Dyes work on the same value principle but react more like transparent or translucent colors (those which you can see through to some degree). These colors are influenced by the background or underlying material and are lightened by being thinned with water or other clear thinner; a tint is achieved by adding more water to the color (or using less dye, as discussed under Dyeing Materials). A more saturated color is achieved by increasing the proportion of dye in the solution; to shade the color, add dye stuff from darker colors.

Use the color wheel as a guide for mixing dyes to get the desired color. Colors can be mixed by any of the following procedures:

1. The dye powders can be measured and combined dry. Careful notation of the ratios used is important for duplicating the color. The dye is then pasted and normal procedures followed.
2. Equal amounts of the dye powders can be pasted and dissolved separately and then mixed in the desired ratio, for example, ¼ cup yellow to ¾ cup blue for blue-green.
3. The colors can be mixed in the dye bath by eye, and samples tested. Since the length of time in the bath influences the color, this is the least accurate method and almost impossible to match. It is effective as a quick one-time project for an experienced dyer.

The range of dye colors on hand in a shop usually depends on personal preference and budget. A bright red, yellow, blue, brown, and black are the basic dye hues and can usually be mixed to create a variety of exciting colors.

It should be noted that true black is very difficult to obtain with commercial dyes. Often the best result is achieved by mixing your own. A basic formula calls for 6 parts navy blue, 3 parts scarlet, and 3 parts yellow; the amounts of dyestuff should be mixed for dark intensity.

Additional colors can be purchased for specific jobs. Since mixing colors can be a frustrating experience, often resulting in a definite mud-tone, the beginner will have the best results by using a wider range of colors and by experimenting with color mixing. As indicated, there are many variables present in dyeing fabrics, and the entire process can easily be considered an experiment, but the results provide an effect which can not really be achieved in any other way.

OVERDYEING COLORS.   The color theory is also applicable to overdyeing colored

Overdyeing Color Chart

This chart provides guidelines for overdyeing primary and secondary colors based on the principles of color theory. Dye colors vary as do fabric colors; always test a sample before proceeding to overdye fabric.

Color of Material to Be Dyed

Red	Blue	Yellow	Brown	Orange	Green	Purple	Over Dyed With
Darker Red	Purple	Scarlet	Reddish Brown	Light Red	Brown	Reddish Purple	Red
Purple	Deep Blue	Green	Very Dark Brown	Dark Grey	Bottle Green	Bluish Purple	Blue
Scarlet	Green	Deep Yellow	Golden Brown	Yellow Orange	Light Green	Greenish Brown	Yellow
Brownish Red	Almost Black	Yellowish Brown	Darker Brown	Yellowish Dark Brown	Greenish Brown	Chocolate	Brown
Light Red	Dark Grey	Light Orange	Tobacco Brown	Deep Orange	Yellowish Green	Reddish Brown	Orange
Almost Black	Greenish Blue	Light Green	Olive Green	Myrtle Green	Darker Green	Dark Green	Green
Reddish Purple	Plum	Almost Black	Very dark Reddish Brown	Light Dull Purple	Dark Purple	Darker Purple	Purple

To overdye fabric black, another dye color needs to be added to black dye, otherwise the dyed fabric will have a brownish cast.

Example: Add 1 part navy blue to 2 parts black over green, brown, or yellow fabric
Add 1 part dark green to 2 parts black over red or purple fabric
Add 1 part orange to 1 part black over blue fabric

Figure 15-5 Overdyeing color chart. Courtesy of Putnam Color and Dye, P.O. Box 1267, Gailsburg, IL 61401.

fabrics. For example, overdyeing a piece of light blue and white striped fabric, such as pillow ticking, with yellow will produce yellow and green stripes, as the combination of the yellow dye on the blue stripe creates a green while the white stripe turns yellow. A pink overdye on the same fabric will produce a lavender and pink stripe. Figure 15-5 is a color chart for overdyeing colors in fabrics. Applying the color mixing principles greatly increases the versatility of fabric. For instance, overdyeing a plaid fabric will create an amazing change as the various colors take the dye. Lengths cut from the same bolt can be overdyed in different dye baths and will result in a different appearance for each piece of the same fabric.

Tie-Dyeing Guidelines

Tie-dyeing is an old technique for creating patterns and interesting effects in fabrics. In recent years, the process has emerged again as a popular decorative effect in fashion. The process is accomplished by tieing, knotting, stitching, or otherwise controlling sections of cloth in tight layers to form a "resist" to the dye. The term *resist* means a process of blocking out areas of cloth so the dye cannot penetrate. A characteristic of tie-dyeing is the irregular edge of the pattern where the dye has *bled* into the resist areas.

The basic steps in the tie-dyeing process involve (1) planning the design; (2) preparing the fabric (washing to remove sizing, and drying); (3) tieing or otherwise setting the resist areas; (4) dyeing and rinsing, and then retieing or over-tieing for dyeing in additional colors if needed; and finally (5) untieing and pressing the fabric.

The pattern for tie-dyeing must be planned in advance so the appropriate steps can be followed. Planning the design requires working out the design for the cloth pattern and the color scheme involved. The basic color theory principles must be observed. All tie-dyeing requires washing from light to dark, unless color is to be removed with bleach. Also, the number of colors (and dye baths) must be carefully planned, since each bath will alter the colors from previous baths if the area is not tied to resist the dye. For example, if the first dye bath is yellow and the second red, the unresisted yellow areas will over-dye to orange.

The tieing process can be done with rubber bands of various widths, rope or cord, wire, dental floss, pipe cleaners, or by any means which will draw the cloth up tight. Additional resist effects can be achieved by tieing the cloth itself in tight knots or wrapping it around such things as beads, washers, or coins, and wrapping it with masking tape or a plastic bag. Punching tiny holes in the bag allows the dye to seep in and creates yet another interesting effect.

Additional effects that have tie-dyed characteristics can be created by applying dye or bleach to the fabric with a small eyedropper, squeeze bottle, or poultry baster. If the fabric is dry the dye will not bleed as much as when it is wet.

Natural fibers are the most receptive to tie-dyeing. Except for wool, which uses cold throughout, the dye bath should be hot and the rinse cold. The dye process can usually be repeated up to five times using different colors or stronger dye solutions. However, the more colors involved the greater care must be taken in order to maintain clear colors.

Batik Dyeing Guidelines

Batik or wax-resist is another method for creating patterns with dye (Fig. 15-6, p. 241). Essentially, this method is accomplished by laying out a pattern on the cloth and covering the pattern areas with a wax-resist to keep the dye from penetrating the fibers. The fabric is then immersed in the dye, rinsed, and air-dried. The wax is then removed by melting it with a warm to hot iron. Layers of paper are placed on both sides of the waxed fabric to absorb the melting wax.

A characteristic of batik dyeing is the "crackle" effect. Crackle is the veining created by cracking the wax before dyeing. The results can be very exciting, and intricate patterns can be created through this addition to the batik process.

The process works best on natural fibers. The steps involve preparing the fabric as you would for all dyeing processes, washing to remove finishes. After the fabric is dried, draw the design on the fabric with tailor's chalk or a soft pencil. This process can be considered the reverse of normal drawing. With batik, the light areas are retained by the wax and the nonwaxed areas are colored, since these are free to take the dye.

When the design is sketched out, stretch the fabric taut on a frame or on the open side of a cardboard box to allow the wax to penetrate the fabric. The fabric can also be pinned to a cork-top table, but it is best to place a layer of paper under the fabric, especially if the fabric is sheer or lightweight, to prevent the wax from soaking through onto the cork surface.

The wax, either paraffin or a half and half mixture of beeswax and paraffin, should be melted in a double boiler or in cans set in hot water. The wax is ready to use when it is translucent; if it is smoking, it is too warm. (Wax needs to be kept warm while working with it, but it should never be left untended while on the heat since wax will burn, and wax fires can be very dangerous.) Apply the wax with a soft, inexpensive natural bristle brush. These brushes will not be usable for any other type of project once they have been used in wax. To prevent accidental drippings of wax, hold some paper or other catch container under the brush.

The wax should have a translucent appearance on the fabric; if it goes on white or cloudy it is probably too cool and will not penetrate the fabric. When waxing the design, do not cover the lines. Wax about ⅛ in. from the line and wax the areas that are to be light in color, since the wax is the resist.

After the wax has dried, wet the cloth in cool water, soaking it for a few minutes to wet-out the fabric and harden the wax; then immerse the piece in the dye solution. The dye must be cool, 90° to 100°, which is just below the melting temperature of the wax. Cold-water batik dyes, such as fiber-reactive dyes, are the best, but union dyes at a cool temperature can also be used. Add any assistants that are required. As with all dip-dyeing, the bath should be thoroughly mixed before the cloth is added.

Follow the appropriate dip-dyeing procedures for the type of dye being used. Spread the fabric on wax paper or plastic to dry; hanging the fabric is not recommended, since the colorant may sink to the bottom of the cloth. When the fabric is dry, sandwich it between layers of absorbent paper and iron with a hot iron to melt the wax. The paper will pull the wax out of the fabric and must be changed frequently. Excess wax or residual wax can be removed by soaking the fabric in a cleaning fluid in a well-ventilated area. Dry cleaning will also remove excess wax.

A faster method of batiking is done by using colored batik wax or crayons to provide additional colors. The pigment from the wax will penetrate the fibers and several colors can be worked at one time. The crayons need to be broken up and melted together with an equal amount of paraffin. A muffin tin set in water in an old electric skillet makes an excellent container for several colors, or tin cans set in water can be used for larger amounts of wax. The colored wax is applied in the same manner as the clear wax, and it is equally important that the wax penetrate the fabric. Be sure to clean the brush before shifting colors in order to maintain accurate colors. After the wax has dried, standard batiking processes are followed.

Many effects can be achieved through the tie-dye and batik processes, and there are numerous methods and approaches to the processes which go beyond the scope of our coverage. Sources for additional information are cited at the end of this chapter.

Stenciling Guidelines

A third method of applying patterns to fabric is stenciling. With this method, dye or other mediums are applied to fabric using a stencil as the resist. The stencils can be lace or some type of open-weave cloth, such as erosion cloth which is normally

Figure 15-6 An example of batik and tie-dyeing. The yoke has been batiked using colored waxes which reduce the amount of "crackle"; the rest of the garment has been tie-dyed using various tieing techniques to create variety in the pattern. Photo by Robert Izzo.

used to hold new grass or seedlings in place. Spraying dye or bleach through materials of this nature can create interesting textures on fabric.

For specific designs, heavily oiled or waxed paper is a traditional stencil material. Clear, unexposed X-ray film also makes an excellent stencil and has the added advantage of being transparent, so placement of the stencil is simple and accurate. It is easy to keep clean and does not deteriorate when wet.

Typical stencils must be cut with bridges, or ties, to connect all the sections within the pattern. However, if the fabric is laid out on a plastic-covered cork-top table, similar to that described in Chap. 2, the stencil sections can be thumbtacked in position, and no bridges are necessary, as shown in Fig. 15-7. A light coating of spray adhesive or rubber cement on the back of the stencil is also a good method for holding the stencil in place on fabric.

The steps involved in stenciling begin with preparing the stencil. After the pattern, with any necessary bridges, is laid out on paper, it is transferred to the stencil material with carbon paper or fabric tracing paper. The stencil material is placed on a hard surface, taped in place, and the pattern is traced through with a hard pencil or a tracing wheel. If carefully done, the wheel perforates the lines and makes cutting easier. To cut the pattern, place the stencil material on a hard surface (glass works very well) and cut on the lines with an X-Acto knife or a mat knife, leaving any necessary bridges. If a bridge is accidentally cut, it can be repaired with tape on both sides of the stencil. A design may call for more than one color, in which case separate stencils are cut for each color unit within the pattern.

There are several mediums which can be used on fabrics in stenciling, including dyes, bleach, textile paints, inks, and acrylic

paints. Several of these mediums are discussed under painting techniques. Regardless of the medium used or the application thereof, the stencil edges must be kept clean and sharp to prevent fuzzing edges. The medium is applied at right angles to the stencil to prevent the medium from working its way under the pattern.

Unless the medium is opaque, the original color of the fabric will influence the final color. As with all other forms of fabric modification, the fabric should be prepared to remove size, and so on, and tested for reaction to various mediums as well as for color fastness.

PAINTING

Theatrical garments are often treated to enhance texture and detail, to create greater depth and fullness by highlighting and shadowing, to add a pattern on the fabric, and to create the illusion of age, deterioration, and a general breaking down of the fabric or garment. Treating a garment involves various processes and mediums. The processes range from creating formal patterns with stencils to aging and breaking down the fabrics. The

mediums generally include those already cited for stenciling as well as canned spray paints and French Enamel Varnish (F.E.V.) among others.

The selection of what medium to use is guided by a number of factors. A primary consideration in the selection is related to the fabric and the effect desired. Will the colorant bleed through the fabric? Should the medium be opaque or translucent? Will the addition of colorant stiffen the

242

ic, and, if so, is that problematic? How ⁀anent is the medium on the specific ⁀c? How must the treated fabric be cleaned to maintain the effect? The answers to these questions can only be found through experimentation with the medium and the actual fabric. However, there are characteristics and typical application procedures for the mediums which can serve as guidelines for appropriate selections.

First, let us look at typical methods of application and the supplies which are necessary. For our purposes, application methods fall into two basic categories: spraying and brushing.

SPRAYING SUPPLIES.   Intended for general use to add texture and to age costumes, spray applications can be operated either manually or with mechanical assistance. The manual devices include *pump spray bottles,* such as plant sprayers, or those with an attached air tank, such as insect sprayers. Both of these units require a fairly thin solution in order to pass through the nozzle. Those with adjustable nozzles offer the most control in applying the medium. Mechanical spraying equipment generally operates on compressed air that is built up with a motor. These units provide air pressure which can be regulated to drive the medium through the nozzle. *Airbrushes* are available in various sizes and offer a great deal of control. The spray can be regulated from a thin line to fairly wide coverage.

With all spray equipment it is important to mix the paint or other medium to the proper consistency for the spray unit if it is to operate at full efficiency. Some units require a thinner consistency than others, but experimentation may be necessary to determine just what the consistency should be. All spray equipment must also be cleaned thoroughly after each use if it is to continue to function properly.

Canned spray paints are also useful for quick application of color. They are available in matte, gloss, and metallic finishes. Paints which have rust inhibitors should be avoided since they dry very slowly and have been known to have strange chemical reactions with certain materials. Typical colors to have on hand are black, grey, olive green, dark blue, brown, bronze, copper, gold, and aluminum (silver).

BRUSHING SUPPLIES.   These are used for texturing, defining patterns, and aging costumes. Three types of brushes are useful in a shop. *Natural bristle brushes* in flat sizes ranging from ½ in. to 2 in. and a collection of large, number 10 and up, round watercolor brushes are useful for detail work with several mediums. *Stiff nylon-bristle, flat brushes* in the same general size range are available for use with acrylics, fiber-reactive dyes, and other mediums that require stiff bristle brushes. *Stipple brushes* are made specifically for stenciling. They are round brushes with short, stiff bristles.

Other supplies which can be considered at this time include natural sponges with large irregular holes. The sponge is used like a stamp or block print to create interesting textures on cloth. The color is picked up by the sponge, except in the holes, and the irregularity is transferred to the cloth. The medium must be fairly thick to be used in this manner.

Felt-tip markers in an assortment of colors are good for quick application of color and will work well on many synthetics. Permanent colors are generally recommended.

Brushing equipment, with the exception of the markers, must also be cleaned thoroughly after each use. Brushes which are used in non–water-soluble mediums should be used only for those mediums; those used in water-soluble mediums are interchangeable.

Additional supplies for treating costumes depend on the medium used, the effect desired, the type of solvent called for, how the medium is mixed, and how it can be stored.

Painting Mediums

The concept of painting costumes centers on overlaying color onto the fabric, but the mediums used for this purpose may not be "paint" as we generally think of it. The types of mediums commonly used are listed in Fig. 15–8 to provide a quick overview of some of their characteristics. Each can be used in various ways to overlay the color in the form of patterns, general texturing, and defining and accentuating, or for various other effects that may be needed. Since the methods and uses are so varied, the emphasis of this section is placed on the mediums and their characteristics rather than on how to use them. The applications are dependent on what the effect is to be. The list is not meant to be all-inclusive, but it should suggest typical mediums and methods.

PAINTING WITH DYES. Many of the characteristics and application techniques for dyes have already been discussed. Additional uses include spraying for highlight and shadow, aging, and direct application with a brush to create a pattern, accents, or sharper definition of details. Some dyes, if properly prepared, can even be used with silk screen techniques or with stamp-block printing.

A stamp-block print has a pattern raised in relief above a flat surface; if the raised pattern is coated with the color medium, it will print in reverse (mirror image) when pressed onto the fabric. The pattern can be cut out of a wood or linoleum block, or even a potato. The pattern can also be made by gluing cord or wire to a flat surface of the block. Wood is easy to use for the block, but if it is made of transparent plexiglas, the pattern can be more easily aligned on the fabric.

Union dyes mixed for a deep c strength are useful for spraying and s brushing. These dyes may have to have assistant added, and the solution needs strained before it is added to the spray container. The solution should be hot or warm for the best application. If crystals form while dyeing, the amount of dye in the water is too strong, and it should be thinned with more water, otherwise it will rub off (called *crocking*). Since dye sprayed on dry fabric will tend not to bleed, the spray pattern will be fairly distinct. Dyes applied by spray or brush can be set to some degree by ironing with a warm to hot iron while the dye is still damp. Since dye applied by this means generally does not penetrate the fibers, it should not be considered wash-fast.

Fiber-reactive dyes can be used for painting, but several steps and additional materials are needed to prepare the dye for painting use, and the steps vary according to the painting technique to be used. However, always check the instructions that come with the dye; some manufacturers include some or all of the chemicals in the packaging.

In all cases, it is necessary to prepare the fiber-reactive dye with a solution known as *chemical-water* which helps fix and set the colors. Regular water will not work, but chemical-water can be made up in quantity in advance and stored indefinitely for later use. To make one quart of chemical-water use

> 1 teaspoonful Calgon or other water softener
>
> 10 tablespoonfuls urea (available from chemical suppliers, dye suppliers, or garden stores—it is a fertilizer)
>
> 2 cupfuls hot water
>
> 2 cupfuls cold water
>
> Dissolve the Calgon and urea in the hot water, add the cold water, and shake well. Cover tightly if the mixture is to be stored.

Medium	To Thin	To Thicken	Application	Best Fibers	Permanence	Penetrates fabric
Dyes:						
Union	Water	—	Spray (Hot) or Brush (Warm)	Natural and Viscose Rayon	P–F*	No
Fiber-reactive	Chemical-water	Sodium Alginate	Spray Brush Print / Requires special solution	Natural and Viscose Rayon	G–E	No
Inkodye	Water	As Is	Brush Print / Color develops	Natural and Viscose Rayon	G	No
Leather Dye	As Is	—	Spray Brush	Natural and most Synthetics	F–G	Very moderate
Paints:						
Textile	Turpentine (check instructions)	As Is	Spray Brush Print	Natural and some Synthetics	G–E	Very moderate
Acrylic	Water and Matte Medium	—	Spray Brush Print	Natural and many Synthetics	G–E	Moderate
Can Spray	As Is	As Is	Spray	Natural and many Synthetics	G–E	Yes
F.E.V.	Alcohol	Shellac	Spray Brush	Natural and many Synthetics	G–E*	Yes
Inks:						
Silk Screen	Water (check instructions)	As Is	Print Brush Spray	Natural and Viscose Rayon	G–E	Very moderate
Drawing Inks	As Is	—	Spray Brush	Natural and many Synthetics	G	No
Felt Tip Markers	As Is	—	Direct	Natural and many Synthetics	G	No
Dye Crayons			Direct	Natural and many Synthetics	G	No
Bleach	Water	—	Spray Brush	Natural and some Synthetics	G*	No

Code: P — Poor; F — Fair; G — Good; E — Excellent; * — Dry Clean Only

Figure 15–8 Characteristics of mediums used for painting fabrics.

To dissolve the dye in the chemical-water, it is necessary to make a paste using a small amount of the chemical-water and the following measurements of dyestuffs to obtain the color strength desired. The quantities indicated should be added, in paste form, to one quart of chemical-water. water.

1 to 2 teaspoonfuls dye for pale color strength

4 to 6 teaspoonfuls dye for medium color strength

8 to 10 teaspoonfuls dye for deep color strength

To prepare the dye solution for use, it is necessary to activate the dye. Dissolve 4 teaspoonfuls of baking soda and 1 teaspoonful of washing soda in a small amount of hot water and add this to the one quart of dye and chemical-water; for larger or smaller amounts of dye solution, adjust the ratios in proportion to the amount needed. The sodas cause the dye to react with the fibers and are added only when the dye is to be used. Once the sodas have been added, the dye cannot be stored, since the activation process lasts only a few hours. This activated dye solution can be used for spraying, but it should be strained to remove any small solid particles that may remain undissolved. It can also be used for some brush applications, but for most brushwork or for printing the dye can be controlled better if the solution is thickened before use.

To thicken fiber-reactive dye, add sodium alginate to the chemical-water. Sodium alginate is derived from seaweed and is available from chemical supply houses and dye suppliers. Using 1 to 4 teaspoonfuls per quart, sprinkle the sodium alginate into the chemical-water and stir or shake vigorously for about 10 minutes, or stir with an electric mixer or blender. This mixture can be used immediately or it can be left to stand overnight, which will make the blend smoother. Generally, the work done with the thickened mixture does not require a full quart of dye, so the quantities should be adjusted accordingly.

This mixture can be applied to fabric with a brush or squeeze bottle, or by printing with a stamp or by silk screening. As a general rule, it is best to mix a thick solution and then thin it as necessary with the chemical-water. For brush application, use a stiff nylon-bristle brush since natural bristles soften and become uncontrollable in the mixture.

To simplify some of these processes, you may want to make up a *stock solution* for storage and use it as needed. As stated, the chemical-water by itself can be stored. The sodium alginate can be added to the chemical-water, and as long as it is tightly covered and kept cool, this stock solution can also be stored for some months. If the dye is added, the solution can be stored only for a few days, and if the activating sodas have been mixed into the solution, it cannot be stored at all.

Fabrics which have been sprayed or painted with fiber-reactive dyes require steam to set the colors to prevent crocking and to ensure their permanence. For most costume shops, this means improvising some sort of equipment for steaming, since most do not have access to a steam cabinet or an autoclave (found in hospitals).

For small amounts of fabric, a large pot with a rack that is set about 2 in. above the waterline can be devised. The fabric should be rolled and tied in absorbent paper or cloth to keep the dyed fabric from touching itself and to prevent the colors from running together. After the water is boiling, place the tied fabric on a pad of cloth or paper on top of the rack and cover the fabric with more cloth or paper to protect it from spatters or condensation inside the pot. Put yet more paper on top of the pot, under the lid, to help "seal" in the steam; the lid may need to be weighted. Steam the fabric until there is a strong odor of urea (about 30 minutes). When the steaming is finished, unwrap the fabric as quickly as possible. Rinse it in cold water until the water runs clear; then rinse in warm water and finish by washing with mild detergent followed by a final rinsing.

Leather dye is yet another medium that has several uses. It is quick to apply, dries fast, does not appreciably stiffen the fabric, and is generally opaque. It is more economical when purchased by the gallon and can be applied with a brush or sponge. Large containers need to be shaken well before the solution is worked, since the pigment settles to the bottom. Leather dye should only be used in a well-ventilated area, since the fumes are overpowering.

Inkodye is a vat dye that can also be used to create patterns on fabrics. Inkodye is specifically marketed for crafts projects and, therefore, already contains the necessary assistants (lye and caustic soda). The colors develop in warm direct sunlight (or the equivalent), which means that the application should be done in strong warm light in order to see exactly what is developing with the colors. Complete instructions come with the dye for setting and finishing. Inkodye will not stiffen the fabric to any great degree.

PAINTS ON FABRICS.   Paints are also a valuable medium for treating fabrics. Paints differ from dyes in that they coat the fibers (dyes tend to penetrate) and are more opaque than dye. These pigments also generally need to be set with heat after they have dried, but ironing is usually sufficient. Many kinds of paints can be used on fabrics, but, as with all materials, the manufacturer's instructions should be followed, and the application techniques and permanence should be tested on the actual fabric before work is begun on the yardage or garment.

Textile paints, such as "Versatex," can be brushed or printed on in the thick state or thinned with turpentine (or a thinner specified by the manufacturer) for spraying or airbrushing. They can also be applied freehand or stenciled. For stenciling, paint pigments are usually applied with a stipple brush or thinned for use in an airbrush. The latter has the advantage of essentially forced-air drying the pigment as it hits the cloth and thereby speeding up the application process.

Acrylic paints applied with an airbrush dry very quickly; however, the degree of consistency (thickness) of the paint varies from color to color for ease of flow through the airbrush. Some colors tend to clog the nozzle more quickly than others. Acrylic paints are thinned with water and mixed with *matte medium* as an assistant. The addition of matte medium helps the paint adhere to the cloth and lessens the stiffening factor of acrylics. Use equal amounts of water and medium to thin the paint.

INKS ON FABRICS.   Many types of ink can also be classified as pigments. *Silk screen inks* which are specified for textiles can be used successfully on most fabrics without stiffening the fabric too much. Some inks, such as Hunt's Speedball Silk Screen Ink, are water-soluble. That is, they can be thinned with water (and the screens cleaned with water) but are permanent on fabric after the ink is heat set with an iron or in a dryer. These inks can be applied with standard silk screening processes, or used for block prints, or applied with a brush. Figure 15–9A illustrates the silk screening process; Fig. 15–9B shows the completed costumes.

Drawing inks, sometimes called architect's inks, are useful for quick applications of color. These tend to bleed on many fabrics, so testing is important. The colors are vibrant and permanent after the ink is heat set.

Waterproof *felt-tip markers* are also very useful for quick fast-drying small applica-

Figure 15–9   A. An example of silk screening a border print on skirt fabric. Photo by David P. Bosworth. B. Examples of completed silk-screened costumes for Master Owen and Susan the cook for a production of Fielding's *The Grub-Street Opera,* a world premiere produced by the University of Rhode Island. From the author's collection.

tions. The colors are permanent in most instances, applicable to many synthetics, and do not bleed as readily as the drawing inks. *Dye crayons,* often called liquid embroidery, are equally useful for similar purposes, particularly if thin lines are desired for quick embroidery.

COMBINED AND METALLIC MEDIUMS. *French Enamel Varnish* (F.E.V.) is a mixture of dyestuff, or other powdered mediums, and shellac thinned with denatured alcohol. F.E.V. is a frequently used medium for treating costumes because it provides a versatile means of achieving good permanent coloration quickly. The mixture calls for one part shellac to four parts alcohol. The dyestuff is pasted with a small amount of alcohol, dissolved, and added to the shellac-alcohol mixture. The

amount of dye varies with the dye and color. The solution should be tested on the fabric for color and more pasted dye added as necessary. Once the correct color is achieved, F.E.V. can be applied with a brush, sprayer, or airbrush. This mixture will stiffen the fabric. Bronzing powders can be used in place of the dye to create metallic effects.

Bronzing powders, which come in a rainbow of colors as well as in bronze, gold, silver, and copper, are a means of creating eye-catching highlights in a costume or on accessories. They are available from most hardware stores, theatrical suppliers, and art supply houses. These can be mixed with F.E.V. or with banana oil (Grumbacher makes "Banana Bronzing Lacquer") which is thinned with lacquer thinner. The oil dries quickly and has a matte finish; F.E.V. is more glossy. To mix: Add the liquid to the powder, first pasting with a small amount of liquid and then thinning with the liquid until the desired consistency is achieved. Mix only as much as needed at one time because it will thicken after several hours and cannot be reused.

Additional metallic finishes include canned spray paints and pasted metallics, such as "Treasure Gold." The sprays are quick-drying but do stiffen fabrics consid-erably. Application of these is most successful by overspraying. For example, overspraying black with gold and copper and highlighting with silver creates a more realistic warm gold "metal" than the straight gold spray. The pastes can be used to highlight hot-melt glue reliefs (see Chap. 19), trims, or other hard surfaces. The pastes are not very successful on soft fabrics.

TEXTURING AND AGING (DISTRESSING) TECHNIQUES

For some productions a bright, sparkling "new" look in the costumes is appropriate, but for a large percentage of modern productions the costumes are greatly en-hanced (and require) texturing and an overall illusion of worn or aged garments. Techniques for achieving this kind of illusion have been developing rapidly in recent years. Many of these techniques have been borrowed from scene painting.

Texturing Guidelines

Typical texturing processes include dry-brushing, spattering, spraying, and spong-ing. *Dry-brushing*, as suggested by the term, is worked with an essentially dry brush; the tips of the bristles are dipped in a small amount of the medium (paint, dye, and so on). When applied to the surface, the bris-tles create a pattern of lines; scenically, the technique is often used to create graining in woodwork.

Spattering is a texturing technique that calls for sprinkling or lightly showering the surface with small droplets. Spattering calls for the tips of the bristles to be dipped in a small amount of the medium; the brush is then slapped sharply against the fleshy part of the hand or a stick. This method is messy; the paint goes back as well as forward, and it requires practice to control the application. The major dif-ference between spattering and spraying is that the latter has very tiny droplets and is usually used for a light overlay of color. Controlled spattering is a good technique for shadowing and highlighting folds in costumes.

As suggested earlier, a natural sponge is also useful for creating a texture. The sponge is not saturated with the medium; the sponge is used in a manner similar to that used with stamp-blocks. The irregular surface of the sponge is dabbed into the medium and pressed onto the surface to create the pattern.

Flaked graphite, available from hard-ware stores, is a medium that can be used to create the appearance of steel. It is mixed with white glue, which may need to be thinned with water, and painted onto industrial-weight felt to give the effect of steel plate. After it is dry, it can be buffed with a soft cloth to bring a gleam to the surface. Since the glue stiffens the fabric, the heavyweight felt will hold a shape and make very convincing armor.

Liquid latex, commonly used for theat-rical make-up, also creates a very rough texture on fabrics. The latex is painted onto the fabric and rubbed while it is still wet to build up irregular thicknesses. This treatment is permanent and can be used

age is by careful application of bleach with a brush, sponge, or spray. Bleach lightens the color and suggests a threadbare appearance or loss of color through age. Bleaching to lift off color is termed *discharge dyeing* and can be done on the fabric or on the garment. Generally the bleach needs to be thinned with water, since bleach can be harmful to the cloth or react too quickly (to the point of eating holes in the fabric). To stop the bleaching reaction, rinse the treated area in water. Working with bleach is extremely effective on fabrics which have been dyed.

Experimentation with any of the processes and techniques discussed here is crucial. The processes are time-consuming and require careful thought and a deft hand. The only true test of how effective the execution of any of these methods has been is to view the garment onstage under lights. It is also wise to start with a light application and add to the effect as necessary. All of this implies time. Therefore a period of time for texturing and aging garments must be planned into the over-all construction schedule.

Figure 15–13 An example of felt treated to look like leather for Hotspur in *Henry IV, Part 1,* as produced by The Champlain Shakespeare Festival. Designed by Edward Feidner. From the author's collection.

APPLIQUÉING TECHNIQUES

The function of appliqué ranges from putting patches on something like hobo pants to creating an ornamental design, such as heraldic symbols as shown in Fig. 15–14, on a garment, to creating unique fabric similar to a collage. Fabrics can be applied to other fabrics or garments by sewing or by laminating (gluing). Certain criteria must be considered in either instance.

Fabrics that are to be sewn on must either be ravel-free or the edges need to be finished. Fabrics which ravel need to be finished either by rolling the edges or overcasting with a tight zigzag stitch before stitching into place. Felt is an ideal ravel-free fabric for appliqué; the hand-sewing techniques are described in Chap. 3. But felt is not satisfactory if the garment must be washed or if a different texture is needed.

LAMINATING. Fabrics can also be laminated—sticking or adhering the appliqué by other means than sewing. Lamination is generally faster than sewing, allows application in difficult-to-sew areas, and eliminates bunching or pulling when working large areas. The drawbacks to laminating include stiffening of the treated area and a somewhat limited permanence in wear and cleaning.

As with all forms of fabric modification,

Figure 15–14 An example of appliquéd heraldic emblems for the character of "Regnier" in *Henry VI, Part 1*, as produced by The Champlain Shakespeare Festival. From the author's collection.

the materials must be tested before the final project is begun. Several adhesives are discussed in the Glossary in Chap. 2. Generally, adhesives that are water-soluble cannot be washed but can be dry cleaned; however, the actor's perspiration can reactivate the glue and loosen the appliqué. Glues which are thinned with chemicals cannot be dry cleaned and can rarely be washed. Hot-melt glue is flexible enough for cloth but is problematic if the fabric of the appliqué is thin and flat, since the glue must be very hot in order to bond. Basically, all of these adhesives work well for appliqués on such things as millinery, footwear, and armor, but each has some drawback for clothing.

Another medium for laminating is "Stitch-Witchery" (brand name) or similar products. This product forms a bond between fabrics when heat is applied and is quick-drying. It is very sheer and flimsy and can be difficult to work with, since Stitch-Witchery must be cut to match the appliqué shape and then sandwiched between the fabric and the appliqué and ironed. Care must be taken when ironing; if the medium does not melt completely, the appliqué will not bond to the fabric. If it touches the iron, it will bond to the iron and is very difficult to clean off.

Ply-on Film is a medium that Irene Corey[3] has used for laminating with great success. This material is a plastic that melts at a low temperature and was originally developed for commercial iron-on patches. Ply-on Film has a definite advantage over Stitch-Witchery. The fabric to be appliquéd is pressed onto the film before the pattern shape is cut out. After the shape is cut, the heavy paper layer on the back side of the film is peeled off and the piece is ironed onto the fabric. The film also "seals" the raw edges of the appliqué so that it does not ravel. Ply-on Film is a boon to appliquéing techniques but is more successful on some fabrics than others. For example, it is not effective with lace, knits, and nonabsorbent synthetics but is very effective with satin, cotton, and similar fabrics.

To apply the film, work with pieces about one-half yard or smaller for easiest handling; set the dry iron on low (275°F.) and press from one edge to the other with a slow, firm stroke. Work in small areas to avoid wrinkling and bubbling; if bubbles do appear, the iron is probably too warm. Allow the ironed piece to cool completely and then cut the shape needed. If the plastic separates, replace the paper and iron again. Then peel away the paper and iron the piece to the garment fabric.

[3] Corey, Irene, "Shop Experiments with Miniature Lighting and Fabric Lamination," *Theatre Crafts*, 11, no. 4 (May/June 1977), 13–15, 34–35.

Ply-on Film is the most secure of the laminating materials, but, depending on the length of run of the production, how often the costumes need to be cleaned during the run of the show, and the strain the garment must endure, laminating fabrics with any of these methods is quite functional and usually time-saving. However, in the long run, sewing appliqués in place remains the most dependable means of attachment.

QUILTING.   Another form of appliquéing is quilting. This consists of two layers of fabric with a filling, or batting, sandwiched between and an overall pattern of stitching to hold the filling in place. The fabrics may be uniform, with only the stitching creating the pattern, or the pattern can be created by joining several fabrics together, as in a patchwork quilt. Quilting techniques can also be used to make three-dimensional appliqués as was done on the Oedipus tabard, see Fig. 19–8.

Theatrically, relying on the stitching to create the pattern is too subtle; it will not be visible over a distance. Patchwork quilting is strong enough to be seen and creates some very interesting fabrics (and uses up all the scraps of fabric that accumulate in a shop). The filling may or may not be necessary for the patchwork, depending on how stiff the finished fabric is to be. In addition, shadows to give the illusion of padding can be painted on the patchwork to enhance the overall texture of the fabric.

An easy method for making patchwork quilting is to start with the underfabric that is cut to the size and shape of the garment; this is called a *block*. Assemble a collection of fabric scraps for the top patchwork and cut the scraps to the sizes and shapes of the "patches." These may be uniform in size

Figure 15–15A   Patchwork quilt detail showing stitches painted on with acrylic paint. Photo by Robert Izzo.

and shape to create a regular pattern or they can be of assorted sizes and shapes for an irregular free-form pattern.

To begin, stitch a patch to the corner of the block, through the batting if it is being used. Next, place the second patch, with the right sides together, on top of the first patch and stitch along the edge so the patch can be folded over to cover the raw edges of the seam. Place the third patch, right sides together, over the edges of the other patches, stitch and fold over to cover the seam. Continue in this manner until the block is completed. By carefully overlaying the patches, all the seams and raw edges can be hidden by the patches. The edges of the block can be bound or concealed in seams if the patchwork is made up for something like a skirt.

Figure 15–15A shows an example of this type of quilting; the complete pieces are shown in Fig. 15–15B (color plate). This particular piece has a muslin block. The quilting was done and the edges bound before the unit was dyed. The muslin became a solid color, and the patches were muted and unified by the effect of overdyeing. The patches were defined with acrylic paint, and the entire unit was sprayed to enhance the overall texture.

The patchwork quilt becomes a good example of the essential steps involved in fabric modifications. The unit had to be planned carefully, and fabrics had to be tested in order to know how they would react to the treatments planned. The piece was then prepared, and several treatments were applied. A combination of the processes we have discussed was used to get the desired result.

Fabric modification covers many mediums and techniques. It offers the costumer an area for creating unique and dramatic theatrical garments. No two fabrics will react exactly alike, and the applications of the techniques vary according to the special effect required. In a very real sense it is always experimental in nature. Everything must be tested and explored. The processes require careful thought and time to execute effectively, but the results can be satisfying, successful, and exciting. The following sources provide in-depth studies for several of the techniques for modifying fabrics that have been discussed.

ADDITIONAL SOURCES

BIEGELEISEN, J. I., *The Complete Book of Silk Screen Printing Production.* New York: Dover Publications, Inc., 1963.

DAY, JOANNE, *The Complete Book of Stencilcraft.* New York: Simon and Schuster, 1974.

GIBBS, JOANIFER, *Batik Unlimited.* New York: Watson-Guptill Pub., 1974.

MEILACH, DONA Z., *Contemporary Batik and Tie-Dye.* New York: Crown Publishers, 1973.

PECKTAL, LYNN, *Designing and Painting for the Theatre.* New York: Holt, Rinehart and Winston, 1975.

PELLEW, CHARLES E., *Dyes and Painting.* New York: Robert M. McBride and Co., 1928.

sixteen

shaping the body

It seems that people have always had a fascination for "improving" or altering the shape of the human body, particularly since the sixteenth century. Men have been somewhat less susceptible to practices of this nature, though certainly not immune. But women have often overindulged themselves, encasing their bodies in rigid cages or expanding clothing dimensions to the greatest extreme possible. Of course, it has been suggested by many that this contrast is due more to the vigorous physical activities of men in given eras than to their inclinations.

Whatever the reasons for the fascination over the centuries with altering or distorting the natural body lines, the practice has been carried through in all conceivable manners. A costumer, then, must investigate the practices and know how to achieve the effects for theatrical uses, since the means of shaping the body that were part of the process for creating the "correct" silhouette for a given period are still the means by which it can be achieved today. Also, because the contrivances are unnatural, they have a marked influence on posture and movement which becomes uniquely characteristic of given periods. Without simulating the devices, these characteristics cannot be captured.

At the same time, for theatrical purposes, it may be necessary to alter the body form of a particular actor in order for that person to play a specific role. Adding weight or musculature for a heavier or stronger appearance, creating a more voluptuous figure, or providing the illusion of sagging muscles, distorted posture, or physical deformities that come with age or from illness, are only a few of the ways in which costuming can contribute to the complete realization of the character.

Methods for shaping the body fall into three basic categories: padding, corsets, and skirt supports. Each of these has been used separately and in combination. Originally these methods were used to make the wearer more attractive to look at, according to a particular fashion. Theatrically, they can have other functions as well; this is particularly true of padding. We also tend to think of the practice of shaping the body as purely feminine; however, there were periods when men were corseted, and corsets for men are available on the market today.

As mentioned before, undergarments—though usually not seen by the audience—are fundamental in achieving an appropriate silhouette. This is true whether the goal is to depict the dress of a specific period, or to create a nonrealistic, perhaps fantastical character, or to give the illusion of a particular body form beneath the clothes. The undergarment level of the costume is where the body shape is formed and the supports for elaborate outer garments are worn.

PADDING

Padding the actor is often important to help establish age, occupation, character, or period silhouette. The almost automatic uses for padding occur when costuming a character like Falstaff ("that hill of flesh"), Sir Toby Belch (Fig. 16–1), or a pregnant woman. Additional uses of padding are often overlooked. For example, observation readily indicates the difference in the shoulder and arm structure of the young athlete when compared with someone who spends hours hunched over a desk. The aging process often means a developing paunch or sagging breasts due to loss of muscle tone, or it may mean a thickening of the neck and shoulders or the waist, hips, and thighs. This can easily be suggested with padding.

The use of padding is also often necessary in establishing a period silhouette. A "well-turned leg" to an eighteenth-century male meant that he needed a well-developed calf muscle. In fact, if he lacked this physical attribute, he resorted to padding. Other periods emphasized full, rounded buttocks, especially for women in the late nineteenth century and mid-twentieth century, and this kind of padding is still available in stores and from mail-order catalogs.

As a general rule, padding should be made as a separate piece, fitted to the actor, and worn under the costume supported by the actor's body. There are some exceptions to this rule; the shoulder pads in the garments of the 1940s, for example,

Figure 16–1 An example of padding used for the character of "Sir Toby Belch" in *Twelfth Night* as produced at The Ohio State University. From the author's collection.

are attached to the garment. But if the padding is to suggest an enlargement of the body, accentuated muscles, or physical deformities, it must be supported by the actor's body. The padding then moves with the body naturally, rather than moving as the garment moves.

Building realistic, effective padding requires skill, which means practice to gain experience. A key factor in creating padding is to ascertain exactly what the padding is to depict; for example, is it to depict well-developed muscular structure or layers of fat (sometimes referred to as "sagging muscles")? Essentially, for realistic padding the reason why fullness in a given area has developed must be determined before construction can begin.

For the padded actor to move realistically, the padding must have direct contact with the body and be held in that position to conform with the actor's movement. It needs to be durable, yet light enough to be worn comfortably and worked in easily. It must also be cleanable to stay fresh. Since the actor must have time to work with and become accustomed to the adjusted figure, the padding needs to be completed early in the rehearsal process for the actor to rehearse with it. Early completion is also important in order to make the costume to be worn over it, since the padding must appear to be part of the body, and the costume must be made to fit that body.

GUIDELINES FOR CONSTRUCTING PADDING. Padding should be mounted on a foundation garment which has been fitted to the actor. Torso padding for such areas as the shoulders, chest, or stomach will need to be mounted on a foundation which covers the torso and is held down with a crotch piece, as shown in Fig. 16–2, or which has short legs attached to prevent the padding from riding up on the body. Complete foundations of this nature will allow the padding to move as the body moves. Arm padding generally needs to be

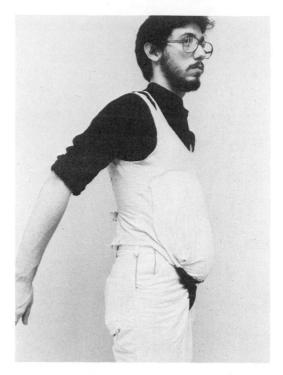

Figure 16–2 An example of paunch padding built on torso-supported foundation. Photo by Robert Izzo.

mounted on a fitted sleeve foundation which is attached to a torso foundation. Leg padding also generally needs to be mounted on fitted foundations from the waist to the knee for additions to the thigh area, from below the knee for calf additions.

Foundations can be constructed of muslin (for small to medium padded areas that are lightweight), of drill cloth or canvas (for medium to large padded areas that are heavier), or of a sturdy jersey or knit (for ease and flexibility of movement). If the padding is to be mounted on stretchy material, the built-up sections should be tacked to the foundation while it is in place on the actor, otherwise the stretch of the fabric will be lost, and it will not fit. Remember that large padding suggests a heavy or fat figure, which automatically limits flexibility in movement.

To pattern the torso foundations, use the basic bodice/jacket patterns with extensions for the hips as described in Chap. 13. The location of the closing for the foundation will depend on the type and placement of the padding. The use of lacing to close the garment is advisable for adjustability, since mounting the padding usually shrinks the foundation to some degree. Adjustability also means that the completed piece can be reused for other actors. The seams and darts in the foundation should be merrowed or double-stitched, and the raw edges should be finished for strength and neatness. If a crotch piece is used, it should be fitted on the actor and closed with hooks and eyes in the back or front. This type of closing makes the unit easy to get into and out of and allows the actor to answer the "call of nature" without removing the entire piece.

For sleeve foundations, use a fitted sleeve pattern. A closing is usually not required for the sleeve, but care must be taken to prevent the foundation from shrinking too much when the padding is added. Arm padding should be attached to a vest or some type of torso foundation for control.

The nature and length of leg foundations depend on the type and location of the padding. Calf padding, for example, can be mounted on a foundation which covers the leg from below the knee to just below the calf, or it can be held in place by wide bands of elastic at the top, center, and bottom. Narrow elastic tends to cut into the leg and cuts off the circulation. Padding for the upper leg and hips can be mounted on a foundation similar to the knee-length slacks pattern in Chap. 10, or it can be attached to a cut-off pair of tights or to fitted briefs. Suspenders are usually necessary to hold up padding supported by the waist.

After the foundation is fitted and stitched, the actual padding can be added. The construction process is time-consuming and requires care and thought if the padding is to resemble human structures rather than a "wad" or lump. For the most effective results and the best fit, the padding must be sewn in a curve that matches the curvature of the body at the given location. The padding stitch, described in Chap. 3, should be used to help shape and hold the curvature of the padding piece.

Controlling the curve(s) in a section of padding is the key to making effective, realistic padding. This is done by carefully adjusting and distributing the thickness of the padding material. It should taper to nothing where the fullness is to blend into the body, and the fullness should be distributed as needed in natural bulges or sagging areas.

The padding stitch provides the means of rounding the flat padding material to match the body. The stitches are executed on the inside of the curve since they draw or pull the piece into the curve. A series of stitches is required to make an even curvature; how many are needed depends on where the piece is to go on the body. Padding over the top of the shoulders, for instance, needs more curvature than padding over the abdomen.

Typical materials to use for building up the padding include cotton or polyester *batting, fiberfill*, sheet or shredded *foam* (polyurethane), and *nylon net*. Construction techniques vary slightly for each material. Batting is built up in layers with each layer firmly stitched to the foundation with the padding stitch. Sheet foam is shaved or trimmed to the shape needed and stitched in place. As a cost-saving material, *bottom sheeting* (or "skins") is very inexpensive foam that can be purchased from manufacturers; it is generally ½ in. (1.3 cm) thick.

Shredded foam is useful for stuffing large pieces. For sagging paunches, for instance, a muslin pocket with darts at the bottom for the full sag can be attached to the foundation and the foam stuffed inside. This approach is quick and effective for exaggerated, comic, or nonrealistic distortions. Shredded foam does tend to be magnetic and sticks to everything. It can also form lumps in the padding if it is not carefully smoothed as it goes into the pocket, and it will shift if it is not packed firmly enough.

Nylon net is useful for small lightweight sections. It needs to be shaped before it is added to the foundation. Keep the top layer smooth to prevent "points" and irregular surfaces.

Sheet foam is probably the most popular padding material; it is lightweight, easy to work with and to shape, and washable. It should be air-dried or dried in a dryer at low heat. Batting is also easy to work with, and the layering process generally allows for excellent realistic shaping; however, it is also very warm and should be dry-cleaned. Nylon net is acceptable for small sections and for short performance runs since it is less resilient than the other materials. It is lightweight and hand-washable but should be air-dried; tumbling in a dryer may cause the net to bunch up or to shift within the piece.

After the padding is mounted on the foundation, it should be fitted before it is finalized. The padding should be checked under a garment—a rehearsal costume or a mock-up of the costume—in order to see the appearance and proportions of the shape. The proportions are very important. The padding may overwhelm an actor of small stature or may not be sufficient for a larger actor. The padding needs to be checked for proportion relationships to the size and shape of the rest of the body. The head, for example, can appear to be tiny and out of proportion if the padding creates too large a body. The hands—especially the wrists—and legs may also present proportion problems.

After the fit and proportions have been approved by the designer, the padding is ready to be finished. Make sure the built-up sections are stitched securely to the foundation. This means that a number of stitches must be stabbed through the padding and foundation with a long needle and heavy thread. The final step is to cover the padding with a soft lightweight material such as muslin or lining taffeta. The latter will limit the amount of cling between the costume and the padding. Remember that new measurements will need to be taken of the actor in the padding to make the external costume fit the adjusted figure.

PADDING THE BUST. For centuries, women have utilized padding, as well as other means, to "improve" their figures, particularly at the bustline. From padded bras, "falsies," and "improvers" to steel and whalebone corsets, the bustline has been stuffed, flattened, or lifted according to the fashions of the particular era.

An all-too-typical approach to creating a full bustline is to stuff a bra. However, for theatrical purposes, lifting the bust to create cleavage is the most effective means of achieving a full bust appearance. To create this type of look, thin layers of a padding material are placed in the lower half of each bra cup. The layers should be shaped to conform to the curvature of the bra cup and the breast; place the thickest part of the layering next to the body and taper the padding to nothing at the nipple. When the appropriate shape is achieved, the padding will need to be stitched in place, using the padding stitch. This approach lifts the bust and has a natural realistic appearance which is effective with high necklines as well as with low-cut revealing necklines.

SHOULDER PADS. Unlike padding used to alter the apparent shape of a body underneath clothing, shoulder pads are usually understood by an audience to be a part of the clothes, so they are attached directly to the garment. They are used in many men's coats and are appropriate for wom-

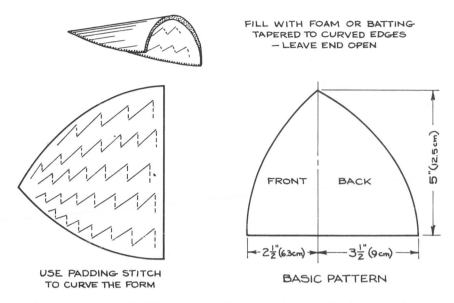

FILL WITH FOAM OR BATTING
TAPERED TO CURVED EDGES
— LEAVE END OPEN

USE PADDING STITCH
TO CURVE THE FORM

FRONT BACK

5" (12.5cm)

2½" (6.3cm)   3½" (9cm)

BASIC PATTERN

Figure 16-3 Basic shoulder-pad pattern showing stitching detail and completed pad.

en's clothing from specific periods like the 1940s.

However, shoulder pads that are available in stores are usually too small for the more exaggerated effects frequently desired in theatrical costumes. Therefore they must often be made in the shop. On the other hand, making these pieces provides simple but good practice in padding construction techniques and also builds up a supply of pads to have in stock when the need arises.

The base of the pad, as shown in Fig. 16-3, is muslin cut to size. The thickness is built up with layers of batting or with trimmed foam tapered to the curved edges. This is held in place and drawn into a curved shape with the padding stitch. After the pad is secured and shaped, the top is covered with muslin or lining taffeta. The cover can be laid in place, cut to size, and stitched around the curved edges. The edge over the armhole is left unstitched to keep the height of the pad intact.

CORSETS

The use of cast iron, steel, wood, ivory, whalebone, and other substances to shape or mold the torso had become fashionable by the sixteenth century, and, with few exceptions, corseting has continued as an important element in feminine fashions until recently. Many names have been applied to corsets; they have been referred to as bodies, stays, corps, whaleboned bodies, and corsets. The term *corset* be-

came fashionable early in the nineteenth century and is used here, generically, to refer to stiffened torso-shaping undergarments.

Corsets are absolutely essential in creating the proper silhouettes for many periods. The cut or pattern of the corset and the angle of the corset stays mold the shape of the torso; this has varied from period to period to be in accord with the fashionable silhouette. For example, an eighteenth-century corset, which emphasizes a high, rounded bust with cleavage, is not appropriate to the flattened bust of the sixteenth-century Tudor silhouette.

An excellent resource for specific patterns and location of the stays is *Corsets and Crinolines* by Norah Waugh. The patterns are clear and drawn to scale. They generally fit sizes 10 to 12 but are easy to scale up or down according to the actor's measurements. If a specific corset pattern is unavailable, the corset can be patterned on the same lines as the bodice of the costume. Keep in mind that the function of the corset is not just to stiffen the torso or to make the waist smaller. Its function is to mold the torso into a particular shape. Therefore, the number and shapes of the corset pattern pieces are important to shaping the body appropriately.

GUIDELINES FOR PATTERNING CORSETS. There are basic guidelines to observe when patterning any corset. Patterns can be taken from the Waugh book, patterned the same as the torso garment, or developed by using the principles cited in Chap. 13. The pattern pieces should be cut with ½ in. (1.3 cm) seam allowances all around, except for the closing which should have a 2 in. (5 cm) seam allowance. Each piece should be carefully identified with notations indicating what seams are to be joined and which is the top and the bottom of each piece; corset pattern pieces are unusual shapes which can be confusing if not clearly identified. Most corset patterns should be developed with separate shoulder straps in order to provide easy adjustment in the fitting.

The finished corset should be 2 in. (5 cm) smaller than the actor's measurements at the bust, waist, and hips to allow the corset to be laced tightly; the closing should never meet completely when laced closed. Generally, the lacing is in the back in order to keep the front flat and smooth.

GUIDELINES FOR CONSTRUCTING CORSETS. The tools and equipment that are necessary when constructing corsets have been described in Chap. 2. These include flat, ½ in. wide spring-steel corset stays which can be cut to the necessary length with wire cutters or tin snips. Any cut metal edges will need to be smoothed with a metal file and then dipped in liquid plastic, available at most craft supply shops, to round and smooth the ends.

Grommets and a grommet set are necessary to finish the laced closing. The grommets are metal eyelets with two pieces, top and bottom, set in place with the fabric sandwiched between the units. They are much more durable than small single-piece metal eyelets. Cotton shoe lacing works very well for the lacing.

The fabric for the corset should be heavy cotton, drill, or duck cloth. Bias tape to finish the edges and heavy ¾ in. (2 cm) wide twill tape are also used in corset construction. There are two typical methods of corset construction; one method uses twill tape as a casing for the stays (see Fig. 16-4, p. 264); the other method sandwiches the stays between the corset and its matched lining. This latter method requires cutting two matching corsets, the good and the lining.

With both methods, the fabric is cut and stitched together for the first fitting. Since the corset is form-fitting, it is fitted with the right side out because the two sides of the body are not symmetrical. As with all fittings, make sure that the seams are in the right place and that the neck and arm holes are correct and comfortable. Mark the waistline and center-back closing before the fitting is completed. Additional markings to show the top and bottom of the corset stays will need to be made in the first fitting, especially if the stays do not go to the full length of the corset. Also, mark the preliminary location of shoulder straps; these will be finalized in the next fitting.

After the corset has been fitted and all the fitting marks have been transferred, stitch the corset together. Double-stitch or merrow the seams and press them flat. If the stays are to be sandwiched between the corset and the lining, make sure that the lining and the good fabrics match each other. To finish the back closing, draw a line 1 in. (2.5 cm) from the marked closing line on each side of the corset to make the corset 2 in. (5 cm) smaller than the actual fit. These new lines are foldlines.

To finish the closing, fold the fabric on the foldlines, with the extra seam allowance inside so that there are three layers of fabric. The folded edges should be wide enough to fit under the grommet, about 1 in. (2.5 cm) for the number 0 grommets. Press and stitch each edge before setting in the grommets, which are usually placed about 1½ in. (3.8 cm) apart. There should be a grommet at the top and bottom of each edge of the corset closing, with the rest evenly spaced between these.

To mark the stay locations, determine the layout pattern of the stays according to the silhouette of the period. Several sources for this are cited at the end of this chapter. The location and angle of the stays are crucial in achieving the appropriate silhouette. Many authentic patterns also call for horizontal stays, but these are not generally necessary for theatrical use.

If twill tape is to be used, use the tape to mark locations by pinning it in the correct locations. The ends of the tape should be folded under to hide the raw edges, and the tape is left unstitched at the top so the stay can be slid inside. If the stays are to be sandwiched, mark the stitch lines of the stay locations on the right side of the lining with a pencil, using a stay as a guide for the correct width. The marked corset lining will quickly become a mass of lines if there are several stays, so keep the lines distinct and clear. Number the spaces and the stays for easy identification if different sizes are to be used.

If the tape-casing method is used, stitch the sides and bottom edge of the tape. The stitching must be straight and accurate to allow the stay to slide into place. Insert the stays, slip the end under the top fold of the twill tape, and tack the top of the tape to the corset to secure the stay.

Add the lacing. Fit the corset on the actor to make the final adjustments in the shoulder straps, check the corset neckline with the costume neckline to be sure the corset will not show, and check for comfort and ease of movement. To finish the corset, bind the raw edges at the neck, armhole, and bottom with bias tape. Figure 16–4 shows a corset finished in this manner.

If the corset is lined, stitch the lining to the good fabric at the neck and closing with the right sides together. Make sure the seam lines match, with the lining and the good fabric in perfect alignment. Remember that the closing will be 1 in. (2.5 cm) smaller on each side. Clip the seam allowances and turn the corset through the bottom. The marked stitch lines for the stays should be visible on the right side of the lining. Carefully sew through both the lining and the good side on the stitch lines at the sides and top and slip the stays in from the bottom; then finish the bottom edge with bias tape. Be careful with this stitching; if the needle hits a stay, it will break. The final steps to complete and fit the corset are the same as described above.

Well-made corsets are surprisingly comfortable. They must be laced for a snug, tight fit; a loose corset is very uncomfortable and virtually worthless. Generally, the corset will need to be relaced after the actor has had it on for about half an hour. The body adjusts to the corset, and retying will make it more comfortable and allow it to function properly. The corset will impose the correct posture and carriage for the period in a manner that is not possible to achieve with any other means.

The corset should be completed early in

Figure 16–4 An example of a completed corset with the corset stays in a twill-tape casing; the natural waistline is marked by a running stitch. Photo by Robert Izzo.

the rehearsal process so the actor can become accustomed to it in rehearsals. The actor must also wear the corset at all subsequent fittings of any garments to be worn over it.

SKIRT SUPPORTS

The term *skirt support* refers to any unit or undergarment which extends or distorts the natural body line below the waist and holds a skirt in a shape appropriate to a particular fashion. The audience rarely sees these units, but they are as necessary to achieving the correct silhouette as the corset. Those periods which utilized corsets also often featured some form of skirt support, although there were eras when skirts were artificially widened and corsets were not in vogue. The most recent example of this is the full, starched, ruffled petticoats of the 1950s.

Skirt supports fall into three major categories: pads and rolls, hoops, and starched or otherwise stiffened petticoats. The pads and rolls rest on the hips to extend the hip line of the skirt which then falls free below the support.

Hoops may also be used to expand the hips, and they have been used just to stiffen the hemline. But they are usually used in a series of suspended rings of graduated sizes to form conical or bell-shaped supports for wide or elaborate skirt styles. In more complicated configurations and complex assemblies, hoops also form the basic structural parts for such skirt supports as bustles or panniers, as shown in Fig. 16–5.

Starched petticoats are generally used to hold out the hem of a skirt and give fullness to the rest of the skirt from the hipline down. This is the simplest form of skirt support, since layers of petticoats suggest volume of fabric but do not distort the natural body lines as extremely as the other forms.

All skirt *underpinnings* (the term really refers to women's undergarments) tend to reflect the line and style of the garment. Therefore petticoats are patterned to mirror the gown. Additions such as ruffles are sometimes made to catch interest or to give added fullness. The traditional "cancan" skirt is an obvious example of this. Virtually all women's period costumes require at least one petticoat; many require more than one, and all need to be planned with the costume.

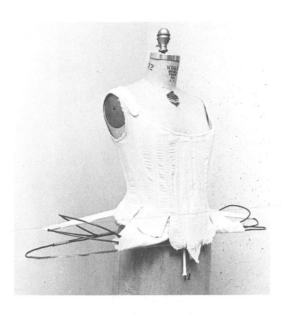

Figure 16–5 Corset and copper-tubing pannier on dress form. The pannier is suspended from the waistband with strips of cloth for balance. Photo by Robert Izzo.

BUM-ROLL PATTERN AND CONSTRUCTION. The practice of artificially supporting skirts had become common by the mid-sixteenth century. A popular form at that time was a padded roll or bolster referred to as a "bum-roll" or as a "French vardingale" or "farthingale" (there are many spellings of the latter). Contemporary illustrations show this as a stuffed tirelike piece which was tied to the upper section of the hips under the skirt of the garment. Theatrically, a common variation of the bum-roll is a crescent-shape which has added fullness at the sides and back but leaves the front flat.

Constructing a crescent-shape bum-roll is a simple process. The following pattern provides only basic guidelines for laying out the shape; the dimensions are generalized and adjustments in the curves may be necessary, but they can be done easily after the shape is drafted. Two shapes need to be cut, one for the top and one for the bottom of the roll. The 12 in.

(30.5 cm) circumference of the roll thickness shown here is fairly standard, but it can be made larger or smaller by adjusting the outside curve. Seam allowance is included in the pattern draft.

1. Lay out the pattern on a piece of muslin that measures at least one-quarter of the actor's hip measurement plus 12 in. (30.5 cm) in one dimension; the other dimension should be at least one-half of the hip measurement plus 18 in. (46 cm). Fold this latter dimension in half so that the distance from the fold to the double edge is one-quarter of the hip measurement plus 9 in. (23 cm) as shown in Fig. 16–6. Draw in a right-angle line perpendicular to the foldline and at the bottom of the rectangle.

2. Set point A on the fold at the right-angle line; measure up 7 in. (18 cm) on the foldline to set point B. Line A–B (foldline) is the center-back line of the pattern.

3. Take one-quarter of the hip measurement minus 6 in. (15 cm) and measure over from point B to set point C; connect points B–C with a straight line that is parallel to the right-angle line.

4. To establish the front of the inside curve, take one-quarter of the hip measurement plus 2 in. (5 cm) and measure up from point B on the fold to set point D^1 for reference. Then measure across one-quarter of the hip measurement and set point D. Line D^1–D should be parallel to the right-angle line.

5. To complete the inside curve, start from point B which is at the center-back of the wearer's body. Measure up the foldline 6 in. (15 cm) and set reference point E^1. On a line parallel to the right-angle line, measure across one-quarter of the hip measurement plus 1 in. (2.5 cm) and set point E. With a french curve, connect points D–E–C.

6. To establish the outside curve, measure up 2 in. (5 cm) from point D and set

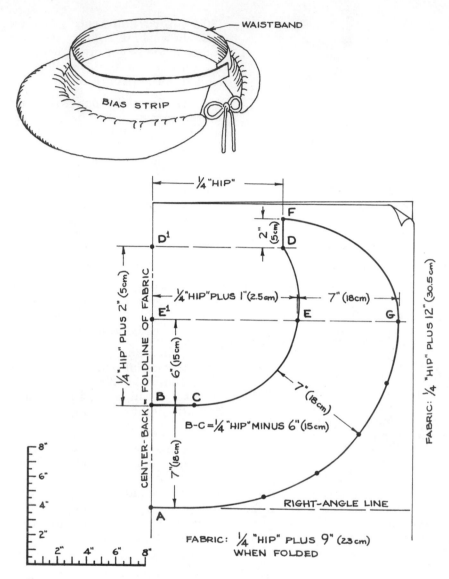

Figure 16-6 Bum-roll pattern and completed bum-roll.

point F. Connect points D–F with a straight line.

a. For the front portion of the curve, set point G 7 in. (18 cm) across from point E on an extension of line E¹–E. Connect points F–G using a french curve.

b. From point G to point A, the pattern piece is 7 in. (18 cm) wide, and the outside curve is equidistant from the inside curve. Set additional points for the outside curve by measuring 7 in. (18 cm) from line E–C–B; connect these points using a french curve.

Figure 19–8A "Oedipus" in *Oedipus Rex* as produced by The Ohio State University. The tabard features three-dimensional appliqués and the actor is wearing shoes with 3-in. high cork soles.

Figure 20-12 Girls and Boys in Act I of *The Boy Friend* as produced by the University of Rhode Island. The 1920 and definition of character types are captured by the use of lines, textures, colors, and details, including a variety of from head decorations to hose and garters, which combine to create the total costume for each character.

This pattern is for a bum-roll that is 12 in. (30.5 cm) in circumference when finished; seam allowances of ½ in. (1.3 cm) are included. Adjustments in the thickness of the roll can be made by increasing or decreasing the measurement between the inside curve and the outside curve. The inside curve (line D–E–C–B) should remain constant, and along the curve it should measure one-half of the hip measurement minus 2 in. (5 cm) since the roll will not meet at the center-front. Adjust the curves as needed, but remember that the bum-roll will be flexible and that it must rest securely on the hips.

Cut two of the pattern shapes and stitch them together, leaving an opening between points C–B to turn the seams inside and to stuff the roll. Clip the seam allowances on the curves, turn the roll, and press the seams. Stitch a length of tape, about 20 in. (51 cm) long to each end, between points D–F. These will be used to tie the roll at the center-front. Next stuff the roll through the back opening with shredded foam, fiberfill, or nylon net until the roll is firm and smooth. Hand-stitch the opening closed.

To suspend the bum-roll from the waist, cut a bias strip of muslin 3 in. (7.5 cm) wide and long enough to match the inside curve of the roll. Overcast or roll-hem the raw edges. Attach a waistband (see Chap. 9) to the top of the bias strip. Then stitch the roll to the bottom of the bias strip. Be sure to keep the roll level on the bias strip so that it will be level on the body.

Fit the waistband to the actor and finish the closure with two pairs of hooks and eyes placed for an accurate fit; for more adjustable fit, work a drawstring through the waistband.

HOOPED SKIRT SUPPORTS. Keeping a skirt support level and evenly balanced is the key to all successful skirt supports. It is particularly important for hooped supports, since they do not rest directly on the body. Since even a modest hooped skirt has a diameter of 36 in. (91.5 cm), which is wider than an average door opening, and a pannier skirt (see Fig. 16–7) is not unusual at 4 ft (1 m 22 cm) wide, poorly balanced skirt supports are almost impossible to wear; they look strange, and movement in them is very awkward.

Specific patterns for several hooped skirt supports can be found in *Corsets and Crinolines*. The necessary tools and equipment are similar to those used in corseting.

Flat ½ in. (1.3 cm) wide spring steel is available from theatrical supply houses; it is recommended for the hoops when a round shape is required. It is flexible, springs back into shape, and is easy to work with. A flexible wire can also be used, but avoid materials that bend or "dent" like hanger wire. Spring steel can be joined by overlapping the ends and riveting, or by using clips available with the spring steel that are crimped with pliers, or by wrapping the join with reinforced packaging tape. The tape should be double-wrapped to prevent the steel from cutting through.

For shapes that are oval, such as the eighteenth-century *panniers* associated with Marie Antoinette, ³/₁₆ in. copper tubing works very well (see Fig. 16–5). It is lightweight, easy to shape and yet does not dent easily, which makes it well worth the expense. Copper tubing can be joined by flattening the ends of the tube and popriveting or soldering the junctions.

GUIDELINES FOR CONSTRUCTING HOOPED SKIRT SUPPORTS. The construction process for a nineteenth-century hoop applies the essential principles for making other types of hoops, whether round, oval, or half-circle, and regardless of the hoop material used. These principles involve suspending the hoop(s) from a waistband with strips of cloth or twill tape and balancing the hoops by adjusting the points where the hoops are joined to the tapes. By the methods which follow, these adjustments

Figure 16–7 An example of a gown with the skirt supported by a pannier. Photo by Robert Izzo.

are easy to make, and the points of attachment can be securely sewed in place after the balance is achieved.

The hoop-supported skirts designed for a given production may take a number of forms in elaborateness and details, but a great many of them can be effectively supported by a simple circular hoop arrangement.

The number of hoops used can also vary; typically, four to six are used with more added if needed. But for theatrical use, we have found that four hoops are usually sufficient; this number makes the garment lighter in weight and easier for the actor to control when worn. It also reduces both the time and effort needed for construction.

For any skirt that can use a circular support—regardless of the size of the skirt or of the actor—it is possible to determine how to construct the hoop support from two dimensions, one from the design and one from the actor's measurements, and a simple formula to find the sizes of the individual hoops. This planning process also provides the information needed to order the right amount of material.

As shown in Fig. 16–8, the simplest form creates a moderate fullness at the hipline, descending into a straight-sided skirt silhouette. To plan this support, first obtain the width of the skirt from the design; this should be the diameter of the largest hoop at the bottom hem position. This information should be readily available from the designer as a specific measurement determined early in the design process since it also affects doorway openings, furniture placement, and the movement of the actor onstage.

Next determine the size of the uppermost hoop by taking the actor's hip measurement and adding 24 in. (61 cm). When suspended approximately at the hipline, a hoop of this size provides a comfortable fullness for the actor's posture and movement. It can be increased in size for greater fullness or raised on the body to create an Elizabethan "drum farthingale."

Since the top hoop measurement is a circumference which also begins to suggest the length of the steel needed to make the hoop, it is necessary to convert the known diameter of the bottom hoop to a circumference in order to know the length of the steel needed for it. This is done by multiplying the diameter by *pi* (3.14 is sufficiently accurate for this purpose).

To determine the differences between

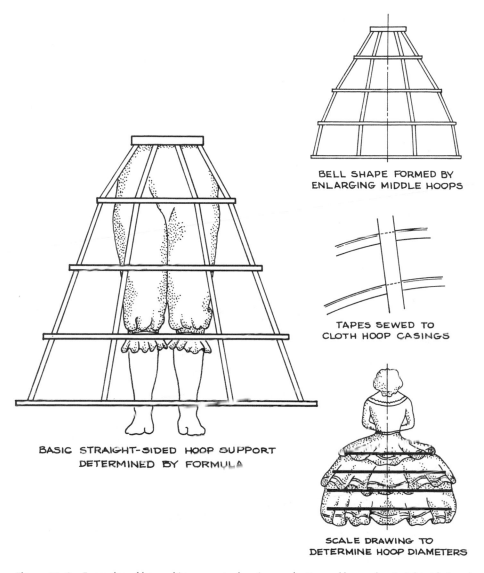

BELL SHAPE FORMED BY
ENLARGING MIDDLE HOOPS

TAPES SEWED TO
CLOTH HOOP CASINGS

BASIC STRAIGHT-SIDED HOOP SUPPORT
DETERMINED BY FORMULA

SCALE DRAWING TO
DETERMINE HOOP DIAMETERS

Figure 16-8 Examples of hoop-skirt supports showing graduations of hoops for straight-sided and bell-shaped configurations.

the circumferences for a straight-sided hoop support, subtract the circumference of the top (smallest) hoop from the circumference of the bottom (largest) hoop. Divide that result by a number equal to one less than the number of hoops. Using the example illustrated in Fig. 16–8, which is based on a hip measurement of 36 in. (91.5 cm) and a skirt/hoop diameter of 42 in. (107 cm), the calculations would be:

269

Circumference of largest hoop (diameter times *pi*):

42 in. (107 cm) diameter times 3.14 = 131.8 in. (335.9 cm); round to: 132 (336)

Minus circumference of smallest hoop (36 plus 24): 60 (153)

72 in. (183 cm) divided by 3 (4 hoops minus 1) = 24 in. (61 cm)
$$\frac{60 \ (153)}{72 \ (183)}$$

This number is the increment which is the difference in circumference length of each pair of adjacent hoops. This formula applies regardless of the number of hoops, but to complete the example, the four hoops would have circumferences of: 60 in. (153 cm), 84 in. (214 cm), 108 in. (275 cm), and 132 in. (336 cm). Before cutting the hoop steel, add 1 in. (2.5 cm) or more to each of these measurements for overlap to join the ends of the steel into the hoops.

If these hoops are equally spaced along the suspension tapes between the hip and the ankle, they will form a straight-sided conical support for the skirt. To obtain a more curved or bell-shaped silhouette with a four-hoop support, merely increase the circumference of the two middle hoops. The curved form shown in Fig. 16–8 is created by increasing each of those hoops by 12 in. (30.5 cm). For this type of curve, both hoops should be increased by the same amount, but be careful not to exceed the size of the largest hoop and to keep the proportions appropriate to the design.

For more elaborate curves in which the size of the hoops does not increase in regular increments, it is best to plan the construction with the aid of a scale drawing or on graph paper to determine the diameters of the individual hoops. Multiply them by *pi* (3.14) to get the circumferences and add 1 in. (2.5 cm) or more for overlaps in the lengths of the hoop steel.

Once the steel is cut, each hoop should be enclosed in a casing; cut, stitch, and turn muslin casings for each hoop length. The casings should be finished ½ in. (1.3 cm) wider than the hoop material for allowance to attach the hoops to the suspension tapes. Insert the hoops in the casings; overlap and secure the hoops in a circle with rivets, clips, or tape, and handstitch the casing closed.

Next, make a waistband; a tie-closing is preferable to hooks or buttons for easy adjustability. Attach a number of lengths of 1 in. (2.5 cm) twill tape or strong cloth strips to the waistband; space them equally around the band and about 2 in. to 3 in. (5 cm to 8 cm) apart. If the length of the tapes is equal to the waist-to-floor measurement plus one-half of the diameter of the largest hoop, there will be more than enough to go over all hoops.

Secure the waistband on a dress form for attaching and balancing the hoops; this process can be done on the actor, but it is time-consuming and the live body is not necessary.

Since the top hoop shifts the lines of support from the oval of the waist to the circle of the hoops, start with that one. Pin the casing of the hoop to each of the suspension tapes so that the hoop hangs at the hipline or at the point called for by the design. Adjust the pins until the hoop hangs level and balanced all around the figure.

The rest of the hoops can then be pinned in place. Space them evenly along the suspension tapes according to the number of hoops and the distance from waist to ankle. The bottom hoop should hang at ankle level.

Once the hoops are pinned in place, adjusting and shifting the hoops to find the proper levels and good balance points is more important than accurate measurements. After the proper balance is achieved, securely hand-stitch each tape and hoop in place with heavy button thread since there is a good deal of strain at each intersection. Should the skirt need to be shortened, adjust the distances between the hoops.

The hoop support and all other skirt supports should be worn under at least one petticoat to soften the lines or ridges of the hoops. Remember, too, that the use of any type of skirt support means that extra length must be cut in the good skirt so that it will cover the support and still reach the proper hem length. If there is doubt as to what the extra length should be, the "waist to hem" measurement can be taken with the actor in the support. Also keep in mind that the shoe and heel height worn with the costume will influence the position of the final hem.

Early completion of any skirt support and accompanying petticoat is important so that the actor has ample rehearsal time to become accustomed to the piece and to learn how to maneuver in it. These supports must also be worn for all other fittings for garments to be worn over them.

As with padding, ascertaining the proper proportions is a key element in making skirt supports. Since the originals were intended to be out of proportion with the body, proper proportions in this instance include the relationships to the stage space, the stage business, entrances to the stage, and furniture as well as the designed proportions of the costume. It is next to impossible for an actor in a set of wide panniers to sit in an armchair, for example. All of these will influence the appropriate proportions for skirt supports and are the concern of the set designer and director as well as the costume people and performers.

ADDITIONAL SOURCES

The following reading list contains sources for additional information on body and skirt supports. These sources are suggested as part of the research that is necessary to create proper period silhouettes.

BENDER, LYNDA, "Creating the Right Silhouette," *Theatre Crafts*, January/February 1978, pp. 20–23, 53–57.

CUNNINGTON, C. W., and P. CUNNINGTON, *The History of Underclothes.* New York: Gordon Press, 1976.

EWING, ELIZABETH, *Underwear, A History.* New York: Theatre Arts Books, 1972.

TOMPKINS, JULIA, *Stage Costumes and How to Make Them*, pp. 146–54. New York: Plays, Inc., 1969, reprint 1972.

WAUGH, NORAH, *Corsets and Crinolines.* New York: Theatre Arts Books, 1954, 2nd printing, 1970.

seventeen

hairstyles and wigs

While some actors can work with their own hair, many others find it difficult to restyle or even set their hair without help. This is particularly true for the hairstyles of different periods and especially for the more elaborate hairdos that may be required for a given production. In other situations, the period of the play, the production design, or even the completion of the appearance of a specific character may call for the use of wigs. Working with hair and wigs has become an important part of modern theatrical productions. The growth of the specialized field of hair design and hair dressing in commercial theatre testifies to the importance of this area.

While the designer is responsible for determining the appearances that are appropriate for each of the various characters, the responsibility for actually executing the hairstyles will often fall to the costumer. Consequently, the costumer needs to learn about and be familiar with the hairstyles from the past as well as from the present and with the techniques needed for working with hair and wigs. Since the variety in hairstyles is so extensive, the following coverage is intended to provide only the basic guidelines for the working techniques, but they can be applied to any hairstyle.

WORKING WITH NATURAL HAIR

Working with the actor's own hair is usually the simplest and least expensive means to create the necessary style. Therefore, actors involved in a production should be

cautioned not to have their hair cut or restyled before getting permission from the director and designer. Occasionally, a different hairstyle will involve nothing more

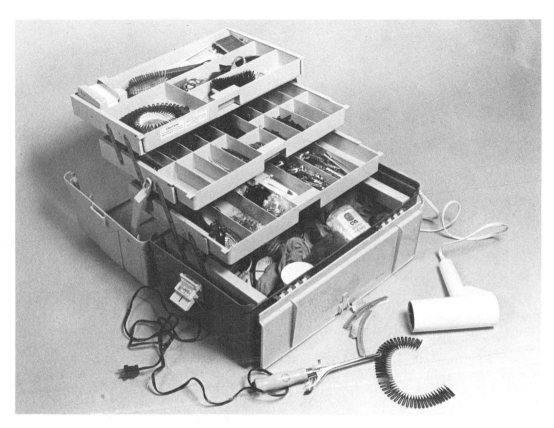

Figure 17-1 Hair supplies kit with a curling iron, flex comb and wave clips, and a portable hair dryer. Photo by Robert Izzo.

than changing a part or combing the hair a different way and controlling it with clear hair spray. At other times, it may require curling, piling the hair up on the head, or "slicking" it down as major departures from the actor's normal hairstyle.

Electric curling irons and electric curlers ("hot rollers") are invaluable for a quick curling and restyling of the hair, and these items are standard tools for working with hair. Other supplies for setting and combing out hair include combs (rattail combs are particularly valuable), bobby pins, hairpins, clips, wave clips, barber's scissors, brushes, wig brushes (these have widely spaced metal bristles), setting gel,

various sizes of rollers, and a hair dryer. We keep these supplies in a portable kit as shown in Fig. 17-1.

The actor's hair should be clean, since clean hair is easier to set and restyle. It is also much more pleasant to work with than dirty, oily hair. Sets done with curling irons or hot rollers are done on dry hair, but these sets do not hold up as long as those done when the hair is wet. Setting the hair when it is wet generally gives a firmer, longer-lasting curl, especially when a setting gel is used. Actually, the method used for setting hair depends on how durable the hairstyle needs to be and the nature of the actor's hair. Some hair takes and holds

273

a set very easily, and some hair does not. Actors usually have a good idea of whether or not their hair will take a set easily.

SETTING THE HAIR. Whether the hair is set wet or dry, the key to successful hair sets is to pull the hair taut and maintain a firm grip on it; loosely set hair will not take a curl well, and it tangles quickly. Anyone who has ever had a hot roller tangled in the hair knows the discomfort and frustration of trying to remove it; often it ends up being cut out of the hair.

To avoid tangles, irregular ends of hair lengths can be controlled by folding endpapers, small rectangles of tissue paper, over the ends from the side of the hair section as shown in Fig. 17-2. The amount of hair in each section for a curl is also a factor in whether or not the hair tangles; too much hair in a curl leaves loose hairs that are not taut. These loose hairs will get tangled. How the curl is held to the head is also important. If the curls are not secure, set too loosely to the head, they will fall out and tangle.

The principal rule for securing the curl to the head is to make sure the pins or clips are anchored to the hair and head. Pins that have straight prongs, such as hairpins or hot-roller pins, should be started into the hair in the opposite direction to catch some hair, and then flipped and pushed home in the other direction to support the curl. Pins that grip, such as bobby pins, should always be used in pairs and crossed to hold the curl secure.

Typical methods of curling the hair are setting it on a roller or pin-curling it. Rollers give a bouffant soft curl when combed out, or the curls can be combed into sausage or banana curls. The use of rollers gives body to the hair; therefore, they are often used to set hair that will be dressed in an upswept hairdo. Pin curls give a tight curl and can be used on both long and short hair. With both methods, the amount of hair in each curl influences how tight or firm the results will be: the less hair, the tighter the curl.

The fundamental element in working with hair is to hold on to it and keep it under control. Loosely set fly-away hair tangles easily and does not hold a curl well. The same is true in regard to controlling the hair when it is combed and arranged. All too often, a hairdo will begin to fall apart because the hair was loose and the pins were not securely anchored. A large number of pins and a lot of hair spray will not ensure the permanence of a hairdo. Firm control of the hair and careful application of the pins will hold the most elaborate hairstyle. Remember that the bobbypins need to be used in pairs and crossed and that the hairpins need to be started into the hair in the opposite direction, with a small amount of hair caught by the pin, and then flipped in the other direction and pushed into place. If the pin direction is not reversed, the pin will fall out.

These hairpin techniques are also used to anchor combs for the hair. Small hair-combs and stretch-combs, also called *flex-combs,* are useful for holding sections of hair in place and for securing upswept hairdos. Stretch-combs are particularly valuable for sweeping up a lot of hair. But these combs also need to be anchored with the reverse flip described for hairpins and secured with bobby pins crossed through the teeth.

Fear of hurting the actor's head is probably the major cause of loose sets and hairdos. Firm control can be maintained without pulling the hair, and pins can make contact with the scalp without drawing blood. Use care, but remember the importance of control; a loose set or hairdo is uncomfortable and makes the actor feel very insecure.

TEASING HAIR. A standard technique for building height or fullness in a hairdo is to tease the hair. *Teasing* is the gathering of the hair into loose cushiony bunches placed to support covering outer layers of hair in order to give fullness and shape to the hairdo, see Fig. 17–3. But if teasing is done incorrectly, the hair can be harmed and may even require cutting out the teased section because it cannot be untangled. If executed correctly, though, teasing is an excellent method of shaping a hairstyle.

The most important rules for teasing

Figure 17–3 Hair being teased by the use of straight single strokes ending at the top of the previous stroke. Photo by Robert Izzo.

hair are to hold onto the hair and to tease from the ends toward the scalp in straight single strokes. The hair is divided into sections, and each section is teased separately. Grip the hair section tightly between the fingers and the fleshy part of the palm and hold it straight out from the head. Run a rattail comb or a teasing comb (which has alternating length teeth) through the hair from the ends toward the scalp, *one* straight stroke at a time. Each stroke pulls some hairs from the section held in your hand and bunches them where the stroke ends. Make each successive stroke slightly shorter than the previous one so that the individual bunches are not forced together and become entangled with each other. This process is repeated, one stroke at a time, until the hair is sufficiently teased for the style.

This method allows the hair to be combed out easily and does not damage the hair. The secret to teasing is the single stroke. The hair must be held taut and firmly, and the comb must not be moved back and forth in the hair. This procedure takes practice to perfect. This practice can be gained by experimenting on wigs.

To comb out the tease, work from the ends of the hair, gently combing out from the tips first, then moving slowly up the strands of hair. Never start at the scalp because that locks in the tease and ties the hair in knots that will not come out. This same technique is used to comb out tangled hair. Always work from the ends to straighten out the hair.

COLORING AND GREYING HAIR. Colored hair spray is a simple, relatively inexpensive means of coloring the hair. It is temporary and will wash out. It does not damage the hair, and the colors do not change on the hair. Rinses, hair dyes, and bleaches can result in strange, unexpected colors. These should be applied by a professional hairdresser in order to minimize surprises.

Colored hair spray is available in a wide range of colors and is easy to apply if properly handled. A major error in the application of the spray is splotching the hair, scalp, and skin. This can be avoided by holding sections of the hair out from the head and applying the spray evenly, holding the can 6 in. to 8 in. away from the hair. This process should be done in a well-ventilated area, and there should be enough space to move around the actor easily during the application. When spraying around the face and hairline, hold a tissue at the edge of the hair to prevent splotching the skin.

Another common error when applying hair spray is to attempt to color every hair on the head. Coloring every hair looks artificial because natural hair has many colors in it. Therefore, allow the actor's natural hair colors to blend in with the spray and use more than one color of spray.

To color streaks or to touch up the hairline, eyebrows, and facial hair, spray some color into the cap of the can and brush the color on with an old toothbrush. This prevents splotching the skin and gives a very natural effect. The toothbrush is also effective for coloring hair roots. Use only a small amount in the cap at a time because the spray dries quickly.

These criteria also apply to greying the hair. Usually, a combination of white and silver sprays is effective because white alone is very dull, and the silver is very shiny. Greying blond hair is a problem because there is not enough contrast between the hair and the spray color. Applying a brown spray first will provide the necessary contrast for the greying agent.

Additional hair-greying materials include white pancake (applied with a dampened toothbrush), liquid hair whitener, liquid white mascara, and white cream stick make-up; shoe polish should not be used: It is made for shoes not for hair. These hair whiteners tend to be fairly lackluster, but all of these materials are temporary and can be washed out after the performance. The cream stick also tends to rub off if there is a lot of physical contact with the hair.

WORKING WITH HAIR FOR PRODUCTIONS. As stated, the designer will specify the details on hair color and style, but the execution of the hair designs often falls to the costumer. However, a local hairdresser, jobbed in for special or elaborate hairdos, can be a valuable addition to the production staff. A person of this background can teach the actors and members of the crew how to execute the styles or can be hired to execute the work for the run of the show.

An area set aside specifically for the hair and wig work during the production is very useful and allows the supplies to be centralized so they are available when needed (Fig. 17–4). Collecting the hair

Figure 17–4 Hairstyles being prepared for performance in a room equipped with hair supplies. From the author's collection.

tools and materials in a specific cabinet or in a portable carrying case, which may be more convenient, will keep the supplies together and, hopefully, keep them from being lost or misused.

Directions on how to set hair for particular contemporary styles are often found in women's fashion magazines. Compiling a collection of these provides a valuable resource for determining how to set hair to get a specific appearance. Sources for period hairstyles are cited at the end of this chapter.

WIGS

Several historical periods require wigs to complete the silhouette. In other cases, the actor's hairstyle, hair length, or hair color may need to be so altered that it can best be accomplished by the use of a wig.

The type and shape of the wig cap, the foundation, and the color blend of the hair are important in determining the quality of a wig. Wigs made up of synthetic hair mounted on a heavy, solid, shallow wig cap and sewn in circles around the cap are the least natural-looking and the least adaptable for different hairstyles.

The wig cap must be deep enough to come down over the top of the head to the hairline and be large enough to go completely around the hairline. Wigs with shallow crowns always look as if they are about to pop off the top of the head.

How the hair is attached to the cap is important in determining whether a wig can be restyled. Hair sewn flat against the

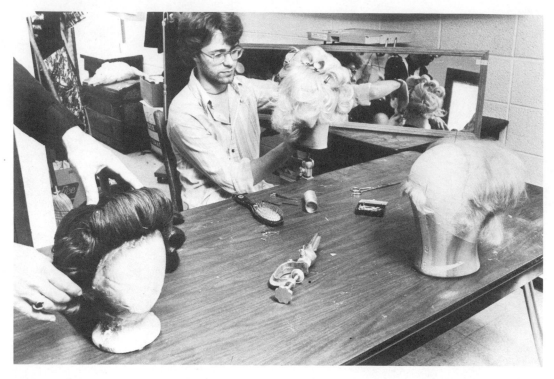

Figure 17–5 Examples of wigs, wig blocks, and tools: stretch wig styled for an eighteenth-century man (*on styrofoam head, left*); stretch wig being set and styled on canvas wig block; ventilated wig and mustache on wooden wig block. Selected tools, including a wig stand, wig brush, curler, barber's scissors, and box of T-pins, are on the table. Photo by Robert Izzo.

cap has severely limited restyling possibilities. Hair that is looped through the cap so that the hairs move easily in any direction can be dressed in numerous styles because that method of attaching the hair is most like the way human hair grows.

Good theatrical wigs are made by a process called *ventilating*. This means that the hairs are looped onto a cap made of netting, and because the hairs can move freely, the wig can be set and combed into numerous styles. A lighter netting is used at the front hairline to form the *lace-front* (see Fig. 17–5). This blends into the skin tones at the forehead so there is no harsh, unnatural hairline like that which is typical in an inexpensive wig.

The type, color blend, and amount of hair used in a wig are other factors that are related to its quality. Wigs made with human hair will take a set the same way an actor's own hair will. Synthetic hair is not easy to curl because heat is required, and the heat from electric curling devices is not sufficient to produce a curl. Blends of human and synthetic hair will generally take a loose set. Hair blends also include the use of different colors of hair in the wig; solid colors are not natural-looking. The amount of hair in the wig is another guide in assessing the quality of a wig. Surprisingly, inexpensive wigs often have too much hair and thus do not have a realistic appearance.

A wig that is to look realistic, as though

it were the actor's own hair, should be a ventilated lace-front wig, particularly if the playing space is small with the audience close to the performers. Wigs that are to look like wigs, the eighteenth-century styles for example, can be made up from the less expensive wigs or rented. Costume rental houses and wig suppliers have a wide range of wigs available. Rented wigs are usually styled according to the period or the design; therefore, arrangements for the rental should be made in advance. Necessary measurements for renting or buying wigs are cited in Chap. 5.

STYLING WIGS. Many of the tools and supplies that are needed for styling wigs are described in the Glossary in Chap. 2. These items include wig blocks, wig stands, T-pins, and the standard hair-setting and comb-out supplies. Canvas wig blocks are the most appropriate for wig styling. They are made in a range of head sizes, they are easy to anchor a wig onto; and they are very durable.

A stock of wigs is valuable to have available. Unstylized stretch wigs with 22 in. to 24 in. length hair have many uses and can be styled in various ways. The hair is a blend of synthetics on a webbed, stretch wig cap, and the hair is not stitched flat against the cap. These wigs can be arranged in roll curls, waves, upsweeps, or other styles, and "set" in the arrangement and held in place with hair spray or a mixture of dry starch and water sprayed onto the wig; 3 parts starch to 1 part water is a basic formula. Figure 17–6 shows an example of one of these wigs teased, set, and sprayed with starch and water.

Setting wigs involves the same process as setting hair. Human hair wigs can be set while wet using setting gel and dried or set with electric curling devices when dry. Synthetic wigs can be set as described above, using hair spray or starch and water, but they can also be encouraged to take and hold waves or a soft set by steaming the set

Figure 17–6 Examples of styled and unstyled wigs: stretch wig teased, set, and sprayed with starch and water formula (*top*); stretch wig with added topknot and curlers (*center*); and an unstyled lace front wig (*below*). The front hairline on the lace-front wig has a more natural appearance than the stretch wigs. Photo by Robert Izzo.

curls for a minute or two and then allowing the set to dry completely overnight.

Color hair spray can be used to change the wig color or to blend in added hairpieces. Highlights of blond and silver spray will enhance the texture and appearance of the wig.

Another technique for doing up elaborate hairstyles with wigs is to make up pieces to attach to the wig, or to the actor's hair, out of rayon horsehair (used to make the wigs for display mannequins). The horsehair is bought by the pound and is inexpensive. It is useful for making stiff pieces, such as topknots. It is wrapped around rollers or cardboard shapes cov-

Figure 17–7 Example of a finished wig with added rayon horsehair pieces sprayed to blend with the wig color for the character of "Gertrude" in *Fashion* as produced by the University of Rhode Island. From the author's collection.

ered with waxed paper over aluminum foil, coated with a half and half mixture of white glue and water, and set aside to dry. Then the hair is taken off the mold (the waxed paper serves as a parting agent) and attached to the wig with thread and needle, or to hair clips with hot-melt glue, to attach to the actor's hair. The rayon horsehair can be sprayed any color with color hair spray to blend with the wig color as shown in Fig. 17–7.

RESTYLING WIGS. Wigs that have been set into a style with hair spray or starch can be cleaned and restyled. Basically, the process of cleaning a wig involves "swishing" the wig around in a basin of mild detergent or in carbon tetrachloride (a dry-cleaning fluid). The detergent-washed wig needs to be rinsed by moving the wig around in clear water. Gentle "swishing" of the wig is important to keep the hair from getting tangled. Never shampoo a wig. After cleaning, place the wig on a wig block that

is the correct size, anchor it with T-pins, and let it dry. A hair dryer, on a low styling setting, can be used to speed the drying.

Comb out the wig and ease the tangles out with a wig brush; the widely spaced bristles do not pull out a great deal of hair. Work gently with the wig, as though the block were a real head of hair.

PUTTING ON A WIG. Before the wig is put on, the actor's own hair should be controlled. If the hair is long, it should be distributed evenly over the head as smoothly as possible. A typical method is to set the hair in a series of large pin curls. A nylon stocking, cut off to about 10 in. to 12 in. long and tied in a knot at one end, can be pulled on the head to the hairline. This holds the hair tight against the head and is easy to pin through. A cut-off stocking can also be used to control short hair to keep it from poking out from under the wig.

Next, holding the wig at the back with both hands, place the wig on the head, starting in the front and moving to the back. This method allows for easy matching of the front hairlines. A small amount of spirit gum (make-up adhesive) is placed at points on the forehead just below the hairline and in front of the ears; the wig is pressed to the glued areas to secure the front. Do not get the spirit gum in the actor's hair. Once the spirit gum has dried, which takes only minutes, the wig can be pinned to the head. A few strategically and correctly placed pins will do the job. Hairpins generally work well, and bobby pins can be used for additional anchoring.

To remove the wig, reverse the process by removing the pins and, taking the back edge with both hands, pulling up and forward. Work carefully to peel the glued edge from the front. The glue should be removed from the wig with acetone, available from most drugstores, and a toothbrush. Excess glue or make-up left on the wig will interfere with the adhesion for the next wearing.

STORING WIGS.   When in use for performances, wigs must always be kept on a wig block between wearings to hold the shape of the cap and the set of the hairstyle. The block should be the correct size, and the wig should be anchored with T-pins.

For long-term storage between productions, efforts should be made to protect the investment which wigs represent. Ideally, all wigs should be stored on wig blocks and protected from dust, but in most shop situations this is rarely feasible.

Cheap synthetic wigs can be collected in a box or drawer if need be to conserve space. But placing each wig in its own separate sack or see-through plastic bag will minimize tangling or damage and make them easier to work with when they are used the next time.

The good, well-made wigs containing natural hair are usually quite expensive and should be treated accordingly. These should definitely be stored on wig blocks and placed out of harm's way. Storage cases offer the best protection, but if they are not available, a cloth dust cover should be placed over the wigs. As with fur, do not encase natural-hair wigs in plastic, which does not breathe.

ADDITIONAL SOURCES

Additional information for working with hair and wigs, and on other tools which may be needed, can be found in Richard Corson's *Stage Make-up*. Wigs can also be made from other materials such as yarn, rope, felt, or cotton. The following references provide information on other techniques and ideas for creating hairstyles and wigs.

ASSER, JOYCE, *Historic Hairdressing*. London: Pitman, 1966.

BAYGAN, LEE, *Make-up for Theatre, Film, and Television: A Step by Step Photographic Guide.* New York: Drama Book Specialists (Publishers), 1980.

BOSS, RICHARD, "Making Low-Cost Wigs from Acrylic Fur," *Theatre Crafts*, 10, no. 1 (January/February 1976), 24, 64–67.

CORSON, RICHARD, *Fashions in Hair*. Atlantic Highlands, N.J.: Humanities Press, 1971.

———, *Stage Make-up* (6th ed.). Englewood Cliffs, N.J.; Prentice-Hall, Inc., 1981.

SEEMAN, BETTIE, "Yarn Wigs," *Theatre Crafts*, 10, no. 3 (May/June 1976), 19–21.

Perhaps one of history's most consistent displays of imagination and inventiveness can be found in headdresses and millinery. From the simplest kerchief to the most complex oversized structure balanced on the head, methods of decorating the head have been used to indicate financial and social status and rank through the ages. There are an infinite number of ways to adorn the head, whether it be with an Indian war bonnet, a ship under full sail, Cleopatra's cobra headdress, or a simple flower. The types of decoration and methods of making the adornments are equally varied. A primary means of ornamenting the head is by the use of hats, which is what this chapter is all about.

Hats not only reflect social status, they can also indicate an individual's personality traits, mood, or intended activity. Hats have even been used as symbols of philosophical or political movements; Jacques Louis David used the *Phrygian cap* as a symbol of liberty during the French Revo-

lutio...
simil...
liberty...

Obv...
a total l...
must kn...
size, shap...
the whole...
create spec...
beyond the...
riety is too b...
has been dea...
provide the ru...
Working from...
terns, a wide v...
treatments can be...
there are no speci...
tions here on how to...
or a calash (shown in...
ing the basic princip...
tumer to understand...
make either of these or...
hats. The instructions f...
vide enough information...

Figure 18-2 An example of a steeple hennin on the "Little Queen" in Anouilh's *The Lark* as produced by The Ohio State University. The headdress is worn over the actress's hairline. From the author's collection.

priate measurement to use...
head measurement locatio...

READY-MADE HATS. E...
shop should maintain a colle...
part of the stock. Occasiona...
be used just as they are; in o...
can be covered to coordinat...
tume, sprayed with dye or pa...
color or texture, or reworked...
appropriate shape. The coll...
include a variety of men's fe...
made with a deep crown and...
piece are the most valuable...
are relatively easy to reshape...
not easy to find (the crowns a...
most men's hats are separate...
they are worth looking for a...
onto. A selection of men's a...
straw hats is also valuable.

A common problem with hat...
is in maintaining the freshness...
There are several techniques wh...
used to rejuvenate old, musty,...
and hat decorations. Of course,...
ner in which the hats are stored...
nite influence on the condition of...
Hats should be stored so they w...
crushed or bent out of shape, a...
should be kept covered to keep...
dust-free as possible.

REVITALIZING HATS. There are...
things that can be done to rejuvena...
For example, most hats can be fre...
to some degree by brushing, vacu...
or sponging with a slightly damp s...
Black straw can be freshened by br...
it with denatured alcohol. Color c...
changed or brightened with leather...
shoe polish, which is particularly eff...
on straw hats, and a weak solutio...
lemon juice or hydrogen peroxide...
bleach straw hats.

Crushed felt hats can be revitalized...
steam. A hat steamer, shown in Fig...
or an industrial steam iron (see Chap...
can be used to steam out the "dents" o...
reshape the hat. Generally, a hat...

surements periodically as you build it up. Wigs can also be placed on the block to simulate hairstyles and to check the hat as it is being completed. The block should be mounted on a wig stand to hold it in place. Finally, you must know how the hat is to be worn in order to make it the proper size. Some hats, such as the top hat or homburg, are intended to be worn rather squarely on the head so the standard head circumference measurement is appropriate. Other hats, such as the steeple hennin of the fifteenth century (Fig. 18-2), are worn over the hairline, and in this instance the hairline measurement is the appro-

Figure 18-3 A hat steamer for reshaping or revitalizing hats. The basic felt hat with deep crown and brim in one piece can be easily reshaped; the basic pillbox hat has been decorated. Photo by Robert Izzo.

steamed on the inside and from the underside of the brim. Then it is smoothed and shaped with the hands onto a wig block of the correct size where it can be steamed from the outside and molded to final size and shape. The hat should then be pinned or clipped to hold the new shape until it is dry.

If a hat is limp, it can be stiffened (termed *sizing*) with shellac, lacquer, or millinery sizing. You can make your own sizing by mixing dry starch with equal parts of water and a white glue such as Elmer's glue. Any of these can be used on felt or straw. On the other hand, if the straw is brittle, it should be oiled with petroleum jelly, glycerine, or olive oil applied with a flannel cloth before the sizing is applied. Straw hats can be reshaped by dampening the hat and supporting the new shape until it is dry. Sizing is applied after the hat is dry.

Feathers and flowers are usually first to show the age and condition of the hat. Flowers can sometimes be given new life by steaming them and then shaping the petals with the fingers. For best results, the flowers should be removed from the hat, treated, and then tacked back on. The shape of a flower can also be controlled by covering it with fine netting to hold its shape. Leaves, stems, and even petals can be reinforced by gluing florist wire (available from florist shops) or any fine wire to the back of the piece. Coloration on the flower can be revitalized by painting it with dye, florist's flower spray, or water-soluble magic marker which blends into the fabric when denatured alcohol is brushed onto the color. As with any color alteration, the fabric and materials should be tested before working on the actual piece.

Feathers are trickier to bring back to life. Occasionally, dusting the feather with common salt and steaming it will help. The *flue* (the downy spur projecting from the feather spine) of ostrich feathers can be recurled in the same manner as curling the ends of paper ribbon. The feather must be steamed first, and then, working with three or four flues at a time, curled by drawing the back edge of a knife against them in a quick upward stroke. Begin this process at the large end of the feather and work carefully to avoid pulling or breaking the flues. The spine of the feather can be repaired by gluing a fine wire along its length. Bird wings or breasts, so popular in hats at the beginning of this century, can also be repaired by careful gluing and covering the piece with fine net.

Veils from old hats can be freshened by washing them in mild soap and rinsing in a solution of water and gum arabic (available at most pharmacies). The solution calls for 2 teaspoonfuls of gum arabic to 1 pint of water. After washing, stretch the veil to its shape, pin it onto a wig block, and let it dry. The gum arabic is a sizing which gives the washed veil enough body to hold its shape.

RESHAPING HATS. Hats in the collection can also be altered or reshaped to create different styles. The one-piece men's felt hats with deep crowns can easily be remade for several period styles. Shaped, undecorated felt shells, called *hoods* in the millinery trade, come in a range of colors with various brim shapes. These offer a greater variety of bases for hats than do men's felt hats. Felt hoods are available from millinery supply houses and are occasionally found at hat counters in department stores.

Reshaping or *blocking* a felt hat takes time, patience, and care. To begin, the felt needs to be made soft and pliable by steaming it heavily on the inside. After this initial steaming, it is placed on a wig block and steamed on the outside. When the felt is soft and pliable, slowly pull and stretch the hat into the desired shape. Felt will break or tear if it is pulled too hard or if the felt has not been softened enough, so several applications of steam during the process may be necessary. After the hat has been reshaped, it must be left on the head block until it is completely dry. If necessary, the dried shape can be stiffened with one of the sizing mediums mentioned above.

Reshaped felt hats can be painted, spray-dyed, covered, or decorated in virtually any manner. A supply of felt hats to use as bases for different styles saves time and provides resources for a variety of hats.

HAT-MAKING GUIDELINES

Creating headgear for the stage is a relatively simple process once the basic principles are understood and observed. Essentially, we need to know the size and shape of the head, what the hairstyle will be, and how the hat is to be worn. This information, combined with the concept of providing sufficient ease for proper fit, is necessary in making up a hat. For our purposes, hats fall into two categories: (1) a stiffened hat, often used as a foundation that is covered or built upon (Fig. 18–4) and (2) a soft hat or cap.

The shaped hat, or foundation, has a reinforced, nonflexible head opening; it is generally stiffened or sized. The shape can be formed by blocking felt or straw and sizing as necessary, or it can be formed by making a foundation (traditionally made of buckram or wire) and covering it with a finishing material. The shaped hat can be brimless or with a brim, and the pieces can be patterned in paper. The soft hat has a more flexible head opening; it has little stiffening or sizing, and the form varies in degree of shape and flexibility. It generally has little or no brim, and is usually made of fabric, lightweight felt, or other soft materials, so patterns are best made in muslin rather than paper. Shaped hats include top hats, pillboxes, cowboy hats, and tricorns. Soft hats include caps, berets, bonnets, and skullcaps. Obviously, there are many variations in each classification, and the characteristics of each can be mixed and matched.

In order to determine how to pattern and construct a hat, you need to know the general classification of the hat and its characteristics. Each style of hat will require its own pattern, and the specific construction techniques will vary. However, regardless of the hat style, the center-front and center-back must be marked on all parts of the hat.

The parts of a hat include the *brim* (the

Figure 18–4 Example of a stiffened hat foundation covered and built upon; the turbanlike brim is stuffed with nylon net to keep the hat lightweight. The character is the "Second Merchant" in *Comedy of Errors* as produced by The Champlain Shakespeare Festival. From the author's collection.

projecting edge) and the *crown*. The *tip* (top surface of the crown) can be cut separately and attached to the sides of the crown, called the *sideband*. The crown can also be in one piece, like men's felt hats, with the cover over the top of the hat and the sideband formed out of one piece of material.

BASIC CONSTRUCTION MATERIALS. A wide variety of wooden hat blocks and other devices are used by commercial milliners. These include hat and cap *blocks,*

in numerous sizes for all types of crown shapes, and *flanges* for brim shapes and degree of brim roll or curl. These are used in the same manner as molds: the hat material is shaped with steam and sizing to conform to the block or flange. Other devices include wooden *crowns* and *hat stretchers*; the latter are used to stretch head openings only. These items are very useful for blocking (molding) hat shapes; however, they tend to be expensive when purchased new and are usually worth the cost only if a large amount of blocked millinery work is done. Sources for these items are listed in Appendix B.

Buckram, a heavily starched open-weave fabric, is a standard material for making hat foundations. It comes in black and white and is available in three weights (light, medium, and heavy) or in double thicknesses which are more opaque and durable than the single piece. Buckram hat frames can be flat-patterned, using the methods described under Patterning Foundations, or blocked over a mold. Since buckram is sized with starch that is water-soluble, it cannot be used for items that will be washed; however, the starch can be used to bond seams or layers together when the buckram is ironed. Tissue paper should be used between the iron and the buckram to keep it from sticking to the iron. Buckram frames can be covered with fabrics (Fig. 18–4), used alone when painted and decorated, or covered with tissue paper and white glue for a hammered metal effect.

Felt is a basic material for making hats. The typical felt found in most fabric stores can be used; however, it is a thin felt and usually needs to be used with two or more layers and should be heavily sized to hold a shape. Industrial-weight felt that is at least 70 percent wool (designated as 70/30 felt) is the most appropriate felt to use for millinery purposes. It comes in several thicknesses (1/8 in. to 3/16 in. is a good weight) and in a limited range of colors. Sources

Figure 18–5 An example of a blocked and sized industrial-weight felt hat with millinery wire added to help support the brim shape. From the author's collection.

for industrial felt are cited in Appendix B, and many of those suppliers provide price lists. All-wool or 70/30 industrial-weight felt is recommended because it has sufficient body to hold a shape (Fig. 18–5), and it can be blocked easily on a mold (Fig. 18–6).

Foam "rubber" (more accurately termed *flexible foam*), which is available in various thicknesses and sizes, is not really rubber at all. It is now made from a combination of chemicals that make up into a spongy material that has many theatrical uses. It has good body, can be shaped, glued, sewn through, covered or colored with paint or dyes, and it is lightweight (Fig. 18–7). We generally buy 4 ft by 8 ft "bottom skins" of *ether* foam, typically used for upholstering furniture. Bottom skins, cut from the foam blocks by the manufacturer to clean up the edges of the block, are about ½ in. thick and are less than half the price of material cut from the blocks. *Ester* foam is used when items are to have extensive use over a number of years, since it has a longer life span and does not yellow with age. Ester foam can also be dyed with household union dyes; however, it is very expensive. Another type of foam is *aerated* foam,

primarily used for air-conditioner filters. This is an open type of foam that creates an interesting texture. It can also be covered or left uncovered and painted for unusual effects.

Horsehair, now made of nylon, is a

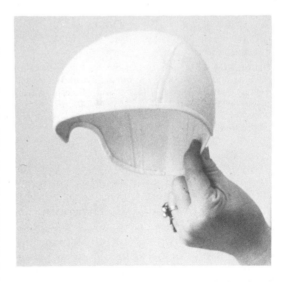

Figure 18–6 An example of a sized hood of industrial-weight felt. The felt has been flat-patterned in sections, zigzagged together, steamed and molded to a wig block, and then sized. From the author's collection.

288

STORING WIGS. When in use for performances, wigs must always be kept on a wig block between wearings to hold the shape of the cap and the set of the hairstyle. The block should be the correct size, and the wig should be anchored with T-pins.

For long-term storage between productions, efforts should be made to protect the investment which wigs represent. Ideally, all wigs should be stored on wig blocks and protected from dust, but in most shop situations this is rarely feasible.

Cheap synthetic wigs can be collected in a box or drawer if need be to conserve space. But placing each wig in its own separate sack or see-through plastic bag will minimize tangling or damage and make them easier to work with when they are used the next time.

The good, well-made wigs containing natural hair are usually quite expensive and should be treated accordingly. These should definitely be stored on wig blocks and placed out of harm's way. Storage cases offer the best protection, but if they are not available, a cloth dust cover should be placed over the wigs. As with fur, do not encase natural-hair wigs in plastic, which does not breathe.

ADDITIONAL SOURCES

Additional information for working with hair and wigs, and on other tools which may be needed, can be found in Richard Corson's *Stage Make-up*. Wigs can also be made from other materials such as yarn, rope, felt, or cotton. The following references provide information on other techniques and ideas for creating hairstyles and wigs.

ASSER, JOYCE, *Historic Hairdressing*. London: Pitman, 1966.

BAYGAN, LEE, *Make-up for Theatre, Film, and Television: A Step by Step Photographic Guide*. New York: Drama Book Specialists (Publishers), 1980.

BOSS, RICHARD, "Making Low-Cost Wigs from Acrylic Fur," *Theatre Crafts*, 10, no. 1 (January/February 1976), 24, 64–67.

CORSON, RICHARD, *Fashions in Hair*. Atlantic Highlands, N.J.: Humanities Press, 1971.

_____, *Stage Make-up* (6th ed.). Englewood Cliffs, N.J.; Prentice-Hall, Inc., 1981.

SEEMAN, BETTIE, "Yarn Wigs," *Theatre Crafts*, 10, no. 3 (May/June 1976), 19–21.

Figure 18–5 An example of a blocked and sized industrial-weight felt hat with millinery wire added to help support the brim shape. From the author's collection.

for industrial felt are cited in Appendix B, and many of those suppliers provide price lists. All-wool or 70/30 industrial-weight felt is recommended because it has sufficient body to hold a shape (Fig. 18–5), and it can be blocked easily on a mold (Fig. 18–6).

Foam "rubber" (more accurately termed *flexible foam*), which is available in various thicknesses and sizes, is not really rubber at all. It is now made from a combination of chemicals that make up into a spongy material that has many theatrical uses. It has good body, can be shaped, glued, sewn through, covered or colored with paint or dyes, and it is lightweight (Fig. 18–7). We generally buy 4 ft by 8 ft "bottom skins" of *ether* foam, typically used for upholstering furniture. Bottom skins, cut from the foam blocks by the manufacturer to clean up the edges of the block, are about ½ in. thick and are less than half the price of material cut from the blocks. *Ester* foam is used when items are to have extensive use over a number of years, since it has a longer life span and does not yellow with age. Ester foam can also be dyed with household union dyes; however, it is very expensive. Another type of foam is *aerated* foam,

primarily used for air-conditioner filters. This is an open type of foam that creates an interesting texture. It can also be covered or left uncovered and painted for unusual effects.

Horsehair, now made of nylon, is a

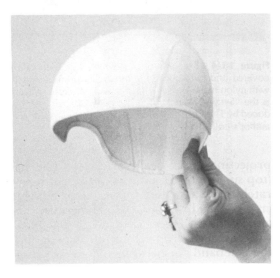

Figure 18–6 An example of a sized hood of industrial-weight felt. The felt has been flat-patterned in sections, zigzagged together, steamed and molded to a wig block, and then sized. From the author's collection.

Figure 18-7 An example of a large headdress with a foam foundation that has been covered and decorated for the "Aristocrat" in *Boccaccio* as produced by the University of Rhode Island. Designed by Ken Holamon; photo by Jane Brawley.

sturdy, glossy, open material that is available in yardage and braid widths. It can be used to make lightweight translucent hats, but we also use the braid inside the head opening on large hats. Because it is an open weave, hairpins go through it easily, and it is easy to secure the hat to the hair. This technique is useful for securing all types of headgear, from simple headbands to large "picture" hats. Horsehair can be made into flowers and other decorative features on hats; and it also is useful to soften edges of brims and to reinforce or give added dimension to straw hats.

Millinery wire is a wrapped flexible wire that comes in three weights in either black or white. It is used to reinforce edges (as shown in Fig. 18-5), to support hat shapes, or it can be tied together to make a hat frame. It can be glued to the surface or machine-stitched on with a wide zigzag stitch.

In order to make hats, whether they are flat-patterned or blocked, certain additional supplies are needed. Both methods require *wig blocks* and *wig stands*.

The blocks need to be the correct head size to ensure the proper fit of the hat. *Pushpins* and *T-pins* are necessary to secure the hat onto the block while it is being worked. A supply of *white glue, hot-melt glue,* a *glue gun,* and standard sewing supplies are also useful during the construction process.

A steam source is necessary for blocking hats. This can be a *steamer* (Fig. 18-3) or a tea kettle if a steamer is not available. *Millinery sizings,* described under Revitalizing Hats, are a basic supply when blocking hats. Heavy paper is needed for flat patterns.

Flat-Patterning Shaped Hats

To begin to pattern a hat, you need to determine the correct headsize. As stated before, two factors influence this: (1) how and where on the head the hat is to be worn, and (2) what the hairstyle is to be. When these two factors are known, the appropriate measurements can be taken, if the information is not already on the mea-

THE TIP. For the tip pattern, draw the desired size and shape and then add ¾ in. (2 cm) seam allowance around the outside. The top of the closed sideband can be used as a guide for the pattern. In the seam allowance, draw in tabs at about 1 in. (2.5 cm) intervals in the same way used for the brim allowance, and cut out the tabs to the stitching line. These tabs will be folded down to connect with the sideband as shown in Fig. 18–11.

Mark each pattern for size and style for inclusion in the pattern library. These patterns can be mixed and matched to make up a wide variety of hat styles.

Constructing the Foundation

What materials are selected to make up a hat depends on the degree of stiffness required. Typical materials for the base form include buckram, pellon, and millinery wire. Other wires, such as piano wire, can also be used. Essentially, a hat can be made from anything that does the job. The materials cited are used to create the base, or foundation, of the hat, which is then covered or finished by other means to look like the design.

The construction process for hat bases that are to be covered follows a general order; the actual step-by-step details vary. The order, however, is also applicable to hats finished in other ways.

First, the material for the base is cut from the pattern and marked. Because of the stiffness of the base, no seam allowance is needed for the outside edge of the brim. The tabbed seam allowance for the head opening and the tip, however, must be on the base. Then the good fabric to be used for covering is cut and marked; two pieces, with seam allowance for all edges, including the outer edge, are needed for the brim—one for the upper side and one for the under side. The good material is usually cut about 1 in. (2.5 cm) larger than the base to provide seam allowance and ease.

Before the brim, sideband, and tip are put together, the wire, if needed, is stitched to the base. Millinery wire can be sewn to the base pieces with the zigzag stitch on a machine and is often needed at the outside edge of the brim, the edge of the head opening, or any other reinforcement areas required by the design. If the covering fabric is thin, the wire may need to be sandwiched in the base material to eliminate the ridge of the wire; or the hollow created by the wire can be filled in with a thin layer of batting similar to the method used when covering shoes with welts as discussed in Chap. 19.

Next, the good fabric is stitched to the sideband and tip on the stitchlines. Then the fabric for the upper and under brim pieces is stitched at the outside edge, with right sides together. The seam allowance is clipped, and the piece is turned through the head opening and pressed. The brim base is slipped inside the good fabric through the head opening and stitched in place at the head opening stitchlines. If the brim is too stiff for this method, the good fabric can be sewn directly onto the brim, and the raw outside edge can be bound with bias strip, turned under and top-stitched, or glued to conceal the raw edge.

After each piece is covered, assemble the hat. The sideband is stitched or glued together into a ring; be sure the head opening is the right size. Then attach the tip to the band; this can be glued or stitched, with the tabbed seam allowance on the inside as shown in Fig. 18–11. The crown is then attached to the brim with the tabbed allowance on the inside. Since it is often difficult to sew on the inside of a hat, hot-melt glue is a good means of joining hat pieces because it forms a bond in just 60 seconds.

To finish the inside of the hat, add a strip of heavy cloth or ribbon that is about 1 in. (2.5 cm) wide and a little longer than the head opening to the inside to cover the seam allowance. If the hat is to be lined, the strip is added after the lining, When this is completed, the hat is ready for any trim or decoration and finishing details.

Blocking Hats

The techniques involved in blocking hats are basically the same regardless of the material being used. Traditional materials include felt, buckram, and straw. Since the use of felt is common for blocking hats, the process described here will center on methods used for blocking felt hats.

Essentially, the process involves converting the flat material into the rounded forms required by the style of the hat and then sizing the material so it will retain the rounded form. This means that certain portions of the material will need to be shrunk while other portions are being stretched. A major ingredient in achieving the shrink-stretch quality is steam. With felt, the material is softened by saturating it with steam before it is carefully molded over the form. Figure 18-12 shows felt that has been steamed being stretched over a wig block.

As the felt is stretched and shrunk over the block, the shape is controlled by pushpins, and the felt is kept soft and pli-

able by frequent application of steam. This process needs to be done carefully so that the felt is pulled evenly to prevent it from tearing and to reduce wrinkles. The stretching should be done by working from opposite sides of the block for even distribution of the felt.

How evenly the felt is distributed during the blocking is the key to a well-blocked hat. Therefore, center the steamed felt on the block and, starting with the center-front and center back, stretch the felt downward. Use firm, even pressure to pull the felt down. Next, grasp the center of the sides and repeat the process. Then stretch from the opposite corners and continue to stretch the felt, always pulling on opposite sides, all around the block until the felt is smooth over the mold. The felt needs to be evenly distributed around the mold. Secure the shape with pins and cord if necessary, and let it dry. There will be excess felt at the bottom of the mold; this will be trimmed away after the felt has dried.

This method of stretching felt can leave a thin layer of felt at the top of the crown. An alternative approach to avoid this is to first pattern and cut a tip and sideband, without the seam allowance tabs, and zig-zag them together before the felt is

Figure 18-12   An example of felt blocked on a wig block. Steam is applied to keep the felt soft and pliable. Photo by Robert Izzo.

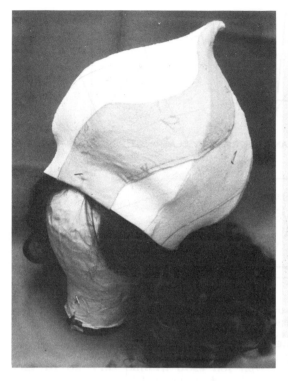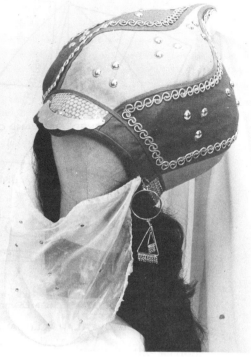

Figure 18–18 A. An example of sectional crown pattern used to construct a turban foundation made of flexible foam. The foam is butt-joined with glue, and the seam edges are covered with lightweight felt to soften the ridges. Photo by Jerry R. Emery. B. Completed and decorated turban with flexible form foundation for *Boccaccio* as produced by the University of Rhode Island. Designed by Ken Holamon; photo by Robert Izzo.

create shapes or for flat-patterned hats to keep the work neat and manageable. Steam can also be used to enlarge many ready-made hats. First, remove the headband in a ready-made hat, steam the inside and then stretch the head opening. Place the hat on an appropriately sized wig block and allow it to dry before stitching in a new headband.

Securing hats or headdresses on the head so they stay put during the performance can be accomplished by adding a band or tabs of horsehair to the inside band. The horsehair can be pinned to the hair so the hat is secure and the attachments cannot be seen. For large headpieces, it may be necessary to use elastic under the chin. If this is necessary, a Y-shaped elastic attached in front and behind the ear with a single piece of elastic under the chin provides a comfortable, secure anchorage for the headpiece.

There are many variations possible in millinery. The guidelines are defined by the shape and size of the head and by providing enough body and support for the headpiece. The headpieces should be kept as lightweight as possible and made so they can be balanced and supported on the head. Whether the headdresses are developed with patterns or blocked shapes, marking center-front and center-back and working on an appropriately sized wig block are basic to successful millinery.

The few examples in this chapter are cited as a reminder that the basic principles have many applications. These principles and patterns provide the basics for working with millinery, and numerous variations can be developed. Additional specific and unusual patterns for period headdresses can be found in the following sources.

COLLINS, WANDA, *Complete Book of Home Millinery.* New York: Funk and Wagnalls, 1951.

KLINGER, ROBERT L., *Distaff Sketch Book: A Collection of Notes and Sketches on Women's Dress in America— 1774–1783.* Union City, Tenn.: Pioneer Press, 1974.

KLINGER, ROBERT L., and RICHARD A. WILDER, *Sketch Book '76: The American Soldier—1775–1781.* Union City, Tenn.: Pioneer Press, 1967, reprint, 1974.

LOEWEN, JANE, *Millinery.* New York: The Macmillan Co., 1926.

MONTAGNA, PIER, *The Key to Millinery Design: How to Make Smart Hats.* Max Padell, 1962.

PATTY, VIRGINIA C., *Hats and How to Make Them.* Chicago and New York: Rand McNally and Co., 1925.

TOMKINS, JULIA, *Stage Costumes and How to Make Them.* Boston: Plays, Inc., 1969.

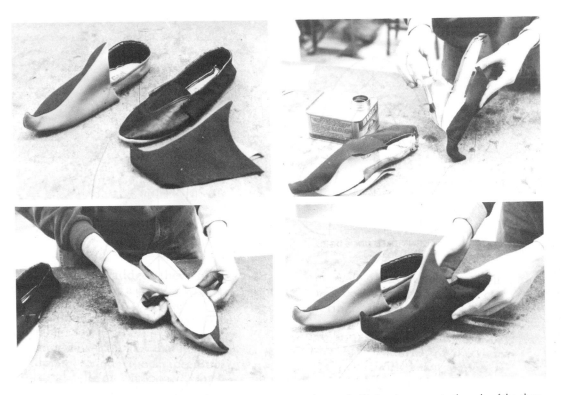

Figure 19–3 A. Shoe covers prepared and added to gymnastic slipper. B. Gluing the covers to the sole of the shoe. C. Separate sole glued over the shoe cover and original sole. D. Finished covered shoes. Photos by Jerry R. Emery.

acrobatic slippers, the shoe cover can be cut, lined, stitched, turned to finish any raw edges, and then stitched directly to the sole. This stitching should be done with strong thread to prevent the stitching from wearing out quickly. The upper portion of the cover can be tacked or glued in place.

If it is not possible to stitch the cover to the sole of a shoe, the fabric can be wrapped around the shoe and a new sole added as shown in Fig. 19–3. In this instance, gymnastic slippers are used as the base. The patterns were cut with a separate heel and vamp (Fig. 19–3B). The vamp had a center seam to allow for the up-curved toe, which was stuffed with lint from our dryer. The edges of the fabric pieces were finished before the heel section was machine-stitched to the top of the

shoe. The vamp was slipped over the shoe, pinned in place, and the fabric of both sections was wrapped around the shoe and glued to the sole. Then a new separate sole was glued over the original sole and the edges of the cover fabric to finish the appearance (Figs. 19–3C and D). We used a pebble vinyl for the sole; however, leather, felt, chamois, or canvas could have been used.

If the shoe has a hard sole, carefully pry an opening all around the edge of the sole, being careful not to cut the stitching or to pry too deeply. The opening should be just deep enough to push the fabric into; glue the fabric in place so there are no raw edges.

To cover a hard-soled shoe, start at the center-back and work forward, or start at the sides if the seams are there, but always work toward the toe. Secure the heel or side-seams with pins and, keeping the fabric taut, work first on one side of the shoe and then on the other side to progress evenly along the length. Use a dull knife to push the fabric between the sole and the upper shoe and secure the fabric with glue as you work; any excess glue can be wiped away with a damp cloth.

To finish the top of the shoe, the allowance at the top needs to be clipped to make a smooth curve; fold the allowance over and glue it in place. Bias tape can be glued over these raw edges to finish the inside of the shoe. Shoe decorations such as buckles, rosettes, pompoms, or whatever is called for in the design can be added as the finishing details.

MAKING SOFT-SOLED SHOES.   Soft-soled shoes are relatively easy to make. To make the sole pattern, have the actor stand in stocking feet on a sheet of paper and then trace around both feet. The tracing should be made with the pencil straight up and down at the edge of the foot. Before the foot outline is cut, round and extend the toe edge about 1 in. (2.5 cm) and add about ¾ in. (2 cm) around the rest of the outline for seam allowance. The paper patterns should be identified with the actor's name and with right- and left-foot designations since they can easily be turned over and confused.

Soft leather, chamois, heavy felt, or canvas can be used as a sole. There should be at least one inner sole and an outer sole. The number of layers is determined by the wearability of the material used for the sole. A material made to repair worn tennis shoes (one brand is called "Shoe-Patch") can be coated on the bottom of the sole to help prevent slipping when the shoes are worn onstage. It is available from sporting goods suppliers and comes in a tube along with instructions for applying it.

Upper-shoe patterns are developed on the same premise as the shoe covers. The important rule to observe when putting the shoes together is to allow room for the width and thickness of the foot. Slipper patterns are also available commercially, and other patterns can be found in books cited at the end of this chapter.

MAKING BOOT TOPS.   As has been stated, a selection of basic boots in the costume collection is invaluable, but if boots are not available or are not within the budget, boot tops can often provide an acceptable substitute. They may also be the best means of completing an unusual design. Figure 19–4 suggests some basic boot-top patterns. Allow ample time to develop the proper pattern, and work with materials which will provide the necessary stiffness.

Boot tops can be made from leather, vinyl, suede cloth, felt, or other fabrics according to the design. The material must have enough stiffness to stay up, which means that some materials may have to be lined for stiffening. The tops can be added to shoes or slippers as the base. If the material can match the shoe base, or contrast with it effectively, the top can be added to the vamp (upper section) of the shoe. Otherwise it must be attached at the sole line, preferably with glue, in the same manner as covering a hard-soled shoe.

Boots which are fitted or shaped around the ankle must have an opening to allow the foot to pass through. If lacings are not appropriate, hidden zipper openings are possible; they should be placed at the inside of the leg in order to be least noticeable. Boots that are loose at the ankle may not need an opening. The space required for the foot to pass through must be equal to the measurement around the foot from the heel over the top of the instep; this is approximately 16 in. to 18 in. (40.5 cm to 46 cm).

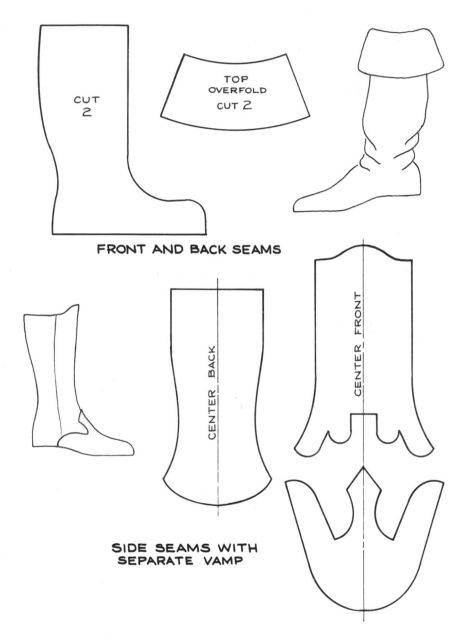

CUT 2

TOP OVERFOLD CUT 2

FRONT AND BACK SEAMS

CENTER BACK

CENTER FRONT

SIDE SEAMS WITH SEPARATE VAMP

Figure 19-4 Examples of some basic shapes for boot tops to cover shoes or slippers.

9-7 A. Character of "Olivia" in *Twelfth Night* as produced by the University of Rhode Island. The overskirt ...rated with bows stiffened with ply-on film and a border of bunches of grapes. From the author's collection. ...il of the overskirt border showing grapes made of hot-melt glue and leaves laminated with ply-on film. Photo ...ert Izzo.

...esting "found objects" such as sea ..., buttons, furniture hardware, or ...ever, which provide sources for re-...ucing any number of pieces for future ...Craft supply houses carry a range of ...g resins, such as lucite, that can be ...with the molds, and many of the "li-...metals" and sculpturing metal pastes ...well. Duplicates of any number of ...s can also be made by vacuforming ...Molding Materials for more details). ...ll of these materials can be painted or ...d to finish the appearance. Essen-..., the tools, materials, and techniques ...imilar to those used in making theatri-...properties. Also, many of the tech-

niques and materials have been adopted by craft and boutique suppliers. Sources with more detail on step-by-step processes for working with these and other materials are cited at the end of this chapter.

Three-dimensional decorations can be used separately or linked together to form an ornate unit which can be worn by itself or be suspended from a chain. In the first instance, if the piece is to be pinned to the garment, a safety pin can be sewn or glued to the back of the ornament. If the pieces are to be linked together or suspended, some means of joining them needs to be planned with the piece. Small screw eyes, loops of heavy thread, large electric

Creating theatrical jewelry and ornamentation, such as buckles, clasps, medals, necklaces, and the like, is perhaps one of the most inventive aspects of costuming. With the possible exception of modern realistic plays, most productions require larger-than-life jewelry and ornaments, and ready-made pieces are not usually large enough or in the right style to meet requirements.

The information contained here is primarily to stimulate the imagination and to suggest the numerous possibilities available for creating theatrical ornamentation. A number of materials are cited, but how they are to be used, what can be accomplished with them, or what other usable materials can be found, depends only upon your imagination and the requirements of the design.

READY-MADE JEWELRY. Ready-made jewelry, in order to work effectively on stage, should be selected from pieces that are large and essentially uncluttered with detail. Pieces which appear very gaudy up close are often quite appropriate for costumes seen from the audience. For theatrical purposes, ready-made jewelry is often taken apart, reworked, added to, and reassembled. A collection of earrings, for instance, can be very useful in putting together a necklace, shoe decorations, or finger rings. For example, rings can be the large adjustable costume jewelry sold in novelty shops, but they can also be made from flexible wire or other pliable materials with an earring glued or wired in position on top.

Ready-made jewelry, intact and broken, is part of the basic stock of materials for a costume shop. The pieces that are kept for the stock need to be large enough to be in proportion with the costumes and so they can be seen from a distance. A costumer

should always be on the lookout for large, even gaudy, jewelry which can be adapted for theatrical use. For instance, the jeweled bra and hip chain for the harem girl costume (Fig. 19-5) were made from sections of necklaces, bits of chain, and a variety of broken-up ready-made jewelry pieces. Places like thrift shops, discount jewelry houses, and flea markets generally offer a good selection of pieces at prices that are within a show's budget.

Large pieces of broken jewelry should be kept, since much of the ornamentation required is based on reworking items or making up pieces which fulfill the design. Often, groupings of small stones, pearls, or beads are combined to make a large "jewel." Individual pieces or strands of beads can be mounted on ribbon or nylon net to make an elaborately jeweled necklace or bracelet. Heavy, bold lace can also be stiffened with flexible glue, gilded with a metallic medium, and set with jewels to make up into an elaborate, even elegant, piece of jewelry.

The primary guidelines in selecting and using ready-made jewelry are the proportions of the pieces to the costume, whether the scale is such that it will project over the distance from the actor to the audience, and whether the piece is historically appropriate.

Generally, the designer will have specified the style, type, and number of pieces required. The costumer as well as the designer must know the historical trends in jewelry. This means researching the numerous sources on the history of jewelry and ornaments and translating that information into theatrical terms. Usually, this requires simplifying and broadening, or even exaggerating, for richness and clarity to create effective stage jewelry and ornaments. If the pieces are too intricate or elaborate, the rich effect is often lost.

Figure 19-5 Examples of broken up ready-made jewelry assembled to make the jeweled bra and hip chain for a "Harem Girl" at the costume ball in *The Boy Friend* as produced by the University of Rhode Island. From the author's collection.

Guidelines for Constructing Jewelry

Finding the right materials to use in capturing the design is a challenge. While a large collection of jewelry is invaluable to a costume shop, construction materials should by no means be limited to these items. Things found in a hardware store, such as washers, cogs, curtain rings, wire, rubber tubing, and the like, are useful for creating a wide range of ornaments. For instance, two or three cogs of different dimensions glued on top of one another can

be the start of an interesting decorative medal; rubber tubing tied in open loops (crocheted) and gilded can create an exciting decorative chain which is lightweight and inexpensive.

In a production of *The Boy Friend*, Maisie went to the costume ball as "Cleopatra." The "cobra" on her headdress (Fig. 19–6) was made of a piece of lightweight ethafoam rod (see Chap. 2) reinforced with millinery wire and then gilded and decorated with hot-melt glue and a red pipe cleaner for a tongue. It was mounted on a felt headpiece that was sized

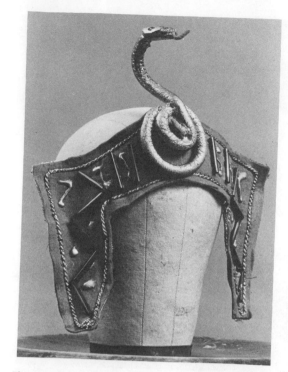

Figure 19-6 Etha foam rod (used in building construction), pieces of rattan, hot-melt glue, and a pipe cleaner are used to decorate a "Cleopatra" cobra headdress. Photo by Robert Izzo.

and supported with millinery wire and then decorated with pieces of rattan, hot-melt glue, and cord. The key is to look at things, not in terms of their designated functions, but in terms of how the shape, texture, and dimensions can be transformed into that which meets a given theatrical need.

Thinking of items beyond the specific function for which they were originally made vastly increases the range of materials available for creating all kinds of ornaments. The selection of materials is governed by such criteria as durability, weight, availability, ease of working with them, and their cost.

RAISED ORNAMENTS. There are some basic techniques which are pertinent to

making jewelry an
ple, pieces which
such as brooches
large stones, and t
some form of bac
be as simple as h
felt, buckram, leat
the purpose. The
basic overall shape
tail or ornamentat
the backing is to
with other mater
additional treatmer
pletely hidden, the
of the backing is se
requirements of th

The raised detail
other costume or
wire, or similar thi
the backing in th
colored according
Hot-melt glue is a
creating raised orn
decorative detail. Fi
photograph of the
showing beads of
make the "bunch of
skirt. Hot-melt glue
used to create many
and can be gilded,
honey color.

Several other mate
useful for making
pieces. Products li
Spackle, traditionally
and walls, can be scu
den by air-drying. D
out of soft wood
mounted on a backi
felt or thin sheets of
to create raised orn
papier-mâché is an ol
three-dimensional ob
molding materials li
and casting rubber ca
raised ornaments.

Numbers of decora
made by casting a m

Figure
is deco
B. Deta
by Rob

inter
shells
what
prod
use.
casti
used
quid
work
item
(see

A
gilde
tially
are
cal

Creating theatrical jewelry and ornamentation, such as buckles, clasps, medals, necklaces, and the like, is perhaps one of the most inventive aspects of costuming. With the possible exception of modern realistic plays, most productions require larger-than-life jewelry and ornaments, and ready-made pieces are not usually large enough or in the right style to meet requirements.

The information contained here is primarily to stimulate the imagination and to suggest the numerous possibilities available for creating theatrical ornamentation. A number of materials are cited, but how they are to be used, what can be accomplished with them, or what other usable materials can be found, depends only upon your imagination and the requirements of the design.

READY-MADE JEWELRY. Ready-made jewelry, in order to work effectively on stage, should be selected from pieces that are large and essentially uncluttered with detail. Pieces which appear very gaudy up close are often quite appropriate for costumes seen from the audience. For theatrical purposes, ready-made jewelry is often taken apart, reworked, added to, and reassembled. A collection of earrings, for instance, can be very useful in putting together a necklace, shoe decorations, or finger rings. For example, rings can be the large adjustable costume jewelry sold in novelty shops, but they can also be made from flexible wire or other pliable materials with an earring glued or wired in position on top.

Ready-made jewelry, intact and broken, is part of the basic stock of materials for a costume shop. The pieces that are kept for the stock need to be large enough to be in proportion with the costumes and so they can be seen from a distance. A costumer should always be on the lookout for large, even gaudy, jewelry which can be adapted for theatrical use. For instance, the jeweled bra and hip chain for the harem girl costume (Fig. 19–5) were made from sections of necklaces, bits of chain, and a variety of broken-up ready-made jewelry pieces. Places like thrift shops, discount jewelry houses, and flea markets generally offer a good selection of pieces at prices that are within a show's budget.

Large pieces of broken jewelry should be kept, since much of the ornamentation required is based on reworking items or making up pieces which fulfill the design. Often, groupings of small stones, pearls, or beads are combined to make a large "jewel." Individual pieces or strands of beads can be mounted on ribbon or nylon net to make an elaborately jeweled necklace or bracelet. Heavy, bold lace can also be stiffened with flexible glue, gilded with a metallic medium, and set with jewels to make up into an elaborate, even elegant, piece of jewelry.

The primary guidelines in selecting and using ready-made jewelry are the proportions of the pieces to the costume, whether the scale is such that it will project over the distance from the actor to the audience, and whether the piece is historically appropriate.

Generally, the designer will have specified the style, type, and number of pieces required. The costumer as well as the designer must know the historical trends in jewelry. This means researching the numerous sources on the history of jewelry and ornaments and translating that information into theatrical terms. Usually, this requires simplifying and broadening, or even exaggerating, for richness and clarity to create effective stage jewelry and ornaments. If the pieces are too intricate or elaborate, the rich effect is often lost.

Figure 19-5 Examples of broken up ready-made jewelry assembled to make the jeweled bra and hip chain for a "Harem Girl" at the costume ball in *The Boy Friend* as produced by the University of Rhode Island. From the author's collection.

Guidelines for Constructing Jewelry

Finding the right materials to use in capturing the design is a challenge. While a large collection of jewelry is invaluable to a costume shop, construction materials should by no means be limited to these items. Things found in a hardware store, such as washers, cogs, curtain rings, wire, rubber tubing, and the like, are useful for creating a wide range of ornaments. For instance, two or three cogs of different dimensions glued on top of one another can

be the start of an interesting decorative medal; rubber tubing tied in open loops (crocheted) and gilded can create an exciting decorative chain which is lightweight and inexpensive.

In a production of *The Boy Friend*, Maisie went to the costume ball as "Cleopatra." The "cobra" on her headdress (Fig. 19–6) was made of a piece of lightweight ethafoam rod (see Chap. 2) reinforced with millinery wire and then gilded and decorated with hot-melt glue and a red pipe cleaner for a tongue. It was mounted on a felt headpiece that was sized

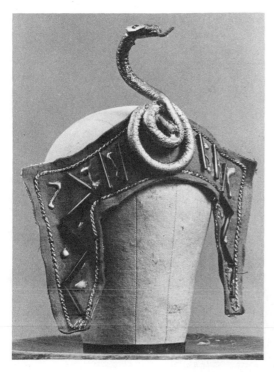

Figure 19-6 Etha foam rod (used in building construction), pieces of rattan, hot-melt glue, and a pipe cleaner are used to decorate a "Cleopatra" cobra headdress. Photo by Robert Izzo.

making jewelry and ornaments. For example, pieces which have definite shapes, such as brooches, buckles, settings for large stones, and the like, are mounted on some form of backing. This backing may be as simple as heavy cardboard, canvas, felt, buckram, leather, or whatever serves the purpose. The backing provides the basic overall shape on which the raised detail or ornamentation can be mounted. If the backing is to be completely covered with other materials, it may need no additional treatment; if it is not to be completely hidden, then the color and texture of the backing is selected according to the requirements of the finished piece.

The raised detail of a piece of jewelry or other costume ornaments can be cord, wire, or similar things which are glued to the backing in the desired form and colored according to the specifications. Hot-melt glue is also very effective for creating raised ornaments or for adding decorative detail. Figure 19-7B is a detail photograph of the overskirt in Fig. 19-7A showing beads of hot-melt glue used to make the "bunch of grapes" border on the skirt. Hot-melt glue is versatile and can be used to create many effects. It cools quickly and can be gilded, painted, or left in its honey color.

Several other materials and methods are useful for making three-dimensional pieces. Products like Plastic Wood or Spackle, traditionally used for furniture and walls, can be sculpted and left to harden by air-drying. Designs can be carved out of soft wood or styrofoam and mounted on a backing piece, or layers of felt or thin sheets of foam can be built up to create raised ornaments. Of course, papier-mâché is an old standby for making three-dimensional objects, and the newer molding materials like Celastic, Polysar, and casting rubber can be used to create raised ornaments.

Numbers of decorative items can also be made by casting a mold of unusual and

and supported with millinery wire and then decorated with pieces of rattan, hot-melt glue, and cord. The key is to look at things, not in terms of their designated functions, but in terms of how the shape, texture, and dimensions can be transformed into that which meets a given theatrical need.

Thinking of items beyond the specific function for which they were originally made vastly increases the range of materials available for creating all kinds of ornaments. The selection of materials is governed by such criteria as durability, weight, availability, ease of working with them, and their cost.

RAISED ORNAMENTS. There are some basic techniques which are pertinent to

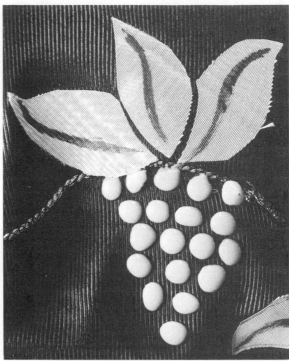

Figure 19-7 A. Character of "Olivia" in *Twelfth Night* as produced by the University of Rhode Island. The overskirt is decorated with bows stiffened with ply-on film and a border of bunches of grapes. From the author's collection. B. Detail of the overskirt border showing grapes made of hot-melt glue and leaves laminated with ply-on film. Photo by Robert Izzo.

interesting "found objects" such as sea shells, buttons, furniture hardware, or whatever, which provide sources for reproducing any number of pieces for future use. Craft supply houses carry a range of casting resins, such as lucite, that can be used with the molds, and many of the "liquid metals" and sculpturing metal pastes work well. Duplicates of any number of items can also be made by vacuforming (see Molding Materials for more details).

All of these materials can be painted or gilded to finish the appearance. Essentially, the tools, materials, and techniques are similar to those used in making theatrical properties. Also, many of the tech-

niques and materials have been adopted by craft and boutique suppliers. Sources with more detail on step-by-step processes for working with these and other materials are cited at the end of this chapter.

Three-dimensional decorations can be used separately or linked together to form an ornate unit which can be worn by itself or be suspended from a chain. In the first instance, if the piece is to be pinned to the garment, a safety pin can be sewn or glued to the back of the ornament. If the pieces are to be linked together or suspended, some means of joining them needs to be planned with the piece. Small screw eyes, loops of heavy thread, large electric

Figure 19–8B Detail of the Oedipus mask and neck-chain. The chain is knotted and gilded rope; the Celastic mask is decorated with sized felt, gilded, and highlighted with other paints.

the local hardware store may be appropriate. Chain can also be made from cord, rubber tubing, or heavy wire; macramé techniques can be applied to create very decorative "chains." For instance, the neckpiece on Oedipus in Fig. 19–8 (also see color plate) is made from knotted rope that has been gilded. Bamboo chain, from import or garden shops, is effective and makes up into excellent chain when textured with paint. Novelty shops and theatrical suppliers also often have lightweight snap-apart plastic chain in various sizes that can be painted for a metallic effect.

GEMS AND BEADS. Gems can be fabricated or purchased from boutique and theatrical suppliers. The term *gem* refers to semiprecious and precious stones and pearls which have been polished to some degree. Historically, the craft of gem cutting (faceting stones to reflect light) was not practiced until the fourteenth century. Earlier stones were usually polished or carved, or else they were displayed in their natural state. Opaque stones, such as turquoise or agate, can be made from styrofoam, papier-mâché, foam, or other materials. Actually, anything that can be shaped and painted to resemble the stone can be used. Translucent stones can be duplicated with clear plastics. Many craft suppliers sell "cracked marbles" and other items which work very well for the translucent stones, and they can often be colored with a translucent paint. Faceted stones are also available from craft suppliers and theatrical supply houses.

Wooden and plastic beads are also readily available. In addition, common pasta, such as macaroni, shells, and twists, can be used to make up unusual pieces as has been demonstrated by the numerous Christmas-tree decorations made from them. Bamboo tubes, often found in window and door curtains, are also valuable for use as elongated beads. Those items

staples, or metal links can be built into the pieces so they can be joined together or to a chain.

CHAINS. Obviously, a normal jewelry chain for an enlarged piece will probably be out of proportion, and a substitute will be needed. Chain belts are often large enough in scale, or something like dog-leash chain or other types of chain from which have a hole punched through the center are easy to work with because they can be strung or threaded through, but the various forms of beads can also be glued to a backing.

Settings for gems or beads are mounted on a backing with some form of adhesive; typical adhesives are cited in the Glossary in Chap. 2. The selection of the proper adhesive is determined by the items to be joined and the effect desired. For example, a large glob of hot-melt glue with a gem pushed into it will create a rough unsophisticated setting for the stone. For a more sophisticated setting, the gem can be attached with a white glue and surrounded with decorative cord, which is also glued. When selecting the type of glue to use, check the label for information on what the glue best adheres to. Generally, liquid glues are absorbed into porous materials and will not adhere well to them, but they will adhere to nonporous substances.

Guidelines for Finishing Jewelry

Finishing techniques are as diversified as the construction techniques. A basic theory of working with paints for metallic finishes is discussed in Chap. 15, but any medium used in finishing should be tested before it is applied to the piece. Styrofoam, for example, dissolves and disappears when painted with many canned spray paints. However, it can be sealed with latex or casein paint and then sprayed; the sealing action protects the styrofoam from the chemical ingredients in the spray paint.

Fabricated or ready-made jewelry may need to be toned down if it reflects too much light, or it may look too new. Reflection can be dulled by using a "dulling spray" (from paint or hardware stores) or by rubbing a dampened bar of soap over the surface. Leather dye or paint dry-brushed onto the piece will tone it down and can also be used to make it look old or antiqued. Covering the piece with fine black net will also accomplish this appearance.

As stated earlier, there are so many variations possible in creating jewelry and ornaments for the stage that specific details on how to make individual pieces are beyond the scope of this chapter. The elements mentioned here are to trigger ideas and to introduce some possible areas to explore.

MOLDING MATERIALS

No discussion of costume construction techniques would be complete without mentioning the molding materials which have become indispensable in costuming for making jewelry, masks, helmets, armor, and other assorted items. The number of products on the market today have simplified and speeded up the processes involved, and the results are versatile and very durable. The products discussed here include Celastic, Polysar XB470, fiberglass, thermoplastic sheets, and molding and casting rubbers. Some techniques for working with these prod-ucts and for sizing (stiffening) and molding felt are included in the discussion.

The properties of each of the products, the amount of time required to complete a unit with a given product, the cost of the materials, and the space and equipment needed to execute the process are all factors to consider in selecting the most appropriate material to use to achieve the best results. For example, fiberglass is very durable, lightweight, and nonflexible; however, it is expensive, and special equipment and space are necessary in order to work with it.

Celastic, which resembles stiff felt, is a plastic-impregnated fabric which softens after a few seconds in acetone or other commercial solvents and is self-adhesive. After it is softened, Celastic can be formed either on a positive or in a negative mold. Celastic dries quickly, is lightweight, strong, and very durable; it can be sanded, cut with scissors, painted, and glued to. This versatile material can be used to make any number of items. The masks in Figs. 19–8, 19–9, and 19–12 are all made of Celastic with pieces of felt, rope, or fur added. Celastic is available in light, medium, and heavy weights from theatrical supply houses.

While Celastic can also be draped and wrapped, typical uses in a costume shop generally involve working with a positive mold that is covered with aluminum foil, which allows the dried Celastic to separate easily from the mold. The Celastic should be torn into small- or medium-sized strips to follow the contours of the mold; the edges should overlap each other, and the torn edges will blend more smoothly than cut edges. The strips are dipped in acetone and smoothed onto the mold. Since the wet Celastic dries fast, each strip is dipped and applied individually. Do not leave the Celastic in the solvent too long because it will lose its self-adhesive and moldable characteristics. Celastic will stretch when wet and then shrink as it dries so it should not be pulled too tightly. The edges should be smoothed and blended as each strip is added; additional acetone on the fingers often helps the blending process.

Always wear rubber gloves and work in a well-ventilated area when working with acetone and use only small amounts of the solvent because it evaporates quickly. It will also dissolve many containers other than glass or metal.

Polysar XB470 is a synthetic rubber that is semirigid at room temperature and softens when heated at temperatures around 170°F. Polysar can be heated in hot water,

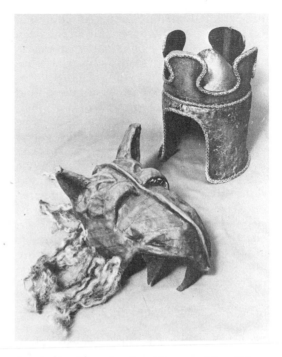

Figure 19-9 Examples of molding materials: a Polysar helmet painted and decorated, and a Celastic mask painted and decorated with frayed rope, hair, felt teeth, and red sequin eyes. Photo by Robert Izzo.

in an oven, or with a heat gun, and then formed on a mold. Unlike Celastic, Polysar can even be molded directly, but with care, on the body for something like exact-fitting body armor. It hardens as it cools, about ten minutes at room temperature, and will retain its shape through heavy use. It can be sprayed with non–oil-base paints and overpainted with thin layers of water-base paints as necessary. Polysar comes in 24 in. by 24 in. sheets which are available in light, medium, and heavy gauge from theatrical supply houses.

Polysar does not require any additional solvents. It can be cut to the needed size and shape; cutting is easier if the material is heated to about 150°F. The piece is heated for use; the higher the temperatures (but not over 200°F.) the more quickly it will soften. If heated in an oven, place the Polysar on a sheet of aluminum foil to prevent it from sticking to the oven racks. Dry heat permits the material to adhere to itself provided both surfaces are cleaned with a dry-cleaning fluid prior to heating. Needless to say, do not use a fluid that is flammable. If heated in hot water, the Polysar must be allowed to become very soft in the water. Then the excess water is dried off, and both of the surfaces to be joined are coated with acetone in order to make the Polysar self-adhering.

Polysar can be reheated if it cools too quickly, and the hardening process can be speeded up by immersing in cold water. The finished product is light and durable and has a small degree of flexibility. Figure 19–9 shows an example of a helmet made of Polysar.

Fiberglass is available in several forms including mat, chopped, woven roving, and cloth. The latter is most used in a costume shop. Glass fibers are woven into cloth which, in use, is saturated with polyester resin; it is more accurately called fiberglass-reinforced polyester. Items made from this are hard, strong, and very durable, but the process of working with fiberglass is more complex than working with Celastic or Polysar.

The materials needed to make a fiberglass unit include the glass cloth (8 oz to 10 oz per square yard has good bias), a solution of resin, a catalyst hardener, rubber gloves, and a filter mask. The gloves and mask are to protect the individual working with the glass fibers because of the nearly invisible glass splinters which get under the skin and can be inhaled.

Directions and proportion formulas for mixing, along with instructions for application, are usually found on the resin and catalyst labels and must be followed closely. The mixture begins to congeal quickly and must be applied to the glass before the resins harden. The solution saturates the glass cloth so that it conforms exactly to the shape of the mold. It also creates a perma-

nent bond, so the finished product has an extremely hard surface when it "cures"— that is, hardens and dries completely.

Fiberglass can be worked on a mold of plaster of paris, plasticine (a nondrying clay), regular clay, and several other materials. In all cases, the mold needs to be coated with a parting agent so the mold will separate from the item. The cloth is cut into strips that are appropriately sized for the mold and saturated with the resin solution by soaking the strips in a container of resin or by brushing the resin over the glass. To add to the strength of the piece, layers of the strips (applied perpendicular to each other) can be built up to the desired thickness.

When the molded unit is almost dry, it is lifted from the mold to assure separation and then replaced in the mold to dry completely.

The expense and complexity of the process for making fiberglass pieces limits its usefulness in a costume shop, but if extra strength or durability is required, it is an excellent material to use.

Thermoplastic sheets are made of plastics that can be softened with heat and then harden when cooled. Vacuforming, a method of producing three-dimensional hollow replicas of an object or mold, has become a popular method for creating jewelry, masks, armor, and other three-dimensional objects. Essentially, the sheet is heat-softened and drawn over or into a mold from which the air is sucked out, creating a vacuum. The molded object is lightweight and fairly durable. It will take paint and additional decoration easily. Vacuforming is also an excellent means for mass reproduction of an item.

Details for making the vacuform equipment and the procedures for vacuforming are found in Nicholas Bryson's *Thermoplastics for the Stage* (see Additional Sources), and prevacuformed sheets of armor, jewelry items, and ornaments are also available from some theatrical supply houses. Since the vacuformed object is hollow, the form may have to be reinforced at flex points and edges where tears might occur with felt, papier-mâché, or additional layers of plastic or cord. Celastic also works well as a reinforcement material.

Felt has numerous theatrical uses. As mentioned in Chap. 18, felt can be softened and shaped when it is steamed. This technique can also be applied to making jewelry, armor, helmets, and numerous other items. Often, in these instances, the molded felt needs to be stiffened (*sized*) with a flexible adhesive to hold and support the shape. Sizing felt also alters the surface texture and is often used to simulate a leather (see Fig. 15–13) or metallic appearance.

Industrial-weight felt, because of its thickness and body, is recommended for these purposes. The felt is cut and formed into the desired shape with steam and blocked in that shape until it is dry; then it is coated with layers of flexible adhesive and allowed to dry again before it is removed from its mold. The flexible adhesive sizes the felt so the shape will be maintained but does not allow the unit to be somewhat flexible, unlike Celastic or fiberglass units.

Felt can also be patterned, cut, and zig-zagged together to get the molded shape as was done for the felt hood in Fig. 18–6. With the thickness of industrial-weight felt, the seams are butt-joined with the zig-zag stitch catching each side of the seam. Darts can also be made in the felt using this technique. The codpieces in Fig. 19–10 were initially shaped with a center seam, placed on the mold, which was nondrying clay covered with aluminum foil, and sized with white glue and water. These were then covered with fabric and decorated.

Any raised detail or ornamentation can be glued directly onto the surface of the sized felt and, if necessary, another coat of sizing can be applied. Metallic powders or flaked graphite can be mixed with the size and painted or dry-brushed onto the felt to simulate metal. An undercoating of black, grey, or any desired color, applied to the surface before the metallic colors are added enhances the metallic appearance, and the piece can be accented with paint, hot-melt glue, or metallic pastes.

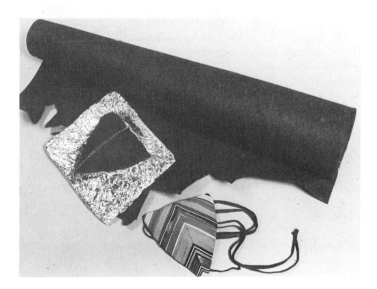

Figure 19–10 Example of molded, sized industrial-weight felt. The felt is butt-joined and zig-zagged, blocked on a mold, and sized before it is decorated. Photo by Robert Izzo.

MOLDING AND CASTING RUBBERS. Mold- and casting rubbers are substances that can be used to create flexible lightweight pieces for armor, masks, raised decoration or any number of other items. The rubbers have different properties which distinguish them; however, both require the use of negative molds, which are discussed under Making Molds.

Molding rubber needs to be air-dried; therefore, it is cast in a waterproof mold, which can be a plaster mold sealed with varnish or shellac. Thicknesses of molding rubber are built up in layers; each layer must be allowed to dry before the next layer is applied; a fan will speed up the drying process. Since molding rubber sticks to itself, these layers will not separate. Pieces made of this rubber can also be reinforced by laminating cheesecloth into the layers of latex. This process was developed by Frederick Nihda for the flexible body armor in the original Broadway production of *Pippin*. The armor had to be lightweight and very flexible because of the strenuous dance numbers.

Since molding rubber sticks to itself, it needs to be dusted with talcum powder before it is pulled from the mold. The reverse side then needs to be dusted with the powder and allowed to continue to dry and set up (*cure*) for up to 24 hours after it is out of the mold. Before the dried pieces are painted, the powder needs to be washed off. Molding rubber items can be painted with bronze powder in lacquer, acrylic paint, or spray shoe dyes.

Casting rubber dries through evaporation, which means that it is cast in a pure, unsealed plaster mold. The plaster absorbs the moisture from the latex, which means that casting rubber will shrink slightly and pull away from the mold. Casting rubber does not stick to itself; therefore, the mold is filled to the brim. To make a hollow piece, the latex is left in the mold to allow the curing process to begin. After the edges have set up, the still liquid center is poured out. This technique is referred to as *slush* molding. The curing process can be speeded up by using warm air, but not heat.

Since casting rubber does not stick to itself, it does not need to be dusted with powder at any point in the process. It can be glued to itself and to other objects with Barge cement. Molding rubber will also stick to casting rubber; therefore, it can be reinforced using the molding rubber and cheesecloth combination.

Casting rubber can be colored with the same materials as molding rubber, and both can be tinted by using a small amount of food coloring mixed into the rubber itself. It will dry translucent, but the color can be distorted by the natural yellow cast of the rubbers. Therefore, the food coloring that is used needs to be selected with an eye to counteracting the yellow cast. For example, if blue food color is used, the finished color will have a definite green tone.

Since both rubbers set up when exposed to air, both must be stored in airtight containers. Excess casting rubber from the slush mold can be returned to its original container or poured into smaller molds to make decorative ornaments.

Items made of either rubber must be stored carefully to maintain the original shape since they can be distorted; they will also take on and keep any crease marks made by folding them.

Both molding and casting rubbers are available from craft suppliers; other sources are cited in Appendix B. As with any molding process, the latex needs to be poured slowly and evenly into the mold to avoid air bubbles. It can also be applied to the mold with a nylon bristle brush. Before beginning to work with either material, always check the instructions that come with the rubber for the methods recommended for working with it. Both rubbers require a degree of time to allow for the curing process, which cannot be rushed or ignored, to get successful pieces. As with every material and technique, a certain amount of experimentation is necessary to master the processes involved.

A mold is either positive or negative. A positive mold is a form which has the molding medium overlaid on it and, when dried, the inside of the molded item duplicates the mold. A negative mold is the reverse of a positive mold and has the molding medium pressed or poured into it; the resulting good side of the molded item duplicates the surface of the mold.

A positive mold can also be used to make an item in which the exposed surface is intended to be the finished side. Building up a shell over a positive mold with something like Celastic or papier-mâché is common practice. The quality of the results, though, are dependent upon the skill of the person doing the work rather than on the quality of the mold as anything other than a starting point.

Making molds for masks illustrates the processes involved in making both positive and negative molds of all types. A set of procedures commonly used to develop a mask that is fitted to a particular actor starts with a casting made of the actor's face. That casting is a negative mold.

A positive mold can be cast directly from that negative to obtain a so-called "life-mask" duplication of the actor's face. This life-mask can then be altered as needed to form the base for the mask being made. Typically, this means building up certain areas or features of the face with plasticine or other materials to approximate the shape of the mask.

Once the final shape is achieved, the mask can be made in one of two ways. The first is to cast yet another negative mold from the altered life-mask base; this new negative mold can then have the desired molding material pressed or poured into it to obtain the thin shell of the mask. The second means is to build up the shell of the mask directly on the altered life-mask, obtaining the external appearance of the mask as the shell is molded.

MAKING MOLDS

Casting Negative Molds

An appropriate casting compound and certain tools are needed to make a negative mold of an actor's face.

CASTING COMPOUNDS. Various materials are available for taking impressions of an object, and obviously molds for casting final products are made from any number of materials from rubber to metal. But the four compounds mentioned here are those typically used for casting faces or other areas of the body. The first two, *moulage* and *flexible dental plaster*, are particularly good for direct application to the face or body. The other two are not recommended for direct application, but they are valuable for making the more permanent positive molds.

Moulage is a flexible self-releasing reusable compound that is heated to a liquid state and applied to the face as soon as it is cool enough to touch. Once the cooling process has begun, it must be applied quickly. Moulage is easy to work with and gives an exact impression of the face, including pores and hair. When applied to the nose area, the subject needs only to exhale through the nostrils for clear, easy breathing; no straws or special breathing devices are necessary. Moulage is packaged under several brand names and is available from theatrical and artist suppliers. Follow the directions on the label.

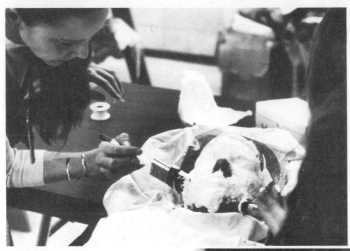

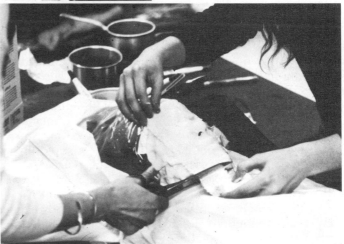

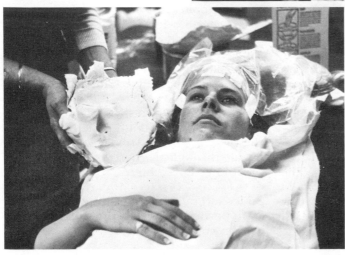

Figure 19-11 A. Applying moulage for a life-mask to the actor's face; her hair is protected by plastic, and the clothing is covered with a piece of fabric. The moulage is brushed over the nose last; no straws or special breathing apparatus is necessary. B. Applying plaster bandages over solidified moulage. Notice the clear nostrils in the moulage. C. Completed life-mask's negative mold removed from the actor's face. Photos by Jerry R. Emery.

Flexible dental plaster (also known as dental impression powder) is mixed with cold water to a puttylike consistency and used immediately, since it sets up faster than reusable moulage. The dental plaster requires petroleum jelly as a separating agent since it is not self-releasing. The petroleum jelly is coated on the face with an extra amount placed on the eyebrows and any other facial hair. This compound does not require special breathing apparatus; the subject needs only to exhale to clear breathing passages. Flexible dental plaster is sold under several brand names and is available from dental supply houses.

Plaster of paris is an inexpensive nonflexible molding material, but it is not recommended for casting face molds. It is heavy, heats up uncomfortably during the curing process, and requires extra breathing devices such as straws in the nostrils which can distort the shape of the nose in the mold. Plaster of paris is mixed with water and is excellent for making positive molds from the negative face mold.

Dental stone is also nonflexible, but it is finer and less porous than plaster of paris. It was developed for use in dental work. Essentially, dental stone has properties similar to plaster and is used in the same manner.

Tools for the Casting Process

Double-boiler, used to melt down moulage

Brush or spatula, used to apply the casting compound

Plastic bowls, used to mix the casting compound

Chaise longue or something to support the actor in a reclining position; the folding lawn version is quite satisfactory for this

Shower cap, used to hold the hair out of the way

Plastic make-up cape or sheet to drape around the neck and shoulders to protect the clothing

Cardboard with an oval opening cut out for the face to keep the compound from running into the ears; if the compound is thick enough it may not run, in which case cotton ear plugs are sufficient

Petroleum jelly to coat the actor's face and facial hair when using flexible dental plaster

Plaster bandages (gauze impregnated with plaster) to reinforce the mold; they are dipped in water and then layered in different directions to hold the shape of the mold; three to four layers are recommended. We use 2 in. (5 cm) wide bandages.

The Casting Process.   While the flexible casting compound is being mixed for application, the actor should be settled in a reclining position with hair and clothing protected and, if necessary, petroleum jelly applied to protect the facial hair. Two people working on the preparation and the application of the compound will speed up the process. When applying the compound, it is important to talk to the actor and to explain what is being done and where the compound is to be applied next. This is particularly important when applying it over the nose area; have the actor take a deep breath, apply the compound, and then tell the actor to exhale through the nose. This action will clear the breathing passages.

The compound should be applied in a thick layer over the entire face and allowed to solidify, which usually takes 10 to 15 minutes. Then apply wet strips of the plaster bandages over the compound. The strips should be built up in three to four layers that are applied perpendicular to each other for additional strength. Allow this to dry, again about 10 minutes, before the cast is removed.

To remove the cast, gently lift the edges of the mold around the edge of the face and then have the actor lean forward so the cast can fall away from the face.

Set the mold into a box or pail that is

strong enough to support both the mold and casting compound for the positive mold. Make sure the mold is well-supported and not twisted out of shape.

Positive Molds

The inside of the negative mold should be checked for air bubbles, which can be filled in with more compound, if necessary.

While the actor is cleaning up, the compound for the positive mold should be prepared. The mixed nonflexible compound is poured into the negative mold carefully so as not to distort the shape of the mold. The compound is added immediately because the flexible compound shrinks as it loses moisture. The plaster should be poured slowly and gently or spooned into the mold, to avoid creating air bubbles. When the plaster has dried, the flexible compound is broken away to reveal the positive mold of the face. (Moulage can be stored in an airtight container and reused up to three times; the flexible dental plaster cannot be reused.)

Additional shapes and details for a mask can be built on the positive mold with plasticine, which is preferred since it is nondrying and reusable. Avoid strong *undercuts* in the mold because the molded item may not pull away from the mold. An undercut is a section that creates an overhang or a projection that may catch in the molding material, making it difficult or impossible to remove the object from the mold. If an undercut is required by the design, the pieces may have to be cast and molded separately and joined. Materials like Celastic or Polysar can be cut to open the area and then rejoined after the object is off the mold.

Once the mask contours are completed, cover the mold with aluminum foil for a Celastic mask, with a silicone release agent for a Polysar mask, or with plastic food wrap for fiberglass. No parting agent is necessary for a thermoplastic mask.

Positive molds for masks can also be made without casting a life-mask first. By taking strategic measurements of the actor's face, a mold can be made by applying plasticine to a styrofoam wig block. The necessary measurements are

> Across the forehead (hairline to hairline)
>
> Across the bridge of the nose from ear to ear
>
> From the top of the head to the tip of the nose, and to the tip of the chin
>
> From the front hairline to the nape of the neck
>
> Length and width of the nose
>
> Hairline to eyebrow
>
> Distance between the outside points of the eyes.

These measurements are used as guides for building up the clay on the styrofoam

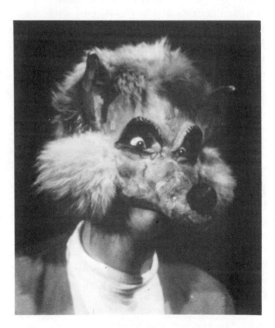

Figure 19-12 Celastic mask for "Brer Fox" in *Brer Rabbit* as produced by The Ohio State University. The mask was made on a positive mold made of plasticine built up on a styrofoam wig block. From the author's collection.

head. They are used to check the proportions of the mask as the mold is developed and completed. This method eliminates the time-consuming process of making the life-mask mold. Brer Fox's mask (Fig. 19-12) was made with this method, as was the Oedipus mask (Fig. 19-8).

To cast a negative mold of a face mold that has been developed with plasticine on a block for a mask made of molding rubber, cover the smoothed surface of the mold with varnish or shellac. (Grease-based parting agents, such as petroleum jelly, will cling to the plaster used to make the negative mold and cause problems when varnishing the mold for the molding rubber.)

To pour the negative mold, first build a "dam" of clay or other material to create a basin to hold the plaster over the positive mold. After the plaster has been poured (carefully to avoid air bubbles) and dried, it is lifted off the positive mold. The new negative mold is then ready to be used following the procedures outlined for molding rubber. Figure 9-13 shows masks made of molding rubber.

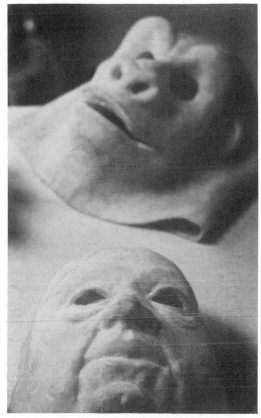

Figure 19-13 Examples of masks made of molding rubber by the Frederick Nihda Studio. From the author's collection.

COSTUME PROPS

It is often difficult to define the difference between costume props and costume accessories. Both can be broadly defined as anything the actor wears or carries. The details of who is responsible for producing items for the production are usually worked out by the designers and the production staff.

Generally, however, the costume shop is responsible for such things as parasols, walking sticks, fans, and purses. Soft items, such as spats, gloves, and handkerchiefs, are traditionally provided by the costume shop, while items such as weapons like swords, daggers, and the like, may be made in the scene shop because they generally have the tools to do the job. The belts and hangers for the weapons may need to come from the costume shop. The belt shown in Fig. 19-14 has a hanger for a sword added. In this instance, we used D-rings, from the local hardware store, that were attached to the belt; a heavyweight chain was attached to and suspended between two rings. Additional decoration includes buttons and broken bits of jewelry glued to the belt.

Most costume prop items should be con-

Figure 19–14 Example of a belt with a simple sword hanger made by suspending a strong chain between two D-rings attached to the belt. Photo by Robert Izzo.

sidered as part of the basic stock. Since many of these items are purchased and then reworked as necessary to meet the design specifications, a costumer and resident designer are usually on the lookout for things that will build up the stock from thrift shops, flea markets, yard sales, and even the local dump. Once procured, many of these items tend to be unique, and they often require special and secure storage so they will be available when needed.

The basic principles involved in adapting a costume prop to meet the requirements of the design are similar to the basic principles of costuming. For example, a parasol can be painted, re-covered, and decorated to create the appearance required. The original cover can be used to pattern a new cover or the principles of patterning a sectional crown (see Chap. 18) can be adapted to fit the sections between the ribs of the parasol.

The term *costume accessories,* as used here, covers a broad range of items, and the techniques for making, finding, or buying them are equally varied. Some of the methods and principles involved are outlined in this and several other chapters; additional information on specific techniques can also be found in books on theatrical properties and scenography books. Selected sources are given in the following bibliography and in other bibliographies throughout the book.

ADDITIONAL SOURCES

BRYSON, NICHOLAS, *Thermoplastic Scenery for Theatre, Vol. 1, Vacuum Forming.* New York: Drama Book Specialists/Publishers, 1972.

CONWAY, HEATHER, *Stage Properties.* London: Herbert Jenkins, 1959.

CORSON, RICHARD, *Stage Makeup* (6th ed.), Chap. 14. Englewood Cliffs, N.J.: Prentice-Hall, Inc., 1981.

EVARD, GWEN, *Twinkletoes: Footgear to Make and Wear.* New York: Charles Scribner's Sons, 1976.

INGHAM, ROSEMARY, and ELIZABETH COVEY, *The Costumer's Handbook: How to Make All Kinds of Costumes.* Englewood Cliffs, N.J.: Prentice-Hall, Inc., 1980.

KENTON, WARREN, *Stage Properties and How to Make Them* (2nd ed.). London: Pitman Publishing Ltd., 1978.

MACKAY, PATRICIA, "Master Prop Builder for Broadway and Television." *Theatre Crafts,* 11, no. 3 (May/June 1977), 7–11, 30, 32, 34.

BLACK, ANDERSON, *Jewelry Through the Ages.* New York: William Morrow and Co., Inc., 1974.

BROOK, IRIS, *Footwear: A Short History of European and American Shoes.* New York: Theatre Arts Books, 1971.

Motley, *Theatre Props.* New York: Drama Book Specialists/Publishers, 1975.

Pecktal, Lynn, *Designing and Painting for the Theatre,* Chap. 10. New York: Holt, Rinehart, and Winston, 1975.

Richards, Sheila, "Loafers to Restoration Slippers." *Theatre Crafts,* 11, no. 6 (November/December 1977), 25–27, 66–68.

Russell, Douglas, "Use of Felt at the Shakespeare Memorial Theatre." *Educational Theatre Journal,* 7, no. 3 (October 1955) 202–9.

Smith, C. Ray (ed.), *The Theatre Crafts Book of Makeup, Masks, and Wigs,* pp. 155–220. Emmaus, Pa.: Rodale Press, Inc., 1974.

twenty

planning and preparation for production

Organization is the key to completing the costumes on time; there is no option on deadlines in the theatre. The costumer must know what needs to be done to complete all aspects of each costume for the show in order to allow the work to progress smoothly. The process of producing costumes incorporates three major phases: preconstruction planning, construction and fitting, and the performance phase. The procedures during each of these phases must be carefully planned and organized in order to allow the costume shop to function efficiently and for the costumes to be completed on time.

THE PRECONSTRUCTION PLANNING PHASE

In consultation with the designer, the costumer must organize the work to be done and be able to communicate that information to the various people working on the costumes. This communication is essential and can only be done if the costumer knows *what* work needs to be done and *when* it needs to be done. In a sense, it is like working a giant crossword puzzle; it requires time and a great deal of homework to make everything fit together at the right place and in the proper combi-

nations and sequence. This process is facilitated by the use of several charts and lists.

THE SHOW CHART. The costumer must be as familiar with the script as the designer and must also use various methods of keeping track of the myriad of things that are part of costuming a show. A standard means of collating the requirements of the script is a *show chart* (Fig. 20–1). This chart, usually put together by

EXAMPLE OF SHOW CHART

[TITLE OF SHOW]

	I-1 [INDICATE (IF APPROPRIATE) LOCATION TIME OF YEAR TIME OF DAY]	I-2	I-3	INTERMISSION	II-1	II-2	II-3
CHARACTER NAME ACTOR'S NAME	X = APPEARS IN SCENE [INDICATE SPECIAL BUSINESS OR ACTION]	[INDICATE GARMENTS]			[INDICATE CHANGES] [NOTE PRESETS]	[INDICATE ANY EFFECT ON TIMING OF CHANGES]	
HENRY JOHN DOE	X "Garments: - - - - - - - - - - " "uses handkerchief"	X "no change"	X "no change"		X "same — add jacket" "Exit pg. 60 –DSL"	X "Enter pg. 75 –USR" "change to: - - - - - - - - - -"	X "same as II-2"
ALICE JANE SMITH		X "Garments: - - - - - - - -"	X "no change" "puts gun in purse"		X "Garments: ① - - - - - ② - - - - -" "changes to ② during scene"		X "same as end of II-1" "adds overcoat" (PRESET)

Figure 20–1 A sample show chart suggesting the kind of information that needs to be included on the chart. From the author's notebook.

the designer early in the designing process, breaks down the script by scenes and the appearance of the characters in the scenes. The chart can be drawn up on a large sheet of paper or on cardboard with the characters' names down the left side and the act and scene and intermission designation across the top. The character designation should also include enough room to add the actors' names; the act and scene space should also include the locale, key action of the scene, or other appropriate designations.

The chart is gridded off so that each character has a separate square for each scene that is large enough to write in necessary information. This information will include the appearance of the character in a scene, a brief description of the garments, and any special stage business that has a bearing on the costume. This business can range from "gets into disguise on stage" to "takes out handkerchief and cries." In the first instance, we learn that the costume will probably need some special construction so the actor can get into it quickly and easily; in the second instance, we learn that the character has to have a handkerchief and a place to keep it, like a pocket or a purse. The function of the

ROMEO AND JULIET

	PROLOGUE	CAPULET'S HOUSE (Ball) 1-5	CAPULET ORCHARD (Night) 2-1	ORCHARD BALCONY 2-2	FRIAR L. CELL 2-3	STREET (next day) 2-4	CAPULET ORCHARD 2-5	FR. L. CELL (WEDDING) 2-6	STREET (FIGHT) 3-1	CAPULET ORCHARD (Banishment) 3-2	FR. L. CELL 3-3	CAPULET'S HALL 3-4
(Chorus)	X											
Escalus		X same ADD mask							X basic			
Capulet		X same							X same as 1-5			X same
Mercutio		X same ADD mask	X same			X same NO MASK			X same – draws weapons – KILLED			
Benvolio		X same ADD mask	X same			X same NO MASK			X same – weapon (sword only)			
Tybalt		X same ADD mask							X basic – draws weapons – KILLED			
Romeo		X same ADD mask	X same	X same NO MASK	X same	X same		X CHANGE	X same as 2-6 – draws weapons		X same	
Gregory		X same ADD mask							X basic – weapons (sword only)			
Friar John		X same ADD mask							X basic – weapon (dagger)			
Abraham		X same ADD mask							X basic			
Apothecary		X same ADD mask										
Juliet		X same ADD mask		X CHANGE			X CHANGE	X ADD cape	X basic	X same as 2-5 (no cape)		X same
Lady Capulet		X same ADD mask					X same					X same
Nurse		X same				X ADD large veil				X CHANGE back to 1-3	X same	

INTERMISSION (between scene 2-6 and scene 3-1)

Figure 20-2 Segment of a show chart for a production of *Romeo and Juliet* showing the characters arranged in the order in which the actors doubled in certain roles. From the author's notebook.

chart is to provide an overview of the show and to help keep track of the costume requirements since the charting also shows what characters appear together and if a character has a fast change or other special requirements.

The designer should discuss the chart with the costumer to make sure that the costume needs are clearly understood. The chart can also be revised with information provided by the director to meet the needs of a specific production. For example, Fig. 20-2 is a segment of a chart for a production of *Romeo and Juliet*. The characters were arranged to show how the actors doubled in certain roles. After a chart has been compiled, it should be posted in the costume shop for quick reference and for any additions or changes that may need to be made.

THE COSTUME PLOT. Another standard list is a *costume plot* which is an itemized list of all the garments and accessories worn by each actor in the production, listed by act and scene. It is the instrument that outlines the workload for the production. Usually, there are two versions of the costume plot: a preliminary plot which outlines the work necessary for the preparation of the costumes, and a final plot which details the use of the costumes during the performances.

The preliminary plot is compiled with the designer after the designs have been approved and are ready to go into the workshop. It is drawn up specifically to outline the workload with a listing of all the garments and accessories, suggested sources for each item, and additional remarks concerning each item as shown in Fig. 20-3. We have found that a 5 in. by 8 in. card for each character and the actor playing the role is an easy way to set up the preliminary plot. Additions and corrections are easy to make, and the cards can be put in alphabetical order when the final plot is written.

Setting up the preliminary plot with three major headings: Garments and Accessories, Source, and Remarks is an effective method of organizing and communicating information for each costume. A complete list of all items the actor needs to wear or carry details the full extent of what is required. A possible source for each item should be determined, whether it be from storage, the actor's wardrobe, rented, purchased, or made. The identification of a source for each item provides information for the costume budget since it indicates what needs to be bought or rented. It also suggests the extent and nature of the workload for the shop; if many items are to be made, the workload in the shop will be greater than if the bulk of the items are available in the costume stock or are to be obtained elsewhere. Additional notations concerning special treatment of any item should be included under remarks. For example, if a garment needs to be made to allow for a fast change, this information needs to be recorded.

Since there are so many items and details which must be brought together to realize a complete set of costumes, it is imperative that all information pertaining to each costume be recorded in a logical form. If a detail is not noted, it will undoubtedly be forgotten and create unnecessary work and frustration later.

The preliminary plot not only provides a record of the information, but it also helps determine exactly how many and what types of items are needed. It will help establish working priorities when preparing the costumes. For example, if a corset or padding is required, these items must be completed before the outer garments can be fitted. The plot also indicates if there are many items which require special treatment. If fabric needs to be dyed before it is cut, or if the garment needs to be painted or aged, time needs to be scheduled in order to do the work in proper sequence. The information on the

Preliminary Costume Plot—Form Layout

Name of Show:		Period of Show:	

ACTOR (Character): Last name first; list actors alphabetically; separate Men and Women

Act and scene	Garments and accessories	Source of item	Remarks
(Script pg. no. can be used)	Garments (list items singly)* Accessories and Costume Props**	E.g. "build, buy, pull, borrow" (indicate source if known)	Include any comment pertinent to the entry; e.g. "rig for fast change"

*Garments should be listed in a consistent order and described clearly for easy identification.

**Accessories include all pieces worn, such as jewelry, hats, gloves, hairpieces, etc. Costume Props include articles which are used in addition to the costume; the procurement and design of these items are to be worked out in consultation with the Director, Scene Designer, and Properties Master.

Preliminary Costume Plot—Sample Entries

THE NIGHT THOREAU SPENT IN JAIL			Period: 1840s
SMITH, Jim (Williams)		Source	Remarks
Act 1	grey trousers	buy	age & rag
	brown plaid frockshirt	build	age & rag
	tan felt hat	pull (in stock)	age & rag
	brown shoes (no sox)	actor to provide	
	rope belt	pull (Scene Shop)	age
	slave collar & chain	build	vinyl; close with elastic
DOE, Jane (Lydia Emerson)		Source	Remarks
Act 1	wine & print dress	pull & alter	see Design Plate
	long petticoat	pull (in stock)	
	black heels	actor to provide	
	rings (2)		
	cameo	pull (jewelry stock)	
	wedding band	actor to provide	
pg. 1	long black cape	borrow (Mrs. Jones)	strike after X-over
pg. 2	beige apron	buy	strike after scene
pg. 40	blue knit shawl	pull (in stock)	
	blue poke bonnet	build	see Design Plate
pg. 65	beige nightgown	pull & alter	

Figure 20-3 Preliminary costume plot for layout and segment of a plot for a production of *The Night Thoreau Spent in Jail*. From the author's notebook.

MOON CHILDREN

WOMEN:

DOE, Jane (Ruth)

I-1	jeans	
	man's blue work shirt	
	sox	
	suede boots	
	denim jacket	preset on S. L. chair on-stage
	brown corduroy cap	preset in jacket pocket
I-2	red flannel shirt	preset off S. R. (remove work shirt)
I-3	No change	add dirt, etc. during scene change
I-4	green/brown sweatshirt	preset in vomitorium (FAST CHANGE)
	olive corduroy jacket	preset on S. R. hook on-stage
II-2	Mike's yellow/orange shirt	change in dressing room
II-3	No change	

JONES, Ann (Shelley)

I-3	hip-huggers	
	braid belt	
	stretch top	
	multi-stripe vest	
	tweed jacket	
	moccasins & bag	
I-4	brown cloth coat	change in dressing room (remove tweed jacket)
	green/white long scarf	
II-1	black leotard (underdress)	preset cloth coat on S. R. hook at Act break
	green print blouse	
II-2	yellow shirt	preset off S. R. (remove print top and moccasins)
	sandals	

Figure 20-4 Segment of a final costume plot with notations for the wardrobe crew for a production of *Moon Children* (actors' names altered). From the author's notebook.

preliminary plot is vital in determining specific needs, priorities, and requirements for setting up the work schedule.

The final plot (Fig. 20–4) is collated when the costumes are ready to go into dress rehearsals. The final plot is organized with the entries alphabetized by the actor's last name; the character name is also indicated. Each item is listed in order of appearance for the actor's and dresser's information. Additional notations concerning any costume changes and the location of those changes are noted on the plot for further information. The final plot is the worksheet for the wardrobe crew; it is the checklist detailing all the items for which they are responsible, and it specifies any costume changes that take place.

THE BUDGET. The costume plot and the costume sketches are used to make up the shopping list. The budget for the costumes for the show will determine the types and amounts of items that go onto the shopping list. The amount of money available for the costumes may be specified at the outset of the production planning. In that case, the designer will have designed the costumes with the budget in mind. In other situations, the amount of money required may be determined after the preliminary designs are done, in consultation with the producer, director, and costumer. In either case, the costumer needs to know how to set up budget estimates and how to stay within the production budget.

While each costume has specific requirements, certain guidelines can be followed to estimate what the cost per costume is going to be. The preliminary plot will provide information on what is on hand and can be pulled out of storage. It will also detail what might be possible to borrow, or to rent, and what needs to be bought, whether the items are to be ready-made or to be constructed from scratch.

Drawing up budgets for costumes that are to be constructed is a matter of analyzing the design sketch and applying the information on the costume plot. First, we need to determine the amount of fabric required for the complete costume. This means specifying the yardage and the estimated cost of the fabrics for the garment and for any accessories. We also need to determine the amount of material and costs for trims and decorations on the costume and the type and cost of the materials used to close the garment. Additional budget considerations include the footwear, hose, headgear, jewelry, and the like. For example, when analyzing the sketch for the gown in Fig. 20–5, we determined that we needed to have 10 yards of satin for the gown, 3 yards of chiffon for sleeves and stole, 15 yards of lining taffeta for lining, petticoat, and underruffles, 1 yard of net to line the sleeves, 12 buttons to be covered for the closing, plus shoes, and hose. We also needed to estimate corset yardage and number of corset stays for the torso undergarment, and it was easy to see that we would need lots of fabric flowers and rhinestones.

When setting up the plot we decided we could pull the shoes from our stock; however, we would probably need to buy shoe dye (we keep a large amount of shoe conditioner in stock). The notations on the plot also indicated that we would make the jewelry from our stock of supplies and that no dyes, fabric paints, or other treatments were necessary, so we did not have to include those items in our budget estimate for this costume.

Since our shop is in an educational system, we did not have to include the cost of labor in our budget; the commercial costume shops do have to include labor and overhead in their budgeting calculations. However, we do add 10 percent to 15 percent of the total estimated costume costs to the total budget as a contingency fund for miscellaneous items and dry cleaning.

This process of itemizing the materials for a costume needs to be gone through with each costume to determine the total costume budget. In order to estimate the costs of the items needed to put together any costume, some knowledge of the costs of fabric and related items is necessary. Including price ranges of fabrics in the Fabric Morgue provides a good resource for calculating costs. In addition, we maintain a file of local sources and costs for stock shop items as well as catalogues with current price lists from theatrical suppliers. We also use the telephone to learn the current prices of many items.

For rented costumes, the rental house will supply an itemized list of what each costume "unit" will include and the rental fee of each for the production period. Rented costume units usually include

Figure 20–5 Finished costume for "She" in Shaw's *How He Lied to Her Husband* as produced at the University of Rhode Island. Designed by Ken Holamon. Photo by Ken Holamon.

things like shirts and neckwear with men's costumes. Women's garments may have an underskirt attached to the garment. The specifics are usually included in the costume plot from the rental house; however, undergarments are usually not included, and footwear, if available, is generally rented separately. If it is at all possible, when renting costumes, go to the rental house and select the things you want. In all cases of renting costumes, send a complete, accurate set of measurements and clearly detail any special design requirements that you have. It is also very important to make the rental arrangements in advance to allow the company ample time to fill your order.

Budgeting for ready-made items is somewhat more difficult than for constructed or rented costumes, since it is difficult to predict what you are going to find and what the cost will be when you do find

things. Of necessity, most budgets for ready-made clothing are developed with thrift shops in mind. Our resource file also includes a listing of all the second-hand clothing stores, thrift shops, discount stores, and mill outlets in our area.

Another approach to developing a budget is to set a limit on the dollar amount for each total costume in the show and multiply that figure by the number of costumes, then add a contingency fund to set a total budget. Since each costume will probably not need the same amount of money, the specific amounts per costume can be juggled according to needs, and the final costs can be kept within the budget. For example, an inexpensive fabric used in quantity can take on a very lush appearance and still keep a costume within budget. The sideless surcote in Fig. 20–6 is made of an inexpensive fabric; however, the skirt on the gown is a full circle with the

Figure 20–6 Example of a quantity of inexpensive fabric used to create a rich appearance; the skirt is a full circle. "Margaret" in *Henry VI, Part I,* as produced by The Champlain Shakespeare Festival. From the author's collection.

body opening cut off-center to create the train. We also found the fabric for the gown in Fig. 20–7 on sale for less than 50 cents a yard. The gown has over 5 yards in the skirt.

THE SHOPPING LIST. The preparation of the show chart, costume plot, and the budget automatically provides the information needed to put together the shopping list. This list includes all the items that are needed to construct the costumes and includes necessary tools and equipment to do the job. For instance, we did not have a rhinestone setter in our shop when we were planning to make the costume in Fig. 20–5. The breakdown for the budget established a need for one, so it went on our shopping list.

Shopping for a show is time-consuming and needs to be planned carefully in ad-

vance to use the time efficiently. As stated earlier, the designer will often shop for the fabrics and related items; the costumer, however, is expected to maintain the stock supplies, such as threads, needles, and other standard stock items cited earlier in the book. It is very frustrating to have to stop construction in order to go and buy needles for the sewing machine because the supply has run out.

Part of the early planning, then, includes checking the shop supplies to be sure the construction phase will go smoothly. Organizing how the time will be spent for efficient use of the construction period requires yet another chart for the working schedule.

WORK SCHEDULES. Once the preliminary charts and lists are drawn up, and the priorities are known, the costume produc-

Figure 20–7 Inexpensive fabric used in the costume for "Mrs. Higgins" in *Pygmalion* as produced by the University of Rhode Island. Notice the use of grain in the skirt and the angle of the waistline to accent the straight line in front and fullness at the back of the gown. Photo by Robert Izzo.

tion schedule can be laid out. A large calendar is useful for setting up the schedule; it is simplest to work backwards since opening night is the specific deadline. The schedule is used to establish the working plan for completing the steps involved in finishing the costumes. Each show will present different challenges; however, generalizations can be used for setting up a typical schedule. The sequence of events discussed here is arranged according to progression of the costumes from start to finish rather than being reversed.

Measurements need to be taken as early as possible. The preliminary plot will indicate if special measurements for such things as wigs or dancewear will need to be taken. We usually arrange to meet the cast and take measurements of everyone at the first company meeting.

This first contact with the actors is also an excellent time for the designer to show the costume sketches and outline what the costumes will be for each character. It is also a good time to tell the actors how the fitting calls will be arranged and where they will take place; any other specific costume information can be given to the cast at this time. Communicating this information at the first company meeting lets everyone meet one another at the outset and gets the pertinent information to all the actors at the same time.

Shopping sessions need to be scheduled early so the necessary material and items will be available when needed. All expenditures for the show should be recorded so the status of the budget is known at all times. Numerous shopping trips waste time and money; therefore, as complete a shopping list as possible should be drawn up prior to the shopping sessions.

Fitting days should be penciled in; definite times usually cannot be scheduled until later when the actors' schedules are set. As discussed earlier, the number of fittings needed varies according to the requirements of the design, but notations of fitting times in the schedule establish goals and are useful for making work assignments to the costume construction crew.

There may be other *deadlines* which should be scheduled, such as completion of dyeing, millinery, masks, or other accessories. If costumes need to be aged or

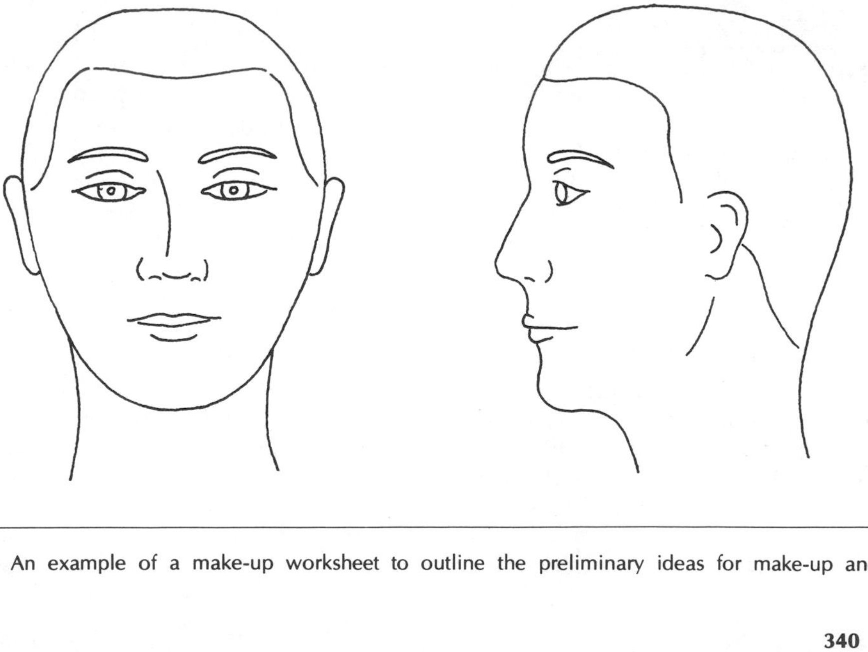

Figure 20–8 An example of a make-up worksheet to outline the preliminary ideas for make-up and hairstyles.

EXAMPLE OF WORK SCHEDULE

SUN.	MON.	TUE.	WED.	THUR.	FRI.	SAT.
27	28	29	30 Dyeing Fabrics: CRUCIBLE	31	1	2
	Construction: CRUCIBLE ——————————————————————————→					
	Measurements: CHARLIE BROWN					
3	4 Construction: CRUCIBLE ——————————————————————————→	5	6	7	8	9
	First Fittings: CRUCIBLE ————————————————→					
	Shopping and Construction: CHARLIE BROWN ——————————→					
10	11	12	13	14	15	16 All Rehearsal Garments Into Rehearsals: CRUCIBLE
	First Fittings (Cont'd.): CRUCIBLE ——————————————→					
Fittings:	CHARLIE BROWN ————————————→					
17	18	19	20	21	22 Wardrobe Crew Meeting – C.B.	23
	Accessory Construction: CRUCIBLE ——————————————————→					
	Final Fittings: CHARLIE BROWN					
24 Second Fittings:	25 CRUCIBLE —————————————→	26	27	28	29 OPEN CHARLIE BROWN 8:00	30 2:00 C.B. Perf. 8:00 C.B. Perf.
			Ageing Garments: CRUCIBLE			
		DRESS:	CHARLIE BROWN ——→			
1 2:00 C.B. Perf. STRIKE	2 Final Fittings: CRUCIBLE ——————————————————→	3	4	5	6 Wardrobe Crew Meeting CRUCIBLE	7 Make-up and Hair Workshop: CRUCIBLE
8	9	10 Measurements: OUR TOWN	11 OPEN CRUCIBLE 8:00	12	13	14 Photo Call
DRESS:	CRUCIBLE ——————————→			CRUCIBLE:	8:00 Performances	
15 2:00 CRUCIBLE Perf. STRIKE	16 Shopping: OUR TOWN ——————————————————→	17	18	19	20	21
	Clean-up and Re-stocking	Construction: OUR TOWN ——————————————→				

Figure 20–9 A sample work schedule showing schedules for three overlapping productions. From the author's notebook.

treated in other ways, the sewing and fitting should be completed early enough to allow time for this work. Special rehearsal garments may be required, and their use should be scheduled in consultation with the designer and director. The inclusion of *rehearsal garments* is important for shows that have costumes which are not contemporary in order to allow the actors to adjust to the garments. As mentioned earlier, such things as corsets, padding, and skirt supports need to be used from early rehearsals on. Other items such as long skirts, large headdresses, full-length capes, and various other items that influence movement should be included in the rehearsal clothes list.

The designer may wish to schedule a *dress parade* prior to the first dress rehearsal so the costumes can be viewed individually and in groups by the designer, director, and costumer in order that notes on adjustments and changes can be made. The dress parade should be conducted on the set under the lights to be used for the production and in sequential order.

We like to schedule a *make-up and hair workshop* before the first dress rehearsal to work out the specifics for each make-up and hairstyle with the actor. Make-up worksheets (Fig. 20–8) are effective for preliminary ideas for the actor to work from. After the make-up is checked under the lights, corrections and alterations are made on the sheet for reference during dress rehearsals and performance.

Dress rehearsals are usually set by the entire production staff; these are noted on the schedule. Final dress rehearsal should be considered the same as the opening of the show, so all the costumes and accessories should be completely finished by that time. *Performance* dates and times should be included in the schedule; with the scheduled cleanup (called the *strike*) following the final performance. *Photo calls* for a pictorial record of the show are usually scheduled after a performance during the run of the show.

The amount of time for the construction process varies somewhat; however, four to six weeks is fairly typical. In some situations, construction of two or more shows may overlap. In this case, the work schedules for all the shows that overlap construction time in the shop would be included on one calendar as shown in Fig. 20–9.

THE CONSTRUCTION PHASE

Primary considerations for constructing costumes are the amount of time for construction, the number and complexity of the costumes, the number of people to work on the costumes, and their skill levels. The costumer needs to break the construction phase into working units or areas and make the necessary assignments.

The specifics of what each unit will be vary according to the requirements of the production and the amount and complexity that is involved in each area. For example, there was a great deal of silk screening to be done for Fielding's *The Grub Street Opera* shown in Fig. 20–10; therefore, silk screening was a major unit for that show. Other units which are usually typical include millinery, corseting, footwear, jewelry or other decoration.

Of course, garment construction is a major unit. Job assignments in this area can be divided up in several ways; we have found two methods particularly successful. One is to assign a garment to one individual to work on from start to finish. The other method is to assign an individual to make all the pants, shirts, or other duplicated items. The first method provides the individual with a stronger sense of accomplishment and gives a consistent quality to

Figure 20-10 Full cast of Fielding's *The Grub-Street Opera* suggests the amount of silk screening, wig construction, and other work units that needed to be planned in the schedule. Production by the University of Rhode Island. From the author's collection.

the costume. However, this method requires a lot of people on the construction crew, and each must be able to put in a lot of time, so this method may not be practical in all situations or for all shows.

The second method, strongly related to the assembly-line approach, is faster and more efficient. The individuals assigned to this type of unit, however, have less of a sense of accomplishment and do not learn as much as the individuals who have complete costumes to work on. Therefore, in addition to the construction time available, the number of people involved, and their skill levels, job assignments are also influenced by the type and function of the costume shop. In educational theatre shops, the emphasis is on developing and learning construction skills; in commercial shops the emphasis is on speed and efficiency.

The *construction crew* is the work force

for making the costumes. In educational theatre and other noncommercial situations, the work force is generally part-time, and the degree of skill and experience varies. How the specific job assignments are made depends on the number of individuals, the skills they represent, and the amount of time they have available to work on construction.

WORKSHOP ORGANIZATION. Most of the preceding discussion centered on formulating what needs to be done for a production; however, how that information is then communicated to the construction crew is fundamental to successful completion of the costumes.

First of all, those working on the costumes should be familiar with the script so they have a better understanding of how the costumes are appropriate to the script and the characters. Knowing the script also makes communication easier, since most designers and costumers refer to the costume by character identification rather than by an actor's name.

Since the sketches are the major reference point for costume construction, displaying them on a bulletin board in the shop permits everyone to refer to them readily. The fabric swatches on the sketch provide further reference.

Notes to identify who the fabric is for can be pinned onto the yardages of fabrics to further simplify the communication process. We set aside a specific location for fabrics that are designated for a show and pin character names and specific garment notations on the fabric. After the fabric is cut, the scraps are folded and pinned together and put into a scrap box that is earmarked specifically for the show. This makes locating additional matching fabric for a costume or accessories very easy.

Specific construction notes for each costume are kept on a clipboard that is assigned to the show. This clipboard is kept in a designated area for easy access by the construction crew. Another clipboard contains an ongoing shopping list so that things we are running low on can be compiled in one place; this list is always ready when someone is going out shopping.

The actual pattern drafting and cutting may be done by the costumer, or a member of the construction crew may take on some or all of the assignment. Once the garment is cut and marked, it can be assigned to someone to prepare it for the first fitting. If the actor has more than one costume, it is advisable to prepare as many of the costumes as possible so they can all be fitted in the same fitting session. Of course, if cor-

sets, padding, or the like, are needed, these must be completed first before the other garments are cut.

Preparing as many of the costumes for a given actor as possible allows for more efficient use of time, the actor's as well as the costumer's and the designer's. Scheduling the amount of time needed for the fitting depends on the complexity and number of the costumes; 30 minutes is usually sufficient for a simple costume, 1 hour is needed for more than one costume. Ideally, a fitting should not be longer than 90 minutes; otherwise, it becomes very tedious. An actor should never be called for a fitting if the costumes are not ready.

The construction process after the fitting should be organized and geared to the various steps of completion as established by the deadlines on the work schedule. While the completion of the garments is under way, the costumer can then turn attention to the accessories and direct preparation of these items so they can be introduced in the subsequent fittings.

The final phase of construction can be the most exciting and the most frustrating. It is very exciting to watch the costumes take on the full dimensions of the costume design. It can be frustrating and tedious to concentrate on the final hand-sewing, particularly where snaps and hooks and eyes are concerned, because it is often difficult to see how the careful execution of these details is really important. However, careful alignment of snaps and hooks and eyes is absolutely necessary for the finished costume to look right, and careful securing of these items is necessary so that the work does not have to be redone.

DRESS REHEARSAL PREPARATIONS

As the costume construction enters its final phase and the last fittings are being completed, the final costume plot should

be assembled and prepared for the dress rehearsals. The final plot needs to include details about any stage business that has been developed in rehearsals which involves the costumes. For example, the plot in Fig. 20–4 indicates that Ruth's denim jacket has to be *preset* (put there before the scene begins) on stage on the stage-left chair with the hat in the pocket. The arrangement and placement of the jacket was determined in rehearsal. Attending rehearsals before preparing the final plot provides information on this type of stage business as well as the locations of exits, entrances, and possible backstage locations for fast changes. This and any other costume-related information can also be discussed with the actors in the final fittings for inclusion in the final plot.

Prior to the dress rehearsals, dress shields should be tacked, or pinned with small safety pins, into nonwashable garments. All costumes, accessories, and related pieces should also be tagged and arranged in units. Garments should be labeled with the actor's name on the inside. A laundry marking pen is ideal, since the ink is permanent and will not bleed through the cloth or tape label. Iron-on tape or twill tape sewn into the garment where a manufacturer's lable is placed will provide easy identification. Adhesive tape or masking tape can be used on nonwashable items. The use of tape gives clear identification and keeps the inside of an often-used garment from looking like a who's who of actors.

Accessories, such as hose, socks, shoes, and jewelry, are difficult to tag in this manner. Names on tape in shoes, for example, quickly smudge and become illegible. Spring-hinge clothespins, with the actor's name taped on, will keep the shoes in pairs and give quick identification. Sandwich-size, or larger, plastic bags will keep jewelry and other small accessories together and can be attached with clothespins to the hanger. All costume items must be set up in some manner so they can be identified accurately and quickly.

Costume racks should be organized for easy access. Markers like those used on clothing racks to separate sizes are valuable for organizing the racks. The markers can be made of heavy cardboard with the actor's name taped on. All the costumes can be hung behind the marker, with shoes and hats placed on the shelf or on the floor under the garments. To prevent loss and frustration, all costume items should always be returned to the proper location when not in use.

The *wardrobe crew* is responsible for working with the costumes and the actors during the dress rehearsals and performances. The crew must be familiar with the script and the production since they serve as dressers, helping the actors in and out of costumes at the right time and place. This means that the crew must know where each costume item is and have it ready for the actor to use.

To acquaint the crew with its duties and the requirements of the particular production, we schedule a crew meeting prior to the first dress rehearsal. Each crew member is given a copy of the final plot, and the details of the plot are explained. The final plot is the primary working document for the crew, and corrections and additional information will be written on the plot. Therefore, the crew will keep their copies of the plot through the run of the performances.

The crew then checks the plot against the costumes to make sure everything is there and to associate the plot entry with the actual costume piece. They also check to see that everything is marked or tagged with the actor's name.

The duties of the crew are also explained at this meeting. These include maintaining the appearance of the costumes during the run of the show. A portable sewing kit with needles, thread, scissors, seam ripper, extra fasteners, safety pins, clothes brush, cleaning fluid, and other related items is prepared for use in

Figure 20–11 Pierrot and Pierrette costumes for "Tony" and "Polly" in *The Boy Friend* as produced by the University of Rhode Island. The feather trims were attached to the costumes with snaps for easy removal so the costumes could be washed for the performances. From the author's collection.

the dressing room so the crew can make necessary repairs or alterations in the costumes. An iron and ironing board are also provided so the costumes can be pressed prior to the rehearsals and performances.

A washing chart of the costumes that will need to be laundered is also prepared. Preplanning for the construction phase can simplify this process. For example, the feather trim and pompoms on the white costumes in Fig. 20–11 were attached to the outfits with snaps so they could be removed and reattached easily. The white costumes could then be washed for the performances with no damage to the feathers. The washing chart should also indicate items that have been dyed, what can be washed with what, and any instruc-

tions for special care that may be necessary. The schedule of when items will need to be washed and who will be responsible can be worked out during the dress rehearsal period.

The wardrobe crew is also responsible for taking repair notes from the actors. Those notes that cannot be taken care of with hand-sewing are given to the costumer so that those repairs and alterations can be made in the costume shop. No alterations in the appearance of the costume should be made without the designer's consent.

One member of the crew is designated as crew head and is responsible for the work of the crew members and will assign the specific duties and dressing stations to them. These specific assignments will vary according to the production needs, but they usually include helping the actors get into costume when necessary, doing up back closings, or assisting them with other difficult costume pieces. The actors are responsible for hanging up their costumes and for normal costume changes, but they may need help getting into and out of some of them. As dressers, the crew members check the actors to be sure they are dressed properly for their entrances. The assigned dressers also help on the necessary costume changes; if it is a fast change, the dresser also hangs up the costume that has been removed.

Once the rehearsal or performance is completed, the crew must check all the costumes to make sure everything is where it should be and that everything is in good repair. This process is repeated prior to the next rehearsal or performance before the actors get into the costumes.

Since the wardrobe crew works very closely with the actors, it is important to establish a good working rapport between the crew and the performers. The crew members should be introduced to the cast and the dressing assignments announced so the actors will know who is working with them and where the costume changes will take place. It should be understood by the cast and the crew that the function of the wardrobe crew is to service the production and to facilitate the performance. The dressers are not personal valets for the actors.

The actors should also be informed about what is expected of them in relation to the costumes. Such things as where to get the costumes, that they should apply make-up before getting into the costume, that they are supposed to hang up their costumes and replace tags in shoes and other items, and so forth, are typical instructions for the actors.

Good organization of the costumes facilitates their introduction into the rehearsal process. A dress parade, prior to the first dress rehearsal, can also ease the process. Ideally, the dress parade is held on the set with the proper lights so the director, designer, and costumer can concentrate on the costumes and take notes for any corrections which need to be made. The costumes should be viewed in their proper sequence under what will be performance conditions. Unfortunately, the ideal is not often possible; therefore, the value of a dress parade varies from production to production.

The number of dress rehearsals varies according to the production schedule and the type and style of the costumes. A minimum of three or four dress rehearsals is essential if the costumes are of a style or period that is different from contemporary clothing or if there are a number of costume changes during the performance. It is essential that the actors know how to work with, and in, the costumes and be comfortable with them. It is also necessary to provide the wardrobe crew with sufficient rehearsal time so they know what to do and how to do it.

THE PERFORMANCE PHASE

Maintaining the appearance of the costumes is the primary function of the costumer and the crew during this phase. The procedures established with the wardrobe crew during the dress rehearsals are continued through the run of the show so that the costumes look the same for each performance.

RESTOCKING AND CLEANUP. The performance period is usually a time that is relatively free of activity in the shop. This time should be used to compile a list of the supplies which need to be replaced. Hopefully, there will be money left in the budget to permit the restocking. Otherwise, these expenses will have to come from the next show budget. Restocking basic supplies is important in order to avoid frustration when the item is needed later, which will always be in the middle of the next production. The shop should also be completely cleaned, items returned to storage, scraps removed from the show scrap box and put away, and everything put in order to receive the next show.

STRIKE. The term *strike* means final cleanup after the run of the show. The costumes are stripped of such things as jewelry or flowers, cleaned, and put into storage. Borrowed costumes are cleaned and returned; rental costumes are packed and returned. Dressing rooms are also cleaned and checked for stray costume items.

The strike should be done immediately after the final performance. All the costumes, sewing kit, and other shop items should be returned to the costume shop. The costumes need to be checked off on the costume plot to be sure everything is there. The costumes are then sorted into units according to the type of cleaning necessary. Items that cannot be cleaned, such as shoes, or that do not require cleaning can be put back into the stock. However, no soiled clothing should be put into the stock.

Before things are sent to the cleaners or laundered, trimmings that cannot be cleaned or laundered and the dress shields must be removed. A list of the costumes that are to be sent out for cleaning needs to be made up. We usually have things cleaned, but not pressed, before they go into storage, since the items will get wrinkled in stock anyway. This approach saves money on the cleaning bill. We do have such things as men's suits, tuxedos, and borrowed clothing cleaned and pressed.

Rental costumes do not need to be cleaned before they are returned, so they can be packed and made ready for shipment. Rented items should be returned immediately so there will be no additional fee charged to the show.

The dressing rooms should be cleaned as soon as the costumes have been removed. Any personal items left by the actors should be given to the stage manager or put in a central location so the actors can retrieve them.

COSTUME PRODUCTION

Each phase of costume production is equally important, and, while certain aspects are more fun and more rewarding than others, equal concentration on each aspect helps to ensure a smooth running and exciting production. An efficiently operated costume shop, with workloads for the production and the priorities well thought through, is a pleasant place to work. The amount of organization and preplanning that is done is necessary to complete the costumes on time and with as few frayed nerves as possible.

The costumer is responsible for the production of the costumes. Accomplishing that requires working with many different people, from designers, directors, and actors to other members of the production team, including the construction and wardrobe crews. Therefore, a costumer needs to have a clear idea of what work needs to be done and how to get the work accomplished. A costumer must also be able to get along with people while accomplishing the job and be able to inspire their confidence and respect. A sense of humor makes the job easier and more pleasant.

Theatre is a cooperative enterprise with several segments that need to interweave to create an exciting production. Each segment of the production contributes to the show's success or failure. The costumes and related elements make an important contribution to every production.

Working on the costumes for a production is almost always going to introduce new challenges to the imagination. Solving the problems of how to create various appearances, working with different people, and contributing to the whole of the production is an exciting and stimulating experience.

appendix a

metric conversion chart

The equivalents are the standard ones approved by the Pattern Fashion Industry. They have been rounded by using 2.5 rather than 2.54 as the equivalent of 1 inch; therefore, the centimeter equivalents do not always compute accurately in mathematical terms. The figures in this chart have been used throughout the text, and 2.5 has been used to calculate dimensions which do not appear in the chart.

Available Fabric Widths

(These are the replacements
for standard fabric widths)

21 in.	54 cm	48 in.	122 cm
25 in.	64 cm	50 in.	127 cm
27 in.	70 cm	54–56 in.	140 cm
35–36 in.	90 cm	58–60 in.	150 cm
39 in.	100 cm	68–70 in.	175 cm
44–45 in.	115 cm	72 in.	180 cm

Inches into Centimeters

inches	cm	inches	cm	inches	cm
⅛	0.3 cm	7	18	29	73.5
¼	0.6 cm	8	20.5	30	76
⅜	1.0 cm	9	23	31	78.5
½	1.3 cm	10	25.5	32	81.5
⅝	1.5 cm	11	28	33	84
¾	2.0 cm	12	30.5	34	86.5
⅞	2.2 cm	13	33	35	89
1	2.5 cm	14	35.5	36	91.5
1¼	3.2 cm	15	38	37	94
1½	3.8 cm	16	40.5	38	96.5
1¾	4.5 cm	17	43	39	99
2	5.0 cm	18	46	40	102
2½	6.3 cm	19	48.5	41	104
3	7.5 cm	20	51	42	107
3½	9.0 cm	21	53.5	43	109
4	10.0 cm	22	56	44	112
4½	11.5 cm	23	58.5	45	115
5	12.5 cm	24	61	46	117
5½	14.0 cm	25	63.5	47	120
6	15.0 cm	26	66	48	122
		27	68.5	49	125
		28	71	50	127

appendix b

selected costuming sources

The intention in compiling the sources included here is not to provide a comprehensive list of suppliers. The selection is intended to provide sources for items and materials that are not always readily available or that are difficult to find; it also covers a representative cross-section of the country. Theatrical supply houses have not been included because they are so numerous, and local companies can be found in the telephone book; the same is true of costume rental houses. The entry for Directories of Theatrical Sources lists four detailed resources for finding numerous items and various equipment and includes an overview of what each source provides.

The Costume Bibliographies are included to expand the sources cited at the ends of several chapters. These bibliographies include books on general costume history as well as detailed studies of particular eras, types of garments, and various accessories.

COSTUME BIBLIOGRAPHIES

Anthony, Pegaret, and Janet Arnold, *Costume, A General Bibliography* (revised and enlarged). London: Costume Society, Victoria & Albert Museum, 1974.

Hiler, Hilaire, and Meyer Hiler, *Bibliography of Costume.* New York: Benjamin Blom, Inc., reprint, 1967.

In addition, The Costume Society of America has compiled bibliographies that are available to members and (for a slightly higher price) to nonmembers. These are entitled *A Bibliography of Recent Books Relating to Costume, 1975,* and *Bibliography of Recent Publications Relating to Costume II* and are available from The Costume Society of America, c/o The Costume Institute, The Metropolitan Museum of Art, 5th Ave. at 82nd St., New York, NY 10028.

Colin, Paul, and Deborah Lippman, *Craft Sources*. New York: M. Evans & Co., 1975.

"Directory of Costume-Related Supplies and Equipment" U.S. Institute for Theatre Technology. 1501 Broadway, New York, NY 10036.

Theatre Crafts Directory, Patricia Mackay (ed.). Rodale Press, Emmaus, PA 18049.

Simon's Directory of Theatrical Materials,

Services and Information, Package Publicity Service, Inc., 1501 Broadway, New York, NY 10036.

Sources for local suppliers can also be found in the Yellow Pages of the telephone book, and many state Arts Councils compile sourcebooks for artists and craftspeople which are available from the council office.

ADHESIVES AND MOLDING MATERIALS

Adhesive Products Corp.
1660 Boon Ave.
Bronx, NY 10460
(casting materials, polyurethane foam, flexible rubber)

Cameo House Ltd.
3828 W. North Ave.
Milwaukee, WI 53208
(flexible mold-making material)

Dequsa, Inc.
2 Pennsylvania Plaza
New York, NY 10001
(Celastic)

Modern Display
436 S. 7th E.
Salt Lake City, UT 84102
(Celastic)

Polysar
1795 Market St.
Akron, OH 44301

Sculpture House
38 E. 30th St.
New York, NY 10016
also

Flax's
250 Sutter

San Francisco, CA 94108
(casting materials, flexible rubbers)

Swift & Co. Adhesives & Coatings Div
111 W. Jackson
P.O. Box 45366
Chicago, IL 60645
(flexible adhesive #3917)

ARMOR AND WEAPONS

The Armoury American Fencing Supply
2122 Fillmore St.
San Francisco, CA 94115

Costume Armour, Inc.
Hangar E, P.O. Box 6086
Stewart Airport
Newburgh, NY 12550

Tobins Lake Studios
2650 Seven Mile Road
S. Lyon, MI 48178
(vacuformed armor and decorations)

DANCEWEAR

Baums, Inc. Dancewear
106–112 S. 11th St.

Philadelphia, PA 19107

Capezio
Mail orders:
745 7th Ave.
New York, NY 10019
(several branch stores around the country)

Danskins
1114 6th Ave.
New York, NY 10036

Eileen Holding
110 W. 18th St.
New York, NY 10011
(unitards and tights to order; helenca and elasticized cotton)

Peko Creations
390 Pine St.
Pawtucket, RI 02860
(helenca, elasticized cotton, Milliskin, and tights made to order)

Selva & Sons, Inc.
1607 Broadway
New York, NY 10019

Maxine Fabrics Co., Inc.
417 5th Ave.

New York, NY
10016
(Milliskin, silks,
wools, linens, vel-
vets, synthetics)

DYES AND INKS:
**Equipment and
Supplies**

Advance Process
Supply Co.
4295 Wendell Dr.
SW
Atlanta, GA 30303
(silk screen
supplies)

Calusa Chemical Co.
801 E. Macy St.
Los Angeles, CA
90012

Cerulean Blue, Ltd.
P.O. Box 5126
1314 N.E. 43rd St.
Seattle, WA 98105
(dyes and fabrics)

Crescent Bronze
Powder Co.
Western Div.
1841 S. Flower St.
Los Angeles, CA
90015

Dick Blick
P.O. Box 1267
Galesburg, IL
61401
(art supplies,
dyes)

Fabdec
3553 Old Post Rd.
P.O. Box 3012
San Angelo, TX
76901
(dyes and fabrics)

Keystone Aniline &
Chemical Co., Inc.
321 N. Loomis
Chicago, IL 60607

Putnam Dye Co.
P.O. Box 1267

Galesburg, IL
61401

Pylam Products Co., Inc.
95–10 218th St.
Queen's Village,
NY 11429
(cold water Pro-
cion dyes)

Test Fabrics
P.O. Box 118
200 Blackford Ave.
Middlesex, NY
08846

INDUSTRIAL FELT

A. B. Boyd Co.
8033 N.E. Holman
St.
Portland, OR 97218

Metric Felt Co.
135 S. Peoria
Chicago, IL 60607

Rumpel Felt Co., Ltd.
Mfg. of Wool &
Synthetic Felts
P.O. Box 1283
Kitchener, Ont.,
Can.

Standard Felt Co.
115 S. Palm Ave.
P.O. Box 871
Alhambra, CA
91802

NOVELTIES AND
CONSTRUCTION
ACCESSORIES

Bamboo and Rattan
Works, Inc.
901–907 Jefferson St.
Hoboken, NJ 07030

Cane and Basket Supply
1283 Cochran Ave.
Los Angeles, CA
90018

Gordon Novelty Co., Inc.
933 Broadway
New York, NY
10010

Lapham Hickey Steel Corp.
5500 W. 73rd St.
Chicago, IL 60638

Lee Ward
1200 St. Charles Rd.
Elgin, IL 60120

Patriarch & Bell, Inc.
94–98 Parkhurst St.
Newark, NJ 07144
(spring steel)

NOTIONS AND
DECORATIVE
TRIMS

Fine Brand
411 S. Wall St.
Los Angeles, CA
90013
(corset stays, vel-
cro, underpin-
nings)

Gordon Notion Co.
1410 S. Main St.
Los Angeles, CA
90015

Hammer Bros.
312 W. 8th St.
Kansas City, MO
65105

Lion Notions, Inc.
P.O. Box 2468
South San Fran-
cisco, CA 94080

M. & J. Trimming Co.
1008 Sixth Ave.
New York, NY
10018

South African Feather
Co., Inc.
401 N. Broad St.
Philadelphia, PA
19108

Steinlauf & Stoller, Inc.
239 W. 38th St.
New York, NY
10018

Theatre House, Inc.
400 W. 3rd St.
Covington, KY
41011

Zucker Products Corp.
568 Broadway
New York, NY
10012
  (flowers, feath-
  ers)

SHOP EQUIPMENT

Automatic Steam
Products Corp.
13–20 34th St.
Long Island City,
NY 11101

Fox Sewing Machine Co.
307 W. 38th St.
New York, NY
10001

Jiffy Steamer
P.O. Box 57
Fulton, KY 42041

Juki Industries of
America, Inc.
32 W. 25th St.
New York, NY
10010

Industrial Sewing Co.
333 Market St.
Paterson, NJ 07501

Superior Model Form
Co., Inc.

34 W. 17th St.
New York, NY
10011

Sussman Automatic of
California
1907 2nd Ave.
Los Angeles, CA
90018

Wolf Form Co., Inc.
39 W. 19th St.
New York, NY
10011

WIGS, HAIR, AND MILLINERY

Bob Kelly Wig Creations
151 W. 46th St.
New York, NY
10036

Haentze Hatcrafters
20 N. Springfield
Rd.
Clifton Hts., PA
19018

Ideal Wig Co.
38 Pearl St.
New York, NY
10004
  and

18075 Ventura Blvd.
Encino, CA 91316

Mark Bernstein,
Western Wig Sales
233 Sansome
San Francisco, CA
94104

Manny's
36 W. 38th St.
New York, NY
10018

Milliner's Supply Co.
911 Elm St.
Dallas, TX 74202

Rieder Bros., Inc.
124 Wooster St.
New York, NY
10012

Synthetic Thread Co., Inc.
825 12th Ave.
Bethlehem, PA
18019
  (monofilament
  nylon mannequin
  hair)

Zauder Bros., Inc.
920 Broadway
New York, NY
10003

Several sources are taken from the *Directory of Costume Related Supplies and Equipment* published by the U.S. Institute for Theatre Technology, Inc., 1501 Broadway, New York, NY 10036.

index